D1595905

THE JOHN ADAMS READER

The John Adams Reader

ESSENTIAL WRITINGS ON AN
AMERICAN COMPOSER

Edited by Thomas May

AMADEUS
PRESS

Published in 2006 by Amadeus Press
512 Newark Pompton Turnpike
Pompton Plains, New Jersey 07444

Book design by Mark Lerner

Printed in the United States of America

ISBN 1-57467-132-4

Library of Congress Cataloging-in-Publication Data is available upon request.

www.amadeuspress.com

To Robert Levine, *il miglior fabbro*

CONTENTS

ACKNOWLEDGMENTS

I EXPRESS MY DEEP GRATITUDE to John Adams for offering invaluable advice and support from the moment I approached him with this project. He continued to share information and contacts no matter how much I pestered during the incessant busyness of the months before the premiere of one of his grandest-scale works, *Doctor Atomic.* Thanks as well to all who contributed, and in particular to Ingram Marshall, Sarah Cahill, and Michael Steinberg for being such an integral part of this collection.

I am grateful to Alice Goodman for providing the previously unpublished *Klinghoffer* scene and to Peter Sellars for taking time (also on the eve of the *Doctor Atomic* opening) to share his wonderful insights.

Thanks are due as well for the generosity of the *New Republic,* the *Nation,* Lisa Mark at the Los Angeles Museum of Modern Art, Libby van Cleve of the Oral History of American Music, and Jane Moss and Kate Monaghan of Lincoln Center. I wish especially to single out Larry Rothe for making essays by Michael Steinberg and Ingram Marshall originally published by the San Francisco Symphony program books available—a testament to his exemplary work as chief editor.

I must also thank my publisher, John Cerullo, for his continued support; and everyone at Amadeus Press who has lent support to the project: editorial director Carol Flannery; publicist Caroline

Howell, a fount of information; and my copyeditor, Gail Siragusa, who handled a complex task with grace.

I owe debts of appreciation to my friends at San Francisco Opera—Claire Myers, Kip Cranna, and Pamela Rosenberg, who found time to help while preparing the world premiere of *Dr. Atomic*. Thanks, too, for the excellent advice of Pierre Ruhe and Tim Page. Steven Swartz of Boosey & Hawkes (Adams's publisher) provided invaluable help in research, as did Joy Partain and Brian Mitchell of Houston Grand Opera.

Finally, all gratitude to my editor, Robert Levine, for his untiring good judgment and common sense—and for convincing me to carry on through the rough spots.

INTRODUCTION

JOHN ADAMS HAS BECOME the most frequently performed living American composer in the sphere of classical music. Having won a Pulitzer Prize for his musical response to September 11 (*On the Transmigration of Souls*), Adams went on to be honored in 2005 with three Grammys for the New York Philharmonic's recording of the work and was in the spotlight later that fall as San Francisco Opera premiered his latest stage work, *Doctor Atomic*. His compositions across all the major genres have proved remarkably enduring, in a way that's difficult to compare with the other arts. For despite our era of ubiquitous commissions and corporate sponsorships, the sad truth is that the vast majority of contemporary art music is condemned to a ritual of once-only performance at its premiere, never to be heard from again save, perhaps, in a curriculum vitae listing. In other words, for new music to have "legs" in today's context—music, that is, of substance not defined by its commercial appeal—carries a significance well beyond what might at first appear to be the case.

As we are mercilessly reminded these days, our relation to classical music culture continues to fray—to the point that we seem to be hanging on to it by a mere thread. For all that is great or enduringly meaningful from the store of past music can only thrive in a dialogue with the new. John Adams, going against the odds, has somehow found a way to reinvigorate that dialogue. By this point his achievements can no longer be trivialized as the lucky flash of a passing fad—just as Adams's evolving musical personality has become increasingly resistant to attempts to pigeonhole his music.

Adams burst on the scene during a period, it should be recalled, when "classical music" was considered to be, if anything, in an even direr state than it is today. The story has been often told of his East Coast upbringing and education at Harvard. The subsequent decision to head west in the famous "Volkswagen Beetle" has become a kind of meme of Adams lore (in fact, Adams's itinerary west took him across the landscape of Canada), as has his first stint upon settling in San Francisco, working in a warehouse across the bay in Oakland that exported Bermuda shorts. But the impasse that had been affecting so many emerging composers involved in the knotty politics of postwar aesthetics seemed irrelevant, for a time, in the Bay Area's Shangri-La of experimentalism, in which Adams eagerly took part.

A famous column by *Time* magazine critic Michael Walsh in the early 1980s (back when *Time* actually *had* a classical critic) drew national attention to a movement by then in full ascendancy and named Adams as one of its younger adherents. The boost to his reputation came at a price, though, for the convenient label "minimalist" stuck. Once Adams was classified and stamped, reactions to his music often turned out to be predictable, according to a critic's a priori attitude toward the style. While the premiere of Adams's first opera, *Nixon in China,* at Houston Grand Opera in 1987 is sometimes recalled today as a glowing triumph, the reviews were, in fact, quite mixed, often harsh. Donal Henahan, then chief critic for the *New York Times,* described the landmark opera as if it were a throwaway skit from *Saturday Night Live,* reserving special venom for Adams, who "does for the arpeggio what McDonald's did for the hamburger, grinding out one simple idea into eternity."

The minimalist pigeonhole still sticks for those who fail to pay attention to what Adams has actually written in the past two decades. And even those who have, needing labels, have pounced on the equally inadequate "neo-romantic." Indeed, another seminal moment in the young Adams's career had been the earlier premiere by the San Francisco Symphony, under his early champion Edo de Waart, of the ambitious *Harmonielehre* in 1985. Purists of the minimalist flock were bothered by its reintroduction of a vaster emotional rhetoric that had been a casualty of the aesthetic battles of recent decades. To some, it was akin to Dylan's "Judas moment," when he expanded his palette beyond the folk idiom to go electric.

Yet Adams had only arrived at his version of minimalism in the context of what his friend and fellow composer Ingram Marshall refers to as "an aesthetic openness that admitted of so many influences." His early San Francisco days involved an infatuation with the chance theories of John Cage and a number of experimental projects with the New Music Ensemble Adams led as teacher at the San Francisco Conservatory of Music. Adams's inherent distaste for hard-line doctrine or settled ideas about what a composer should be only encouraged that aesthetic openness.

And so it has been with minimalism, and with all the influences he has integrated during the ensuing years, as Adams continues to redefine his voice in a rich dialogue with the past—Ives, Beethoven, Duke Ellington, Schoenberg, Stravinsky, and Sibelius being some of the most prominent luminaries—that yields an authentic originality: an originality not for its own sake (the simultaneous glory and disaster of twentieth-century music) but in terms of its profoundly compelling urgency of expression. Minimalism may have been the far pendulum swing away from an intolerable situation of modernist music's indifference to audience communication. But Adams has progressed beyond the action-reaction cycle, beyond the straitjacketed ideologies, and beyond the unconvincing, smug inclusiveness of postmodernism, with all its shackling quotation marks.

Adams has instead become a representative twenty-first-century American composer. His Whitmanesque openness to artistic experience has led him to embrace an expansive array of styles and forms. Reflecting this is Adams's astonishing versatility: he has composed monumental symphonic spans, path-breaking operas and multimedia stage works, inventive chamber music, and pieces involving electro-acoustic experimentation. His work might be seen as forming a bridge that connects key aspects of American tradition with the heritage of European art music, and one that links an increasingly neglected past with the vibrancy of present consciousness.

In Adams we find the maverick impulses of Ives, as well as his optimistic eclecticism, philosophical currents from the transcendentalists, and what, according to *New Yorker* critic Alex Ross, is "Copland's populist mission, but without any trace of big-city knowingness," so that his "open prairies became modern, moody spaces, lit up with neon red and bathed in television blue." It's not a coincidence that in his stage works Adams, with his collaborators Peter Sellars and Alice Goodman, has been able to locate the power of myth in figures from contemporary history.

We also find Adams struggling to convey a sense of beauty that transfigures without losing touch with its relevance to life as it is lived: the miracle of birth in *El Niño,* the rhapsodic figurations of the Violin Concerto's "Chaconne," or *Nixon in China*'s depiction of private vulnerability on the public stage. "Wherever serious art loses track of its roots in the vernacular," the composer has said in a sort of credo, "then it begins to atrophy."

The result is a unique sound world that rebalances the opposing forces of simplicity and complexity. It has proved utterly enchanting to audiences in an environment still often assumed to be inimical to new classical music. This is a world of possibility that points toward other composers of a similar synthesist bent who have been gaining increasing recognition, such as Thomas Adès or Michael Hersch.

Surprisingly, given the influence and significance of John Adams for today's cultural fabric, this is the first full-length book in English to be devoted to him. *The John Adams Reader: Essential Writings on an American Composer* gathers a colorful and far-ranging selection of pieces from leading musical commentators and critics who have been observers of (and in some cases participants in) the Adams phenomenon. Included are eloquent essays by Ingram Marshall, Michael Steinberg, Alex Ross, Sarah Cahill, Alan Rich, and other writers offering detailed investigations of his music. From these emerge composite portraits of Adams the man and creative figure. Although this anthology does not include Adams's own writings, in-depth interviews with the composer offer a good dose of his forthright, articulate self-understanding. Ingram Marshall's memory piece also provides a valuable glimpse of those heady early days in San Francisco

Adams's works have generated notable controversy through the years, for he is a composer who has made a point of pressing buttons or tackling "difficult issues." Ever since a few of the establishment local critics took notice in the early San Francisco days with dyspeptic grumblings, Adams has been no stranger to caustic diatribes. The section on critical reception would not present a wholly honest picture were it to ignore some of the more eloquent of the composer's detractors.

By far the longest part of that section is taken up with the matter known as "the *Klinghoffer* controversy." The complex interplay between the 1991 opera *The Death of Klinghoffer* (dealing with terrorism) and our recent tumultuous history has taken on a life of its own—remarkably out of proportion to Adams's wide-ranging output. Yet its reception has played a significant role in the composer's reception. In a 1997 interview with Vivian Perlis for the Oral History of American Music Project at Yale University, Adams lamented how his work had been misunderstood: "It has a sense of *gravitas* and a kind of oracular feeling to it—those choruses that seem to speak from the oldest books of the Bible, and they're cheek by jowl next to these awful jarring violent events, this sort of thing that we see on television everyday. I think that's just a brilliant dramatic invention. It just boggles my mind that people dismiss *Klinghoffer* as being a cheap politically correct opera that had no real meaning."

Bernd Feuchtner's illuminating overview draws together the various points of debate that have swirled about the work; a number of the key articles to which he refers are also reprinted. Also included in this collection is the text of Alice Goodman's "Rumor" scene that was deleted after the Brussels premiere of the opera.

The John Adams Reader traces the evolution of an artist who has never ceased to take on a new challenge. A certain amount of repetition of themes or anecdotes is inevitable, as I have tried to balance the overall flow of the collection with the understanding that a reader may wish to dip in at any particular point. Yet through all the changes he has experienced, all the controversies he has weathered, Adams emerges as an intensely creative figure, passionately engaged in his cultural heritage and in his present milieu. Fortunately, he has never been one to rest on his (now considerable) laurels. Adams is an artist who will continue to evolve, in ways that can only fascinate us.

—Thomas May

THE JOHN ADAMS READER

PART ONE

Portraits of the Artist

John Adams Reflects on His Career

Interview by Thomas May

This interview took place in February 2005 while John Adams was serving a residency at Northwestern University as the inaugural recipient of the Michael Ludwig Nemmers Prize in Musical Composition.

I'm intrigued by how you identified yourself as a composer from an early age. What were those feelings like as a child? What are the earliest pieces of yours we have?

The first piece I remember was a minuet that I wrote for a friend of the family. She was a woman who lived in Vermont who taught at a private school, the Woodstock School, that my sister attended. She owned a harpsichord—very much ahead of her time. I wrote a minuet for her, though I don't remember how old I was— probably nine or ten. The next substantial piece that I wrote was a suite for string orchestra, which was the piece that was performed by the local community orchestra in Concord, New Hampshire, when I was probably thirteen or fourteen.

I think the idea of being a composer started in 1956. That was the bicentennial of Mozart's birth. I went to a small, rural elementary school in a very small village, East Concord, New Hampshire, where my family had moved from Vermont. I had a very enlightened third-grade teacher—a woman who took advantage of that Mozart year to read the class a child's biography of Mozart. It had a huge effect on me: the idea of what it meant to be a composer, to write music, to have a life in music as someone who didn't just play pieces, but created them as well. So that's probably where the notion of being a composer began for me.

Was it a very musical household?

My father played clarinet and my mother sang. She sang in church choir and also in local productions of Rodgers and Hammerstein shows. So, yes, there was a lot of music in the household, and I particularly remember a Christmas—must have been 1957 or '58—when my father brought home a Magnavox long-playing record console. Up to that point there had been no recorded music in our house in New Hampshire. All the music I heard was what my parents performed or what I myself played on the clarinet. But on that critical day at Christmastime my dad brought home the Magnavox—still in the days before stereo—along with a couple of LP records. I remember one was the "Brandenburg" Concertos, and another was a Mozart string quintet, and another was the Mozart clarinet concerto. And then there were some jazz albums. I can't remember what it was—probably Benny Goodman, because both my parents loved his band.

From the moment that record player came in the house, that Magnavox with its four spindly legs and single speaker cone, my life was utterly transformed. I couldn't wait to get home from school and lie on the floor in front of it, listening to music for hours at a stretch. Eventually I began to save money from my paper route or from my allowance to buy recordings, and by the time I graduated from high school I had a substantial LP collection.

This is the era when we were still in the midst of what Virgil Thomson derided as the "music appreciation racket"—where classical music was clearly kind of segmented to this particular audience. But it doesn't sound like this was even an issue at the point—it was all music for you.

I would say everything was a marvel. Both of my parents loved what we call, for lack of a better term, "vernacular" music—jazz, Broadway, whatever. And my sister, who was eleven years older than I and had already left home by then, was very interested in folk music. She brought along the Kingston Trio and Pete Seeger. So I devoured it all. I suppose you could say that it formed my musical pedigree.

I remember going to the A&P market, which was one of the very first grocery chains. At one point—it seems hard to believe—they concocted a promotional scheme that involved a monthly album of classical music. If you collected enough coupons from buying groceries, every month you could get a new album. Can you imagine that happening now? One month, along with your coffee, eggs, and laundry soap, you'd get the Grieg Piano Concerto. The next month *Scheherazade*. These albums even had a host who introduced the music…Milton Cross or Sigmund Spaeth or someone. Today it's easy to make fun of such middlebrow attempts to popularize classical music, but I think it had a very important effect on making the general population at least marginally aware of classical music.

Concord, New Hampshire, then was a relatively small town (about 28,000), but major symphony orchestras still had it on their tour lists. Thinking back, I have to marvel that the Boston Symphony, for example, would come to Concord on a Sunday afternoon and play a concert in the local movie house, the Capitol Theater, with its awful acoustics. During my childhood I heard not only the BSO, but also the Cleveland Orchestra, the Buffalo Philharmonic, and the Robert Shaw Chorale, all of them right in my small hometown.

Orchestra players probably groaned at the thought of playing at Concord, New Hampshire, but who would have known that in the audience was this ten-year-old boy ready to have a life-changing experience? And I always think of that when I do a performance—that somewhere out in that sea of people there might be another person like me as a young kid, a sponge, soaking up every detail of the experience.

Just one person makes all the difference. And this was before Leonard Bernstein's Young People's Concerts?

No, he started televising the Young People's Concerts when I was probably in elementary school. But my parents didn't want a television in the house, since they thought that it would compromise my reading of books. So what little I saw of the Bernstein Children's Concerts, I usually saw on televisions in my neighbors' homes.

When you ended up at Harvard, what was its effect for you on this very democratic attitude toward vernacular music?

I didn't listen to rock until after I graduated from high school. Of course, "rock" barely existed as a style in 1962–65. Most pop music at that point was in that sort of transitional style dominated largely by crooners—Bobby Darin or Elvis Presley—and I didn't listen to Elvis, although I certainly knew about him. I listened to a lot of jazz—Miles Davis and Duke Ellington, etc. When I got to Harvard things changed abruptly. I immediately started listening to all the Beatles albums that were available. And then that branched out into a fondness for other bands. The great thing about being in college between 1965 and 1971 is that it was the golden period of rock. It was an extraordinary time: you could turn even the AM radio on and hear a sort of endless sequence of wonderful songs. So I listened to pop music, to rock and to soul and Motown, continually throughout college. I liked to listen carefully enough to detect the harmonic changes and be able to reproduce them by ear at the piano.

Your first exposure to Schoenberg later became transmuted in your music into elements of parody. Was that the beginning of a sense of the tension of what a "composer" is supposed to be? When did you first experience that clash between the ideal of the composer in our age versus what you wanted to express?

The idea that if you want to be a composer it's going to be difficult and probably unpleasant.

And nobody's going to want to listen....

Actually, I think I was musically quite sophisticated even when I was still in high school. I used to go to Boston every weekend from the tenth grade through the end of high school. And I played clarinet in the Greater Boston Youth Symphony. I would take the train down from Concord every Saturday, go to rehearsals in the morning at Boston University, and then go to the New England Conservatory of Music on Huntington Avenue for a clarinet lesson. In my last year before college I began going over to Cambridge to take theory lessons with a young composer who'd recently been at Harvard. But most important was the fact that in Boston I had high-school-age friends who shared my enthusiasm for music. We traded recordings and scores and information all the time. You know how kids are: they get together and download each other's brains with an intensity that adults rarely attain. It was from one of my friends in the orchestra that I first heard about the Mahler Ninth, for example, and about *Gurrelieder.*

I became aware of Schoenberg rather early. When I was about sixteen I attended a week-long seminar for young people at Brandeis University given by Bethany Beardsley and Robert Koff. Robert Koff was one of the founding members of the Juilliard String Quartet; he had left the Juilliard to teach at Brandeis, and he was a very serious musician of the old school, having made all those classic recordings of Bartók, Berg, Schoenberg, and Webern. He had a gift for making that music seem exciting. I watched him rehearse *Pierrot Lunaire* with the soprano Bethany Beardsley and the pianist Luise Vosgerchian, who later became my theory teacher at Harvard. Of course, I was at a very impressionable age—I think I was probably a sophomore in high school. I was fascinated by the *Sprechstimme* and the eerie chiaroscuro of Schoenberg's instrumental writing. Now I realize that the poetry is really quite bad, but it fired Schoenberg's imagination in just the right way. In 1963 *Pierrot Lunaire* was very challenging for musicians. No one had those kinds of techniques as a part of their conservatory training, and this meant struggling to make coherence of the often ungainly intervals and rhythms.

So I started buying Schoenberg albums after my experience at Brandeis. I bought many of the Robert Craft albums, which were well recorded and informed performances made with Los Angeles studio players. And some of my friends who were in the youth orchestra also bought them, so we all had heated arguments about what was the best performance of the Violin Concerto—and things like that. So Schoenberg was a major figure for me. I think I was drawn to him partly just because he was so prickly. And then I had another significant exposure to Schoenberg when I was an undergraduate at Harvard, during my junior year. I occasionally was called in to substitute with the Boston Symphony as a clarinet player, and during that season they played the American premiere of *Moses und Aron* in the old Back Bay Theater on Massachusetts Avenue. Imagine: the Boston Symphony in the pit, and a grimy, cramped pit it was—probably one of the only times in their history that they ever did that. This occurred in the autumn of 1967. We must have had ten orchestra rehearsals, so that was another way that I got close exposure. Then both of my composition teachers at Harvard were Schoenberg students: Leon Kirchner and Earl Kim.

But when I got to Harvard, I saw a different image of what it meant to be a composer, and it was…(I have to be careful with my words, because I don't want to offend the memory of my old teachers). The paradigm was no longer the one I had received from the *Child's Biography of Mozart,* one of effortless creativity. It was rather the opposite, one in which composing music was presented as a series of problems to be solved, somewhat like mathematics. And although my principal teacher, Leon Kirchner, struggled to draw a link between Mozart and Schoenberg or between Bach and Stravinsky, there was no escaping the subliminal feeling coming from him that the glory days of music composition were long gone, and we were now stuck with the leftover scraps from the feast. I think it was a really dark time for composition in the 1960s and early '70s. I don't understand why the Schoenbergian model had become so prestigious. It may be that, despite his aggressive and querulous personality, he nevertheless represented the Nietzschean model of the outsider—the person who is the visionary, whose language you can't understand nor even find appealing but are nonetheless affected by it. Therefore it's up to *you* to change *your* way of being to accommodate *it*— rather than the music charming or pleasing you into loving it. This image of the composer as perennial outsider was certainly made even more vivid when I later read *Doktor Faustus* by Thomas Mann.

Did you feel the same about Webern and Berg?

The Webernian model, even more popular during the 1960s, epitomized the current paradigm of the "composer as scientist." That was a mindset that emerged after World War II. Early photos of Stockhausen featured a guy who looked like a rocket scientist working for NASA. And, of course, the whole Princeton group, Babbitt and his followers, wrote "papers" for publications like *Perspectives of New Music*, aping the style of scholarly papers delivered by physicists or mathematicians and which now, in retrospect, make me think of a satire by Thomas Pynchon. Some of Babbitt's articles are fantastically ornate, mannerist prose etudes with baroque uses of the English language which revel in their own ellipses and obscurities. When you're a kid and you read that sort of thing, it makes your hair stand up, and you think, "God! This man is in possession of some secret and important knowledge, and I'd better figure it out or I'll be left in the dust!" It took me a long time to realize that these articles by Babbitt were "shticks," almost like nightclub routines. Babbitt was having fun in a professorial sort of way. He was forever the smart-aleck ten-year-old with thick glasses, entertaining the adults and annoying his peers with his quick intellect and verbal facility.

Boulez's book, *Penser la Musique Aujourd'hui* , was equally implacable and, to me, largely incomprehensible. I remember students at Harvard carrying it around in their book bags, referring to it with a knowing look as if they'd cracked the code. In fact, I don't think anyone there could make much sense of it. So it was a period where the model of the composer as scientist/technocrat was more important than the more traditional paradigm of the composer as a free spirit, someone who uses the materials of everyday life to make art. It's interesting, because Stravinsky bought into that ideology too. Once Stravinsky started experimenting with twelve-tone music, then suddenly all the college professors scrambled to follow. "Stravinsky's doing it, then I'd better do it." Some of them were very natural talents. I think, for example, Harold Shapiro, a very gifted composer with whom I studied briefly. He was a class-mate of Leonard Bernstein, student of Hindemith and Copland, and a very skillful composer in the tonal neoclassic style. Suddenly in the 1960s he felt that if he was going to be relevant he had to write twelve-tone music. But the style was so fundamentally inimi-cal to him that he just stopped composing altogether. And that happened also to Irving Fine, another very gifted neoclassic com-poser who also felt that sudden command from on high to follow Schoenberg. And, of course, Copland wrote most of his late works in a very simplistic and strident twelve-tone style—generally un-pleasant-sounding pieces like *Connotations, Inscape,* and the Piano Quartet. I don't think the twelve-tone sound world was quite such a stretch for Copland, because ever since the 1920s, he'd already demonstrated a piss-'n-vinegar penchant for sour intervals, like he did in the Piano Variations. But even so, the rigor of the "method" seemed more to crimp his natural spontaneity than to aid it.

But another way of looking at this is what was happening in the golden age of rock music that you mentioned earlier. That must have seemed like a real antipode, in terms of making music and directly getting the feedback of connection with an audience. Why, for exam-ple, did you decide not to go in that direction? At the time it didn't seem to have the negative connotation of "selling out." You could be in the world of rock and still be a real artist.

I didn't want to become a pop musician because it just wasn't musically challenging. I really loved—and still love—the classical tradition, whether it's Bach or Messaien. I didn't think it was a dead tradition, or even an endangered one. Nevertheless, by the time I was finishing college, I did find myself in a kind of cul-de-sac. It seemed that there were only two possible routes (this is roughly 1967, when I was a junior in college): the Boulez para-digm or the John Cage paradigm.

What didn't interest me in any way was the sort of hangover from the mid-century tonal Americans: composers like Samuel Barber, Menotti, or Bernstein. That just didn't appeal to me in the least. So, feeling that I had to make *some* decision, I opted to follow Cage because I thought that he at least was genuinely American and utterly original. Furthermore, many of Cage's philosophical interests like Zen and Buckminster Fuller appealed to me. Boulez seemed to me very aggressive and exclusive. What particularly offended me about the European serialists and post-war composers like Boulez, Stockhausen, and Berio was their absolute deafness to popular music: to rock and to jazz. I just couldn't believe that somebody could be a composer in the United States and not want to absorb all the Dionysian energy and color in the world of pop music and do something with it. I was keenly aware of how the vernacular tradition had been the wellspring for many of the great European composers, from Bach through Brahms and Bartók and Ravel.

Then comes the first great transition, which is the move west for you. So how did that relate to your Cage-ian choice?

When I left the East Coast I may have been temporarily in a bad mood and said, "I'm sick of this, I'm getting out." But the truth is, I almost went back! After one year in California things looked pretty bleak, and I was seriously considering returning to grad school. Then, just by pure chance, things opened up for me, so I ended up staying. I have to say that I had an extraordinary six years in Cambridge when I was at Harvard. So many of the things that I needed to do, and so many of the skills that I needed to develop, happened as a result of being there. I'm sometimes distressed when I read articles about me that describe me as miserable at the Harvard Music Department or underappreciated or whatever. Actually, I had a fantastic time at Harvard. The people that I came in contact with there gave me an enormous amount—whether it was Leon Kirchner or Harold Shapiro or David Del Tredici or Luise Vosgerchian, all of them wonderful teachers. The same with my experiences playing substitute clarinet with the Boston Symphony, or conducting—I did a lot of conducting when I was there. All of those things came into play in my later, mature career, so I was and I still am immensely grateful for it.

It is also a total myth we students were pressured to write twelve-tone music at Harvard. In fact, nobody wrote twelve-tone music there. Kirchner for sure didn't, and I don't believe Kim did; Don Martino joined the faculty just as I was leaving—he was a serialist, but I had no contact with him. After I left, Mario Davidowsky joined the faculty, and the Music Department and serialism became ascendant, but it certainly wasn't while I was there. Even so, composition was not presented as a particularly joyful, unblocked activity—not in the least! The only person who was really producing freely and spontaneously was David Del Tredici. David was an assistant professor, and he was at the blossoming point of his career, producing two or three pieces a year with remarkable, almost insouciant fluency.

What did you discover as you moved west? The first year was bleak, but how would you describe the atmosphere in general in California?

I went out to California partly just to see what it's like on the other side of the continent. I had read a lot of very evocative literature—everything from Henry Miller's *Big Sur* to Ginsberg's poetry and works by Ferlinghetti and Jack Kerouac. And also I'd read a lot of John Cage and especially liked stories about the West Coast. I might even have known some of Lou Harrison's music— I'm not sure. I had one friend from Boston, Ivan Tcherepnin, a composer whom I had known at Harvard. He'd become a Cage follower and had gone out to teach, first at the San Francisco Conservatory and then briefly at Stanford. Ironically, he went back to Harvard right after I arrived in San Francisco. But other than Ivan I didn't know a soul out there. I just went—just to see what it was like. I'd been listening to the Jefferson Airplane and the Grateful Dead, and I'd heard about Haight-Ashbury. It felt like it would be the right ambience for my radical tendencies. Going to Europe didn't seem right for me, and certainly staying on the East Coast was contraindicated. There wasn't an active downtown scene in New York at that point—it was just getting going, but it wasn't something that appealed to me. I'm very glad I went to San Francisco, I think it was the right place to go.

But the first year I was there I hardly communicated with anybody. I lived with my first wife [Hawley] at the time in a cramped apartment overlooking Telegraph Avenue in Berkeley. She taught yoga in a health club in downtown Oakland. I had a series of very menial jobs: I was a building supervisor and swept the garage and cleaned apartments in exchange for free rent in a building on Telegraph Avenue. And then for the latter part of the year I worked in a warehouse on the waterfront in Oakland. Purely by luck, I was asked to interview for a job at the San Francisco Conservatory. It turned out to be a life-changing moment that happened almost purely by chance.

As you were beginning to establish your voice as a composer, what was your relationship to the minimalists?

That didn't come until I'd been living in California for at least four years. When I started at the Conservatory I was a devout follower of John Cage, even though I still listened to and loved Beethoven quartets, Schumann piano music, *The Rite of Spring*—all of which I taught in my classes. But as far as my creative life and what I thought was important, Cage was the big figure. Cage was very much accepted in the music community in San Francisco, to the point where there was even a class taught at the Conservatory on Cageian theory, if you could call it that: sort of Cageian principles of making art. It's hard to believe that a music conservatory would offer such a course in 1972, but it's true.

The first year I was there, I was teaching kids how to toss coins and consult the *I Ching*. That's kind of charming, isn't it? People were used to going to concerts and hearing crazy "process" pieces or chance pieces or whatever.

But I was feeling a tremendous internal disconnect, because on the one hand I loved reading Cage's books, and I loved the New Age humanism of Cage's writings and his work: the idea that everybody could do art; that art wasn't a stilted, ceremonial activity where people came out on the stage in white ties and tails to perform music by long-dead composers. Rather, Cage seemed to be advocating a much more communal, almost tribal creative process.

We would present concerts with my students of "experimental" music, many of which were stupefyingly tedious, and I'd look out and see the audience sitting there with a blank, bored expression on their faces—what little audience we could ever get! Or we would have pieces in which either something went wrong, or some aspect of the piece suddenly ended up with twenty minutes of nothing happening, and everybody is supposed to sit there in Zen wonderment…in fact, it could be just agonizing. You really did have to be Cage himself to love that sort of thing! Clearly there was something in me that needed more expressive meaning from the music. And, of course, Cage is all about *not* being expressive. We're just supposed to let the "sounds be themselves." When I heard my first minimalist pieces I felt tremendously exhilarated because I suddenly saw that there was a possibility for a music which I could make a life in, create a body of work around—particularly with my kind of incessant rhythmic energy. But I could detect right off that minimalism in its classic embodiment was too chaste and pure for me, that I would have to find a way to make it more expressive and less bound to its procedures.

What were those first pieces you were exposed to?

A friend played the recording of *In C* for me, the famous Columbia LP recording, when I was still at Harvard. And while I was still there, Lukas Foss brought his ensemble from Buffalo and performed *In C* at a concert at Sanders Theater. I didn't go to that concert, but it was a scandal and all the students were talking about it, you know. Most talked about it in disparaging terms, but others talked about it with a kind of secret enchantment. So I was aware of that piece already.

But my awareness of minimalism as a language with serious potential was really launched when I heard *Drumming* in 1974—I'm almost certain that was the year Steve [Reich] came through on a tour with his ensemble. And that had a big effect on me because up to that point I'd been seeing avant-garde concerts at Mills College which were very free-form, kind of messy, with electronic instruments breaking down onstage, and oscillators feeding back, all part of this extremely relaxed and often not particularly satisfying musical experience. But Steve's group was so highly organized and rehearsed; everything was performed in extreme precision. And there was a beauty to that precision—like hearing a great string quartet. Plus, the music was very enchanting.

I also heard Glass about a year later—a tour that he did in San Francisco of excerpts from *Einstein on the Beach.* That disturbed me. I was living at that time by myself in a little cottage way out by the ocean. I heard the concert downtown (in the Art Museum or the Opera House), and I remember driving home alone in the car, feeling very violent emotions about it. On one level I didn't like it because I found some of it just mindlessly repetitive—the structures were so obvious. Yet I think that the reason I was upset was that there must have been something else about it that I found extremely appealing, and I couldn't quite rectify the two conflicting emotions in my head.

What, in retrospect, do you think that was?

First of all, it was something that was absolutely new—just completely original—and that drew a lot of its power from the tradition of rock music. It was very loud, and the performers, when they walked onstage, had the aura, the strut, of rock musicians. Steve Reich's players resembled classical musicians in their discipline and decorum, whereas Philip's musicians appeared onstage with the casual air of jazz musicians, dressed in jeans and T-shirts. Glass's music at the time was sonically very assaulting, very hypnotic. If you took away the highly amped sound and the ritualistic performance practice, the actual musical materials proved shockingly simple. But art is funny that way: Sometimes radicalism reveals itself most powerfully when it's most annoyingly simple.

That really was Philip's greatest period. I heard *Satyagraha* about seven or eight years later. I flew to Brooklyn with Debbie [the photographer Deborah O'Grady], who eventually became my wife, and we heard *Satyagraha,* and that I liked very much. There's no doubt that some of what Philip did in that opera influenced *Nixon in China.*

So where do you identify your authentic voice really as first emerging? Would you actually identify it in a particular piece?

There's a piece that dates back to the pre-minimalist period called *American Standard*. It was a triptych of three American standards: a march, a hymn tune, and a jazz tune. The piece was somewhat influenced by my awareness—if only third- or fourth-hand—of British experimental music. Just after I arrived in San Francisco I started a correspondence with Gavin Bryars.

At the time, 1973, my mature harmonic and rhythmic language was yet to be formed. But *American Standard* did have one aspect that would remain through my later music: a certain kind of Mark Twain American wit. And you see that in works like *Grand Pianola Music* and *Fearful Symmetries, Nixon in China, The Chairman Dances, Gnarly Buttons, Hallelujah Junction, John's Book of Alleged Dances*: they're all pieces with a wryness that I think is very much unique to American culture. Of course, not all of my pieces share this, but it is a common thread in much of my music. I supposed that this streak is in part the product of my habitual reading of American literature. Even when I was in high school I was very aware of H. L. Mencken and Mark Twain and Faulkner and Henry Miller. And later on William Burroughs—I was fascinated with Burroughs and Ginsberg when I was in college.

You've said elsewhere that in recent years you've been a little more focused on contemporary literature. And you've spent a lot of time, too, engaging with classic nineteenth-century American literature. How would you describe the impact of all this on your music?

I think American culture is a vast and rich tradition; it represents the best that we have as people living together. It also expresses the fact that we really are the product of a special ethnic fusion which breathes a unique life into all of our arts, both high and low. We have influences from Africa, China, India, Latin America, as well as Europe. I think my reading has always informed my work. It's one of the reasons why I love working with Peter Sellars, for example—that we both are voracious readers. When we take on a topic, it's always an extraordinary voyage of discovery: for example, to read about physics and Los Alamos and the atomic bomb, as I've been doing recently. Or when I collected so many books about China and the Cultural Revolution to prepare myself for *Nixon in China*.

What role does poetry play for you?

I read poetry but in spurts. I always have a novel going, but I often tend to read poetry for very selfish purposes—if I'm looking for text. For example, when Peter and I were assembling a text for *El Niño,* I remember reading probably in a six-month period more poetry than I've read in ten years, because I was looking for ideas and for something to set. I'm sort of ashamed to admit that, because I feel I should be more faithful in my poetry reading. But I go through periods of being fascinated with a particular poetic voice—Byron, Whitman, Ginsberg, Robert Lowell, Baudelaire. Poetry is not emphasized in most American schools or universities. You have to find your own love for it. When I was very young my sister bought an LP of Robert Frost reading his poems. Frost was already an old man with a gravel voice when he recorded those poems, and he'd probably recited them so many times he was sick of them—"Mending Wall" or "Stopping by Woods on a Snowy Evening." But I was enchanted by the mysterious person behind that voice, and the powerful inner life that his poems gave to the New England landscape I'd grown up with. Later, Frost was invited by JFK to read a poem at Kennedy's inauguration. We don't honor poets in that manner anymore in our society. Or maybe they've become too radical and too difficult to participate in such a public event.

I discovered Dante when I was about thirty. I'd never read him in school and only knew him as a "name." I read him every day for several months, and I could not get over how rich and complex and thrilling his images were. I don't know what's happened to poetry in our own time. It seems that the poet is no longer acknowledged as the prophetic voice among us. Dante and Goethe and Victor Hugo and Pushkin were absolute giants in their countries. When you look at American society and try to find a artist with comparable notoriety and influence now, someone like Stephen Spielberg or Bob Dylan comes to mind. I'm not sure what that means. They are indisputably accomplished artists in their own way, but I don't think they embody the same depth or cultural importance that the great poetic voices of the past poets did.

I should also admit that my intellectual life for the last fourteen years has largely been dominated by my trying to master two completely different foreign languages. First there was German, which I started in '92, and which I studied very hard for about five years. Then, after a pause, in 2000 I started in earnest to learn Spanish.

I can understand why Spanish, living in California. Why German, though?

Because I love German literature and I love the German intellectual and artistic tradition. How can you be a classical musician and not love German culture? And I wanted to be able to read all that great stuff in the original. Even after five years, it's hard! I can't say that I could pick up a book by Nietzsche or Goethe or Thomas Mann now and read it effortlessly, but I got pretty good at it, and I was certainly able to speak it well enough to run an orchestra rehearsal with relative comfort. And I think that Europeans, who generally find Americans rather obtuse and indifferent to their cultures, are always shocked and delighted when an American turns up speaking their language. It's a form of respect that we as Americans, too, rarely show these days.

But Spanish has been an even greater love, and that's something I continue to pursue. I read novels; every day I read the Internet; I read two or three newspapers in Spanish every day. For a while I was even inching my way through *Don Quijote* with my teacher. But after realizing that my vocabulary was becoming largely about horses and chivalry, I decided to concentrate on more recent books. But in any case, that kind of reading takes up a lot of my literary space right now. And then I am also writing a book, a mixture of memoirs and comments on my various pieces. As I get deeper in the writing, I find that some of my other literary ventures are having to be discontinued.

You're very sensitive, obviously, to visual art as well—who are some of the artists that come to mind as general influences or inspirations?

Well, with my wife being a photographer, I'm probably more aware of what's currently going on in photography than I am of what's new in painting. But my father was a pretty good painter, and we always had art books around the house, particularly books of American painting. Now, our daughter has become a very serious painter, and it's a thrill not only to have it as a topic of discussion around the house, but also to witness the growth and evolution of a young twenty-one-year-old who's very plugged into the art world.

Some of my first trips away from home when I was a kid were to the Boston Museum of Fine Arts, where my parents introduced me to all the great impressionists in the Boston collection. At the same time Charles Munch was conductor of the Boston Symphony and was programming a lot of Debussy and Ravel. To this day, my memories of hearing that music are always inextricably bound with walking through the rooms of Monet, Degas, Renoir, and Van Gogh in the Boston Museum of Fine Arts. I know it's a cliché that is forever exploited by record-jacket designers, but there's a common sensibility among that period that is irresistible.

With that said, I'd have to admit that I respond more to architecture than I do to painting. Painting and photography please me, but architecture positively stimulates me on a deep creative level. When I was twenty-eight years old, I had an absolutely key watershed moment that was brought about by my exposure to great architecture. Up to then, I had never been to Europe, and for this first trip I went as a coach for a small group of American teenagers who were at a music camp based in Switzerland. We took a five-day trip to Florence in the middle of a hot, humid August. I was profoundly affected by being around all of that architecture: the Brunelleschi and Michelangelo churches and palaces, the statues, and the overall sensual beauty of Florence. What takes you so unawares when you get to Florence is the variety of the colors in the buildings: all those luminous greens and pinks, side by side with the terra-cotta earth tones of the buildings and public gathering places. I saw the repetition in the structural patterns of the buildings, a repetition of blocks and bricks and stones, all played out in a marvel of organizational harmony. I was deeply impressed by how the Italians, through this beautiful harmonious unity, could create these very expressive and emotionally powerful forms from stone and marble.

Turning to your compositional methods: I've seen you involved in proofreading, which is a massive effort, for your current project [Doctor Atomic]. What is a typical day in your composition process like in general? Does it differ with each work? Are there things in common?

I have two places where I work: my studio at our home in Berkeley and another studio, a mirror image of the first, in our place in northern Sonoma. The Sonoma studio is in a very rural, densely forested part of the county right on the Mendocino border and just a couple of miles inland from the Pacific. I don't work anywhere else, largely because over the years I've become joyfully tech-addicted, and I like to work in an environment where I can mock up ideas with a sampler and a software program. I've never been the kind of composer who can work at an arts colony or in a hotel room or on an airplane or whatever. I'd love to be able to have that freedom, but I can't. I also tend to be extremely protective of my time, to the point where I sometimes feel like I'm so absorbed in my art that I'm not a very good citizen. I see people I know who have very complicated lives, but who still manage to serve on boards, do charitable work, teach, or donate their time for a public cause. Yet I seem always to be fighting a constant uphill battle to finish one piece, and that's pretty much my life—jumping immediately from one large project into the next.

But that must be incredibly satisfying: to be able to give that to the world?

I hope so. I'll have to satisfy myself by knowing that the way I do my public service is by creating good art. I work very much blue-collar hours: I tend to start about eight-thirty or nine in the morning, and I work all day, maybe with some time off to deal with correspondence or proofing. It's a very regular, very predictable routine. I am amused to think that Kant's daily habits were so unchanging that the citizens of Königsberg could confidently know to set their clocks when he went out for his late afternoon walk. I usually work weekends, too, which is a tiresome bore—and I think it's a burden on the family. I'm trying to stop doing that, but projects sometimes are just so huge and time is so limited. Work tends to fill the available space. I take deadlines very seriously and rarely am late delivering.

I usually get my first ideas when I'm walking or on a hike in the mountains. There's something about physical movement that's very productive for creative thinking. When I see pictures of Beethoven walking, I can understand what was going on inside his head. But when it comes time to write something down, I usually start with improvising. I might improvise at the piano. I'm a very poor pianist, but the piano nevertheless tends to give me a helpful harmonic picture. Then shortly after that I start making extremely rough sketches on manuscript paper with a pencil. The next step is to move over into the computer environment where I have a very flexible software system, Digital Performer, a program originally developed for film scoring. It has flexibility of the sort that allows me to take musical structures and stretch them, transpose them, squeeze them, distort them—move large or small structures around in ways that would be extremely tedious on paper. I've become very adept at using it, and, of course, I don't use the software in the way that its developers intended. I can move around in that environment very fluidly...I can do it almost without thinking.

For the last step, after I've made a MIDI realization of my piece, I go back and do a pencil score on manuscript paper, something that most younger composers find charmingly old-fashioned. Nowadays the majority of composers younger than I never move out of the virtual realm until they output the music on a laser printer. For them manuscript paper and pencils are relics of the past.

With big orchestral works, when does the point come that you jot down ideas for the actual orchestration?

I don't go through a whole piece making a pencil "rough draft" in the way that, for instance, Mahler did a "short score." Instead, I keep several spiral-bound manuscript books, and I only use them when I need to figure something out that is not clear in my mind. I might sit at the piano or I might just scribble in the book until I've understood something and seen how it works, and then I go back to the "sequencer" program, and I'll enter it into the MIDI file so that it plays back in real time. I create exceptionally long and complex sequences with the software. They play a whole bank of samples that I have stored in several hard drives. I've collected these samples over ten years, so I have a lot of them, and I update them periodically. I have two hefty computers that I run in tandem when I'm making a MIDI sketch of a big orchestra piece or of an opera. It's like flying several jumbo jets at the same time.

Going back to the early years in California: how much did you mind being pigeon-holed into the minimalist fold when you were emerging as a composer?

I did mind it. For sure it annoyed me. On the other hand, it helped a great deal, because having a "label" helped to establish me in the musical public's mind. It's a depressing fact about the arts that many art consumers, listeners, or potential fans need a frame of reference. They need to know how, as an emerging figure, you fit in. Even if your work is essentially maverick and unallied with any movement, they'll need to place as "maverick." Only after you've become familiar and the public knows your name and work can they really begin to detect what it is that makes you different.

In 1983, when I was thirty-five, a critic named Michael Walsh wrote a major feature on "The Minimalists" for *Time* magazine. It was a serious discussion about a new movement in classical music, and it featured photos of Terry, Philip, Steve, and me. I was obviously the new guy on the block, ten years younger than the others and not as purely "minimalist," but in Walsh's mind I represented the next step or the next generation. Many people read the article. It was one of those rare journalistic events that had a lasting impact. At the time, minimalist procedures were far more evident in my works such as *Shaker Loops, Harmonium,* and *Phrygian Gates.* I think it made sense to see in those pieces the evolution of the style.

What I found that was liberating about minimalist techniques was that through them I found I could build large musical structures: Brucknerian structures even. The control of tonal harmony and the construction by means of repeated motivic cells allowed me to create architectural "events" like the first movements of

Harmonium and *Harmonielehre* or those big opera scenes in *Nixon*. You just couldn't build big structures like that in atonal music.

But your work even then was clearly heading in a different direction, no?

Certainly. You can tell in a work like *Phrygian Gates*, which was written in 1977, that I was uncomfortable with the rigors imposed by the minimalist aesthetic. Right from the start, you can sense that I'm already gnawing at my ropes and trying to get free of that sort of procedural rigor.

I needed to find a musical language that could contain my expressive needs, a language that was formally and emotionally much more malleable, much more capable of a sudden change of mood, one that could be both blissfully serene and then violently explosive within the same minute. This was something that "classical" minimalism, with its chaste purity and monochromatic emotional worlds, couldn't handle. I loved pieces like *Music in Changing Parts* and *Drumming*, but on an emotive level, they struck me as being unwittingly in some weird bondage to the old baroque doctrine of the affections. A structure might gradually evolve, as it does in the best of Philip's or Steve's pieces, but the evolution de rigueur had to be a gradual process. This feeling of slow, steady evolution imparted a ritualistic quality to their music that was, indeed, very attractive, even majestic, especially when, in the case of Glass, it was linked with equally paced visual events on a stage or on film. Nevertheless, I couldn't rid myself of the suspicion that "the minimalists" were in danger of painting themselves into a corner by insisting on a much too confined emotional bandwidth. Now, nearly thirty years later, when I see how little their music has evolved, I'm inclined to think my perception was the right one.

Of course, the seeds of this new "doctrine of the affections" are latent in Stravinsky's neoclassicism. I think Stravinsky, as much as Ghanaian drumming or North Indian ragas, is responsible for the minimalist revolution. But it didn't escape my notice that American listeners have always had a huge need for highly expressive music, whether it's Jimi Hendrix or Duke Ellington or Beethoven and Mahler.

Every good composer has a period of struggling to find a voice. If you're one of the lucky ones and succeed, it's because you've found a way to embrace what you can't live without and do so in a way that's novel and original. In my case, during my formative years, I was striving for a language that had these three critical elements without which I couldn't live: (a) pulsation, (b) tonality and/or modality, and (c) repetition. These elements had been systematically destroyed or "deconstructed" by the serialists, staring with Schoenberg and culminating in the 1960s and 1970s with radical forms of composition by everyone from Babbitt and Boulez to Xenakis, Stockhausen, Carter, and even Cage.

At the time—say around 1975—it was hard to tell whether their music was, indeed, the new Millennium, the Brave New World of the future, or whether it was a brief historical epoch of experimenting that would eventually peter out. There were many critics who bought the whole ticket—Andrew Porter, for example—and wrote, telling us that Carter and Babbitt were to our time exactly as Tchaikovsky and Verdi were to theirs.

Fortunately, the minimalists didn't give a damn about all of that, and they went ahead with their own brand of music. They had the encouragement of very enthusiastic audiences who, significantly, did not come from the academy or even from the classical contemporary music world, but from all different backgrounds. Steve and Philip had their first big successes with dance and theater audiences, people who were artistically very educated, but who couldn't have cared less about Schoenberg or serialism.

There is an intriguing irony there. Minimalism was posited as a kind of antidote to the orthodoxy of postwar serialism, a way of breaking free—and yet it had developed its own strictures and in a way just mirrored what it seemed to replace.

In its early forms, particularly with Reich and Glass, minimalism really still showed a lot of the modernist aesthetic: *here's an idea and we're going to watch this idea evolve according to very strict principles.* They might be simplistic principles, but they were nevertheless strictly adhered to. I think that the reason why the music was so persuasive and so powerful and immediately garnered such a large audience was that it was really enjoyable to listen to, it was pleasurable. As I said in the essay I wrote for Steve Reich's Nonesuch box, the minimalists brought back the pleasure principle to classical music. It's hard to describe how grim and pessimistic the world of avant-garde music had become. Babbitt's famous analogy in which he compared one of his compositions to a paper to be delivered at a scientific conference perfectly sums up the mindset of the era.

This broaches the possible danger of yet another kind of mythologizing, but the idea of landscape in your music seems to be crucial. How literally have different landscapes had an impact on you or your musical thinking, and how you relate to spaces? I think of that image of you composing Harmonium in this tiny studio in the Haight...

That's a true image, and there's a photo of me crunched into that tiny room on the top floor of a Victorian on Cole Street in the Haight, circa 1980! In fact, the studio in Berkeley where I wrote *Nixon in China* was even smaller. That is not a cliché about landscape—it's very true. I do think that my pieces are unlike anyone else's in the way they summon up musical form. Or perhaps it's vice-versa...I don't know for sure. The analogy between the two—musical "space" and geographical space—comes to me from the experience of traveling over a large land mass. To be moving across a surface... let's say: you could be going over part of the central part of the continent in an airplane at thirty thousand feet and looking down and seeing hundreds of miles of the Earth's surface, but what you see moves very, very slowly. Or you could be in a speeding car going eighty miles per hour while the road in front of you changes almost every second, with new objects—houses, trees, signs, people, along the side—whizzing past your field of vision at breakneck speed. The formal idea with my music is that something appears on the event horizon, and then it increases in importance as it begins to dominate the screen, and then it passes you and it's gone. Meanwhile, several other events have arisen and are at various stages of moving towards you. I think that is the essence of how I compose and it's the way I experience my own music. It's very different from rhetorical form, which organized as a dialectical discussion of opposing motives or gestures: an A theme and a B theme, a thesis and an antithesis.

In this sense I think the way I treat musical form is unlike that in any other music. It's even different from classic minimalism where you may have at play a sense of movement and space, but the "main event" is essentially mechanistic. When you listen to a work like *Drumming*, you're really largely involved in the way that the materials are evolving over time. Whereas in my music, I think the listener is less involved in the way the music's playing itself out—how this idea is evolving into that idea. There's more of a sense of surprise and the unexpected, of an event arising, coming up and causing the landscape to shift and the mood to change. Obviously, not every piece of mine is like that, but a lot of pieces are: certainly *Shaker Loops* and *Phrygian Gates* and the first parts of *Harmonium* and *Harmonielehre*. Even recent pieces like *Naive and Sentimental Music, El Dorado,* the "Chorus of Exiled Palestinians" utilize this approach to form. Several of them begin with a kind of strumming, or pulsing, while over it rides a simple melody which over time transforms into something completely different.

But are there real landscapes that actually inspire you visually?

I don't think I ever would have written the kind of music I write had I not spent the larger part of my life living in a geographical environment like California. I move about the state: I have a cabin high up in the Sierras. There was a period when I frequently ventured with my wife out into the Nevada desert, accompanying her on her photo expeditions. Now we have forty acres of dense redwood and oak on the Sonoma/Mendocino border, a few miles inland from the Pacific. So I'm very conscious of the relationship of the land to the ocean as land masses.

Did you do the classic trip west? I mean did you actually drive across? The whole Kerouac kind of thing?

Yeah, except I went through Canada. The first trip went up

from New Hampshire up into Ontario and then across the Great Plains and then down from British Columbia down the coast, in a Volkswagen Beetle.

How does that presence of landscape influence the concept of gates as transitions in your earlier music?

"Gates" was a term actually that I appropriated from electronic music—I don't know if it's used anymore. A "gate" is a module, an electronic circuit that is either in one of two states, positive or negative, and on command it flips instantaneously to its opposite state. As I often did in those days, I would take something from wave theory or from electronic technology and make a musical "analogy." The musical image of "gating" was very simple: a sudden change of state, for instance, a change of tonality or a change of texture or a change of speed or rhythm or whatever. What made it different from, let's say, a Beethoven modulation was its completely unprepared and nonlinear nature. The sudden, unprepared change would produce an expressive shock to the listener. The most successful example was *Phrygian Gates,* where the tonality goes through half the circle of fifths, alternating between Lydian and Phrygian modes. But it's poetic license: it's astonishing to hear how many pianists struggle either consciously or unconsciously to "prepare" the listener for each new "gate."

Do you have any sense of where the tremendous energy in your music comes from? It's such an identifiable thumbprint of the Adams sound.

I am sure that my energy comes from my mother. She was always an extremely energetic person, even to the point of pain. She couldn't control it at times, largely I think because she was a person with an enormous talent and generosity of spirit, but she grew up in a family situation that was compromised by all kinds of problems so that no one really appreciated her gift and no one supported it. She never had any confidence in herself. My father had a modicum of musical talent, having taken some lessons in both music and painting when he was young. Unlike my mother, he was very patient and learned things systematically, even if he wasn't a natural talent. But he was a good teacher, and he instilled in me the right instincts to be a good musician. My mother, though—she was the one with the real talent and energy.

Early on in your music you're so intent on exploring rhythm and harmony and harmonic rhythm—and melody literally becomes an obsession a little bit later on.

Certainly up to 1990, my music was largely "about" strumming on harmonies. If you think about what goes on in *Shaker Loops* or most of *Harmonium* or *Grand Pianola,* it's really a vast strumming, various ways to make a chord ripple in musical space, to make it resonate over time. If there was melody, it was usually an afterthought. What mattered to me was the harmonic flow.

I had to struggle to find a way to work melody back into music. Even to this day, I notice that I'll sketch a harmonic scheme a long way out and then realize that I have to go back and invent melody to reflect that harmonic design. Obviously, the ideal is to have both melody and harmony arise hand-in-hand, but that's not always the way things happen!

It brings us back to the question, what was the real impetus behind atonality? Was it really harmony and harmonic crisis, or the sense of melody as being the crux, where originality could not be found anymore?

I believe that the adoption of atonality was the result of composers trying to find the *essence* of expression. At the core of an expressive moment in music lies some form of pain, no matter how attenuated or muted. Even in Mozart—*especially* in Mozart!—we experience the intensity of emotion because of the composer's expert use of "pain" in the guise of dissonance or the refusal to grant one's wish. A composer like Schoenberg was immensely attuned to Mozart's craft, and he tried to distill this hyper-expressivity, hoping that the resulting atonal music could be pure emotion, pure expression. In works like the *Six Little Pieces for Piano* you can see him trying to whittle away or boil down and distill all the critical intervals, attempting to get at the essence—the absolute mesons, the quarks, of the expressive experience. But in the end, the music lost its capacity to give pleasure. He proscribed too much, and ended with a strangely deformed expressive world that most listeners find alien and unsettling.

Describing your aesthetic overall, Peter Sellars has observed that you're quintessentially a dramatic composer. Do you think that's accurate, regardless of whether the music in question is opera?

One of my first experiences as a performer was being onstage with my mother in *South Pacific*. People tell me I'm sort of a quiet, reserved person, a typical Yankee and not very dramatic in my personal mannerisms. But certainly my response to music is a very dramatic one. My music has always been very expressive, and that was one of the things that alarmed people when I first started writing in minimalist style. I even recall one music critic complaining that I had taken a perfectly good new musical language and "corrupted" its simplicity.

Where would that be perceived?

Probably in a piece like *Harmonielehre*, where I mixed minimalist procedures with a lot of artifacts from the romantic era, tropes such as big, swelling melodies and high-energy climaxes. I've never attempted to squelch the kind of energies inherent in my music in order to avoid a catharsis or a "crisis" or climax. I don't view my expressive world as teleological. Rather, I try to allow what's latent in the material to flower naturally. I think a lot of being a good composer is like being a good gardener. You need to have a gift to know when to water something, to cultivate it, and also when to know that something needs judicious pruning.

The Harmonist

Alex Ross
The New Yorker, January 8, 2001

AS HIGHWAY 1, THE CALIFORNIA COASTAL ROAD, goes north of San Francisco, it holds the eyes like a work of art. The landscape might have been devised by a trickster genius who delights in grand effects and strange juxtapositions. Rolling meadows end in sudden cliffs; redwoods rise above thin patches of beach. Towers of rock rest on the surface of the ocean like the ghosts of clipper ships. Here and there, a lost cow sits on the shoulder, looking out to sea. Side roads go up inland hills at odd angles, tempting the aimless driver to follow them to the end. One especially beguiling detour, the Meyers Grade Road, departs from Highway 1 shortly after the town of Jenner. The grade in question is 18 percent, and the steepness of the ascent causes dizzying distortions of perspective. The Pacific rises in the rearview mirror like a blue hill across a hidden valley.

Not far from here is Brushy Ridge, the forest home of John Adams, who may be the most vital and eloquent composer in America. If you had to sum up his music in a single metaphor, you might say that it sounds like Highway 1. It is a cut-up paradise, a sequence of familiar elements arranged in unfamiliar ways. A gaudy Hollywood fanfare gives way to a trancelike sequence of shifting beats; billowing clouds of Wagnerian harmony are dis-

persed by a quartet of saxophones. Adams is not the only composer who has combined a classical education with a pop sensibility, but he is the one who has made the synthesis stick. His music,
in spite of its discontinuities, has a unifying hum, as if riding on
fresh asphalt. It is probably this sense of a firm foundation which
has given his works their staying power. His first opera, *Nixon in
China*, had a triumphant revival in London last spring. A recent
orchestral piece, *Naive and Sentimental Music*, is making the
rounds of American cities. Before Christmas, the Théâtre du
Châtelet, in Paris, gave the first performance of *El Niño*, a two-
hour-long oratorio on the Nativity, which will be performed again
next week, in San Francisco. Adams wrote much of the work at
Brushy Ridge last summer.

Brushy Ridge is at the far end of the Meyers Grade Road. Even
though Adams supplies visitors with detailed instructions, the last
part of the drive is a matter of guesswork. Unmarked tracks di-
verge in the woods, one leading to a startup winery and another to
a corrugated-metal shack that the FBI must have searched while
looking for the Unabomber. The Adams house is at the top of a
rocky hill. It is a comfortable, spare, rural-hippie kind of place.
The composer is asleep on the couch, with the collected poems of
Allen Ginsberg lying open in front of him. He wakes up, rubs his
eyes, apologizes for a nonexistent mess, and sets about making
coffee. At the age of fifty-three, he has a youthful and friendly face,
framed by a neat, silvery beard. His eyes are sometimes bright with
curiosity, sometimes clouded by a slight sadness. He loves to read,
and his favorite gambit in conversation is to mention a book, such
as the Ginsberg collection, that has excited him. If you saw him in
Berkeley, where he lives most of the year, you might peg him as a
U. Cal. professor—one of those plaid-shirted intellectuals who sit
outside the Cheese Board, on Shattuck Avenue, eating organic
pizza and annotating Wittgenstein.

When Adams is at Brushy Ridge, he is often joined on weekends
by his wife, the photographer Deborah O'Grady, and their two
teenage children, Emily and Sam. But he is also alone for long
stretches, and it takes him a few minutes to adjust to company.
There is an appealing innocence about him, but it is an innocence

sharpened by confidence. He speaks in mild, unhurried tones, halting to look for words that please him. On occasion, he breaks into an unexpectedly aggressive cackle, underscoring it with a clap of his hands and a merry roll of his eyes. There is coiled energy behind his laconic exterior. He does not talk much about his own work, but you sense that some portion of his mind is always occupied by it. After a couple of hours of conversation, he seems to grow anxious about the huge piece that is lying, incomplete, in his studio. But before he returns to work he gives a tour of his property, which occupies forty acres. He points out a few disused irrigation hoses in the woods; not too long ago, the place was a pot farm. He greets one of his neighbors and gets into a "Chinatown" conversation about the water supply and the winery's adverse impact on it.

He makes his way across a steep ravine to a large, modern warehouse. "My composing shed," he calls it. There is a tradition of composers working in the woods; Gustav Mahler wrote many of his symphonies in a one-room hideaway constructed to his specifications, and Adams can claim to have the largest composing hut in history. He raises the overhead door and walks through the warehouse, part of which is rented out to a woodcutter neighbor. There is a sharp smell of freshly cut redwood. Adams goes into a smaller room, where sheets of music paper are scattered around an electronic keyboard and a computer terminal. He fiddles with the keys, commanding the computer to play the aria "Pues mi Dios ha nacido a penar," or "Because my Lord was born to suffer," which opens the second part of the new oratorio. In meekly peeping tones, the computer sings a sinuous, long-breathed Adamsian melody, twisting and turning over lullaby chords. After about fifty bars, the music trails off into a single unharmonized line. The composer stares at the floor, cupping his chin in his hand. Then he goes back to work, chipping away at the silence of everything that remains to be composed.

It is a strange business, composing music in twenty-first-century America. The job is difficult in itself: it is slow, solitary, and intensely cerebral. You have to believe deeply in yourself to get through the process. You have to be possibly a little mad. When you are done, you have in your hands not a finished object—a painting that can be put up on a wall or a novel that can be read at one sitting—but a set of abstract notations that other musicians must learn and perform. Then you step back into the culture at large, where few people embrace, or even notice, what you do. In this country, classical music is widely regarded as a dead or alien form—so much so that jazz aficionados routinely say, "Jazz is America's classical music." To make the counterargument that America's classical music is America's classical music is somehow to admit that the battle is lost. In such a climate, composers easily become embittered.

It is often suggested that American composers thrive in isolation, that they are best understood as lonely mavericks. The prototype is Charles Ives, the putative Beethoven of American music, who made money in the insurance business and in his spare time produced radical collages of hymn-tune, marching-band Americana. Wilfrid Mellers, in his classic book *Music in a New Found Land*, said of Ives, "His integrity is synonymous with his experimental audacity," with his "pioneer's courage." Such sentiments look handsome on the page, but they can serve to rationalize failure. Ives, for all his tremendous gifts, made only sporadic efforts to reach an audience, and was most comfortable sketching in private. Certain of his successors have taken pride in their obscurity, advertising themselves as experimenters, technicians, amateurs, and curmudgeons. There was a time, in the 1930s and '40s, when the boundaries between the classical and the popular were more fluid: Copland listened to Ellington, Ellington listened to Ravel, Bernstein listened to them all. After the Second World War, however, European doctrines of atonality swept the land like a virus, sending composers into university quarantine.

In the 1960s, a band of young composers struck out in a new direction. Their music came to be called minimalism, and, by a curious chain of events, it reversed the trend toward the marginalization of the American composer. A West Coast visionary named La Monte Young became mesmerized by isolated sonorities in the twelve-tone music of Anton Webern; in 1958, he wrote a String Trio in which chords were sustained for minutes at a time. A Californian, Terry Riley, applied Young's "long tone" methods to the simplest chords, such as the C-major triad. With *In C*, Riley's revolutionary work of repetition, minimalism was off and running. Steve Reich perfected the process; Philip Glass popularized it; rock stars of the 1960s appropriated it. The Velvet Underground found its signature sound when it incorporated the eerie viola drones of John Cale, who had played in Young's ensemble. Brian Eno used minimalist techniques to create "ambient music," and from that source grew the electronic sounds that ripple through dance clubs around the world.

America's classical music, then, is alive and well, and thriving in the oddest places. The minimalists' chance discovery of a huge new audience for contemporary music suggests that other avenues are waiting to be found. When, in the 1970s, Steve Reich sold hundreds of thousands of copies of *Music for Eighteen Musicians*, he destroyed a central myth of modernism, demonstrating that music did not have to be esoteric to be audacious. And when, at around the same time, John Adams began writing serious concert works that drew on minimalist techniques, he showed that classical forms were capable of absorbing almost anything. Minimalism, for him, was an art of amalgamation, a way of linking together the widest possible gamut of American sounds. He resumed Copland's populist mission, but without any trace of big-city knowingness. His open prairies became modern, moody spaces, lit up with neon red and bathed in television blue.

When I visited Adams at his house in Brushy Ridge, last June, he was pondering the composer's relationship with the mass culture. "I like to think of culture as the symbols that we share to understand each other," he said. "When we communicate, we point to symbols that we have in common. If people want to make a point, they reach for a reference. It might be a Woody Allen movie, or a John Lennon lyric, or 'I'm not a crook.' When I was young, I came to realize that twelve-tone music, or, for that matter, all contemporary music, was so far divorced from communal experience that it didn't appear on the national radar screen. It would be nice to hear someone say, 'Look at that gas station in the moonlight. It's pure John Adams.'"

He began with the advantage of a memorable name. As far as he knows, he is not related to the Boston Adamses, but he had an almost surreally old-fashioned American upbringing. He was born in 1947 in Worcester, Massachusetts, and he spent most of his childhood in the white-steepled hamlet of East Concord, New Hampshire. His father played the clarinet, and his mother sang in musicals and with big bands. His grandfather ran a dance hall on the shores of Lake Winnipesaukee, and the family would go there to play music during the summer. "It was called Irwin's Winnipesaukee Gardens," Adams recalled in a 1992 interview. "It had a gorgeous hardwood dance floor built out on pilings over the lake. It was incredibly romantic." Duke Ellington's band played at Irwin's once, and Adams was allowed to go onstage and sit on the piano bench next to the Master.

Adams was something of a child prodigy. He wrote music, played the clarinet, and, on occasion, conducted the local orchestra, which was sponsored by the New Hampshire State Mental Hospital. He had to cope with the fact that the hospital patients who played in the group sometimes improvised freely during the performance. When he was thirteen, the orchestra presented his Suite for String Orchestra, and he became the talk of the village. At this time, he was listening to little twentieth-century music, although he did fall under the spell of Sibelius. "I was used to seeing snow and pine trees in New Hampshire," he explained. "When I went into the record store, I bought albums with snow and pine trees on them. They were all Sibelius." Adams has taken on many other influences with the passing years, but he remains loyal to this early one; echoes of Sibelius's slowly evolving musical landscapes can be heard in all his major orchestral works.

In 1965, Adams went to Harvard on a scholarship and heard the surprising news that tonal music could no longer be written. Along with many other young composers of the day, he was led to believe that Schoenberg's twelve-tone method was the only way forward. He even wrote a letter telling Leonard Bernstein that his Chichester Psalms was in the "wrong" style. Adams's teacher was Leon Kirchner, who had studied with Schoenberg himself, and who held sway over Harvard composition students for many years. "I respected Kirchner deeply," Adams said, "but my relationship with him was complicated. He was very severe with me early on. He would tell me, 'Don't bother to bring that kind of thing in.'"

At the same time, Adams was soaking up the culture of the late 1960s. He counted twelve-tone rows by day and listened to the Beatles in the dorm by night. The sense of disconnection between these worlds was so extreme that he wrote almost nothing. "I had to turn something in for my senior thesis," he said, "so I wrote a song cycle for soprano and chamber ensemble, a setting of psychedelic texts by another undergraduate. It is somewhere in the bowels of Widener Library and, to my horror, will someday be exhumed." Most of his energies went into performance. He conducted the Bach Society Orchestra and put on a student production of *The Marriage of Figaro*. His conducting was good enough to attract the attention of one of Bernstein's talent scouts, and, despite his adverse review of *Chichester Psalms*, he was invited to the maestro's conducting seminar at Tanglewood. But he turned down the invitation and decided to devote himself to composition. He had a gift that Bernstein lacked—the ability to say no.

By 1972, Adams had had enough of East Coast musical politics, and he drove to San Francisco in a Volkswagen Beetle. After working for a year as a forklift operator on the Oakland waterfront, he took a low-paying job at the San Francisco Conservatory of Music, as a jack-of-all-trades instructor. He had been studying the writings of John Cage and began organizing elaborately anarchic Cagean happenings. For one piece, *lo-fi*, he and his students assumed various positions around the Arboretum in Golden Gate Park and played 78-rpm records that had turned up in Goodwill stores. This activity proved no more satisfying than the highbrow work that he had done at Harvard. In an autobiographical essay, he wrote that "the social aspect of these events was piquant, and the post-concert parties were always memorable, but the musical payoff always seemed 'lite.' I began to notice that often after an avant-garde event I would drive home alone to my cottage on the beach, lock the door, and, like a closet tippler, end the evening deep in a Beethoven quartet."

The pianist Sarah Cahill, who has known Adams since his early San Francisco years, noticed early on his need for isolation. "He could be, and he can be now, tremendously gregarious," she says, "but it was always understood that he had to be out of touch for long stretches of time." During one of his spells of solitude, he had an epiphany that led him in a new direction. "I was driving to the Sierra Nevadas," he told me, "and excerpts from Wagner's *Götterdämmerung* came on the radio. I was thunderstruck by the simplicity and power of the emotions in the piece. I knew all at once that I wanted to move toward this intense emotionality in my own music. I began to hear it echoing in my mind, as something within reach. But it took me several years to find the technique to accomplish it."

He had another breakthrough during a trip to Florence, with a group of high-school students. "I was struck again," he recalled, "by the immediate and transforming beauty of the surroundings—particularly the architecture. I began to think about how I could create big architectural spaces in music through the manipulation of patterns and repetition. There's great drama to be found in the use of a limited range of notes and then in the sudden introduction of something deep in the bass or high in the treble. Then you achieve a real sense of space in music." When he heard the minimalism of Riley, Reich, and Glass, the pieces of his technique fell into place. He mapped fragments of romantic harmony onto the electric grid of minimalism. Adams announced himself with an astonishing sequence of works, *Shaker Loops, Harmonium, Grand Pianola Music,* and *Harmonielehre,* each of which was more confident than the last.

The title of *Harmonielehre,* which had its first performance in 1985, was aimed directly at the East Coast musical establishment. It took off from a famous text by Schoenberg, in which the inventor of atonal music set out to anatomize the preëxisting tonal system and, at the same time, to demonstrate that the system had become decadent, even degenerate. "Somehow, the word really got to me—the idea of this summa of harmony," Adams said. "I kept thinking about spiritual harmony, too. Schoenberg seemed like some religious zealot cutting off his genitals to prove how totally pure he is, how dedicated to the Lord." Adams laughed, as if surprised by the violence of his image. "Yes, *Harmonielehre*, my version of it, is a kind of parody," he continued. "But I also reached out and embraced all of that harmony that we weren't supposed to touch." The piece begins with a colossal blast of E minor, and, within a few minutes, decadent tonal chords are proliferating everywhere.

The feeling is one of tonality rising from the dead. Although many twentieth-century composers held on to tonality in various forms, few were able to make it breathe with animal life, as Adams did in *Harmonielehre* and its companions. The other American minimalists, for all their insistence on basic chords, had shied away from such textbook progressions as IVI, or CGC. *Grand Pianola Music* lands on that sequence with a vehemence that borders on the absurd. These days, the composer is apt to be embarrassed by his youthful bravado—"This piece is like a barking dog running around with no leash," he told an audience in San Francisco—but *Grand Pianola Music* has aged well: it has a startling transparency, mixing sweetness, sadness, madness, and joy.

In 1983, Adams had another stroke of luck. While visiting his parents, in New Hampshire, he happened to meet a recent Harvard graduate named Peter Sellars, who, in one of the operatic brainstorms for which he would become famous, came up with the idea of dramatizing Richard Nixon's trip to China. For a libretto, Sellars turned to a classmate, the poet Alice Goodman, who extracted an array of half-comic, half-epic archetypes from the documentary record of Kissinger, Mao, Chou Enlai, and the Nixons. Goodman's style, statuesque but wry, reads like politicized Wallace Stevens. One aria is a fantasia on "The Emperor of Ice-Cream," with Pat Nixon, transformed into a poet of American virtues, proclaiming, "Let the band play on and on;/Let the stand-up comedian/Finish his act, let Gypsy Rose/Kick off her high-heeled party shoes."

Faced with this intricate text, Adams restrained his own penchant for large gestures. He took a more neutral tone and reacted to the text line by line. His demands on singers were sometimes hard, but he turned out to have an extraordinary knack for vocal writing. His preset style of musical speech—flexible, irregular melodies, often switching back and forth between duple and triple rhythm—matched the rise and fall of English speech. For example, in Nixon's opening monologue, "News has a kind of mystery," Adams had to set these potentially unwieldy lines:

> And though we spoke quietly
> The eyes and ears of history
> Caught every gesture
> And every word.

Unpacking the images, Adams set the first line three times. The third time, he stretched the word "quietly" into a gentle melisma—"qui-i-i-i-i-et-ly." The up-and-down arc of the voice is not only a lovely addition to the vocal line but also an indication of Nixon's character: he is, at heart, a dreamer, a fantasist. Whether this trait conforms to the historical Nixon is beside the point: in this opera, he is a composite politician, a merchant and consumer of American nostalgia. Adams allows him eloquence, yet remains detached. The minimalist figuration churning beneath the vocal lines is like a camera trained on a subject.

Nixon in China helped set off a fad for operas with contemporary subjects: Charles Manson, Marilyn Monroe, Harvey Milk, and Rudolph Valentino, among others, have been set to music. The genre has been given such condescending labels as "CNN opera" and "docu-opera," but Adams bristles at the idea that *Nixon* was some sort of trendy exercise. "Anyone who uses these terms," he said, "just doesn't begin to understand what opera is about, potentially or historically." Indeed, Verdi, among other composers, kept as up-to-date with current events as the censors would allow. With *Nixon*, Adams plays a very sophisticated game; the subject of the opera, to a great extent, is the idea of political art itself. Much of Act II is taken up with one of Mme Mao's totalitarian ballets, and Adams re-creates it with a transhistorical mix of secondhand pop and secondhand Wagner. He portrays an antimusical phenomenon in a musical way. The irony is worthy of Verdi himself.

In 1991, under intense media scrutiny, Adams, Goodman, and

Sellars reunited for a second opera, *The Death of Klinghoffer*. This one had a harder time. The intention was to use the hijacking of the ocean liner *Achille Lauro* and the murder of Leon Klinghoffer as the basis for a sort of Middle East *Passion* or *Requiem*. Two problems arose: first, Goodman's libretto was not as sharply etched as the one for *Nixon*, and, second, the project came so close to current events as to be singed by them. Sellars wanted to show all the characters, even the Palestinian terrorists, as flesh-and-blood individuals, but the idea of giving voice to the murderers of Jews did not sit well with some listeners—particularly since the American premiere took place in Brooklyn less than a month after the Crown Heights riots. Klinghoffer's daughters said that the opera's sketches of Jews were anti-Semitic, failing to understand that the entire point of the piece was to overcome stereotypes. Perhaps *Klinghoffer* tried to do too much; a forthcoming film version, being produced for Channel Four in Great Britain, may tell more. Certainly, the score is a coolly haunting creation. It shows a turn away from minimalist processes and toward a sort of polyglot lyricism, or "hypermelody," which the composer continues to explore.

The reception of *Klinghoffer* still troubles Adams. "At the time, I was so upset. I couldn't think of anything to say. 'Anti-Semitic Opera Opens in Brooklyn'—you can't shake that kind of thing," he said. "Not long afterward, plans for other productions mysteriously folded. I won't go into details, but I know that some people were deterred by the so-called 'controversy,' which came from a few critics looking to turn their reviews into op-ed pieces. It may be part of the reason I haven't had the inclination to spend another two years working on an opera. It's too depressing." Adams shook a little as he said all this, in the quiet of his Brushy Ridge studio.

The *Klinghoffer* imbroglio was, in a way, a useful experience for Adams. It showed him the outer limits of the popularity of serious classical music, beyond which lay the no-man's-land of media notoriety—the limbo zone of David Helfgott and Andrea Bocelli. "Let's face it, classical music just doesn't sell," he told me, regaining his usual equanimity. "I sell more records than most contemporary composers, and I'm grateful for that, but it's still a pretty puny number compared with some records that my label, Nonesuch, puts out. I can't compete with *Buena Vista Social Club*. I'm not even famous on the level of, you know, Yo-Yo Ma. But the audience isn't an inconsiderable one—I'll just say that measuring it by pop standards doesn't do it justice. I listen to what people say to me directly. If a hundred people say they like a piece of mine, maybe it'll be a thousand people in ten years' time, and the audience will build from there."

Adams is one of the very few American composers who receive a comfortable income from commissions and royalties. Robert Hurwitz, who has been Adams's producer at Nonesuch since 1985, told me that some of the records have sold upward of fifty thousand copies, which is exceptional for a classical release and altogether freakish for new music. (The company recently released a deluxe, ten-CD boxed set, entitled *The John Adams Earbox*.) Musicians of international stature—Emanuel Ax, Simon Rattle, Gidon Kremer, Esa-Pekka Salonen, and Kent Nagano among them—have given Adams's music more than a dutiful once-over. Ax, whose reputation is based on authoritative readings of Beethoven and Brahms, has gone all over the world with *Century Rolls*, the concerto that Adams wrote for him, and he has also recorded it for Nonesuch.

"It doesn't look hard at first," Ax told me, examining the piece in preparation for an all-Adams concert that will take place in Los Angeles in February. "The notes are relatively sparse on the page. With a lot of twentieth-century works, and even with a lot of romantic concertos, such as the Rachmaninoff Third, you're going for gestures, for great waves of sound; if you ride the wave from the bottom D to the top D, it's all right to schmutz a little in the middle. *Century Rolls* is more like a Mozart concerto, where if you play a B-flat instead of a B-natural it's a complete disaster. Once every note is in place, once every rhythmical cell is in synch, the jigsaw puzzle is complete, and the picture is fantastic."

Last June, the composer participated in an American Mavericks festival, in San Francisco, at the invitation of Michael Tilson Thomas. Adams, who conducts about fifteen weeks a year, led the New World Symphony in *Shaker Loops* and *Grand Pianola Music*.

It was interesting to see how briskly his sound world came to life once the musicians had solved a limited number of technical problems. "Very precise on top, very lyrical underneath," he said, at a rehearsal. "Off the string," he told the violins, in *Shaker Loops*, and as the players shortened their bowing the music became bright and crisp. In a passage where most of the strings have to turn their pages at the same time, he asked them to practice doing it as quietly as possible, so as not to spoil the transcendental hush. "The New York Philharmonic would have had me for breakfast if I'd asked them for that," he said afterward.

Over the past decade, as performances of his operas have become mysteriously scarce, Adams has immersed himself in orchestral music. He wrote a Chamber Symphony, whose funky bass lines seem to poke fun at Schoenberg's work of the same title; a Violin Concerto, whose otherworldly passacaglia slow movement can stand comparison with the instrumental lamentations of Britten and Shostakovich; and *Century Rolls*, which has hints of Ellington and Jelly Roll Morton in its easygoing bop and swing. The multiple directions suggested by these pieces sometimes puzzled Adams's admirers, who found the romantic minimalism of *Harmonielehre* so grippingly likable that they simply wanted to hear ten more things in the same style. But Adams has resisted the temptation to repeat himself and often takes pleasure in tweaking his audience.

With *Naive and Sentimental Music*, of 1999, Adams tried his hand at something like a heroic American symphony. The title alludes to a celebrated essay by Schiller that contrasts "naive," or natural, art with the "sentimental," or self-conscious, kind. Adams says, essentially, that he can do both at once. His control of orchestral resources is stupendous, but the real strength is in the thematic writing: the work unfolds as an endless forty-five-minute melody. The theme first shows up as a serpentine aria for flutes and oboes over strumming harp and guitar; for long stretches, it disappears into a series of orchestral mob scenes, only to resume without a pause; in the second movement, it mutates into a slow, sad love song for guitar; and, finally, a fragment of it, run in reverse, is blasted out by brass instruments in the densely minimalist finale. At once rigorous and raw, the piece reveals Adams as a supremely confident symphonic composer. It is strange to remember that he once described himself as an opera composer who wrote for orchestra in order to fill up his spare time.

On December 15, at the Théâtre du Châtelet, Adams witnessed the first performance of *El Niño*, with Kent Nagano conducting. Paris was fairly abuzz over the event, to the extent that the city is ever abuzz over anything in particular; the composer was advertised as a purveyor of "flamboyance orchestrale, luxuriance instrumentale, jubilation rythmique." The audience, an immaculately fashionable one, responded with a long round of rhythmical clapping, which is the French version of a standing ovation. There were also a few boos, but a total absence of scandal would have been discouraging in the city that had famously mixed feelings about *The Rite of Spring*. The press was out in force, and it failed to reach a consensus. The critic of *Libération* praised Adams's "art of polyphony, borrowing from the Middle Ages as much as from Ligeti." The critic of *Le Figaro*, however, asserted that the composer displayed "too many contradictory influences," and that the result was "vaguely Alzheimer-like."

The next morning, sipping coffee on the Place de la Bastille, Adams was in a good mood. He had been in Paris for the rehearsals, and his family had come over for the premiere; he was about to take his children to the Louvre. "I'm usually horrified by my pieces when I first hear them," he said, "but this one feels pretty good. I think I've finally learned how to write for voices. The orchestration didn't overwhelm them—I finally got that right, after having to make so many adjustments to *Nixon*. It's such an astonishing feeling when all these elements come together—voices, instruments, words, action. It makes me think about writing for the stage again, terrifying as that is to contemplate. No more grand opera, though. You end up talking about nothing but the budget. When they were building Notre-Dame, did someone say, 'Put up that buttress by next spring, and, no, you can't have any more money'?"

El Niño looks suspiciously like an opera in disguise. It can be done in concert form, but for Paris, and for San Francisco next week, Peter Sellars has devised a multimedia production in which soloists and chorus are joined by dancers and film sequences. The libretto, which Sellars and Adams created together, draws on the King James Bible, Gnostic Gospels, Martin Luther, medieval mystery plays, and a selection of LatinAmerican poetry on Nativity themes. In the film, which plays behind the stage, Hispanic actors present a dreamlike allegory of Jesus' birth in a Southern California setting. While he was working on the piece, Adams delved deeply into Hispanic culture and learned Spanish from a teacher in Berkeley. He now watches Spanish-language television to keep up with South American news.

El Niño is a piece of grand dimensions and gentle details. The plot is advanced by a neo-medieval trio of countertenors, who function as God's backup singers. Dawn Upshaw, in the role of the Virgin Mary, unfurls an indelible new melody for the familiar words "My soul doth magnify the Lord." Lorraine Hunt Lieberson has a series of ecstatic Marian rhapsodies of her own; one of them, "Pues mi Dios ha nacido a penar," is a painstakingly filled-in and embroidered version of the aria Adams sketched on his computer back in June. Moments of drama land like shocks: when the chorus thunders, "For with God no thing shall be impossible"; when Willard White, in a convincing impersonation of God himself, sings, "I will shake the heavens"; when the massacre of the innocents begins over a sinister vamp of trombones and piano. This nativity is laced with fear: Mary believes that her miracle might be taken away, and hurries through the night. The emotional ambiguity of the work is indicated in the title, which is Spanish for "infant" but also calls to mind destructive weather.

The model is Handel's *Messiah,* but there is no "Hallelujah Chorus," no climax of joy. The first part closes with a movement called "The Christmas Star," in which the star of Bethlehem is represented by a shimmering, intricately ornamented sequence of G-minor and D-major chords. It is not unlike the brazen climax of *Grand Pianola Music,* but the tone is more sombre, more muted. When a D sounds low in the orchestra to anchor the harmony, Adams marks it *mezzo forte* in the trombones—half loud. The miracle seems to hover at a distance, just outside our reach. In the finale, a children's chorus sings in Spanish of the palm tree that bent down to give Mary refreshment. The work closes with their small voices and solo guitar. The tune is Adams's own, but it sounds as if children had been singing it for hundreds of years. I thought back to something the composer told me after he related his youthful encounter with Duke Ellington. "The older I get," he said, "the more committed I am to recapturing my first impressions of the world."

The music of John Adams, unlike so much classical composition of the last fifty years, has the immediate power to enchant. When I first heard *Nixon in China*, fragments of it invaded my head, and they did not leave for weeks. It seems likely that a century from now audiences will still be fascinated by this opera, and that some listeners will have to double-check the plot summary in order to remember who Richard Nixon was. Such is the composer's slow, posthumously sweet revenge. *El Niño*, too, tugs at the memory. As I walked away from the Place de la Bastille in the rain, I hummed Adams's palm-tree song to myself, and it seemed to me that I had just spent the morning with a man who was never going to die.

On Top, but Ever the Risk-Taker

Mark Swed

Los Angeles Times, January 28, 2001

IN 1997, THE YEAR JOHN ADAMS TURNED FIFTY, it was already tempting to call him America's leading composer. The country, of course, is too big and diverse for any such label. But four years ago, this much was incontestable: There was no serious American composer who could consistently get more attention or press; none who could generate the same eager anticipation for a major work at home or abroad; none as much in demand or performed or recorded, none who commanded the same degree of respect from both fellow musicians and general audiences.

Four years hence, we still can't claim that Adams is America's most important composer—Elliott Carter, at ninety-two, is more dazzling than ever; the reputation of Lou Harrison, eighty-three, is finally on the rise; and the profound influence of Philip Glass and Steve Reich has not lessened. But since turning fifty, Adams has produced three masterworks, each grander and greater than the last, that assure his place in history. In a recent profile in the *New Yorker,* the critic Alex Ross concluded, after interviewing Adams, that he had "just spent the morning with a man who was never going to die."

The first of those three works, a rollicking piano concerto, *Century Rolls,* will receive its first Los Angeles performance Friday night, played by Emanuel Ax, the pianist for whom it was written, when the composer conducts the Los Angeles Philharmonic in a program of his music.

Naive and Sentimental Music, which the Philharmonic premiered two years ago under Esa-Pekka Salonen, is a symphony in all but name that began the sweepstakes of monumental millennium symphonies on an extremely high level. Last month, Adams unveiled *El Niño,* a staged oratorio on the Nativity story, as his offering in another millennium sweepstakes, this for oratorios, passions, or operas on the significance of Christ for our times.

The Paris premiere, in which *El Niño* was staged as an opera, directed by Peter Sellars, was an international event. The North American premiere two weeks ago by the San Francisco Symphony and semi-staged by Sellars was a national event.

Still, Adams is a classical composer, which means he isn't about to be accused of taking advantage of the cult of celebrity anytime soon. His picture is a staple in the arts pages of the Bay Area press, but dressed in jeans, a sweater, and leather jacket, he attracts no attention on the day after the San Francisco premiere as he enters a neighborhood café in the Rockridge section of Berkeley for a chat.

He is friendly and tired, and orders a lemonade. His latest problem is the kind all composers dream about, the three performances of *El Niño* are completely sold out, and he cannot find a ticket for his Spanish teacher (the oratorio uses some texts by South American poets, which led him to learn Spanish).

One of the indications that Adams has reached the pinnacle of his profession is how comfortable he is in the role. That was not always the case. When *The Chairman Dances,* an orchestral fantasy on themes from his groundbreaking 1987 opera, *Nixon in China,* received an early performance at the Ojai Festival some fifteen years ago, the audience reacted with astonished enthusiasm. The composer, used to being controversial, was convinced that he must have done something terribly wrong. Now his level of success might make it seem he can do no wrong.

In fact, Adams has managed the considerable trick of writing accessible music that still surprises and challenges its listeners—and he continues to generate controversy.

El Niño is no exception. The flash point, as it has been in all of his works for theater, is the contribution of Sellars. Unlike the operas *Nixon in China* and *The Death of Klinghoffer* or the updated musical *I Was Looking at the Ceiling and Then I Saw the Sky*, *El Niño* is not based on a provocative idea, but rather on Adams's own desire to come to terms with the miracle of the Nativity. The fact that it sets texts from the Bible, the Apocrypha, and the very beautiful poetry of four Latin American writers (three of whom are women, giving the oratorio a uniquely feminine perspective on the Nativity) is not wildly upsetting to most audiences. What bothered many San Franciscans—as they made clear by their complaints at intermission and empty seats for the second part— was sensory overload. There was a lot to look at. Sellars brought the world into the concert hall, a place where many people come for escape. But here, the singers (three soloists and three countertenors) were in contemporary costume and barefoot, acting as well as singing. They were joined by three dancers. The orchestra and chorus performed in street clothes, while Sellars projected a film he had made of Latino street life in Los Angeles. Supertitles spelled out the text in English, and when the singing was in Spanish, in both languages. Adams says he loved it all. A *Wall Street Journal* review of *El Niño* in Paris, however, suggested that all the work needed was "a prefrontal Sellarsotomy."

Adams chalks it up to the shock of the new. Subscription audiences, he says, "have been played down to for so long that they are used to getting the same fare over and over again in the same structure. [The] programming people's ideas of something really novel is a theme. For example, having the orchestra come in not wearing penguin suits alarmed a lot of people."

Actually, even Adams admits he was concerned when Sellars told him that the orchestra and chorus should perform in street clothes. He remembered his experiences with leaving concert dress up to the players in the 1980s, when he led a series with the San Francisco Symphony called New and Unusual Music.

"I told the orchestra to just wear what it wanted. The mixture of clothes was something else. A trumpet player, say, would try too hard to be hip, and he would look very conspicuous. But last night, it was natural and not an event. And I think it was very beautiful."

The singers in the oratorio, he points out, portray Mary and Joseph as ordinary people confronted with a miracle, as every new parent is. "So imagine if the orchestra were in tails. It would have made the impression that we are these kind of people, and the orchestra is here to make us sound better. Whereas now it felt like everybody was celebrating the same thing. Now it was like a village passion play."

Adams and Sellars have worked together long enough not to be too concerned with initial reactions to their collaboration. Their two large-scale operas, which generated considerable antagonism when they premiered, are being newly reconsidered and revived— "Why is it they only speak of terminal patients and operas with that word?" Adams asks. He recalls how many people originally dismissed *Nixon in China* (1987) as fleeting pop art that would be of no interest in five years.

In fact, it has become a classic and is probably the most talked-about American opera of the last quarter-century. In June, when English National Opera staged the Sellars production, the opera was hailed by British critics as a modern masterpiece. It was said to be the hottest London opera ticket of the season, and it will now enter the opera company's regular repertory.

Indeed, after thirteen years, *Nixon in China*—excerpts of which, in a suite called *The Nixon Tapes*, will also be included in Adams's Los Angeles Philharmonic program—could not sound fresher. Some of the musical ideas are so striking that Adams is still profitably mining them. In *El Niño*, Joseph first sings in the same stuttering fashion as Nixon—both are naive, macho characters headed for spiritual revelations. And as Adams explains, Alice Goodman's extraordinarily perceptive libretto for *Nixon* only grows in relevance over time.

"To me," Adams says, "*Nixon in China* is really about the collision of the two ways of looking at how people live their lives. Do they follow market principles of life, which we are in a hectic, orgasmic state over right now? Or should they choose Communism, which, in its purest and most idealistic form, is about a life of sharing? But, of course, the whole issue gets completely messed up in the opera by the fact that you have these two complicated egos banging their heads against each other. That produces the comedy."

There was certainly nothing comic about the protagonists and their points of view in the next Adams/Sellars opera, which was based on the Palestinian takeover of the Italian cruise ship the *Achille Lauro*. The continued relevance of *The Death of Klinghoffer*—a poetic and disturbing vision of religious strife that particularly upset American Jews because it gave eloquent voice to both sides of the Israeli-Palestinian struggle—goes without saying. "Do we still have religious warfare in the world?" Adams rhetorically asks. "I think so."

Klinghoffer is also having what Adams calls "an interesting outbreak." Finnish Opera unveils a new production directed by the British documentarian Tony Palmer on Saturday. And Channel Four, the independent British television network, is about to begin filming a multimillion-dollar, feature-length film of the opera. Thomas Allen, one of Britain's most admired singers, will portray the captain of the hijacked *Achille Lauro*.

The outbreaks are likely to continue. The operas, *El Niño*, and Adams's best orchestral music operate on many levels at the same time. They are simply too rich to be grasped on a single hearing and they invite reinterpretation, which is the hallmark of great classical music.

It is this combination of depth and accessibility that sets Adams apart. Adams doesn't stretch the musical language. He is outspoken in his rejection of the modernism of Pierre Boulez or Milton Babbitt, and he embraces the American vernacular. He delights in Duke Ellington and Miles Davis. His clarinet concerto, *Gnarly Buttons*, swings like Benny Goodman. Glass and Reich were strong early influences, and their minimalism still propels his music. He likes the lush harmonies of early twentieth-century symphonists, particularly that of Sibelius and early Schoenberg. He also admires a good pop tune.

But Adams finds new uses and new contexts for his appropriations, and they always wind up sounding like Adams. World music began to influence his works in the 1990s, but not in obvious ways. The Violin Concerto, one of his greatest pieces, has the long, meandering lines of Indian raga, although there is no indication of Indian scales or rhythms, just the sense of rambling into distant territories.

The *Gymnopédies*—simple, spare, drifting piano pieces by Erik Satie—have taken on a strange and exceptionally moving role in many of his recent works. Leon Klinghoffer falls to his death to slow, unbearably sad music that Adams named after the Satie works. There is a rich, sweeter allusion to Satie in the slow movement of *Century Rolls,* which stands in contrast to the outer movements that celebrate the twentieth century's fascination with automated rhythms, everything from the early piano rolls to percussion machines.

An exhibition of Adamsiana at the San Francisco Performing Arts Library, mounted in conjunction with the *El Niño* premiere, serves to remind us that Adams also has a background in experimental music. When he led the New and Unusual concerts in San Francisco in the 1980s, he programmed and conducted all sorts of pieces by composers from John Cage to Elliott Carter to Diamanda Galas. Whoever was making news got heard, and he took plenty of criticism for it: On display is a review from the *San Francisco Examiner* that dismisses one program as "crap."

Adams, who was born in New Hampshire and received a traditionally modernist music education at Harvard, moved west after graduation, drawn to the freewheeling Bay Area arts scene in the early 1970s. And although he readily embraced that scene, he did find that after an evening of performing wild avant-garde music, he would go home craving the sustenance of a late Beethoven string quartet. Nevertheless, the years spent experimenting had their impact.

Adams got the bug for electronic and mechanical music early, and he has never lost it. *Century Rolls* works through, and not for the first time, his fascination with the rhythmic intricacy and urgency in the experimental piano roll music by Conlon Nancarrow, the American expatriate composer who spent most of his career in Mexico City hand-punching piano rolls to create superhuman effects. Adams's music for orchestra always includes elaborate parts for synthesizers, and he insists that they be programmed cor-rectly—he maintains a Web page devoted to how that can be ac-complished.

And he laments that these days, the music world isn't as lively in its use of technology as it was thirty years ago, when he moved to the Bay Area. "It is sort of strange that now when everything is so tech-heavy, we are in a slightly retroactive period," he observes. "But I suspect the next generation will move forward."

But where Adams would most like to be a pioneer is in the most controversial application of technology—amplification in the concert hall and opera house. He writes for slightly amplified—"sound-enhanced"—singers. He doesn't care for the grand oper-atic voice, with its huge and biologically unnatural sound, or all those rolled *R*s. At the early performances of *Nixon* and *Klinghof-fer*, what he got was a trade-off—intelligibility of words but artifi-cial electronic balances. *El Niño* in San Francisco was more to his liking. The soloists were so subtly enhanced that the amplification was barely noticeable, although the chorus still suffered from the glaring sound from loudspeakers.

"Last night was the state of the art," Adams insisted, "and that's Mark Grey," the composer's favored sound designer. Because of the film, the sound-reflecting "clouds" in Davies Symphony Hall had to be removed, and the musicians had to be set far back on the stage in what turns out to be an acoustically dead spot. "The first rehearsal didn't have any sound," Adams says, "and what Mark did was miraculous." Still, Adams emphasizes that where we are today with sound enhancement is where the Wright brothers were with flight.

"But I want to establish a tradition for it right now while I'm still alive, so that when I'm not around anymore and good halls have sound systems already into them, this will not be a problem. My singers were a little upset when they first heard that they would be miked, but now they are totally into it."

All along it has been the musicians Adams first tries to please, and he credits them with an essential role in creating interest in his work. He is composing a big solo piano piece for Garrick Ohlsson, which will have its premiere at Carnegie Hall in a year, because he so enjoyed conducting Copland's Piano Concerto with him last year in New York. And Adams credits conductors as the ones who set the tone for supporting new music in the community.

"The bottom line is really who the conductor is," he says.

"People can say it's the community or the [orchestra's] executive director. But if you have a conductor like Esa-Pekka [Salonen], MTT [Michael Tilson Thomas], or Simon [Rattle], then things happen."

In San Francisco, Adams says, Michael Tilson Thomas "has created the feeling that going to hear a new piece is a pleasure and an exciting thing, and maybe almost the most exciting thing you can do."

On the other hand, Adams points to an orchestra manager who once asked if his music director might call to pick the composer's brain about new music. "I said, 'All right, but a music director shouldn't be buying a book called "Contemporary Music for Idiots."' He never called."

If conductors are the key, then Los Angeles is perched to become an Adams mecca. Salonen is one of Adams's finest interpreters, and he plans to conduct *El Niño* with the Philharmonic in 2003, shortly after Disney Concert Hall opens. Kent Nagano, the principal conductor-designate of Los Angeles Opera, may be Adams's greatest champion. He premiered *Klinghoffer* and *El Niño*, and he conducted *Nixon* here ten years ago. Grant Gershon, who takes over as music director of the Los Angeles Master Chorale next season, conducted *Ceiling/Sky* in New York and on CD, and Adams wrote the two-piano piece *Hallelujah Junction* for Gershon and Los Angeles pianist Gloria Cheng. John DeMain, now music director of Opera Pacific, oversaw the world premiere of *Nixon in China* in Houston. And it was the Los Angeles Philharmonic's general director, Deborah Borda, who, together with Adams, started the New and Usual Music series when she worked for the San Francisco Symphony.

So now Los Angeles presents Adams with a potential new dilemma—a local Adams battle of the bands. But what better sign than that could there be of Adams's exceptional place in American music?

Composer Captures Essence of Today

Pierre Ruhe
The Atlanta Journal-Constitution, May 23, 2003

AMERICA'S COMPOSER OF THE MOMENT is the man with the all-American name: John Coolidge Adams. Not since the mid-century heyday of Aaron Copland and Leonard Bernstein has one composer so successfully balanced the combination of a genuinely populist spirit with concert-hall popularity and critical esteem.

From the beginning, the John Adams story reads like our national archetype, like the creation of The Great American Composer. Small-town New England upbringing, elite education, he was on a predictable path to safe, academic respectability. Then came the psychic break. "In the summer of 1971," writes Adams, "I packed everything I owned into a Volkswagen bug and drove across the continent to California."

These words, which open an autobiographical essay, have a self-conscious, Melville-meets-Kerouac cadence, suggesting that a coming-of-age story is about to begin. It never seems to run out of gas, this most recycled mythology for a young man in a young country: Go west, hone your instinct, find your own creative space. Away from the establishment roots from which he came, Adams slowly discovered his own voice and, in 1987, a measure of celebrity with his opera *Nixon in China*—a fresh approach to a centuries-old art form, and an effort, as Shakespeare did in his history plays, to turn politics into legend. London critic Andrew Clark has put his finger on it: Adams's music "exists in that halfway house between the heavyweight rigor of the Old World and the feel-good freedom of the New."

At fifty-six, Adams is a soft-voiced speaker, eloquent and observant, quick to find humor, with a graying beard and bemused, professorial air. Colleagues confide that he's an emotional man, sensitive, genuine, and never naive. Poet and librettist Alice Goodman, a long-term collaborator, explains, "John appears to be mellow, but he's very often a bundle of nerves."

Adams's music seems driven by an ambition to speak for America's diversity—to create an American musical sound as surely as Copland created an optimistic, open-prairie style of music. The United States has evolved since Copland's New Deal–World War 1940s; Adams is finding the essence of today. Naturally, Adams shuns such talk. "It's better to do your thing unconsciously," he says, "because if you start wondering, 'Does this C-sharp break new ground?' or, worse, your place in history, it becomes unhealthy for the act of composing. It's just poison."

Yet Adams continues his journey in bold, confident steps. *El Niño,* a dramatic oratorio premiered in Paris in 2000, has quickly become his most celebrated large work. *El Niño* (The Little Boy) shows Adams finding an enviable groove, fusing emotional maturity with his most sophisticated vocal and orchestral writing to date.

When preparing a new version of the birth-of-Christ story, with Handel's *Messiah* as a model, he says, "I knew from the start it had to be told simply, directly, with a genuine sincerity to it," adding, with a mild chuckle, "and not be an essay in stylistic irony." In *El Niño,* the composer says, he "wanted to go back to the feeling of an artist being a servant and a craftsman. Someone who uses his gift to lift the audience's spirit." He tells the story in a mosaic of sources, including the Gospels, apocryphal tales that didn't make it into the Bible, and poems by Latin American women writers on the miracle of childbirth. The music sounds uncommonly spirited, enlivened by the orchestra's neo-baroque/quasi-minimalist pulsations, by the citrusy harmonies from a trio of countertenors, and, perhaps the highlight of the piece, by Rosario Castellanos's poem *La anunciacion,* which Adams gives to a mezzo-soprano, one of three vocal soloists. Atlanta Symphony Orchestra Music Director Robert Spano, who has conducted most of Adams's orchestral works, recalls, "When I first heard *El Niño,* I flipped out. It just towers over the others."

Adams's story begins in the tiny town of East Concord, New Hampsire, where he was a precocious musician. Like his father, he played clarinet, but he also dabbled in composing and conducted a small orchestra whose members were patients at the local mental hospital. His mother sang in an Episcopal church choir and took young John to services. "I thought deeply about spiritual matters," he remembers, "but when I was a teenager I bounced very forcefully between the Christian message and agnosticism. I haven't been a follower of any religion since."

Composer David Del Tredici taught briefly at Harvard in the late 1960s, where Adams was a student. "Even in those days," Del Tredici remembers, "John gave off a visceral feeling about music, it was all so alive to him, and it inspired rather remarkable allegiance in people. He was very ambitious, too; he really wanted to be a success at composing." Still, Del Tredici continues, "there was no way to guess that he'd become John Adams"—the older composer is here using the name like an icon, as if Adams were our composer laureate—"as others in the class were more developed, but they've fallen away. John's just gotten stronger."

Throughout his youth, Adams listened about equally to pop and classical music, with the Beatles, Joni Mitchell, and Pink Floyd spinning on his turntable along with the symphonies of Sibelius. After moving west, he worked as a forklift operator and, eventually, at the San Francisco Conservatory. Composing in his beachside cottage, he experimented with then-fashionable styles. Most enduring is a 1973 spoken-word-and-electronic sound collage called *Christian Zeal and Activity,* where a synthesized hymn tune is mixed with repeated snatches from a fiery Sunday sermon. The composer, at twenty-six, already had an ear for catchy phrases and an unpretentious use of everyday ideas and language—a pop sensibility steering his classical techniques.

By the mid 1970s, he had been introduced to the spare, clean lines of minimalism, where "cells" of notes repeat and repeat, so that when the harmonies shift even a little, it feels like a major event. The orchestral *Shaker Loops* (1978) hints at what would lead to Adams's adult voice, where pulsating, intricate rhythms underscore flowing melodies. Using the repeated cell technique— loops of music—Adams envisioned how the New England Shakers worked themselves into frenzy during religious ceremonies. As we hear in *El Niño*, Adams often finds musical inspiration in earnest, unquestioning beliefs—not organized religious doctrine, but simple, pure, emotional faith.

Next came an altogether higher level of fame: *Nixon in China* smashed known boundaries for what classical music was about and for whom it was written. In Alice Goodman's artful libretto, the president is not the crook of Watergate, but, as Adams says, "an Everyman" who "articulates a vision of American life."

Then there's the ongoing outrage over Adams's second opera, *The Death of Klinghoffer*. In another collaboration with poet Goodman and director Peter Sellars, he here explored the Palestinian-Israeli conflict, focusing on the 1985 hijacking of the *Achille Lauro* cruise ship by Palestinian commandos and their murder of a wheelchair-bound American Jewish passenger. Goodman gave voice to the hijackers, and Adams's music gave all the characters dignity—as symbols of spiraling confrontation and violence.

"While our opera honors the memory of Leon Klinghoffer," says Adams, "we tried to look at the circumstances that came about to make this happen. That's the source of the criticism— people run around saying, 'The opera with singing terrorists,' which is, of course, impossible to refute. What we're trying to say is that if someone does perpetrate some brutal, arbitrary act, they must have a reason."

Other commentators dismiss this attempt at operatic even-handedness.

The distinguished musicologist Richard Taruskin has written that in portraying hijackers onstage and giving them beautiful music to sing, Adams and Goodman are glorifying their actions.

The opera was picketed at its 1991 world premiere in Brussels,

Belgium, and again in Brooklyn a year later. Other co-commissioning opera houses, citing unconvincing reasons, later chose not to perform it at all. Then, for a November 2001 guest-conducting gig with the Boston Symphony, Spano scheduled excerpts from *Klinghoffer*, including the "Chorus of the Exiled Palestinians" and the "Chorus of the Exiled Jews." In preparing the music, the conductor felt it was time to return to this seminal score.

September 11 intervened, reframing the debate. A chorus member's husband died in one of the hijacked planes. In fierce, often nasty debate—on the meaning of this opera specifically, and more generally on censorship and the role of the arts in society—the orchestra canceled the *Klinghoffer* music. At the time, Spano said, "I think it would have been unfair to everyone to perform it then and there, because we were just presenting the provocative part, not the whole opera, and we would have just been pushing buttons."

Now *The Death of Klinghoffer* has been made into a film by British director Penny Woolcock (available on DVD), and Spano is scheduled to conduct the complete opera in Brooklyn in December. "The work is inherently about really volatile issues," Spano says now, "but to be an enduring piece of art—and we're the only people who cannot judge this category—it must having meaning and appeal outside that volatility." For his part, Adams says, "I know that deep down inside, although [Spano] never said anything to me, that he was humiliated about what happened with the Boston cancellation. Doing it complete is his way of answering that."

That too-close-to-judge issue is also the case with Adams's *On the Transmigration of Souls*, which earned him the 2003 Pulitzer Prize for composition. Commissioned by the New York Philharmonic as its musical memorial to the September 11 tragedy, its premiere, a year after the terrorist attacks, held everyone in the Lincoln Center audience frozen in their seats, engrossed in the music, and for moments in the middle, weeping.

With future projects, including another real-life opera based on physicist Robert Oppenheimer—a Faustian tale on the making of the atom bomb—Adams has found his niche as one of America's most vital and appreciated artists. It all makes for a rare catch: the composer of the moment and the one most likely to endure. As David Del Tredici puts it, with only mild irritation in his voice: "What composer wouldn't want to be John Adams right now?"

Voice of America: Composer John Adams Speaks for the Nation

Joshua Kosman
San Francisco Chronicle, May 18, 2003

AN INTERESTING THING HAS HAPPENED to John Adams during the past year or so. With neither discussion nor fanfare, he has become America's composer laureate. Not literally, of course—the last time I checked there was no such position (though we do have a poet laureate, which must rank as an even more marginal gig). But at fifty-six, Adams has become the de facto embodiment of classical contemporary music in this country.

Of course, there have been many observers—myself among them—who have long thought that he was writing the most cogent, beautiful, witty, and technically assured music of anyone in the United States. And that view only gained credence as he spent the past decade turning out one powerful, memorable masterpiece after another.

But that's not the same as being the accepted go-to guy for the musical powers-that-be. Adams took on that role last year, when the New York Philharmonic turned to him for a piece to memorialize the victims and heroes of the September 11, 2001, attacks—a commission he fulfilled with great distinction in the choral and orchestral tapestry *On the Transmigration of Souls.*

And last month, when Michael Tilson Thomas and the San Francisco Symphony premiered *My Father Knew Charles Ives*, Adams went a step further and acknowledged his new role. To an extent unmatched by any of his predecessors but one, Adams is now the exemplary American composer—and he knows it.

The only previous composer to have occupied a comparable niche was Aaron Copland. No other twentieth-century American has been granted quite that iconic status, and for good reasons— Samuel Barber's music, for instance, is too genteel, Ives's too ornery and disruptive, Leonard Bernstein's too inconsistent, Elliott Carter's too ugly. But Copland, like Adams, could blend intellectual rigor and populist directness in proportions that enabled him to be (within reason) all things to all listeners. And his conscious determination to write music that could act as a sounding signifier for American geography and culture—the wide, windswept prairies, the mountains, all those zippy dances— meant that the nationalism of his most famous works was an integral part of what made them distinctive.

Adams steps into Copland's shoes at a time when the idea of being the consummate American composer is a much more ambiguous affair. Nationalism is (or at least ought to be) looked on with considerably more ambivalence than it was sixty years ago, and listeners are more aware of the multiple strains that go to make up any musical landscape.

For that matter, the idea that America's leading musical spokesman would be writing for symphony orchestras is itself passé. It's likely that Bruce Springsteen speaks for, and to, the American populace as a whole more convincingly than Adams or any of his colleagues do; certainly *The Rising* will be heard by more listeners than *On the Transmigration of Souls*.

But the purveyors of orchestral music like the Philharmonic still need someone to call when they want to make a contribution to the national mourning process, just as monarchs employ court composers and poets to mark momentous national events. And it has to be someone whose artistic voice, like Copland's, is distinctively and recognizably American.

Adams answered the Philharmonic's call, and rose to the challenge of creating a public utterance of enormous dignity and tenderness. But it was only with *My Father*, as I hear that score, that he accepted the full responsibility of being the nation's musical representative in the way that Copland was before him.

That may seem an odd interpretation of such a deeply personal creation, what the composer has called a "Proustian madeleine" of a piece. Yet its fusion of personal and cultural history—the way Adams intertwines his own musical past with that of the United States, as exemplified by Ives—suggests that there is more at work here than simple nostalgia. What Adams is attempting, I think—as he has before but more explicitly this time—is to define the terms of an indigenous American musical tradition. And the assertion is twofold: The tradition begins with Ives, and it is encapsulated today by Adams's music.

The second part is not nearly as arrogant as that formulation makes it sound, any more than it was arrogant for Copland to try to invent a musical American West out of his own Brooklyn-born imagination. Yet there is a slightly polemical edge to it, which is made even more direct by the invocation of Ives—still by no means a universally accepted father figure for American composers.

In that regard, Adams reminds me of another unofficial twentieth-century composer laureate, Benjamin Britten. Like Adams, Britten began his career as a Young Turk, embracing heretical musical influences (the Second Viennese School in one case, minimalism in the other) before settling into an entente with the British musical establishment in middle age. Britten was even dragooned into writing an opera, *Gloriana*, to mark Elizabeth II's ascension to the throne, which is about as court-composerish as you can get.

Yet the English tradition that Britten carried forward was embodied for him most crucially by Purcell, who had been dead more than two centuries when Britten was born. And Britten's many homages to his baroque forebear—deliberately skirting such immediate predecessors as Vaughn Williams and Elgar, for whom he felt nothing but impatience—find their echo in Adams's similarly pointed obeisances to Ives.

Of course, being the new front man for the musical establishment has its ups and downs, as was made clear by the mild flap surrounding last month's awarding of the Pulitzer Prize for Music to *Souls*. Adams took the occasion to point out, with justification, that the prize has a pretty poor record when it comes to stylistic diversity; nearly all of the past winners are of the modernist, high-intellectual stripe.

But he was also criticized in some quarters, again with justification, for seeming to overlook the fact that he is now just as prominent and established a figure—and therefore just as uncontroversial a selection—as previous winners like Carter, Milton Babbitt, or Leon Kirchner. That he got the prize for a project as mainstream as *Souls*—rather than, say, the extravagantly inventive *El Niño* or the darkly idiosyncratic *Guide to Strange Places*—only reinforces the point.

Such are the perils of Adams's new situation, and there is no reason to think that the road is going to get any easier for him. But if his current burst of extraordinary creativity and artistic mastery is anything to go by, the music he produces should be enough to sustain both him and us.

Life as Music: John Adams
Goes Public

Alan Rich
LA Weekly, October 3, 2003

THE OFFICE OF COMPOSER LAUREATE does not yet exist; if it did, John Adams would be the hands-down choice for occupant. In the quarter-century since his works reached their first thunderstruck, cheering audiences he has found within his soul the appropriate music for a swath of American history that includes Richard Nixon's visit to China, San Francisco's Loma Prieta earthquake, the hijacking of an American cruise ship by Islamic terrorists, the impact of 9/11 on the streets of New York, and the poetic mystique of California itself. *On the Transmigration of Souls,* the work for voices and orchestra reflecting the 9/11 tragedy, commissioned and first performed by the New York Philharmonic, went on to win this year's Pulitzer Prize; it gets its first local hearing on October 19 at Costa Mesa's Segerstrom Hall, by the Pacific Symphony and Chorale under John Alexander. That poetic obsession with the Californian essence forms the substance of *The Dharma at Big Sur,* first to be heard here on October 24 in one of the three "gala" events celebrating the opening of Walt Disney Concert Hall.

"I had no intention of writing a piece about 9/11," says Adams on the phone from his Berkeley home, in a one-day break between preparing the California performances and leading the inaugural performances at Carnegie Hall's new Zankel Hall, where he seems to have left no room for his own music on the all-American concert he will conduct. "But then the New York Philharmonic called with the offer of a commission, and that was like a command performance. For my generation—and for generations before— growing up with music meant growing up with the Philharmonic: the concert broadcasts on Sunday afternoons, and the educational programs with Leonard Bernstein; this was a totemic orchestra. After 9/11 some people gave blood, some people wrote books; everybody was moved to do whatever possible, and writing music was, for me, the obvious possibility."

Both new works, as it happens, are substantial examples of what Adams refers to as his "public" pieces. "You've known me for now, what, twenty-five years; you know that basically I'm a very private person, the outgrowth of my Yankee upbringing. Lately I've had to reconcile that attitude with the demand for public works; without blowing my own horn I like to link myself with Frank Gehry. Large pieces—operas, orchestra works, concert halls—need to preserve the personality of the maker while pleasing the outside world, and it's not always easy."

Maybe not, but you have to admire Adams for trying, and in so many ways. *Transmigration* feeds on the horror of the 9/11 attack, not as a Straussian tone poem, but from the inside. Its words—for chorus, children's chorus and tapes of people directly affected by the violence—form an emotional core. Voices call out the names of the missing; the sirens mingle with other city noises, and with the large orchestra that seems to vibrate as a horrified eyewitness. "We love you, Chick," intones a boy's voice out of the murk. "I loved him from the start," echoes the children's chorus in the words of a bereaved lover. At the end the chorus calls out a litany of names of the missing: "Juan Garcia...Michael Taldonio...My Mother," and the music dissolves into a pianissimo "I love you" and dissolves in the dust of that awful day.

Dharma is, of course, happier stuff; take it as the latest step in the growing love affair between Adams and California, an affair that began in 1971, when his parents—both musicians of sorts—

presented him with a copy of John Cage's *Silence* upon his graduation from Harvard. "That owner's manual of the alternate arts became for me a summons to abandon the Ivy League and move west," he says. "Thirty years later, I can still remember that first primordial moment, my first viewing of the Pacific Ocean. My own memory resounds with the writings of the others, from Fra Junipero Serra to John Muir to Robinson Jeffers to Jack Kerouac. It resounds in the music of Lou Harrison, who looked out across the Pacific and found other echoes on the far shore." (Harrison's *Concerto in Slendro,* his radiantly beautiful music inspired by Indonesian scales and rhythms, figured in Adams's inaugural concert at New York's Zankel Hall. It's high time the East Coast learned more about the much-neglected Harrison and his westward glance.)

"I planned *Dharma* as a piece about ambiance," says Adams, "and then in addition it became a violin concerto. That happened when I discovered the phenomenal Tracy Silverman, who will play the solo part on his six-string electric violin. One important aspect of the 'Californian' quality is my use of unusual tuning systems, especially that much-misunderstood system known as 'just intonation.' Lou Harrison was a strong proponent of unusual tunings, because they brought us closer to a universal harmony that incorporated a worldwide scope. *Dharma* uses a big orchestra, plus all kinds of electronic devices, plus Tracy; it runs nearly half an hour."

Within the time frame of the two Adams premieres in Southern California, his kinky orchestra piece called *Lollapalooza* will delight audiences at two hearings in Barcelona; audiences at the Prague National Theater will hear two performances of his opera *The Death of Klinghoffer;* and Leila Josefowicz will unleash her phenomenal energies on the Violin Concerto with the Toledo (Ohio, this time) Symphony. Most remarkable among these events is the resurgence of *Klinghoffer* after its troubled premiere in 1991 and a history of summary rejections in the intervening years: the Los Angeles Opera, one of the work's co-commissioners, which reneged on its announced performance, and the Boston Symphony, which canceled a scheduled performance of excerpts that would have taken place a few weeks after 9/11. The problem has never been Adams's music, which remains one of his most emotionally loaded scores, but rather the Alice Goodman text, in which members of an Islamic terrorist cell, now in command of the hijacked cruise ship *Achille Lauro,* sing of their hatreds toward the outside world. "America is one big Jew" did not go over well in 1991; it has taken a decade and more to let these words settle back into perspective and the music be recognized for its eloquence.

The tide turned. I was at the concert performance at London's Barbican, to start a dazzling all-Adams weekend, in January 2002; it was a hot-ticket item that drew an ecstatic, mostly young crowd. At that time elsewhere in London, Adams himself was preparing a film version of the score; that has now been shown in Britain and the United States, and is due for DVD release before the year's end; this month's Prague production is one further step along its road to redemption. "The subject matter is painful," Adams freely admits. "But the best thing is that people have gone back to it."

I Was Looking at the Ceiling and Then I Saw the Sky: a true laureate can even set a California earthquake to music, and this frisky bit of stage biz shook up a few viewers at its 1995 Berkeley premiere. "A few people felt that this was a comedown," Adams remembers. "They just don't know about my lighter side. They forget that my very first performance was next to my mother in a production of *South Pacific* in Concord, New Hampshire. That was me on that stage, with two other stage brats, singing, 'Dites-moi, pourquoi, la vie est belle.'

"When I first came to San Francisco," he continues, "I did some teaching at the Conservatory, but I prefer a less formal framework. Our house in Berkeley is always full of kids—my own and other people's. We work on projects, mostly in musical theater on the level of *Ceiling/Sky,* and it becomes a real workshop. The first boy you'll hear on tape in *Transmigration,* singing, 'Missing…missing…' is one of my kids. My musical life began working with kids, and a lot of it continues that way."

Ingram Marshall on the Early Years in San Francisco

Interview by Thomas May

Composer Ingram Marshall's friendship with John Adams extends back for decades. Marshall shared his memories of that vibrant period in the early 1970s in San Francisco when Adams was discovering his voice. This interview was conducted by Thomas May in August 2005.

How did your paths first cross?

John was teaching at the San Francisco Conservatory. As part of that he also led concerts of their New Music Ensemble. I think I first saw him at a concert that he was giving in the fall of 1973, at the San Francisco Museum of Modern Art, which in those days was located down in the old Vet's Memorial in the Civic Center, across from the Opera House. All I can remember about the concert was the Webern Quartet—John played the saxophone part in it. Later, in 1974, was when John and I really started hitting it off. I had a garage I rented and lived in Hayes Valley—a kind of Bohemian squatter's hovel. The area has become gentrified since, but in those days it was pretty smarmy and dangerous. There was a wood-burning stove and a rowdy all-night blues club adjacent that made the sonic ambience a bit...interesting. It was the San Francisco equivalent of a SoHo loft. So John used to come down and hang out. He and his first wife, Hawley—she was a violinist who used to love playing jazz—must have split up in about 1975. John moved into a little house he had way out on the beach. We would spend a lot of time taking road trips—driving out to the desert for a couple of days or heading out to the wineries. I used to drag him to Calistoga, which is famous for its hot springs. There was a hokey hotel with mud baths we would stay in for a few days. One time we went up there with a bunch of friends. John was working on *Shaker Loops,* and he stayed in the motel room the whole day because he *had* to finish it. We were having a great time, but he wouldn't come out with us. He was always very serious about his work, even in the early days. You couldn't budge him when he was obsessed with a piece. We would also hang out and play a lot of music. I had four loudspeakers up in the rafters of my place that would really shake the building. We'd listen to Bruckner and Sibelius, drinking wine. Back then Sibelius was considered the ultimate retro—this was years before he was seen as modernist.

Would Adams try out his own music for you while he was working on it?

John had built his own synthesizer, which he called the "Studebaker"—a voltage-controlled analogue synthesizer with no keyboard. He got the parts from a place called E-Mu, which is still in business. He started doing live electronic pieces with it, but mostly he just fooled around with it in his room at the Conservatory. I recall one part of what was a set of three pieces called "Discharging Capacitors": it involved a bunch of these little electronic gadgets lying around on the floor of a performance space randomly going off and making noises. John was very influenced by Cage in those days. He was still involved with the experimental/chance school: people like Cornelius Cardew. John used to do pieces by Alvin Lucier, Bob Ashley, and others from Mills College, which in those days was a very experimental place. Most of his new music concerts had a performance art/experimental and theatrical element to them.

For example, I remember him working with contact-improv dancers at a space called Site. That was a movement in modern dance that was the equivalent of free jazz. John was collaborating with some of these dancers and was crawling around on the floor aiming a zoom microphone at their bodies, and that was going back through a synthesizer and some filters. He was creating a live sound environment, almost like a David Tudor piece. John was really into that kind of experimental mode: he was interested in anything that was new or radical. What he wasn't much interested in was the contemporary European avant-garde, although he had made contact with Gavin Bryars and was intrigued by music of Bryars and his colleagues.

But he would definitely share music and let you know how a project was going and when he was blocked. I remember years later when he was working on *Harmonielehre* and he was really stuck. I think he was having Jungian therapy then. John was really into Jung at the time and even wrote music for a documentary about Jung. Well, finally he was able to break through, and he had that famous dream that everyone hears about at the beginning of *Harmonielehre*. It sounds like a cliché, but I think writing music actually is therapy for him.

Describe the larger artistic sensibility your group of friends shared in common. What made the West Coast scene feel so different?

I had had a lot of experience in Indonesian gamelan music. Spending time in Indonesia was an important turnaround in my own music. When I met John, I think he found my interest in Asian music intriguing. I was involved in the World Music Center at Berkeley for a couple summers. That's where I first met Steve Reich, and it may, in fact, be where John did as well. Very quickly he got interested in what was then called pattern or process music (before it became known as minimalism). That was a turning point for him, since John thought it really worked. He may have been the first outside Steve's own group to perform his music, when he did *Music for Mallet Instruments, Voice and Organ*. One name you always hear about in this context is Lou Harrison. But at that time there wasn't much contact with his music on John's part, even though people assume there was.

There was a lot of Asian, world music suddenly coming into

people's ears. It was an anti-academic music, anti-establishment
culture. Composers who were below the radar in academic terms
were being heard. And even back at Harvard, for his master's thesis John composed a tape composition based on the writings of
William Burroughs [*The Soft Machine*] called *Heavy Metal.* So he
was really into the whole beatnik thing even back on the East
Coast.

What were the audiences like?

John got pretty good audiences. He really fit into the wiley coy-
ote maverick tradition. His new music group put on some outra-
geous events. They would perform at different rotating places: the
Museum, or a place called the Hall of Flowers, which was a vast
barnlike building in Golden Gate Park. The hippie thing was still
sort of happening and that atmosphere pervaded these concerts.

*When did you end up living in the same neighborhood, in the post-
hippie Haight-Ashbury years?*

In 1976 I moved out of that garage. By 1978 a friend of mine
who actually made it big in real estate bought a huge Victorian
house off Haight and divided it into four apartments, and John
moved into the apartment next door to mine. So there were a couple years of overlap in that house. There were lots of parties, spontaneous dinners together with groups of friends. We talked as
much about poetry and literature and visual arts as music. We
were good friends with painters and other artists. Sometimes there
were conservatory students, also some of the Mills College folks.

A unique event stands out in my mind as a milestone of the
overall artistic craziness going on in the Bay Area at the time.
There were a bunch of artists who were living in this condemned
hotel south of Market called the Hotel Reno, which had been a
squatter's paradise. Some of the floors were even gone—it was
very dangerous to move around in. But they used to have parties
and art events there. The whole thing culminated one year in a festival of performing artists and composers. John and I both participated in this, but I can't remember the actual programs. The
festival involved all kinds of avant-garde artists, like John Gnazzo,

Bob Ashley, and Charles Amirkhanian. Charles played a very important role at radio station KPFA in Berkley, which broadcast to all of northern California and had good funding then. He always played contemporary music on his show in the morning, from all over the world. Any composer who wanted to get his or her music played on the radio just had to go to Charles. In fact, I first really got to know John was when I interviewed him for that radio program in 1974.

In those early years, how did the live performance art aesthetic influence the direction of Adams's music?

John's openness to technology and to how fooling around with electronics could influence the way you'd write for live musicians was very important—and it was for my own music too. John was much more interested in live electronic than classical tape pieces. His stuff at the Conservatory was aimed for performance. There are some tape pieces in his catalogue: *Studebaker Love Music* is a tape piece that he'd play sometimes, and it was lovely. His experience working with tape recorders and synthesizers actually influenced the way he composed. *Shaker Loops* is more than just a pun—he really is talking about patterns that are like tape loops that keep repeating at a certain time. I think it was probably the experience of fooling around with tape loops in the studio that gave him the idea of doing that piece. A bit later, in the early 1980s, there was the studio piece *Light Over Water,* which was music to go along with a dance project [*Available Light*] choreographed by Lucinda Childs. John recorded a live brass band that he planned to mix into the tape. A happy coincidence was that when he was recording the brass I was also recording my *Fog Tropes*—so we combined the two recording sessions. The players we got had been playing the *Ring* at the Opera and were just wonderful.

Was Adams much interested in cutting through the boundaries between "highbrow" and popular music?

John had a real love of jazz. His early piece *American Standard,* for example, uses Duke Ellington, mixed with Sousa. He was a real lover of Charles Ives and that whole eclectic anything-goes attitude. But I think there's very little influence in his early music of contemporary jazz. It was more of an aesthetic openness that admitted of so many influences. But there wasn't much crossover. Whereas some of the other minimalists like La Monte Young, Philip Glass, or Steve Reich probably show more influence from jazz musicians. But there's another thing that's important to remember: John is a very sensual—almost erotic—personality in an aesthetic way. A lot of his music really deals with longing and passion. That's what sets him about from the other so-called "real minimalists." He took the dressing, the style of minimalism, and turned it into a very expressive vehicle in a way the others weren't interested in doing.

PART TWO

The Musical Works

Shaker Loops (1978; revised 1983)

Ingram Marshall
San Francisco Symphony program book, September 1983

IT IS RATHER UNUSUAL THESE DAYS for a composer to have at his beck and call a group of musicians with whom to try out things. In the eighteenth century, when composers were often associated with court or church and were in charge of resident orchestras, things were different. Composing, rehearsing, and performing were intimately intertwined. In the twentieth century, composers have been set adrift from the human sources of their music and all too frequently write music without much idea of what it will sound like. Two antidotes to this unhealthy situation have arisen. One is to compose in the electronic music studio, where the composer works with sound directly, and another is to found one's own ensemble, as such diverse composers as Steve Reich, Philip Glass, Peter Maxwell Davies, and Karlheinz Stockhausen have done.

John Adams seems to have garnered the best from both approaches. In the ten years he was on the faculty at the San Francisco Conservatory of Music, not only did he work in the electronic music studio there (he also built his own analogue synthesizer), but as conductor of the New Music Ensemble he had a small but dedicated pool of young and talented musicians at his occasional disposal.

Before 1978, Adams had composed a number of pieces for instrumental combinations with electronic processing and sounds. While a student at Harvard, he had composed a few "straight" ensemble works, but in a rather strict, academic style. Working with electronics taught him much about timbre as a compositional force, and when he returned to purely instrumental writing with *Phrygian Gates* for solo piano (1977) and *Shaker Loops,* he brought an "electronic ear" to his composing. He didn't just sit down, however, and write a string septet; he tried things out with string players, recorded them, listened, revised, went back and tried them out again.

In the fall of 1977, he experimented with a trio of violins playing certain tremolo patterns in various repetitive patterns and the following February presented a work called *Wavemaker* at a loft concert in San Francisco. It was not entirely successful, but the validity of highly excited, consonant string sonorities as a compositional basis was established. (Incidentally, the consonance factor is important, for the composer has come to believe strongly that dissonant aggregates in instrumental sonorities tend to null overall resonance, whereas consonance tends to reinforce it.)

A second version of *Wavemaker* was developed for string quartet (amplified) and played by the Kronos Quartet in August 1978 at the Cabrillo Festival. Still unsatisfied with the results, Adams withdrew the work after one performance and once again set to work to refine his vision. Throughout the fall of 1978 he worked assiduously with a group of Conservatory string players, rehearsing and composing simultaneously, and this is, perhaps, the reason that *Shaker Loops* sounds so good: The "laboratory" environment in which it was composed was crucial to its success. As one becomes more familiar with the music, one sees the work and care—the laborious craftsmanship—that went into it. Its effortless and joyous surface belies its arduous creation.

Shaker Loops evolved as a "modular" composition for three violins, one viola, two cellos, and one bass, with conductor. By modular is meant that repeated sections, or "loops," are pieced together by the conductor's cues. At times, the "period"—that is, the number of beats per repeated pattern—of each instrument is different, resulting in a constantly shifting texture of melody and rhythmic emphasis.

Each module, then, is like a tape loop, to use the language of the electronic music studio, that is, a length of the tape with a fragment of sound on it that is repeated ad infinitum—its end attached to its beginning. (Again, the influence of electronic music is seen. The composer may well have hit upon the idea of combining repeating modules of various lengths from "classical" studio tape loop pieces.) These "loops" are an integral part of the music throughout, even in the slower sections, where the repetition may not be as evident.

In the modular septet version, there is a certain amount of latitude in the actual timing and placement of entrances; the conductor decides these things. But in the orchestral version, practicality prevails—all the repeats are written out. So although the loops are still there, their relationship to one another is now fixed and no longer a spontaneous choice of the conductor.

The Shaker part of the title derives, of course, from the frenzied worship activities of the now-extinct cult of the Millennial Church. These communal Christians had colonies around New England and the Midwest and were famous for the ecstatic physical shaking and trembling that characterized their religious ceremonies. It occurred to Adams—he grew up not far from one of their defunct colonies in Canterbury, New Hampshire—that the tremolo style of playing on the strings constituted a kind of shaking. Indeed, the execution is often quite fervid, not to mention exhausting, and requires a nearly religious, if not fanatical, application on the musicians' parts to make it succeed. (It should be made clear that *Shaker Loops* has no real connection with the Shakers, especially not musically; no Shaker hymns are used. The title is something of a poetic whimsy on the composer's part. To my ears, there is a distinct spirituality in the music, and a kind of durable, New England one at that.)

Shaker Loops is divided into four distinct movements, each of which grows almost indiscernibly into the next. The first and last movements consist primarily of rapid tremolo movement—the "shaking." There is a great deal of variety in the way the musicians are asked to perform their tremulous playing: Directives such as "spiccato," "off the string," "on the string," "sul tasto" (on the fingerboard—the piece begins with that soft and distant timbre), "flautando," "brush strokes," "at the point" (of the bow), and "mutes" are in abundance. The second movement and the beginning of the third refrain from the busy-ness of the outer movements and constitute a slow quiescence between the storms. The shaking returns with a vengeance in the latter part of movement three.

Along with *Phrygian Gates, Shaker Loops* is a turning point in Adams's oeuvre, as it marks not only a return to pure instrumental writing, but also a re-engagement with tonality. Those who have heard *Harmonium,* his massive work for chorus and orchestra on texts of Donne and Dickinson, and other recent works such as *Grand Pianola Music* know that John Adams doesn't shy away from good old-fashioned harmony and lyrical expression. In *Shaker Loops* we see him beginning to test the waters; the use of harmony is somewhat tempered by its relative lack of movement (he tends to sit on a chord or modal area for a spell), and melody is really only sensed or implied by combinations of events. Even the tune played by the solo cello in the third movement is in reality no more than a slowly expanding loop, beginning with just two pitches, then adding a third, a fourth, and so on. Indeed, the harmonic rhythm is rather slow, but then it is hardly needed to keep the piece going, with its wound-up motorisms. The resulting harmonies, although "tonal," are not functional in the traditional sense and thus give the music a vague and suspended feeling. Chord changes don't feel "inevitable."

But there is quite a bit of harmonic shifting nevertheless. In the opening, there is at first an ambiguous feeling: we could be in C major, G major, or perhaps E minor, but we finally feel it to be E Dorian. It soon changes to C Mixolydian, but quickly moves on to A Phrygian. The frequency of the modal changes increases as the movement progresses, and I suspect this is a kind of harmonic rhythmic device to increase tension and keep things moving along.

The first movement, "Shaking and Trembling," is divided into four roughly equal parts. These divisions are delineated not only through modal-key changes, but through changes in dynamic tension as well. There is an overall dynamic increase with each succeeding section, so that in the third section, about six and a half minutes into the piece, the shaking is at its most intense, and the dynamic reaches its loudest point. Indeed, where this occurs, at measure 256, the composer has actually written into the score the directive "shake!" which hardly seems necessary, but is indicative of his desire to have the players working at fever pitch at that climactic point.

Immediately following, the last section begins with a *subito piano* violin and viola harmonics on D. Over a series of bass pedal points, various modal shifts and harmonic squeakings, the busyness of the sixteenth-notes is now seriously diminished by an overall quiet dynamic. The movement runs out of steam, resolving on a breathy, triple *pianissimo* chord cluster. Bass harmonics on E-flat carry over into the next movement, "Hymning Slews."

With this movement the frenetic trembling stops and we enter a more fragile world of haunting sounds, suggesting slides and high, squeaking harmonics. The general effect is one of quietude, stasis. Glissandi, or slides from one note to another, are featured prominently here. (A "slew," by the way, is another term from electronic music. When a voltage glides from one point to another, it is said to be slewing.)

The movement's division is roughly tripartite. The first section is harmonically vague, painting a static, gray landscape with just a few harmonics sliding about to suggest life. After a slight, awakening tremolo, the music moves into a more comforting tonal area centered around F Dorian. Sliding harmonics and tentative pizzicato suggest a more alluring landscape. Especially evocative are the pizzicato slews. Gradually, slow trills appear in the upper voices, muted and celestial, but they descend, and a third section brings us to a more earthly feeling. Yet a sense of randomness prevails; the slides, harmonics, and plucked notes seem unattached to a center. This vagueness is finally resolved on a perfect fifth, D and A, on muted violins, which segues directly to the third movement, "Loops and Verses."

The first section of movement three centers around a melodic idea in the solo cello which grows very gradually. Starting on C and B-flat, it hesitatingly slopes down to A. This yearning voice is mimicked an octave lower by the second cellos. It turns around and finds its way up to D. A steady patter of quiet sixteenths on the violins (played "on the point" and *sul tasto*) supports it, as do occasional wisps from viola harmonics. After a darkish interlude by the accompanists, the cellos return, the solo with seconds now following in the same register. The ascending lyricism of the melody is now allowed to develop fully and is eventually picked up by the violas as the basses copy it below in sixteenths. The other strings, chugging along, begin their entry into the latter section of this movement, which is, in the composer's words, "a wild push-pull section that is the emotional high point of the piece." It is, indeed, quite intense, its series of heaving accelerandos leaving us breathless.

The third movement quietly fades into the fourth, "A Final Shaking," with high violin harmonics on F-sharp. This, the shortest of the movements, has more shaking than trembling, that is, a great deal of repetition on one note, as opposed to fast tremolos on two or more notes (of which there was plenty in the first movement). Things are very muted and easygoing at first—we need a rest after the fury of the preceding movement—but the music gathers momentum after a minute or two and we are into a pure Vivaldian sixteenth-note clatter of dazzling speed on unisons, fourths, and fifths. The final, subdued measures of the work feature a gentle rocking over the natural harmonics of the open strings of violins and violas while the cellos and basses hold long pedals. I like to think of these final, disembodied "spirit" shakings as some kind of evocation of the heavenly music the Shakers could never have made in this life.

Harmonium for Large Orchestra and Chorus (1980–81)

Michael Steinberg
San Francisco Symphony program book, April 1981

HARMONIUM IS THE WORK that really put John Adams on the map. Professionals knew about him, especially in the Bay Area, where he had lived the past nine years, but the wildly successful Harmonium premiere was his first performance by a major, mainstream organization.

In April 1981, I was in my second season as the San Francisco Symphony's artistic adviser, and so I had concocted the program on which *Harmonium* had its first hearing. Because it was Holy Week we began with Vivaldi's *Sinfonia al Santo Sepolcro* and a wonderful unknown treasure of American music, George Templeton Strong's *Chorale on a Theme by Leo Hassler*. Then came *Harmonium,* and after the intermission, Alfred Brendel, making his long-awaited first appearance with the orchestra, played Beethoven's "Emperor" Concerto. It was Brendel and Beethoven who caused the hall to be sold out that week, and that great pianist and de Waart together did, in fact, deliver a splendid run of "Emperors," but I think none of us had anticipated how those concerts would stick in our memories primarily as the ones at which we first heard *Harmonium.* Indeed, for almost everyone at the concerts that week it was the first time of hearing any music by John Adams, already known in the new-music world, particularly in the Bay Area, but an unknown quantity to the Symphony's subscription audience.

The concert began in a haze of muddle. I had suggested to de Waart that he go without a break from Vivaldi to Strong. What neither he nor I had expected was that the two parts of this ecumenical pair (Strong being based on a meditation on the "Passion Chorale" that plays such a large role in Bach *Saint Matthew Passion*)—both for string orchestra, quiet, fairly slow, and with a certain "holy" aura—would be heard by many in the audience as one piece. And naturally, when the next piece began, with the chorus chugging out its insistent repetitions of the syllable "no," those same people thought they were now hearing Strong, a composer as new to them as Adams. Only gradually, as syllables became words—some of them words with very secular sentiments, indeed—did the situation become clear. When, thirty-five minutes along, *Harmonium* came to its end, enormous applause erupted. At de Waart's bidding, a lithe young man with floppy hair and glasses, and possessed of electrifying energy, ran onto the stage, to be greeted by an outburst of cheering. That evening John Adams became, unmistakably, a major figure on our musical landscape. And we would often again see that fired-up figure taking possession of the stage, and with orchestras and in opera houses all over. The hair is gray now, but the energy and the lively charm of that figure have not diminished by one iota.

Born and raised in New England, and a Harvard graduate, he decided in 1971, the year he turned twenty-four, to head west. Not that the East had not been good to him: it had given him contact with his Vermont neighbor, Walter Piston, a kind, informative, and encouraging friend to the gifted and inquisitive boy; put Leon Kirchner into his life as an imaginative and intellectually vigorous teacher of composition; allowed him to get to know Kirchner's own teacher, Roger Sessions, a humane and compassionate presence at a time when Adams, like so many of us, was depressed by what was going on in Vietnam; brought him the practical experience of exercising his clarinet skills as a substitute player in the

Boston Symphony; and had afforded his first adventures in conducting as director of Harvard's Bach Society Orchestra. But his parents had unwittingly planted the seeds of unrest by giving him a copy of *Silence,* John Cage's collection of lectures and writings, as a graduation present. Of *Silence,* the *Village Voice* critic Jill Johnston said when it appeared in 1962 that "those who read [it] should find it impossible to curl up inside any comfortable box made before picking up the book." Sure enough, for John Adams it called into question everything that Cambridge 02138 stood for. Packing up the Beetle was the inevitable next step.

Adams first found a job as a forklift operator in an Oakland warehouse, but only a year later he had joined the faculty of the San Francisco Conservatory and had become part of the Bay Area's music community. He got involved with the work of Cage and other figures of the avant-garde; he organized concerts of electronic and chance music; and he built his own synthesizer. Paradoxically, it was what he called his "electronic immersion" and his involvement with technical points of tuning and the harmonic series that led to his "diatonic conversion. It made me realize the *resonant* power of consonance." In 1980, the examples he cited were Beethoven, Sibelius, the orchestral Wagner, and early Stravinsky. That would still be his core list, though on the whole his sympathies are larger than they were then.

In the mid-1970s, Adams encountered the new minimalist music of Steve Reich and others, and saw how its rediscovery of what he calls "the primordial elements of music—pulse, repetition, tonality—might hold the key to creating something closer to my own musical genotype.... Minimalism was a profound breath of fresh air." But even in 1980, in the first conversation I had with him about *Harmonium,* he voiced reservations, describing himself as "a minimalist bored with minimalism. It can really be a bore— you get those Great Prairies of non-event—but that highly polished, perfectly resonant sound is wonderful."

In that same conversation, the future composer of *Harmonielehre,* named for Arnold Schoenberg's great, far-reaching, imaginative treatise, pulled Charles Rosen's book on Schoenberg from a shelf and read: "Originality requires the exploration of a

self-created universe coherent and rich enough to offer possibilities beyond the development of an individual manner." Adams's
hope, he said then, was "to build forms more impacted" than
those of Reich and Philip Glass, "forms that grow," and the big
works he has written since—notably *Harmonielehre,* his operas
Nixon in China and *The Death of Klinghoffer,* the Violin Concerto,
and *Naive and Sentimental Music*—attest to how confidently and
successfully he has realized the program he had assigned himself.
Actually, as we can hear in *Shaker Loops,* whose original version
dates from 1978, and in *Phrygian Gates* (1977), he had already set
out on that path by 1980.

When Edo de Waart, an effective proponent of new music as a
very young man in Amsterdam and later as conductor of the Rot-
terdam Philharmonic, moved to the San Francisco Symphony in
1977, he said he would value the assistance of someone who could
bring him up to speed on the subject of recent American music
and who could keep him informed. Milton Salkind, then president
of the San Francisco Conservatory of Music, suggested that
Adams, who was teaching theory and running a new-music ensemble at the Conservatory, would be ideal for the task, and what
began as an informal arrangement grew into a real position as the
orchestra's composer in residence, an appointment that came to
serve as a model for many such relationships between composers
and orchestras in the United States. At de Waart's urging, the San
Francisco Symphony commissioned *Harmonium* for the orchestra's first season in its new home, Davies Symphony Hall, and this
was followed over the years, going far past the end of Adams's
composer-in-residence tenure, by commissions to which Adams
responded with *Harmonielehre* (1984), *El Dorado* (1991), the Nativity oratorio *El Niño* (2000, commissioned jointly by several
other organizations in America and Europe), *My Father Knew
Charles Ives* (2003), and another work to follow in about 2007.

In 1981 I was in my second season as the San Francisco Symphony's artistic adviser and, given Adams's references to
Beethoven as his ideal consonant composer—I vividly remember
how moved he was by the simplicity of the soft G-major chords
and their lingering resonance in the little Goethe cantata *Meer-*

esstille und glückliche Fahrt (*Becalmed at Sea and Prosperous Voyage*), which he had just heard—I wish I could claim that putting *Harmonium* and the "Emperor" Concerto on the same concert was an inspired programming idea of mine; rather, it was by happy chance.

Particularly in its magnificent first movement, the "Emperor" is one of those amazing pieces in which Beethoven makes amazingly basic and seemingly neutral material—scales and arpeggios and clichés such as "horn fifths"—yield a triumphantly personal music. No less than that great concerto, *Harmonium* is a celebration of "the primordial," most especially a celebration of major and minor chords. That is, in fact, one of the sources of its provocative title. Another was the thought, abandoned almost immediately, that he might set poems from Wallace Stevens's debut collection by that name.

A question I always like to ask a composer is "What was the first thing you knew about this piece?" The answer for *Harmonium,* as Adams formulated it in a 1984 essay, was that the work "began with a simple, totally formed mental image: that of a single tone coming out of a vast, empty space and, by means of a gentle unfolding, evolving into a rich, pulsating fabric of sound. This wordless 'preverbal' creation scene describes the opening of the piece, and it was fixed in my mind's eye long before I had even made the decision whether or not to use a text. Some time passed before I was able to get beyond this initial image. I had an intuition of what the work would feel like, but I could not locate the poetic voice to give it shape." At one stage, Adams considered writing a choral piece with no text, just syllables and sounds. Then, having rejected Wallace Stevens as a voice alien to his own, Adams almost at once and almost simultaneously came across the poems by John Donne and Emily Dickinson that he went on to set in *Harmonium* and which give it its distinctive texture and shape.

Harmonium begins with quietly insistent repetitions of one note—D—and one syllable—"no." (Something else Adams loves about Beethoven is his "rhetorical repetitions.") The Donne poem he had found was "Negative Love." Its title, which Adams found "irresistible," also suggested to him the repetitions—two minutes of them—of no no no no no no no no no no no no no no,—"and I wanted a syllable that I could use as a kind of sonorous building block." "No" becomes "ne," which is repeated equally urgently with the pulsing of what Adams once called "Beethoven quarter-notes" until syllables become words, and the music suddenly opens onto the broad declamation on simple chords of Donne's first lines: "I never stoop'd so low, as they/Which on an eye, cheek, lip, can prey."

Donne, that tough-minded early-seventeenth-century cleric, can be a difficult poet, and that was, in fact, one of the qualities that drew Adams to "Negative Love": "Each time I read it, it seemed to mean something different." In a brilliant essay on Donne in Louis Kronenberger's *Atlantic Brief Lives*, Denis Donoghue summarizes the poet's intellectual temper thus: "Donne's mind delights in conflict, challenge, interrogation. 'I would not that death should take me asleep,' he wrote to Sir Henry Goodyer…. Far from evading paradoxes and problems, he conspired with them, lest he should miss the pleasures of casuistry. He preferred the possible to the probable, because it provided more scope for energy and force."

In dense, characteristically argumentative terms, Donne compares—in order to reject—physical and intellectual love with the love of God. Adams proclaims the first stanza in grandly sonorous block chords. His harmonies are diatonic with an occasional touch of something modal, heading, as the poet rejoices in the braveness of his love, for "Emperor" Concerto E-flat major. But while the harmonies for the most part move and change slowly, the surface of the music is a continuous rippling, an exhilarating surge in relentless crescendo, and—shades of Beethoven again—possessed of a powerfully determined sense of harmonic and rhetorical goal. After an interlude comes Donne's second stanza, with more friction between the chords than before, and with more clash between conflicting rhythms as well. And when Donne finally sets the word "no" as an end-rhyme (with know)—catching up, as it were, with what Adams has been doing since measure one—the music returns to and expands the iterations of the opening pages. Slowly tempo and temperature subside, and a few sopranos sing the last line: "Though I speed not, I cannot miss."

The only well-known musical setting of Donne before *Harmonium* was Benjamin Britten's *Holy Sonnets of John Donne* (1945); several American composers, on the other hand, have been drawn to Emily Dickinson, most famously Aaron Copland, but also Ernst Bacon, Elliott Carter, John Harbison, George Perle, and Michael Tilson Thomas. It is hard to imagine lives of poets more different than those of the eloquent dean of Saint Paul's in London, so much the public figure, and the maiden lady in white who passed almost every day of her fifty-six years in her parents' house in Amherst, Massachusetts.

Emily Dickinson was known to have written a few poems as a girl, and in 1862—she was then thirty-two—she hesitantly showed some more recent ones to the essayist Thomas Wentworth Higginson, asking, did they breathe? No one was prepared to find that on her death she had left 1,175 poems, most of them on sheets of five-by-eight letter paper stitched in fascicles of five or six, but many, the unrevised or unfinished ones, in the margins of letters, on brown paper bags, on bills, programs, invitations, leaves torn from old notebooks, subscription blanks, drugstore bargain flyers, recipes, shopping lists, cutoff margins of newspapers, a Chocolat Meunier wrapper, the insides of used envelopes, and detached envelope flaps—a catalogue I take from Millicent Todd Bingham's introduction to *Bolts of Melody*, a 1945 gathering of hitherto unpublished Dickinson poems.

She used common words as though they were new as, with what the poet Jean Garrigue called "her astigmatic gaze," she saw all substances as rare. Lungs and ears, not the grammar book, determined her wondrous, breathing—yes, breathing—punctuation. Copland, in his preface to his *Twelve Poems of Emily Dickinson*, lists the "subject matter particularly close to Miss Dickinson: nature, death, life, eternity." Like Donne, she wrote about transcendental love, and her words, also aimed at God, are rich with erotic imagery.

Adams begins his setting of "Because I could not stop for Death" virtually without preamble (in contrast to the long one that prepares "Negative Love"), and he proceeds through the poem swiftly and simply. (Adams sets the poem in the version he first read it in, the one generally in circulation before the appearance of Thomas H. Johnson's scholarly edition of 1970 that undid Higginson's taming of Dickinson's punctuation and vocabulary.) Notable here, and in striking contrast to "Negative Love," is the series of sudden and bold shifts of harmonic center. In his 1984 essay on *Harmonium,* Adams wrote that "the 'placing' of the speaker—in a slowly moving carriage while the sights and sounds of her life gradually pass her by—created an irresistible opportunity for a slow, disembodied rhythmic continuum."

Mounting sonority and gathering speed create an overwhelming surge. This makes a bridge to "Wild Nights," words which in this impassioned projection often turn into "wi-hild" or "oho-wild" nights. These are not words we are apt to associate with Emily Dickinson, but this ecstasy is also part of her ever mysterious essence. Propelled by obsessive repetitions of rapid broken chords, the music moves with enflaming energy. The phrase "Rowing in Eden" becomes a series of canons, set over a return of the "Beethoven quarter-notes" and under a broad and powerful declamation of the final lines:

> Might I but moor—Tonight—
> In Thee!

Again I quote the composer: "If 'Negative Love' is a meditation on love and 'Because I could not stop for Death' a sequence of tableau-like images about the arrest of time, 'Wild Nights' embraces both...themes with a poetic intensity that is at once violent and sexual and full of that longing for forgetfulness which is at the core of all Dickinson's works. Her goal is far from being some kind of Apollonian serenity of self-realization, her Eden is the sea, the universal archetype of the Unconscious, an immense, nocturnal ocean of feeling where the slow, creaking funeral carriage of the earlier poem now yields to the gentle, unimpeded 'rowing' of the final image."

Yields, I want to add, after a passage through tempests, winds, and waves that lift us up and bring us crashing down. At the end,

Emily Dickinson's and John Adams's great *Liebestod*—or at least *Liebesnacht*—rises to one last luminous chord of A major (with an F-sharp sounding softly in the bass), and from that height the orchestra, leaving the chorus behind, makes the descent alone to recede into silence.

Grand Pianola Music (1982)

Sarah Cahill
Lincoln Center's John Adams Festival program book
New York City, 2003

ON ITS WEB SITE, the Pianola Institute calls John Adams "that man who wrote *Grand Pianola Music,* not for Pianola, and the piano concerto *Century Rolls* without rolls!!" Pianola fanatics may be the only people still rankled by this piece, which has metamorphosed over the last twenty years from controversy to classic. *Grand Pianola Music,* along with *Harmonium* and *Harmonielehre,* established Adams's gift for enfolding the repetitive patterns of minimalism within sweeping orchestral gestures. It was also one of the first major works in which he incorporated American vernacular music into the classical symphonic tradition. As he puts it, "Duelling pianos, cooing sirens, Valhalla brass, thwacking bass drums, gospel triads, and a Niagara of cascading flat keys all learned to cohabit as I wrote the piece."

Grand Pianola Music is in two movements, titled "Part I" and *On the Dominant Divide.* Part I is actually in two joined sections; Adams describes the second as "a slow serene pasture with grazing tuba."

A considerable amount of tension builds through the first half of *Grand Pianola Music*'s Part I, partly because it appears to be a concerto for two pianos, but it doesn't behave like one. For a long time, the pianos mingle with the orchestral body, echoing the repeated notes and ostinato patterns of other instruments, but never rising above the surface. The pianists often share material, but with one slightly behind the other, a sixteenth-or an eighth-note apart (a technique reminiscent of Adams's 1977 *Phrygian Gates,* whose own modal loops and phasing were derived from the composer's still earlier electronic work). Three women's voices sing wordless harmony in triads; they, too, behave more like symphonic instruments than as soloists. Suddenly, the pianists burst out with arpeggios in B-flat major (which the musicologist Nicolas Slonimsky calls "the key of the universe"), with strong echoes of the piano's heroic entrance in Beethoven's "Emperor" Concerto; we are on the threshold of a real concerto, enhanced by Wagnerian brass.

On the Dominant Divide applies minimalist techniques to the simplest of chord progressions, I-V-I. The oscillation of tonic and dominant phrases generate a melody and chord progression in the key of E-flat major—the key of Beethoven's "Emperor" Concerto and of his "Eroica" Symphony. Each repetition of the melody gains in romantic extravagance, reinforced by ever mounting layers of brass and bass drum and symphonic fireworks. Finally, in Adams's words, "it goes over the top to emerge in the gurgling C major of the lowest registers of the pianos. From here it is a gradually accelerating race to the finish, with the tonalities flipping back and forth from major to minor."

On the genesis of the piece, Adams explains: "As with *Harmonielehre,* which began with a dream of a huge oil tanker rising like a Saturn rocket out of the waters of San Francisco Bay, *Grand Pianola Music* also started with a dream image in which, while driving down Interstate Route 5, I was approached from behind by two long, gleaming, black stretch limousines. As the vehicles drew up beside me they transformed into the world's longest Steinway pianos…twenty, maybe even thirty feet long. Screaming down the highway at ninety miles per hour, they gave off volleys of B-flat and E-flat major arpeggios. I was reminded of walking down the hallways of the San Francisco Conservatory, where I used to teach, hearing the sonic blur of twenty or more pianos playing Chopin, the "Emperor" Concerto, Hanon, Rachmaninoff, the Maple Leaf Rag, and much more."

Light Over Water: The Genesis of a Music (1983)

Ingram Marshall

In the early 1980s, while the Los Angeles Museum of Contemporary Art's permanent building was under construction, the institution had at its disposal a couple of industrial warehouses in downtown Los Angeles to present interdisciplinary programs under the general title of "The Temporary Contemporary." One of these projects was *Available Light*, the collective title for a collaboration uniting John Adams with the dancer and New York–based choreographer Lucinda Childs (who would later choreograph *Doctor Atomic*) and with Los Angeles–based architect Frank Gehry. Also contributing were Beverly Emmons (lighting) and Ronaldus Shamask (costumes). *Available Light* also drew on the work of photographers Grant Mudford and Garry Winogrand, and the project was documented in the Los Angeles Museum of Contemporary Art publication *Available Light*, which includes essays by Jeremy Gilbert-Rolfe, Susan Sontag, and Ingram Marshall. The following is Marshall's essay on Adams's musical contribution to the project, which carries the title *Light Over Water* and was included as an LP record with the original publication.

LIGHT OVER WATER IS A LONG, unbroken composition with contrasting sections whose boundaries are so subtle as to be almost imperceptible. Formally, it is a balancing act among its widely divergent moods. Technically, it is a kind of symphony played by an orchestra of both electric and natural instruments, and frozen into its idealized form by means of a multichannel tape recorder. In its formal scope and approach to orchestration, it departs radically from other music made with synthesizers. Yet to call it electronic music is not entirely misleading.

John Adams has an aversion to the term "electronic music," at least in connection within his own work. He feels it has become a catchword that recalls the era of *musique concrète,* the scraping, screeching, hard-edge days of the first music recording studios and the names associated with them: Varèse, Stockhausen, Ussachevsky. If the term "electronic music" implies a stylistic distinction, John Adams wants no part of it. But such a distinction need not be drawn, for the term is a general one embracing a multitude of persuasions, and can mean simply any music that relies on electronics for its realization.

Virtually every young composer whose musical language grew to maturity during the 1960s and 1970s was affected by the electronic medium's apparently infinite range of possibility and by its otherworldly universe of novel sounds. The potential for a music that could exist in a disembodied state, pure and no longer dependent on the unpredictable midwifery of the live performer, acted as an irresistible magnet to a whole generation of composers fortunate enough to inherit the fruits of a technically advanced society.

But if *Light Over Water* is electronic in a technical sense, in perhaps a purely aesthetic one it is rather a kind of orchestral music clothed in electronic garb. This paradox makes more sense in light of Adams's earlier music. Even though his better-known pieces—*Shaker Loops, Harmonium,* and *Phrygian Gates*—are strictly acoustic (do not involve studio amplification by electrical means), they inspire within the listener subliminal awareness of the electronic experience. The repetition pattern techniques pioneered by Steve Reich are still evident in both *Phrygian Gates* (1977) and *Shaker Loops* (1978). But the complex of slowly shifting rhythms of color and nuances of melodic modulation that Adams superimposes on, and makes grow out of, a highly energized, pulsating surface is more important. This chiaroscuro effect, riding over a bright, dancing, energized surface, came from a heightened sensitivity to sound, which Adams derived from working with the intimate form of electronics. As one could sculpt and mold sound in the studio, using the tape recorder and modular synthesizer, so one could return to the instruments of the orchestra, as Adams did, and compose for them as if they were a breed of super-synthesizers, the most flexible and vital of all.

Shaker Loops, a work that began as a study for three violins and eventually became a half-hour composition for full string orchestra, was influenced by electronic studio techniques. The loops refer to little melodic fragments that are repeated over and over by the players. When each instrument is assigned a loop of different length, the resulting counterpoint among the parts is in constant flux. This technique, an extended and more complex approach to the phase patterns of Steve Reich and Terry Riley, has its analogue in the recording studio, where tape loops (literally, segments of magnetic tape whose tails are spliced to their heads and which generate infinitely repeating melodic or rhythmic figurations) are a common means of creating textural continuity.

The timbral awareness of *Shaker Loops* also reveals Adams's longtime experience with sound synthesis. Much of the haunting, spectral quality of the piece derives from the unusual use of the natural harmonics of the strings themselves: in the shimmering upper resonances of these freely vibrating strings, one is reminded of delicately filtered electronic sounds.

By 1981, Adams's ideas of massed sonorities and a carefully woven internal structure of shifting textures had grown and were realized in immense proportions. *Harmonium,* the huge choral setting of texts by John Donne and Emily Dickinson, for a hundred-piece orchestra and two hundred voices, brought to a logical conclusion the experiments begun only three years earlier with the little study for three violins. Despite *Harmonium's* predilection for traditional orchestral sonorities and resources, one can still discern in it the timbral influences of the synthesizer and electronic studio, particularly in the way Adams uses repetition and harmonic stasis to create sonic washes—great waves of modulating timbres that sparkle with electricity. *Harmonium* shares with *Light*

Over Water an introspective, meditative feeling infused with an intense emotion that is more pronounced than in *Shaker Loops* or *Phrygian Gates.*

In the summer of 1982, Adams composed a score for the film *Matter of Heart,* a documentary about the psychoanalyst Carl Gustav Jung. He worked with the synthesizer, but with a digital keyboard version more sophisticated than the older modular analogue type used during the late 1960s. He combined the "living" sound of a string orchestra with the electronic parts, and a new timbral merging was born. If electronic music had earlier opened up new avenues of instrumental writing, then the opposite was now happening. The instrumental world had begun affecting the way Adams's electronic music sounded. Gone were the swishes and swoops and futuristic sound effects of early tape music—the massed sonic conglomerates, the Varèsian granitic sounds. In their stead comes simple melodic and harmonic invention, but in timbral robes unheard before.

As synthesizers come to mimic the "real thing," they truly begin to live up to their hitherto inappropriate name. Technology offers the possibility of a truly synthetic orchestra. Thus Adams, who has a natural gift for composing the lyrical and expressive sounds of instruments, found a technology that could augment and reinforce the orchestral traditions of several centuries.

This is the nascent situation of *Light Over Water.* Essentially electronic, it was nevertheless born out of the world of the orchestra. In previous works, Adams "electrified" his orchestrations. Now he "orchestrates" his electronics.

Light Over Water was conceived and executed primarily as a processed synthesizer piece, but to the array of electronically produced sounds. Adams added—in the recording studio, of course—a kind of phantom presence in the form of a brass choir (trumpets, horns, trombones, and tubas). It inhabits a shadowy, distant plane and is sometimes so subtle and dark that its addition to the synthesizer music is not even consciously heard. Conceived as an integral part of the score, the brass sound—Adams calls it the music's shadow—adds an expressive voice not available from purely synthesized sound.

There are three kinds of musical artistry at work in this situation. There is the synthesist, working in his own electronic music studio with an assortment of equipment and sound processors (Casio digital keyboards, Serge modular analogue systems, various outboard line delays and harmonizers, and multitrack recording equipment). There is the orchestral composer, working with the brass configuration, using his knowledge of these instruments and their potential for mixed sonorities. There is the composer working precisely and painstakingly in the art of studio mixing, the arduous process of balancing and distributing the many discrete channels of recorded sound (as many as twenty-four in this piece) into a final "mix," a process not dissimilar from the actions of a conductor molding and shaping the dynamic form of the music during a live performance. The craft of studio mixing is becoming a more significant tool for contemporary composers, as the technology of recorded music continues to be refined.

Translucent and meditative, the music of *Light Over Water* rarely jumps out but rather pulls the listener gently along. It is not music of bristling detail that invites a calculated analysis, nor is it music that induces a "trance." Although there are moments of apparent stasis, where one feels almost suspended in time, the careful listener will detect a musical form that is predicated on the notion of constantly evolving gradual change. Sudden entrances are rare. More often than not, the listener finds himself in a new territory without remembering how he got there. These changes are not only purely structural, but are also expressive. There is much subtle emotional modulation in this music.

Light Over Water is very personal and emotive music, although it is not necessarily romantic. (Adams and a number of other very different composers have been indiscriminately grouped by some observers into a "neo-romantic" school.) Most romantic music charges ahead, sparing no effect for its hyper-expressive purposes. Adams purposely leaves something out, something he wishes the listener to fill in. In this sense, perhaps, he is a type of minimalist.

Light Over Water is music for the dance, so it has a kind of subdued physicality. It is not music for a specific dance, the game plan between composer and choreographer being very general from the start. It is music that is given choreographical meaning by the movements of the dance *after* the fact of its composition. Adams always had movement in mind—a sensation of pulse, something for the dancers to hang on to—yet that pulse is barely palpable in the slower, more dreamy sections. But in the faster sequences, it is aggressive, constructed around a rigid, patterned style.

Faced with the task of creating a single, unbroken musical statement nearly an hour in length (Lucinda Childs requested a sustained musical score), Adams eventually settled on the idea of a symphonic structure that would meld together highly energized fast movements with dreamlike, pastoral, and almost motionless slow movements. Six distinct sections are grouped into two larger parts. In Part I, a sforzando attack in the synthesizer and low brasses on a low C slowly decays over a period of a minute, providing a dark, brooding backdrop into which the main body of the dance music, itself bright and glistening, is inserted. This opening up-tempo dance gradually winds down, thinning out, changing both mode and mood, eventually leading into a section of serene calm, a quiescent state full of quiet agitations and episodic excitations not unlike the periodic rustlings of a dreaming sleeper. This inner landscape gives way to a deeper and darker terrain, ushered in by the long, luxurious bottom tones of the synthesizer. Here the shadow choir of muted brass joins the long sinuous lines of the synthesizer in a slow polyphony that is serenely lyrical, disturbing, and unsettling.

The only abrupt surprise in the entire score, a rather buoyant little clock pulse, signals the next section, a quickly moving "shaking" dance. The clock pulse, at first a single stroke, is joined one by one by other little figurations, which transform the music's textural surface into a whole train of bubbling and ticking pulses. The bright colors then begin to grow somber, and the rhythms even out into a more regular pulsation distinctly reminiscent of the shaking tremolando strings of Adams's *Shaker Loops*. As the music takes a darker turn, the mode changes momentarily and mysteriously suggests the slendro flavoring of certain Balinese music. A distant trumpet seems to issue from the music's depths as it rattles around in curiously metallic timbres. As the persistent shaking grows softer and silkier, the motion is sublimated and prepares for the transition to Part II.

The second part of *Light Over Water* has a two-part form: a slow pastorale gives way to a long, gently rolling continuum, which, as it unfolds, gradually acquires power and massiveness, culminating in the heroic music of the finale. The meaning of the title becomes much clearer, as the music, which has seemed watery and submerged, is flooded with a radiant light. Adams composed much of the score in a remote converted cattle barn in the lush, verdant hills along the Pacific coast south of San Francisco. The influence of the natural world is quite apparent in this music, especially in the opening of Part II. Slow, birdlike glimmerings are supported by a deep drone in the bass. These calls are later supplanted by the more human sound of the French horns keening away in a slow, canonic overlay. One feels the pictorial nature imagery giving way to a more plaintive human feeling, to an atmosphere of searching and longing.

Indeed, the title of the piece is derived from the changing vistas Adams witnessed from his hillside perch. The Pacific Ocean, only a few miles distant, was hidden by winter fog and rain, but frequently illuminated by sudden appearances of brilliant light. Introspection is Adams's natural inclination, even if it is more pronounced here that in his other works. The longing restlessness is further heightened by the tonality of this section, with its ambiguous oscillation between E minor and G major.

In the last section of the music, there exist some disturbing—in the context of the overall consonant feeling of the piece—polytonal modulations, which increase the sensation of movement. When the final minutes of *Light Over Water* reclaim the original tonality of E-flat major with a vengeance, one does not feel that one has arrived there without resistance. The brasses are virtually unleashed and make their most assertive appearance, first declaiming then letting forth a volley of unrestrained cries. Compared to the plaintive wails of the preceding section, these cries seem unobstructed, even triumphant. The final moments are almost Brucknerian, and the resemblance is not just harmonic—the hammering away on the tonic—but sonorous as well, for the brasses, with their pure resonating triads, have the last heroic word.

The union of music and movement is a mysterious, almost alchemical event. To be successful, a collaborative relationship, such as the one that produced *Available Light,* requires a delicate balance of artistic sensitivities. In our time, the term "collaboration" has somewhat lost its original connotations of rapport and interchange and is now used loosely to describe almost any simultaneous presentation by two or more artists, even when only the thinnest of threads link together their individual statements. The passive relationship between the mutually coexistent music of John Cage and the choreography of Merce Cunningham is perhaps the most celebrated example of how generalized the idea of collaboration has become. A Cunningham dance can, in many instances, exist independently of the music. The dancers hear the music, but they do not necessarily listen to it. This is not the case with *Available Light,* wherein the choreography is wholly and intricately wedded to the musical score. As the elements came together, there was still much surprise, and many encounters with the unknown. When John Adams was asked about his first impressions of Lucinda Child's completed choreography, he responded:

> It was a shock. I realized at the moment, and it had never dawned on me until then, that I had been all along imagining a choreography, in a very vague way.... What struck me, when I did see the dance, was how Lucinda had responded to the score by creating a kind of overlapping structure in her choreography that often went in opposing directions from the structure of the music. This choreographic structure is frequently on another planet, expressively, from what's going on in the music. For example, there are moments when the music is absolutely still, motionless, yet the dance is extremely active. This is not to mean that there are not moments when the music and the dance are made to coincide harmoniously. In fact, when those moments do happen, perhaps just because they *are* infrequent, there is great beauty and power.

Although it may at times appear that the dance and the music are gong in different directions, the actual detail of the choreography is precisely attuned to the music. Adams commented about Lucinda Childs's way of working with the music:

> She has an extraordinary ear. Picking out the most subtle variations in timbre and rhythm in the music, she has choreographed every single second of the score…. It's not at all a Cage-Cunningham situation, where the music can change with each different performance. I found that even if I left out some minuscule detail from the final mix (and this was easy to do, given that we were at times working with upwards of twenty-four channels of sound), it caused all sorts of chaos with the dancers. Her fidelity to some level of the music, not necessarily emotional, is extraordinary.

When asked if this piece is a collaboration in the true sense, Adams responded:

> I would construe the term to mean work that's built through a continuous consultation and exchange of ideas and feedback. Because of the geographical problem and because of the fact that I was composing the music while she was in France working on another project, there was only a kind of general concord about the larger form, the most important of which was the duration and the fact that she did not want a work that was broken down into little separate movements. She wanted a kind of grand arch. This was an awesome challenge for me because I don't write the kind of gradually evolving, patterned repetitive music that she is used to working with, like Glass [Philip Glass's score to *Dance*] or John Gibson [*Relative Calm*]. This is why I finally settled upon the idea of the symphonic structure, with its slow and fast movements. In fact, that is why there are slow, *really* slow, movements here.

The reference to symphonic structure says much: it allows for a new form of expression in the context of an aesthetic—continuous or minimalist music—which traditionally remains aloof. It appears to be a key to understanding *Light Over Water* and all of John Adams's music. He has adopted some stylistic elements of minimalism, especially the use of repetition, consonance, and pulse, but he has gone far beyond the structural simplicity of so much of that music. Adams makes use of graduated change over sustained periods, but his big, contrasting ideas and dramatic approach to form betray the minimalist aesthetic of "those vast prairies of non-event," leaving behind coolness, detachment, and emotional blandness. *Light Over Water*, as a work of pure music and as a score for the dance, is a manifestation of John Adams's involvement with music as a vehicle of expression.

Harmonielehre (1984–85)

Michael Steinberg
San Francisco Symphony program book, March 1985

I despise those sons who blush to resemble their fathers.

—Francis Poulenc

ABOUT 1977, the year of his *Phrygian Gates* for piano, Adams's musical language became "very pure," as he recalled at the time of the *Harmonium* premiere, "almost rigorously pure in its modal, diatonic expression." ("Diatonic" denotes a harmonic style based primarily on the notes of the major and minor scales; its opposite is "chromatic"—literally "colorful"—a style that draws freely on all twelve notes. *The Star-Spangled Banner* is diatonic, as is the Beethoven Fifth; the Prelude to *Tristan* is chromatic, and so are barbershop quartets.) *Harmonium*, composed for the San Francisco Symphony in 1981, though still diatonic and essentially consonant, is looser in language than *Phrygian Gates*, *Shaker Loops*, and *Common Tones in Simple Time*, the works that preceded it. It has a quicker rate of harmonic change and more dramatic contrast, and it was at the time of completing *Harmonium* that Adams described himself as "a minimalist who is bored with minimalism."

Musical minimalism—in its way as unsatisfactory a label as baroque, classicism, romanticism (to say nothing of neo-romanticism), and most of the others we use—is a style based chiefly on repetition and consonance. Some find it beguiling, some maddening. In the hands of composers as imaginative as John Adams and Steve Reich (whose work was an important inspiration for Adams in his younger years), it has fascinating and delightful possibilities. But Adams was worried about being dead-ended.

Yet it is one thing for an artist to know that it is time to move and quite another to discover where and how to move. Adams found himself deeply mired in a crisis of language. Add to this intrinsic problem the fact that after *Harmonium,* a work that caused a considerable stir and made Adams a much talked-about composer, certainly within the profession, expectations for his next big orchestral work were high; so, therefore, was the pressure.

For a whole year he could keep nothing he wrote. He abandoned a project for the Santa Fe Chamber Music Festival, and he made what seemed like an unending series of false starts during the first eight months of work on his San Francisco Symphony commission. It looked doubtful that the premiere could take place as scheduled. Then, one night, Adams had a dream in which, as he told Jonathan Cott in an interview, he saw himself "driving across the…Bay Bridge, and looking out saw a huge tanker in the bay. It was an image of immense power and gravity and mass. And while I was observing the tanker, it suddenly took off like a rocket ship with an enormous force of levitation. As it rose out of the water, I could see a beautiful brownish-orange oxide on the bottom part of its hull. When I woke up the next morning, the image of those huge [E-minor chords with which the work begins] came to me, and the piece was off like an explosion."

For three months Adams worked like a man possessed. Pages were dispatched to Davies Symphony Hall one, two, three at a time. Verdi once wrote, "Torniamo all'antico; sarà un progresso." It sounds unbearably corny, but Adams had found his future by looking into the past. A musician of wide culture, he has never shared his minimalist colleagues' disdain for the central tradition of Western music. "I don't try to turn my back aggressively on the past," he says. "I try to embrace it."

The title *Harmonielehre* is itself a handshake across seven decades. Adams has always liked referential titles, and if they are punning, so much the better. *Harmonielehre* is the name of one of the great books on music, a rich mix of practical instruction and theoretical speculation, first published in 1911 by Arnold Schoenberg and dedicated "to the hallowed memory of Gustav Mahler." *Lehre* pertains to what is taught. But Adams was thinking more about *learning* harmony. "I'm not trying to teach anyone harmony," he said in 1985. "This is the culmination—so far—of my teaching myself about harmony." Then characteristically, the horizon widens: "I also thought about harmony in the human, the psychological sense, about living with oneself, about balance in life."

I recall when I visited John Adams shortly before he finished *Harmonielehre* that a well-worn score of *Gurrelieder,* the great and magical cantata Schoenberg completed in 1911 (at the same time as his own *Harmonielehre*), occupied a conspicuous place on a shelf by the tail of his grand piano. And before long, Adams mentioned another of the landmark works of the early twentieth century, the Sibelius Fourth Symphony—also, as it happens, completed in 1911. The Sibelius, he explained, was the "primary generating model" for the second movement of *Harmonielehre.*

Harmonielehre is thus "rich with resonances of my personal musical storehouse. I'm not conservative. I'm conserving. But I'm not just playing around in the outtakes of *Gurrelieder* or Berg's Opus 1 Sonata either." Adams sometimes finds his relationship to the past hard to talk about. "It's a waste of a composer's life to do 'imitations.'" When he calls the Sibelius a "primary generating model," he does not mean "model" in the concrete sense—a work whose structure is to be emulated or whose details are to be replicated. What comes through, he said to Jonathan Cott, "is not, say, 'Mahler,' but rather John Adams's personal, private experience of Mahler….And I find that the best art is that way. Certainly, no one takes James Joyce or Thomas Mann or William Gaddis to task for their filtering through of the past."

This "filtering" Adams sees as a way to attain his ideal of an art "which touches you in spirit, which touches you in the center of your soul and affects you." In much twentieth-century work this, he feels, has been "eschewed in favor of sound for its own sake or formal patterns for their own sakes. Most of the best twentieth-century art has been 'thinking art.' There's been a triumph of the thinking portion at the expense of the feeling portion," and he draws a Jungian diagram illustrating head–heart polarity. "So much music has been about its own construction." Musing further about this, he suggests that the reason Elliott Carter commands, for a "difficult" composer, so large an audience is that the dramatic content of his music is so vivid and compelling. He cites Stravinsky as an ideally balanced musical personality, and while he stops just short of saying so, his hope seems to be that *Harmonielehre* might be a work of balance, of *Harmonie*.

And so we come to *Harmonielehre* itself. It is in three parts, the first of which accounts for a little more than half the work. Adams thinks of Part I, which is untitled, as a huge symphonic movement, or perhaps a single-movement symphony like the Sibelius Seventh. The metrical patterns change constantly, but for a long time the pounding beat with which *Harmonielehre* opens is relentless and unchangeably present. It is not until nearly halfway through that the tempo relaxes for an episode of slower music which Adams describes as being "full of *Sehnsucht*" (yearning). The final section is a synthesis of the long lyric lines typical of the middle of the movement and the insistent motoric energy of its opening.

The second, slow movement is called "The Anfortas Wound." This is not the Amfortas of Wagner's *Parsifal,* but his prototype in *Li Contes del Graal* by the late-twelfth-century poet Crêtien de Troyes, of Champagne. Wagner's Amfortas is wounded in his side, like Christ on the cross; but Crêtien's Anfortas sustained his un-healing wound in the testicles. "He was wounded," Adams points out, "due to pride, to hubris, and the wound caused impotence. 'The Anfortas Wound' is a piece about sickness and infirmity, physical and spiritual."

Muted cellos, a sonority borrowed from the Sibelius Fourth and which Adams calls "the key to that symphony," begin this very slow music, playing an expressive rising melody against a background of a softly rolling kettledrum and four-times-divided basses. The harmonies revolve like an agonizingly slow kaleido-scope. In striking contrast to the first movement, the meters here are regular rather than fluid—numbingly regular, which for Adams is part of the imagery of sickness and confinement, "one day after another, just rolling on."

The third movement also begins with slow music ("slowly rocking" is the tempo mark), but where the second movement is wracked, this music brings healing. The title is "Meister Eckhardt and Quackie." Meister Eckhardt is the common name for Eck-hardt von Hochheim, a thirteenth-century Dominican, a specula-tive mystic whose chief subject was the soul's union with God. Quackie was the baby name for the Adams's daughter Emily, nine months old when her father completed *Harmonielehre*. Adams speaks of two principal generating images for this work—the first the dream about the tanker, the other a vision of Meister Eckhardt "floating through the firmament with a baby on his shoulder." Quackie is first of all the archetypical child but also a homunculus. The score includes a note on the third movement's title: "Quackie, who is still too young to walk, rides upon Meister Eckhardt's shoulder as they glide among the heavenly bodies. Quackie whis-pers the secret of grace into Meister Eckhardt's ear."

"At the end," says Adams, "there's an extended passage during which a tremendous harmonic struggle takes place with the differ-ent tonalities vying for dominance. Now, in a more traditionally worked-out tonal piece, there would be a modulatory sequence that would present the outcome in a rather dialectical way. But in this case, I simply place the keys together, as if in a mixer, and let them battle it out. And finally E-flat wins through its strength, and this moment seems like an epiphany."

The Chairman Dances (Foxtrot for Orchestra) (1985)

Michael Steinberg
San Francisco Symphony program book, November 1986

THE CHAIRMAN DANCES IS A BY-PRODUCT of John Adams's opera *Nixon in China,* set in the three days of President Nixon's visit to Beijing in February 1972, one act for each day. The single scene of the third act takes place in the Great Hall of the People, where there is yet another banquet, this one hosted by the Americans. Here is the situation as described in the preface to the score of *The Chairman Dances:*

> Madame Mao, alias Jiang Ching, aka The White-Boned Demon, has gatecrashed the Presidential banquet. She is seen standing first where she is most in the way of the waiters. After a few minutes, she brings out a box of paper lanterns and hangs them around the hall, then strips down to a cheongsam, skin-tight from neck to ankle, and slit up the hip. She signals the orchestra to play and begins to dance by herself. Mao is becoming excited. He steps down from his portrait on the wall and they begin to foxtrot together. They are back in Yenan, the night is warm, they are dancing to the gramophone....

Act III of *Nixon in China,* in which both reminiscing couples, the Nixons and the Maos, find themselves contrasting the vitality and optimism of youth with their present condition of middle age and power, is full of shadows; Jiang Ching's and Mao's foxtrot in the opera is therefore a more melancholy piece than *The Chairman Dances.* This is, uninhibitedly, a cabaret number, an entertainment, and a funny piece; as the Chairman and the former actress-turned-Deputy Head of the Cultural Revolution make their long trip back through time they turn into Fred and Ginger. The chugging music we first hear is associated with Mao; the seductive swaying-hips melody—*La Valse* humorously translated across immense distances—is Jiang Ching's. You might imagine the piano part at the end being played by Richard Nixon.

Short Ride in a Fast Machine
(Fanfare for Great Woods) (1986)

Michael Steinberg
San Francisco Symphony program book, November 1986

THE MOST FAMOUS AMERICAN FANFARE is *Hail to the Chief.* Next comes Aaron Copland's thumping huff and puff in honor of "the Common Man." Most fanfares are brilliant, some even aggressive (etymologists disagree whether the word "fanfare" is onomatopoetic or actually connected with the verbal family that gives us "fanfaronade," meaning blustering and bragging behavior), though John Adams has also explored the possibilities of the restrained and pianissimo fanfare (in his *Tromba lontana*).

Short Ride in a Fast Machine is a joyfully exuberant piece, brilliantly scored for a large orchestra. The steady marking of a beat is typical of Adams's music. *Short Ride* begins with a marking of quarter-notes (woodblock, soon joined by the four trumpets) and eighths (clarinets and synthesizers); the woodblock is fortissimo and the other instruments play forte. Adams describes the woodblock's persistence as "almost sadistic" and thinks of the rest of the orchestra as running the gauntlet through that rhythmic tunnel. About the title: "You know how it is when someone asks you to ride in a terrific sports car, and then you wish you hadn't?"

Short Ride in a Fast Machine is an example of the style called minimalism. Its features are repetition, steady beat, and, perhaps most crucially, a harmonic language with an emphasis on consonance unlike anything in Western art music in the last five hundred years. Adams is not a simple—or simple-minded—artist. His concern has been to invent music at once familiar and subtle. For all of their minimalist features, works such as *Harmonium, Harmonielehre,* and *El Dorado* are full of surprises, always enchanting in the glow and gleam of their sonority, and bursting with the energy generated by their harmonic movement.

Nixon in China (1985–87)

Michael Steinberg
Liner notes for *Nixon in China*, Nonesuch, 1988

THOMAS MANN LIKED TO TELL THE STORY of how his typist, working on some episode in *Joseph and His Brothers,* a three-thousand-page expansion of twenty-four chapters of *Genesis,* remarked one morning, "So that's how it really happened!" *Nixon in China* is similarly seductive. Or more so, because these characters are our famous contemporaries. Famous and familiar. Surely there has been no audience member at any performance of *Nixon in China* who has not heard Richard Nixon speak in actuality, on television, on the radio, on tape in some historical documentary, none who has not seen him and Pat Nixon on television or film, none therefore without an image of what these people sound like and how they move. Andrew Porter pointed out in his *New Yorker* review of *Nixon in China* that the Nixons, Dr. Kissinger, and Madame Mao, had she been released from prison (where she was serving a suspended death sentence for her role in the Cultural Revolution), could all have attended the Houston premiere of the opera in October 1987. It is rare for us to encounter living and real characters on the operatic stage. Indeed, so accustomed are we to seeing singers in tights, crinolines, frock coats, tunics, flowing robes, and the like, that directors and designers can still induce a certain sense of shock just by dressing someone in something clearly recognizable as contemporary—clothes, not costume. In the theater, when James Maddalena and Carolann Page stepped through the door of *The Spirit of '76* onto the rolling stairway at Capital Airport, Beijing, audiences drew in their breath, so "real" were these Nixons.

It was Peter Sellars, a director as serious and as perceptive about dramatic and human issues as he is imaginative and, when need be, iconoclastic, who had the idea for *Nixon in China* and who brought librettist and composer together. The poet Alice Goodman was a Harvard contemporary of his; John Adams was a graduate from the previous decade. Goodman is a poet born in Saint Paul, Minnesota, now living in Cambridge, England. *Nixon in China* is her first opera libretto; a second, also for John Adams, was already in the planning stage at the time of the first *Nixon* performances.

She has described *Nixon in China* as a "polyphonic" collaboration. Her Nixon, she points out in her essay on the making of the opera, is not the same as John Adams's, and "both differ slightly from Peter Sellars's...not to mention James Maddalena's." The "real" Nixon, who stands behind all these, is a polyphonic mélange in himself: whose Nixon, which historian's, which witness's, after all is the real Nixon? Goodman's *Nixon in China* libretto is a wonder of human perception, generosity, wit, and poetic resource. She is as essential to *Nixon in China* as da Ponte was to *Così fan tutte,* Boito to *Falstaff,* von Hofmannsthal to *Der Rosenkavalier.* But an opera is, in the end, the composer's. It stands or falls by its music. We can read a few opera librettos with pleasure away from their music, and *Nixon in China* is one of them, but when we hear an opera or, for that matter, any other piece of vocal music, what we encounter and respond to is not the text itself, but the text as the composer read it and wanted us to hear it. It is the music that delivers the words.

Nixon in China is John Adams's second major composition on a text, the first being *Harmonium* (1981) for chorus and orchestra, setting poems of John Donne and Emily Dickinson. People— some people—dearly love pigeonholes. It is, of course, not true, as some might have one believe, that all composers living between

Princeton, New Jersey, and Princeton, Maine, write twelve-tone music or that all in California follow in the footsteps of John Cage. No question, though, the artistic climates on the two coasts are different. When John Adams made the trek from Cambridge to Oakland it was to give himself permission to write the music he heard in his head, and what he heard was not approved nor even much known around Cambridge. Steve Reich, with whose *Four Organs* Michael Tilson Thomas scandalized Boston Symphony audiences in 1971, and whose music is exciting, transporting, poetic to some, maddeningly simple-minded to the point of idiocy to others, was an inspiration to Adams. So was Beethoven, whose luminous major triads validated for him Arnold Schoenberg's dictum that there was still plenty of good music to be written in C major. (It was more than anything Schoenberg's courageous and inspired explorations of *terra incognita* that had seemed to put C major on the index.)

The minimalists, as Reich, Adams, Glass, and others quickly came to be known, have turned out to be quite as diverse as the twelve-tone composers, the Viennese classicists, the German romantics, or any other such group. Their common ground is easy to define—repetition, steady pulse, and consonant harmony. After that come the distinctions, and that is where it gets interesting. Distinctions of intention and distinctions of ability: how imaginatively does a composer use a restricted harmonic vocabulary, how refined is his or her ear for instrumental color, how sure the sense of how to assemble the elements of a piece (literally of "composition"), how precise the knowledge of when to do more of the same, when to move to something new, when to return, how certain the feeling for tension and release?

Reich's *Four Organs,* my own first introduction to the style, is an exploration for some twenty-five minutes of a single five-note chord. When I first heard it, it seemed like holding five beans, each of a different kind, in the palm of my hand and seeing how many patterns I could make. Accustomed by education, experience, and preference to finding my way into and through complex designs (maximalism?), I found that paradoxically it took work to tune my focus down to a slow rate of change and a small amount of information. But I enjoyed what could be done with those beans—I tried it, literally, in my kitchen—and when the composer was as good as Reich I loved the music too.

Adams's first orchestral work, completed in 1979 and called *Common Tones in Simple Time,* is a pure and beautiful essay in what one might call extreme or truly minimal minimalism, without melody, and with all other elements such as color, rhythm, and harmony treated with extraordinary delicacy. Clearly, though, he had already found a language, a tone of voice altogether his own. His music is like Reich's in the sense that Mozart's is like Haydn's, but it is also as different from it as Mozart's is from Haydn's. Expressively, and thus of necessity technically as well, *Harmonium* goes far beyond the bounds of "classical" minimalism, as for that matter had *Shaker Loops* for string septet (1978, with a string orchestra version made in 1983), and as in their various ways have the major works since then—the exuberant and parodistic *Grand Pianola Music* (1982), the searching, often anguished *Harmonielehre* (1985), and now *Nixon in China.*

Adams believes in the rich possibilities of his chosen musical language. He likes to quote the assertion by the composer Fred Lerdahl that "the best music utilizes the full potential of our cognitive resources." (Lerdahl cites Indian raga, Japanese koto, jazz, and most Western art music as good examples, Balinese gamelan and rock as musics that fail in this respect.) More, Adams, who really is one of those composers who love music, not just their own music, and whose knowledge is encyclopedic, believes in his harmonic style as a human necessity and is willing to risk taking the controversial position of maintaining that our response to tonal harmony is not so much cultural as genetic. "Something tremendously powerful was lost when composers moved away from tonal harmony and regular pulses," he has said. "Among other things the audience was lost." He invokes Walt Whitman: "He has nobility, he was a social radical, and he wrote plain English." And Dickens, one of his "great inspirations": "He had a huge audience, he had profound compassion, he spoke on social issues—and he wrote for money." So did Handel and Verdi, who brought their musical ideals into harmony with the assumption that it is pointless not to please your audience.

Adams's music enters the ear easily, but it is not simple, certainly not simple-minded, and never predictable. At no point, were the music suddenly to stop, could you foresee with certainty what comes next, even when the sense of pattern seems at its clearest. An example: for the first 159 measures of *Nixon in China* the violins, violas, and keyboards in the orchestra play rising scales; moreover, for the first thirty of those measures the scales are the same, Aeolian (the white keys on the piano from A to A) and always rising through one octave. But to these scales, woodwinds add slower scales (about one-seventh the speed of the others), bass instruments contribute a series of pedals on A, F, and C, trombones add a little four-note sputter from time to time, and every now and again the whole is punctuated by a high "ding." You never know when the bass is going to change, how tightly the slower scales will be lapped, when the trombone sputters or the "dings" will appear. The scales come to outline new harmonies; the bass line adds C-sharp and then B-flat to its repertory; the scales stop partway to double back upon themselves or move beyond the compass of a single octave; the pattern of eight notes to the bar is broken by sixes, fives, sevens, fours. Eventually, when the chorus comes in, the scales recede to become background and accompaniment.

This musical fantasy is at the service of a noble idea that has a hard time surviving the essential frivolity of so much of our public operatic industry, the idea that the theater is appropriate for the contemplation and discussion of the most urgent issues in our lives. The double subject of *Nixon in China* is a meeting that changed the world (Andrew Porter cites the meeting of Wotan and Erda in *The Nibelung's Ring* as comparable) and the multiple portrait of those who met—the Nixons, Mao Tse-tung, Chou En-lai, and, nearer the periphery, Chiang Ch'ing (Madame Mao) and Henry Kissinger. (It took another five years after Nixon's 1972 visit to China until formal diplomatic relations were reestablished between the United States and the People's Republic, an event that neither Mao Tse-tung nor Chou En-lai lived to see. Nonetheless, it was Nixon's visit that provided the essential contact. Now that the People's Republic has become a tourist spot with Holiday Inns and Sheratons, we are already in danger of forgetting how utterly and hopelessly remote that country once seemed, the sensational effect at the time of the Chinese invitation to the U.S. Ping-Pong team in 1871, President Nixon's revelation in the same year that Henry Kissinger had made a secret, preparatory visit to Beijing, and Nixon's own visit, which was televised all over the globe.)

At a preview performance in San Francisco in May 1987, Adams joked that *Nixon in China* was an opera for Republicans and Communists. Kissinger is treated without a jot of mercy, but the other portraits seem to reveal something essential of how each character would have seen him- or herself. (Kissinger has little to sing, and so someone who first gets to know *Nixon in China* from the recording probably has little idea of the drearily oppressive force of his cloddish, silent, and nearly constant presence onstage—powerfully realized by Thomas Hammons in the first productions. Melot in *Tristan und Isolde* is a parallel example from the standard repertory of a character who is immensely compelling as a stage presence but who for the same reason—near-silence—does not come across on a recording.)

There is humor—Nixon's excited arrival aria, "News news news news news news news news news news news has a has a has a has a kind of mystery has a has a has a kind of mystery," is an example—but also compassion. *Nixon in China* is not a political cartoon; rather, though it contains elements of both the historical and the comic, Adams and Goodman offer it as a heroic and mythic drama. Hector and Perseus, Cupid and Psyche, no longer get to us directly; we may have to look them up to be sure we understand the allusion. But, as Adams has remarked, "when you say Hitler or Donald Duck or Marilyn Monroe"—Richard Nixon—"any number of buttons in our psyches are pressed." And *Nixon in China* is also an opera about perception and appearance (Richard Nixon's misunderstandings of Mao's literary and historical references, Pat Nixon's intervention in *The Red Detachment of Women* ballet), about illusion (Mao's amplifying/translating secretaries whose English-into-English turns out sounding like some foreign tongue, Mrs. Nixon's sightseeing tour, especially in the episode of the glass elephant), and even an opera about opera (Mao's three secretaries borrowed from the court of the Queen of the Night, the device of ballet as reinforcement of the story, the allusions to a host of operatic conventions from Mozart through Verdi and Wagner to *The Rake's Progress*).

The time covered in *Nixon in China* is five days, February 21–25, 1972, the days of Richard Nixon's visit to Beijing, a visit made in the hope, but by no means the certainty, of seeing Chairman Mao. Alice Goodman's synopsis (© Alice Goodman) of each scene is set off here in italics.

Act I
Scene i

The airfield outside Peking: it is a cold, clear, dry morning: Monday, February 21, 1972. Contingents of army, navy, and air force circle the field and sing The Three Main Rules of Discipline and the Eight Points of Attention. Premier Chou En-lai, accompanied by a small group of officials, strolls onto the runway just as The Spirit of '76 *taxies into view. President Nixon disembarks. They shake hands and the President sings of his excitement and his fears.*

I have described the instrumental prelude and its merging into the opening scene; the subsequent buildup—the chorus itself and the orchestral crescendo as the plane lands and we wait for its passengers to appear—is masterly.

Scene ii

An hour later he is meeting with Chairman Mao. Mao's conversational armory contains philosophical apothegms, unexpected political observations, and gnomic jokes, and everything he sings is amplified by his secretaries and the Premier. It is not easy for a Westerner to hold his own in such a dialogue.

This is where our "so that's how it really happened" feeling is most likely to overtake us. I know only one other operatic political scene of equal verve, sharpness of observation, and polyphonic skill, and that is the—wildly different—"Council of Trent" Act II of Hans Pfitzner's *Palestrina*.

Scene iii

After the audience with Mao, everyone at the first evening's banquet is euphoric. The President and Mrs. Nixon manage to exchange a few words before Premier Chou rises to make the first of the evening's toasts, a tribute to patriotic fraternity. The President replies, toasting the Chinese people and the hope of peace. The toasts continue, with less formality, as the night goes on.

Here is an instance of how music characterizes as precisely as words. The distinct musics of the two toasts—Chou's fluent, flexible, confident, free, Nixon's staccato, nervous (at least first), somehow stiff in its irregularities—speaks volumes.

Act II
Scene i
Snow has fallen during the night. In the morning Mrs. Nixon is ushered onstage by her party of guides and journalists. She explains a little of what it feels like for a woman like her to be First Lady, and accepts a glass elephant from the workers at the Peking Glass Factory. She visits the Evergreen People's Commune and the Summer Palace, where she pauses in the Gate of Longevity and Goodwill to sing, "This is prophetic!" Then, on to the Ming Tombs before sunset.

Here is a great opening-up of human perspective and musical vocabulary. The beginning of the preceding banquet scene had given us a glimpse of the Nixons as private and vulnerable human beings, and now what Mrs. Nixon reveals of herself, her wry humor, her passionate patriotism, falling almost into the idiom of Ferlinghetti's "I am waiting," is profoundly touching. It was in the slow movement of *Harmonielehre*, the writhing and angst-filled "The Anfortas Wound," that Adams first gave free rein to his lyric bent. Here, in "This is prophetic!" he gives us an aria of indrawing melodic sweep. A lovely detail: At the reference to the Unknown Soldier a muted trumpet adds its counterpoint to the soprano voice, its timbre alone sufficient to suggest taps. But Adams goes beyond making this an "effect" in quotation marks, for the trumpet stays to be an organic part of the texture for the remainder of the aria.

Scene ii
In the evening, the Nixons attend a performance of The Red Detachment of Women, *a revolutionary ballet devised by Mao's wife, Chiang Ch'ing. The ballet entwines ideological rectitude with Holly-*

wood-style emotion. The Nixons respond to the latter; they are drawn to the downtrodden peasant girl—in fact, they are drawn into the action on the side of simple virtue. Chiang Ch'ing sings, "I am the wife of Mao Tse-tung," ending with full choral backing.

It was at the beginning of 1966 that Mao launched the "Great Proletarian Cultural Revolution," a movement to recall the Chinese people, especially the young, to the revolutionary spirit. It led to horrors no less vile than those in Nazi Germany and the Soviet Union. Mao's wife, Chiang Ch'ing, was put in charge of cultural affairs and launched a reign of terror in the worlds of education and the arts. Her hatred was directed particularly at European-American cultural traditions and anything that could be stigmatized as bourgeois. Among other things she undertook to reform dance, to get rid of the swans and wilis, and to introduce scenarios of political significance. *The Red Detachment of Women*, which the Nixons saw on February 22, their second evening in Beijing, was her most famous achievement. A dance translation of a film from the beginning of the 1960s, itself based on fact, it is set on a tropical island where a peasant girl is tied to a post and tormented by the landlord's factotum. (Onstage, the slavering factotum bears an unmistakable resemblance to the President's national security adviser; hence Mrs. Nixon's "Doesn't he look like you-know-who!") She escapes, is led away by a member of the army, and herself joins the Detachment of Women. With her comrades she liberates her village. The ballet ends, of course, in celebration. The ferocious action of the ballet itself, the Nixons' intervention in its course, the observation of this bit of dramatic counterpoint by the Chinese officials, make for a lively stage picture and provide a considerable challenge to the imagination of the listener at home. In the earlier part of the scene, Chiang Ch'ing is another example of a visually powerful though largely unheard presence—until, that is, she bursts forth with her triumphant aria, "I am the wife of Mao Tse-tung."

Act III—The Last Night in Peking

Nixon in China recapitulates Adams's development as a composer in that each of its scenes brings an expansion of resources and possibilities, the opera becoming progressively more richly inventive in melody, freer in rhythm, subtler in harmony, more fanciful in texture. This scene was originally intended to be another banquet, that "one event too many," with everyone in a state of exhaustion. In the first production, Peter Sellars changed the venue from banquet tables to beds. This, however, leads the characters to turn away from the externals of their "real" surroundings to the inner landscapes of their minds. With a candor sometimes painful to witness, they contemplate, they relive the paths that have brought them to this place and this moment. Humor, eros, pathos, nobility—each finds its place in this moving scene. The last word, literally, is Chou En-lai's, and stirring and touching it is, in its melancholy poetry: "Outside this room the chill of grace/Lies heavy on the morning grass." The last word, truly, belongs to music, the simple scales with which the drama began now stretched, transformed, into broken chords for solo strings, rising, turning, rising, to disappear at last into silence.

Fearful Symmetries and
The Wound-Dresser (1988)

Sarah Cahill
Liner notes for *Fearful Symmetries/The Wound-Dresser*
Nonesuch, 1989

"ONLY RECENTLY HAVE I NOTICED an odd fact about my work,"
writes John Adams:

> It seems to alternate between two opposing polarities:
> along with every dark, introspective, "serious" piece there
> must come the Trickster, the garish, ironic wild card that
> threatens to lose me whatever friends the previous composi-
> tion might have gained. *Harmonium* required a *Grand Pi-
> anola Music; Harmonielehre* necessitated *The Chairman
> Dances;* and *The Wound-Dresser* seemed to flow directly out
> of *Fearful Symmetries.* I don't consciously choose to manip-
> ulate these polarities. It's more like being engaged in a kind
> of psychic balancing act, dark alternating with light, serene
> alternating with jittery, earnest alternating with ambiguous.
> I know I'm certainly not the first artist to experience this
> need. Ravel would often work on a "demonic" piece (*Gas-
> pard*) and on an "innocent" one (*Ma mere l'oye*) at virtually
> the same time. What may strike others as strange is that I

value my trickster pieces just as highly as my more serious ones. I certainly put just as much effort into them, and in many ways the free air that they breathe has allowed me to try new and even radical ideas that I might otherwise have routinely suppressed.

While *Fearful Symmetries* and *The Wound-Dresser* do, indeed, project the widely divergent sides of Adams's personality, his distinctive musical vocabulary is recognizable in both: the steady pulse and repeated patterns folded into rich, dramatic orchestration; the harmonic modulations which, like those of Schubert, achieve the greatest impact by their simplicity and subtlety; the inventive instrumentation. And just as each of two polar extremes contains the germ of its opposite, so light flickers through the darkest moments of Adams's "serious" works, and the dance-band beat of his most extroverted compositions leads into passages of meditative tranquility.

Fearful Symmetries is audacious, a "confrontational piece," explains Adams, "in the mode of *Grand Pianola Music,* and equally bound to offend. I think one problem of twentieth-century music is that composers feel they have to be serious, unforgiving, and grim. We have lost the kind of composer who is able to use his or her art not only to elevate, but to entertain and amuse as well."

Adams borrowed the phrase "fearful symmetries" from William Blake's "The Tyger," but that is his work's only link to the poem. As he explained in a program note for the first performance by the Orchestra of St. Luke's in October 1988, "I like the joining of the passionate adjective to the precise, almost clinical noun. The combination of passion and precision seemed like a good starting point for a piece. However, in this case the music came first and then the title. Not long into the composition, I realized that the harmonic phrase structures were falling into almost maddeningly symmetrical patterns, and so the Blake phrase sprang to mind."

This work welds precision and passion into an energetic dynamo. With its enormous momentum, the playful whirring of large cogs turning smaller ones, the occasional brassy blurt of a trumpet or rude timpani thump, *Fearful Symmetries* brings to mind the excessively complex and comical machine inventions of Dr. Seuss or Rube Goldberg, or the hilarious kinetic sculptures of Jean Tinguely: each tiny and apparently purposeless mechanism hooked up to another to form a massive, grinding, sputtering creation as riveting as it is undignified.

Of course, we have heard this interplay of autonomous elements in Adams's music before, but not so explicitly, never so clearly defined. While working on Act III of *Nixon in China,* in which the five characters sing distinct lines that weave among each other, Adams renewed his interest in counterpoint, in the "joy of making many events coexist effortlessly." *Fearful Symmetries* is Adams's celebration of counterpoint, and the pleasures he takes in it are endless: the layering of motifs and fragments, each with its own definite character, which submerge and re-emerge throughout the piece as if in a multiple discussion; the terse economy of material; the sheer propulsion of the music generated by the collision and interrelation of these voices.

As in his other orchestra works, here Adams demonstrates his ingenuity and keen instinct for combined instrumental colors and timbres, particularly to achieve a sense of motion within a constantly developing and evolving texture. He scored *Fearful Symmetries* for the same group used in *Nixon in China,* as he explained in his program note, "not because I was short of ideas, but, on the contrary, rather that the peculiar assortment in the *Nixon* pit—winds, saxophones, synthesizer, strings, and lots of brass—turned out to be a remarkably flexible ensemble, and I felt I'd not even begun to see the end of the many possibilities it had in store."

Fearful Symmetries begins with an upbeat rhythm ticked out by a sampler, joined two bars later by piano, synthesizer, and strings. While these add richness to the steady pulse, the melodic line is suavely crooned by the "lounge lizard" quartet of saxophones, English horn, and bassoon. Brass, piano, and synthesizer often assume percussive roles, aggressively puncturing the fabric of sound, but no instrument is relegated to one task: each gets a chance at melodies and ostinato accompaniments until they all join forces in a great theatrical buildup before the recapitulation, the accumulated sound of the whole orchestra swinging like a gigantic pendulum.

As he has in almost all his recent orchestrations, Adams includes synthesizer in this ensemble for its flexibility and its unusual resonance. "One thing that keeps me composing," says Adams, "is the possibility of discovering new sound worlds. I have always been interested in electronic instruments, but I use them differently now than I did in the sixties, when they were attractive to me more for their crude 'sci-fi' noises than for real musical potential. Since then they have become more technically sophisticated, more malleable, and combining them with acoustic instruments is like a new form of alchemy." The protean synthesizer assumes many roles in this piece. At one point it becomes a campy silent-movie organ to ascend and descend by chromatic half-steps with concurrent harmonic modulations, joined later by the piano in galloping iambs—"Liberace in Hell," Adams calls it. "The essence of minimalist music," he explains, "has been its wonderful smoothness of transitions between tonalities, usually between thirds, which I like to compare to automatic transmission. *Fearful Symmetries* goes in the opposite direction by using the most jagged modulation available, which is by half-steps—it's like shifting without a clutch. The moment I used half-step modulations the piece suddenly acquired the melodramatic quality I had wanted."

With these musical jokes, and with his incorporation of syncopation, dance music, boogie-woogie riffs, and big band sounds into his "trickster" compositions, Adams has often violated stereotypes about music for the concert hall. But as he points out, popular music *is* the folk music of twentieth-century America, and just as Copland immortalized the Shaker tune *Simple Gifts* and Ives used songs and hymns in his symphonies, Adams is creating his own version of inherently "American" music.

The Wound-Dresser was first performed in February 1989 by baritone Sanford Sylvan and the Saint Paul Chamber Orchestra conducted by the composer. The work takes as its text Walt Whitman's poem of the same title, part of a sequence about the Civil War entitled "Drum-Taps." Whitman assumed the task, during the war, of visiting the sick and wounded soldiers crowding the hospitals. He talked with them, wrote letters for them, nursed them, and comforted them. "*The Wound-Dresser,*" says Adams, "is the most intimate, most graphic, and most profoundly affecting evocation of the act of nursing the sick and dying that I know of. It is also astonishingly free of any kind of hyperbole or amplified emotion, yet the detail of the imagery is of a precision that could only be attained by one who had been there."

Adams chose to omit the prefatory section of the poem, in which the narrator as an old man is asked to talk about his experiences, to "be witness again, paint the mightiest armies of earth./Of those armies so rapid so wondrous what saw you to tell us?/What stays with you latest and deepest?" The main body of the poem, then, is a flashback in which the narrator tells not of wondrous armies but of the suffering war victims. By beginning his piece with the hospital scene—"Bearing the bandages, water and sponge"—Adams places us firmly in the immediate present. "It was mostly a matter of tone," he explains. "The first section is an overture to the actual event, the vision, and seems very dated, but the moment Whitman says, 'Bearing the bandages,' he is speaking very plainly."

There is a powerful tension in Whitman's poem between the physical and the metaphysical, between bodily sickness, which he records with almost scientific detachment ("From the stump of the arm, the amputated hand/I undo the clotted lint"), and a spiritual transcendence of the corporeal. Whitman the attentive nurse coexists with Whitman the visionary, and Adams is acutely sensitive to this dual role in his setting.

The instrumental character changes between stanzas almost like panels of a painted screen. A plaintive rocking figure in the violins creates a ghostly atmosphere to evoke the "dreams' projections" through which the poem is filtered. A solo violin in its highest register hovers above the baritone's opening lines; at the beginning of a later stanza the voice is paired with a solo trumpet, which seems to echo from the distant battlefield. From the elegiac restlessness of the opening, the mood is gradually transformed to one of warmth and affirmation.

Adams had already shown his sensitivity to language in his 1981 chorus-and-orchestra work *Harmonium,* which sets poems by Emily Dickinson and John Donne, and in *Nixon in China,* using Alice Goodman's libretto. With the opera he particularly concentrated on transferring the natural rhythms of speech exactly into music. The obvious danger of setting a poem is that the poem's own music—its inflections, its dips and curves, its pauses and cadences—will be impeded by the music accompanying it, a danger to which many contemporary composers have succumbed. Adams, however, has re-created the rhythms of Whitman's "The Wound-Dresser" so that the poem retains its integrity: the music enhances and deepens, rather than distorts, Whitman's lines. For example, a phrase like "But a day or two more" becomes two sixteenth-notes, a triplet, and a half-note, with a slight melodic rise on "day or two" to reflect that of the spoken phrase.

The narrator struggles with grief, with perseverance ("I am faithful, I do not give out"), and with revulsion at the horrors he confronts daily ("Cleanse the one with a gnawing and putrid gangrene, so sickening, so offensive"), all of which force an emotional climax in the middle of the poem. The music, too, becomes highly agitated and feverishly charged; the trumpet solo, paired with the voice, develops from stately quarter-notes to an erratic, disturbed comment on the text, punctuated by a steady percussive toll. The piece ends on a strong, comforting note, with an extended tender chord. Whitman's sympathy and compassion for the dying soldiers shines through. The honest portrayal of hope in the face of suffering, gentle attendance and direct human contact, was as much an act of courage in Whitman's time as it is in our own, and Adams has captured both the blunt realism and the inspiration of Whitman's humane vision.

While Whitman wrote "The Wound-Dresser" more than a century ago and about an event which may seem remote to us, few of us remain untouched by its message. We are caregivers or patients; our friends and relatives may be afflicted by cancer, AIDS, or the illnesses of old age; but whatever our individual situations, *The Wound-Dresser* resonates with immediacy. While he was working on the piece, Adams's own father was dying of Alzheimer's disease and his mother was devoting her life to caring for him. "I was plunged into an awareness," remembers Adams, "not only of dying, but also of the person who cares for the dying. The responsibility is tragic and also incredibly exhausting, and the bonding that takes place between the two is one of the most extraordinary human events that can happen—something deeply personal of which most of us are completely unaware." But *The Wound-Dresser*, he points out, encompasses far more than either Whitman's or his own experience: "It is a statement about human compassion that is acted out on a daily basis, quietly and unobtrusively and unselfishly and unfailingly. Another poem in the same volume states its theme in other words: 'Those who love each other shall become invincible…'"

The Death of Klinghoffer (1990–91)

Michael Steinberg
Liner notes for *The Death of Klinghoffer*, Nonesuch, 1992

THE DEATH OF KLINGHOFFER is John Adams's second opera. He began it in 1989 when the United States was lavishly supporting Saddam Hussein, completed it on February 12, 1991, while we were dropping "smart bombs" down Baghdad ventilator shafts, and the first performance was given five weeks later, on March 19, at the Théâtre Royal de la Monnaie in Brussels. The same production, with choreography by Mark Morris, sets by George Tsypin, and costumes by Dunya Ramicova, came to the Brooklyn Academy of Music for the American premiere that September.

Klinghoffer has important things in common with Adams's first opera, *Nixon in China* (1987). The composer worked with the same librettist, Alice Goodman, and with the same director, Peter Sellars. Goodman and Sellars were contemporaries at Harvard, where Adams had been a student a decade earlier, and it was Sellars who got the trio together and who proposed the subjects of both operas. Several of the *Klinghoffer* roles were written with members of the original *Nixon* cast in mind: Sanford Sylvan, the Chou En-Lai, is Leon Klinghoffer; James Maddalena, the Nixon, is the Captain; Thomas Hammons, Henry Kissinger, is the First Officer and "Rambo"; and Stephanie Friedman, Second Secretary to Mao, is Omar.

Both operas deal with brief but emblematic events in recent history. Richard Nixon visited Beijing from February 21 to 25, 1972; the hijacking of the Italian cruise liner *Achille Lauro,* when the wheelchair-bound Leon Klinghoffer was murdered, lasted from October 7 to 9, 1985. These historical events also have an immediacy that goes beyond when they occurred on the calendar. Mention of the *Achille Lauro* instantly conjures up images of that handsome ship at anchor in Port Said, of armed guards quayside, of tourists in buses headed for the Cairo airport—images vividly remembered from the nightly news or the morning paper. This is our life.

There the similarities between the two operas stop. What the *Nixon* and *Klinghoffer* stories have in common matters less than what divides them. *Nixon in China* is a comedy tough; in the words Goethe used to describe his own *Faust,* these are ""very serious jests." *Nixon* is parade/charade/masquerade, a picture drawn with compassion and humor of the meeting of two self-important, experienced, shrewd, confident statesmen who, because of the cultural chasms between them and because of recent political events, were perfectly equipped to misunderstand each other. In *Klinghoffer,* there is nothing comedic or masked. The deep religious and economic conflicts that drove the terrible events of October 7 to 9, 1985, are weighted by millennia of history. We can read about them in the Old Testament, and guaranteed, on whichever day you read these words, there will be some new installment in the morning paper. When the curtain went up on the *Klinghoffer* premiere it was in the immediate, dread, and oppressive shadow of the Gulf War.

Nixon in China is, for the most part, naturalistic in pacing and presentation: theater audiences gasped with delight when James Maddalena and Carolann Page stepped from *The Spirit of '76* onto the rolling stairway of the Beijing airport, so true to life were these Nixons. Only the wondrously moving final scene, with its interlocking soliloquies and fragments of conversation, turns away from the "reality" of airstrips, pig farms, and banquet halls to the inner landscapes of the characters' minds.

There is no such "reality" in *The Death of Klinghoffer.* The original production was placed in a versatile and evocative but quite abstract set by George Tsypin; Ramicova's clothes were likewise designed to distance and to neutralize (no Bermuda shorts, no smart marine whites). Singers double in divergent roles, and many of the principal singers-actors have dancer-doubles in the manner of Anna!/Anna II in the Brecht-Weill-Balanchine *Seven Deadly Sins*. Captain Gerardo de Rosa has lost his name and is simply the Captain; the First Officer is given the fictitious name of Giordano Bruno (the historical Giordano Bruno was a formidable Renaissance intellectual and scientist who was burned at the stake as a heretic in 1600). The words *Achille Lauro* occur just once.

Concerning the dramaturgy of *The Death of Klinghoffer,* John Adams has noted that one does better to seek a model in Johann Sebastian Bach's *Passion* settings than in any opera. Peter Sellars likewise cites the Bach *Passion*s as points of comparison, along with Greek tragedy, Persian *Ta'ziyeh*, and Javanese *Wayang Wong*, all works "made up of multiple layers" and all religious.

The Bach *Passion*s are extraordinary in their complex layering. You have two primary strata, narrative and commentary. The narrative itself divides into two layers, the Evangelist's storytelling ("And it came to pass…he denied…there was darkness" and so on) and the actual words of the participants. This last layer subdivides further into the statements and questions of individuals and the exclamations of the crowd.

The commentary also falls into two divisions, one complex, the other simple. The former consists of the arias and choruses with their newly invented, elaborate poetry and their involved musical textures and designs; the latter is found in the congregational hymns or chorales, every word and note of which would have been familiar to every listener from childhood. Moreover, these two categories can overlap when a congregational hymn is superimposed on a chorus or aria. Part of the time we attend to the telling of a story, but often the story stops and we are bidden to reflect on its meaning.

To one degree or other, all operas alternate between event and reflection: for instance, ensembles and recitatives might move the action forward, whereas arias are freeze-frames in which a character allows us to observe the present state of his or her heart and mind. *The Death of Klinghoffer*, too, brings both events and episodes of reflection. Realistic interpretations of actions are, however, almost nonexistent, and, notably, they do not include the incidents that most of us would first have thought to put into the libretto: for example, the moment at which the terrorists reveal themselves or the one when Leon Klinghoffer is killed and his body pitched overboard. (That Mr. Klinghoffer was thrown overboard still in his wheelchair is not unbelievable, and certainly the story was rapidly accepted; it is not, however, known to be a fact and may well be a media myth.) Reflection dominates, in the sense both of meditation and remembrance.

For the Klinghoffers and the Palestinian terrorists, everything happens in the present tense, but the Captain and the other survivors reminisce in the past tense. A series of choruses stands outside "real" time altogether. Oracular and metaphysical, these choruses are high-water marks of poetry in *The Death of Klinghoffer*, as well as being the occasions for some of the musically richest moments in the opera. (Parallels that come to mind are the psalms in Honegger's *Le roi David* and the spirituals in Tippett's *A Child of Our Time*.) Adams points out that "you have a constantly shifting scale of closeness and distance…. At one moment you feel as though you're right there on the deck under the blistering sun with the rest of the passengers, and a moment later you feel like you're reading about it in some very ancient text."

In what follows, Alice Goodman's synopsis (© Alice Goodman) is set off in italics. The synopsis refers several times to events and facts she thinks it useful for us to know about, but which are not to be found in the opera itself.

Prologue
"Chorus of Exiled Palestinians"

Steady F minor chords set pace and key, and some of the central issues—exile, and the void between having and not having—are delivered as clearly as a stone through your window: "My father's house was razed/In nineteen forty-eight." Women's voices and flutes begin the weary, tender melody. Plain to begin with, it soon blossoms into quietly ecstatic melismas as the singers remember the beauty of the crescent moon on a summer night. The words grow angry—"Of that house, not a wall/In which a bird might nest/Was left to stand"—and the music becomes faster, stronger, an engulfing flood. The chorus ends explosively, the word "teeth" set as a dissonant two-chord appoggiatura. ("My father's house" brings to mind the most famous of all operatic exile choruses, "Va, pensiero" from Verdi's *Nabucco*. It is an interesting twist that in *The Death of Klinghoffer* the yearning in that beautiful song of the Jews in their Babylonian captivity in Nabucco is reflected not in the "Chorus of Exiled Jews" but in the "Chorus of Exiled Palestinians.")

[The deleted scene involving the Rumor family, friends of the Klinghoffers, was originally placed here as an interlude between the two opening choruses. The scene is reprinted in full in the Appendix.]

"Chorus of Exiled Jews"

Most of the choruses in *The Death of Klinghoffer* are paired—Palestinians and Jews, Night and Day, Desert and Ocean—and this "Chorus of Exiled Jews" completes what was begun in the opening chorus. It is a love song to the Daughter of Zion, to the distant but ever promised land. This chorus is in dark G minor and the tempo is very slow. It begins in a rich four-voice texture. The address, "O Daughter of Zion," is an aria for the chorus tenors; the reply, "I am an old woman," comes in a pungent three-part harmony of women's voices. The music fades away into silence.

The Prologue is now over; the cruise can begin.

Act I
Scene i.

The cruise liner, Achille Lauro, *has been hijacked just a few hours out of the port of Alexandria, where a large group of passengers disembarked for a tour of the Pyramids. Those remaining on the ship are old, the very young, those desiring a rest amid the comforts of a floating hotel, the crew and service staff. The hijackers are an unknown number of young Palestinian men. Not until much later is it discovered that there are only four of them. Their purpose is not clear.*

Their actions, however, are definite. A waiter has been shot in the leg. The ship's engines have been shut down. The First Officer has a gun against his head. Passengers, who had gathered in the dining room for lunch, are transferred to the Tapestry Room, which is more easily guarded. Americans, Britons, and Jews are identified. The Captain urges calm.

It is the Captain whom we meet first, recalling as though from a great distance the way the events of October 7, 1985 began. Long before *The Death of Klinghoffer* was finished, John Adams put it to me that in preparation I should reread *Lord Jim,* and in an interview shortly before the premiere he said: "The figure of the Captain is heavily indebted to Joseph Conrad. He reminds me of Marlow (the Conradian mouthpiece in *Lord Jim* and several other tales) in the way he likes to spin out a good yarn and intertwine events with his own psychological and philosophical musing." (Most famous among the other tales are *Youth, Heart of Darkness* and *Chance. Benét's Reader's Encyclopedia* describes Marlow as "a kind of detective of the conscience, who studies the moral dilemmas of others in order to understand himself better.") Reflecting on the fact that the role was written for James Maddalena, the first Nixon, Adams suggests a connection between these two characters, each tending "to overrate his own ability to control the events that are unfolding before him."

The Captain's "aria" is really a duet, chiefly for voice and oboe, another Bachian device: most of the arias in Bach's cantatas and *Passions* are duets between a voice and a solo instrument. This texture also has a strong presence in the score that immediately preceded *The Death of Klinghoffer,* Adams's Whitman setting, *The Wound-Dresser.* The Captain's admission of how much he is moved by his passengers' happiness at the beginning of each cruise elicits an almost Wagnerian surge from the violins.

His account carries us to the point where the excursion group goes ashore for the trip to the Pyramids. Now the narratives are undercut. One of the passengers, an elderly Swiss woman, tells her version of the story up to the same point. She had remained on-board with her two-year-old grandson, while the rest of the family took the tour. A flute adds an obbligato to her aria. Then the Captain, now with the counterpoint of a powerful bass line, recounts how the First Office came to his cabin just as the ship was ready to leave Alexandria: "*We've terrorists on board.*" Then, in short, choppy phrases—no Marlow, no philosopher he—the First Office tells the story of the takeover. The agitated orchestra, with its rushing triplets, strings slapped col legno, yapping brass, and mallet instruments evokes the chaos of the alarm bell that would not be silenced, of the first shot, of people confused and afraid. For a time, the voices of the Captain and the First Officer tumble over each other as they recount what happened. Toward the end their personae become blurred as we hear the First Officer sing what he imagines to have been the Captain's words—"Everything will be just fine/If everybody will remain/Calm...."

Now, for the first time, we hear one of the Palestinians. It is Molqi, their leader, who speaks, who gives orders for the segregation of Americans, Israelis, and Britons, as well as for the setting up of emergency housekeeping arrangements. His phrases are short, almost always anchored to the same two notes, E and E-flat, over and over. Quick figurations for strings, woodwinds, and the electronic keyboards that are so distinctive a part of the Adams orchestra swirl around his bright tenor voice. The Swiss grandmother resumes her story. There is no trace now of her earlier lyric calm. Her memories and Molqi's commands are telescoped into a duet. She recalls how, to her horror, she caught herself thinking, "At least we are not Jews." That is her piercing moment of truth. Each character has one such moment.

Another of the Palestinians appears, Mamoud, who, with contempt in his voice, contrasts the passengers' desire to live with his and his comrades' wish to die. The Captain orders that sandwiches and coffee be brought, and in a gesture of gallantry that now seems strangely out of place, he tells the Palestinians they may choose from which cup he should drink and which sandwiches he shall eat.

"Ocean Chorus"

After the Prologue, the sea is ever present in the opera. The words here evoke the deep kinship between humankind and ocean. The chorus sings slowly, quietly, in rich harmonies, while violins and synthesizer spin a broad and eloquent melody across their song.

Scene ii

The Captain is on the bridge, guarded by the teenager Mamoud. Mamoud tunes in to various local radio stations. He signs of the night, of his love for this music [the Arabian pop songs broadcast by these stations], *and his memories. The Captain confides his thoughts on the nature of travel. (One passenger, an Austrian woman, has locked herself into her stateroom, where she will remain the next two days.) Just before dawn a bird lands on the ship's railing, almost at the Captain's elbow. He starts. Mamoud rebukes him.*

Mamoud's appearance in the previous scene was brief and gruff. He is the most complex of the four Palestinians, and now we see another side of him as he rhapsodizes about the music he loves and the magic of music traveling over water. A succession of bass instruments, beginning with the bassoon, seconds his song. These obbligatos are alive with sinuous, expressive melismas, and the language is akin to that of the "Chorus of Exiled Palestinians." Adams has said that he wanted "to convey a sense of 'otherness'…if only to point up the fear of the unknown that must have gripped these American and European tourists [but] at no point did I try to imitate Arabic music…. What I did instead was to develop certain harmonic and melodic modes that were dedicated to one group and not shared by another. Beyond that, the only specific influence I could name would be the music of Abed Azrié, a Syrian composer and singer whose songs I was listening to while composing the long scene in Act I between Mamoud and the Captain."

Mamoud, whose first toy was a gun, a real one, turns from romantic fantasies engendered by the songs to the grim and exceedingly unromantic memories of his childhood. The Captain is moved by Mamoud's account of his brother's death and by the religious fervor with which Mamoud tells the story. "*I think,*" the Captain says, "if you should talk like this/Sitting among your enemies/Peace would come." But over slow, still chords, Mamoud tells him

The day that I
And my enemy
Sit peacefully
Each putting his case
And working towards peace
That day our hope dies
And I shall die too.
My speech is slow
And rough. Esau
Cannot argue.

There is Leon Klinghoffer's death sentence.

For the Captain, Mamoud's words close a door. He does not reply; rather, he embarks on another of his reflective soliloquies, this one taking from the thought of how unlike a ship in the old sense is "this hotel, *Achille Lauro*." A solo violin becomes partner to his voice. Another voice joins in, that of the Austrian woman who had locked herself in her cabin with her fruit basket and her stash of chocolate. She is not a character who arouses sympathy, but she is impressively certain about herself: "Even if one were going to die/One would avoid the company/Of idiots.... I have no fear/Of death. I'd rather die alone,/If I must, though I'd hate to drown." She uses *Sprechstimme*, that halfway house between speech and song that was the invention of her compatriot Arnold Schoenberg, whose music and whose Jewishness she would surely hate. We hear her voice and the Captain's together, but not in dialogue. Bach cantata duets with their simultaneous-but-not-together voices come to mind. Rapid woodwind lines accompany the words of the Captain and the woman. Mamoud, with all his vulnerability, his touching gift for farsight and fantasy, speaks again, reflecting upon the free and peaceful ways of birds—peaceful at least as compared to ours. The music becomes slow and still. "As things stand now," he sighs, "This will not be/An easy day."

"NIGHT CHORUS"

After the meditative music of the scene just ended, the determined quick motion of the "Night Chorus" is startling. The wordless obbligato of the chorus basses also makes it frightening. Composing this scene, Adams had in mind "the image of a pogrom, the terrible fear of a hunted person": "The taped voice unwinds in the widow's backyard. No one bothers to look up from his work." What power there is in the dissonance between the noncommittal tone of the words and the dread they evoke! The August 1992 film clips of Bosnian prisoners, terrified into silence, have shown us this scene in yet another situation and language.

A smaller group of voices adds a new strand, distinct in harmony and rhythm, at the words, "Elijah will return, the Jews believe…." Voices and instruments grow to a pounding fortissimo, and it is with this that Act I roars to its close.

Act II
CHORUS: "HAGAR AND THE ANGEL"

Hagar, whom you will find in chapters 16 and 21 of Genesis, was the Egyptian handmaid (read "slave") of Sarai, the wife of Abram. Because Sarai was barren, she gave Hagar to her husband as a secondary wife that she might bear him a child. Hagar did, indeed, become pregnant and crowed about it rather too tactlessly, angering Sarai, who "dealt hardly with her," causing her to flee. Finding her by a fountain in the wilderness, an angel of the Lord commanded her to return and submit herself to Sarai. At the same time, the angel made her a promise: "I will multiply thy seed exceedingly, that it shall not be numbered for multitude." He ordered her to name the son she would bear Ishmael, also telling her that Ishmael would be "a wild man; his hand will be against every man, and every man's hand against his."

Thirteen years later, the Lord himself appeared to Abram, making a convenant whereby he would become "a father of many nations…and kings shall come out of thee." His wife, Sarai, would at last conceive, and their names would be changed to Abraham and Sarah. Not wanting to have her son, Isaac, share the inheritance with Ishamel, Sarah, to the great grief of Abraham, again expelled Hagar and her son. As Hagar and the child Ishmael wandered in the desert of Beersheba (or Bir es Saba), their water spent, there occurred the incident described in this chorus, the miraculous revelation at the well. (According to the account in Genesis, Ishmael was fourteen when Isaac was born and presumably something like fourteen or fifteen when he and Hagar wandered in the desert. By poetic license, Alice Goodman makes Ishmael an infant.)

Aside from the psychological richness of this tale, it is of paramount historical significance. You could almost say that it is with the rivalry of Isaac and Ishmael—instigated not by them, it is worth remembering, but by Sarah—that the story of *The Death of Klinghoffer* begins. Both Jews and Palestinians make some claim on Hagar and Ishmael: these exiles were protected by the god of Abraham and Isaac, but Muslims also venerate Ishmael as the ancestor of Muhammad. For this reason "Hagar and the Angel" is the only chorus in *The Death of Klinghoffer* that is not one of a pair. (The other, paired choruses represent, among other things, the voice of the natural—as distinct from human—world, and in this sense, too, the "Hagar and the Angel" chorus stands as an exception.) The music is of extraordinary beauty. The chorus unfolds the tale against trudging eighth-notes in the bass; counterpoint and rhythm are powerful; and there is a real sense of wonder to the epiphany of the final line: "Then the angel struck open the abandoned well."

Scene i

It is 11:30 a.m. The Achille Lauro *awaits permission to enter the Syrian port of Tartus. The air corridor is deserted, as is the sea-road. Americans, Britons, and Jews have moved on deck to the Winter Garden, which is the only place a helicopter might hope to land. Leon Klinghoffer's wheelchair cannot be lifted onto the platform, so he sits a little below the others. There is no shade. Differences between the Palestinians are becoming clearer, as is their isolation from their commanders. Molqi, the leader onboard the ship, has not revealed his orders. Everyone is on edge. One Palestinian torments some of the passengers. Another, Omar, invokes the holy death he longs for. Mamoud believes that their radio contacts have betrayed them. Omar and Molqi fight. Molqi wheels Klinghoffer away.*

The opening music is quick, the marking "nervosa." As Molqi spits out his rapid-fire lines, trumpets snarl and the keyboards keep up a constant tattoo. An ominous ticking like that of a time bomb begins; Mamoud declaims the key words: "Now we will kill you all."

At last we hear the voice of Leon Klinghoffer, who, in an aria of rich-textured music, in measured rage denounces the terrorists:

> You don't give a shit.
> Excuse me, about
> Your grandfather's hut,
> His sheep and his goat,
> And the land he wore out.
> You just want to see
> People die.

The most brutal of the four Palestinians, the one who came to be called "Rambo," replies. His taunting of his helpless adversary is nasty. At the same time, his words are eloquent and horribly truthful. As Adams notes, this tirade, with all of its "foul" imagery, delivered to his prosperous bourgeois audience, is "a speech of a lifetime for him." Klinghoffer attempts to comfort his wife. The scene ends on a thought so prosaic as to set the situation into unbearably poignant relief: "I should have worn a hat."

Now we meet another passenger, a young Englishwoman, flirtatious, perky, confident, with a powerful drive for self-preservation, and with a good nose for the people and events around her. Her brief scene is another scherzo. Through the power of contrast, this intermezzo heightens the intensity of our response both to the Klinghoffer/"Rambo" scene we have just heard and to the one that comes immediately after, the first appearance of Omar, the youngest of the Palestinians.

The Englishwoman had mentioned him in her account: "[He] was extremely nice,/Kept us in ciggies the whole time." This is not the Omar we meet. He is very young, young enough for Adams to make him a mezzo-soprano, a grim descendant of Cherubino and Octavian. He has known life only from the confines of a refugee camp. His soul is "all violence," and he is possessed by the idea of Holy Death:

My heart will break
If I do not walk
In Paradise
Within two days
And abandon my soul
And end the exile
Of my flesh from the earth
It struggled with.

Like the Captain, Omar philosophizes. Behind his words we hear the wailing, anguished and urgent, of a women's chorus with tenor solo, as well as the nervous rapping of mallets. The mallets begin with a three-note figure, which, however, constantly erupts into longer and more elaborate firebursts. The vocal line becomes strong and broad ("Let the tent of your exile/Blow away in the gale"). The waves of orchestral sound become overwhelming in preparation for Omar's invocation of Holy Death; we drown in the flood tide of Wagnerian brass. This is unbridled passion beyond anything we have so far experienced in the opera. The aria's end, Adams has said, "should feel like being in a truck loaded with TNT, driving straight into a marine barracks."

"DESERT CHORUS"

From the *ffff* ending of the Holy Death aria, there emerges the quiet opening of the "Desert Chorus." Like the "Chorus of Exiled Palestinians," it begins with women's voices in unison ("gently, without vibrato"), and just a few instruments join them. As in the "Ocean Chorus," to which it is complementary, and the "Night Chorus," Goodman sets the atmosphere with a question: "Is not their desert the garden of the Lord?" Later, at the line "And the sky is nothing but cloud pouring out rain," the oboe adds its expressive obbligato to the very simple and beautiful vocal line. (A word on a detail in the text, the line "Rain falls, and not lightly, on the bituminous land": I thought I had better look up "bituminous," and predictably I found "like or containing bitumen." Bitumen I knew as a substance found in asphalt and tar, but the *Oxford English Dictionary* yielded more treasure. Bitumen is a mineral pitch particularly prevalent in "Palestine and Babylon," and it is also known as "Jew's pitch." As for "bituminous," it also refers to the flaming Lake of Hell, and is so used by Milton in *Paradise Lost*: "The Plain wherein a black bituminous gurge/Boiles out from under ground, the Mouth of Hell.")

Scene ii

Klinghoffer is shot. Mrs. Klinghoffer, sitting on the deck in wretched discomfort, has no idea that her husband is dead. The Palestinians announce the murder to the Captain. He must inform the authorities onshore and let them know that other hostages will die. He considers it his duty as Captain to sacrifice his life for others. Molqi decides that no further killing is necessary. During the ensuing radion operations, the Captain assures Abul Abbas, among others, that no one has died. It is thus agreed that the ship will proceed to Cairo, where the Palestinians will be allowed to disembark. As the ship begins to move, Klinghoffer's body is thrown over the side. It will drift ashore in Syria.

Seated on the ground and leaning against an oil drum full of kerosene, Marilyn Klinghoffer talks to her dancer-double—thus really to her anima—about the pain that consumes her cancer-ridden body. She speaks about her husband and how he had coped with his paralysis; she gives vent to her anger about medical fashions. In spite of her own consuming physical pain, her concern is always and first for her husband. As Adams puts it, "They have become like limbs of the same body." The theme of physical decay and the contrast, set before us throughout the opera, implicitly or explicitly, between the Klinghoffers' age and infirmity, and the youth and robustness of the terrorists, is a powerful thread in the telling of this story.

Then the orchestra takes over as great chains of trills begin a furious crescendo. It is during this fearsome orchestral noise that Leon Klinghoffer is murdered. In the theater we see two things, the four terrorists running across the stage, and then Klinghoffer's body being lowered slowly, infinitely slowly, from ceiling to floor. But Marilyn Klinghoffer still believes her husband to be safe in the ship's hospital. She does not hear the orchestra, and when that storm has passed, she resumes her chatter about the "meshugaas" of their present situation.

She leaves, and Molqi bursts in with the only spoken words in the opera: "American kaput. Take his passport." Mamoud and "Rambo" have their brief say, the latter again gratuitously brutal. The Captain recollects his offer to be the next to die.

"ARIA OF THE FALLING BODY (GYMNOPÉDIE)"

Now Klinghoffer's death is brought before our eyes, not realistically, but symbolically. We have not seen the death; only the music has implied the shot that killed. Now, Klinghoffer's dancer-double drags him away in a great white sheet like a shroud. It is a dance between Leon Klinghoffer and his body, performed to a slow and solemn oboe solo. It is at once lyric and exceedingly formal. Adams has borrowed the title *Gymnopédie* and the musical flavor from the hauntingly solemn yet gently physical piano pieces of Erik Satie. (Satie himself borrowed the title from the Spartan athletic festivals called *gymnopaidiai,* a word that is derived from the Greek *gymnos* [naked] and *pais* [boy].) Mamoud adds a brief epilogue, musically as dry and casual as the *Gymnopédie* is rich and formal.

"DAY CHORUS"

Here is another meditative chorus that begins with a rhetorical question: "Is not the day made to disperse their grief?" Men's voices start, but as the music progresses, the register shifts upward until there are only female voices. The close is given to the entire chorus.

Scene iii

The Achille Lauro *has docked in Cairo, and the Palestinians have disembarked. The Captain calls Mrs. Klinghoffer to his cabin and breaks the news of her husband's death.* None of the passengers is aware that Leon Klinghoffer is dead: they assume that he has been moved to another part of the ship where he would be more comfortable. Breaking the news to Marilyn Klinghoffer, the Captain is kind and ineffectual. There is nothing to be but ineffectual in this situation. Nor is consolation possible. Marilyn Klinghoffer sings out her grief—and we know it to be only the beginning of her grief—in music of searing intensity. She moves from rage to happy remembrance (at this point a wordless women's chorus joins in her threnody) to incredulous sorrow. And there, in desolation, in the dark G minor that was also the key of the "Chorus of Exiled Jews," *The Death of Klinghoffer* ends.

But here is also a second beginning. We have heard the poetry and the music, the music that delivers the poetry to us and heightens and sharpens its meaning. Now, in the silence into which Marilyn Klinghoffer's song dissolves—"They should have killed me—I wanted to die"—these words and this music and what they have told and shown us, all this can begin to resonate in our memories and minds and hearts.

Peter Sellars has said: "I didn't want to stage the images we saw on CNN." The point of writing and composing *The Death of Klinghoffer* was not to produce a documentary, real or fictionalized. That, as Sellars implies, would have been redundant. Music can achieve more than that, penetrating deeply, finding its way to places otherwise unreachable. To do that was the ambition behind *The Death of Klinghoffer*, an ambition largely fulfilled.

By chance, as I first began to study *The Death of Klinghoffer*, I came across a poem by William Meredith, titled "About Opera." It speaks to this point. Meredith writes that the appeal of opera for him is neither in the tunes nor in the plots; rather

An image of articulateness is what it is:
Isn't this how we've always longed to talk?
Words as they fall are monotone and bloodless
But they yearn to take the risk these noises take.

What dancing is to the slightly spastic way
Most of us teeter through our bodily life
Are these measured cries to the clumsy things we say,
In the heart's duresses, on the heart's behalf.

El Dorado (1991)

Michael Steinberg
San Francisco Symphony program book, November 1991

THE LEAD PIECE in the *New Yorker* of October 14 [1991] was a shrewd and somewhat bemused contemplation of anger in public life today, commenting on such phenomena as Jimmy Conners, the audience at the recent Lincoln Center Film Festival, Hate Radio, the *New York Post*'s coverage of Buddy Harrelson's firing as manager of the Mets, and the political success of George Bush [Senior]. (Had the article been written a week later, another topic might have been the political success of Judge Clarence Thomas.) "Anger," the essay proposed, "is to our time what angst was to the nineteen-fifties."

We seem inclined today to look at recent history decade by decade, even giving each a label of its own. I don't know whether this is to be attributed to a new kind of Zeitgeist vanity, to historical short-windedness or myopia, or some other cause. To those who did not live through them, the dreary, far from cheering 1950s now seem as exotic as the 1920s and the object of nostalgia. We all know about the 1960s, a decade that, in fact, lived some way into the 1970s. The 1980s have already been identified as the decade of greed and "me first." As the *New Yorker* suggests, the 1990s might become known as the Age of Anger. Discomfort about the 1980s may have something to do with it.

In this spirit, *El Dorado* is an authentic 1990s piece—an often angry look at the deplorable 1980s by an artist in his mid-forties, whose personal, political, and social sensibilities were formed in the 1960s. My first question to John Adams regarding the piece was about its title. Was it one word or two? "Two words," he replied. "It's not the Cadillac." But the Cadillac would not go away from our conversation. Adams recalled growing up in the 1950s, "the time of Eldorados and electric kitchens. And it's disturbing the way the eighties repeated the fifties—disturbing, that is, to anyone with a transcendental vision of life." Musing about this, Adams recalled a recent magazine advertisement for an imported and expensive automobile: "The black car is blurred, to suggest speed, and the caption says something like 'Feel how good aggression can be.'"

The house that Adams and his family—photographer Deborah O'Grady (once the San Francisco Symphony's operations manager) plus Emily and Sam, seven and six, respectively—moved into last spring is a peaceful place. Wherever you look there are signs of people busy and happy in their lives. The smell of good coffee hangs in the air. The room where Adams works is filled with synthesizers and other bits of electronic equipment that allow him instantly to realize his ideas in sounds that at least approximate the orchestral colors and textures to come. It is a far cry from the familiar old image of the composer at the piano, pencil in hand. It is also a blessing to the program annotator who can be given not only a score but also what Adams calls an "electronic mock-up" of the as yet unperformed composition.

But there is a piano in the room as well. A copy of Jon Backus's formidable text on *Acoustical Foundations* lies on its lid, but on the music rack there is a volume of Mozart sonatas, as well as Hrimaly's *Scale Studies*. These last belong to Emily, who plays the violin. Adams himself is a good enough clarinetist to have been a regular substitute and extra with the Boston Symphony during his student days at Harvard; nowadays he is more and more in demand as a conductor. His programs, like the one tonight, almost always include music other than his own, and the "other" might be anything going all the way back to Haydn. The sense of connection with musical tradition is strong in him. He was proud of the way his *Harmonielehre* in 1985 was nourished by Schoenberg's *Gurrelieder* and the Sibelius Fourth Symphony; now, with equal pleasure, he mentions Sibelius No. 6 as music whose harmonic language has left its mark on *El Dorado* and points to Bach and Bruckner as models for other aspects of his work.

"I am unable and unwilling to filter out my response to the world around me," says Adams. The major event in his professional life this year has been the series of performances in Brussels, Lyon, and New York of his second opera *The Death of Klinghoffer.* Adams wants to write music that presses buttons. It can happen that pressing buttons produces explosions. *Klinghoffer* has. Its unconventional dramaturgy, which owes more to the Bach *Passions* than to the operatic tradition with which Adams played so comfortably and sometimes so amusingly in *Nixon,* has bothered some people. But the subject is inherently dangerous, and because Adams and his collaborators, librettist Alice Goodman and director Peter Sellars, have tried to illuminate both sides of a deeply rooted, ancient, and tragic conflict, *Klinghoffer,* especially in New York, has given rise to accusations of anti-Semitism. (More Jews than Palestinians go to the opera.)

In a purely instrumental composition you can say *j'accuse* to a specific addressee only by cuing the audience by means of the title: Luigi Nono's "Y su sangre ya viene cantando" from his *Epitaph for Federico García Lorca* and Krzysztof Penderecki's *Threnody for the Victims of Hiroshima* are examples from a generation ago; the *Lacerations* of Bright Sheng are a more recent one. Adams describes *El Dorado* as his "response to surviving the eighties," with special emphasis perhaps on his feelings on witnessing the continuing despoilment of our planet. One could imagine Adams, Goodman, and Sellars making an opera about the *Exxon Valdez.* In fact, though, Adams has chosen to make his subject, so to speak, the European conquest of this continent.

The name of El Dorado, the Gilded One, was first given to an early sixteenth-century Colombian chieftain who covered his body with gold dust at certain festive ceremonies. The tale of El Dorado drew the Spanish conquistadors to the region in the

1530s. El Dorado was not found, but the Spaniards remained, and *El Dorado* gradually came to mean a fabulous region of untold riches. You can see it on old maps of Brazil and Guiana, and those who named cities in the United States resorted to the name more than once. Milton mentions El Dorado in *Paradise Lost,* and so did Voltaire in *Candide.* Throughout the sixteenth century, the seekers continued to come: Pizarro, Orellana, and Jiménez from Spain, Raleigh from England, Coelho de Sousa from Portugal.

The first movement of Adams's *El Dorado* is titled "A Dream of Gold," but it was originally called "Pizarro's Dream." There were three Pizarros, all explorers and conquerors, the brothers Francisco and Hernando, and their half-brother Gonzalo. Francisco, who took Peru from the Incas, is the most famous, but it was Gonzalo who sought El Dorado in 1539, crossing the Andes from Quito. These stories are told in *History of the Conquest of Mexico* (1843) and *History of the Conquest of Peru* (1847) by William Hickling Prescott, a historian with exceptional gifts of imaginative insight and dramatic narrative. From the point of view of scholarship, Prescott is in many respects outdated and superseded; but like Gibbon's great and similarly "obsolete" work on the Roman Empire, Prescott's histories are classics, still read, and irrepressibly alive.

Adams, who must be one of the best-read and most widely curious of composers, of course read Prescott. The question of historical perspective interests and troubles him. It is too easy to simplify a story like that of the conquest—or, as we are beginning to learn not to say, the discovery—of the Americas. "The Incas," Adams points out, "were no saints either." He continues: "I'm suspicious of the current trend of self-loathing. You see a lot of this in all the arts," mostly, he suggests, as response to equally unattractive self-congratulation. "I also don't want to overdo, to romanticize 'the romance of the Virgin Continent.'"

Nonetheless, "A Dream of Gold" is music with fire in its belly. Taking just under fifteen minutes, it is the first of what Adams has called the two "panels" that make up *El Dorado.* (The second, "Soledades," takes just over fifteen minutes.) Describing the formal and emotional structure of *El Dorado,* Adams speaks of "a punishing first part and a 'pure' second part. I imagine they constitute my two notions of El Dorado: one with man, the other without him."

"A Dream of Gold" is quiet and tranquil to begin with, but this calm is overtaken by what Adams calls "the most terrifyingly aggressive music" he has written. Very simply—too simply—put, it is one huge crescendo. The music begins with what has almost become the Adams signature, a steady pulse of quick notes, played here on the cabaza, which is soon joined by the high-hat cymbal. Basses and a synthesizer anchor the music to C, and it is something like two and a half minutes before that note relinquishes its hold on the harmony. Meanwhile, though, much has happened. For one thing, the other strings have gradually added sustained, softly dissonant notes. For another, the steady rat-tat of the sixteenth-notes in the percussion is reinforced from time to time by single accented notes on marimba, piano, and harp.

Just as the first high G added by the second violins is just the beginning of what will become a considerable stack of notes, so these single accents turn out to be the starting of the rhythmic motor that drives this movement. The single Cs become pairs of C/E-flat; then D-flat is added to the repertory of available pitches, eventually E-natural, F-sharp, and so forth. These notes also occur in ever quicker succession. A flute takes these notes and turns them into a sustained melody that starts shyly, but quickly learns to assert itself as it climbs across two and a half octaves. The harmonic range grows wider, and the harmonies also change more frequently. With these materials and ideas—the insistent tattoo of quick notes, the contrast of these fast, metrically defined patterns against lines of longer notes that move around the beats rather than on them, and the constant use of small rhythmic units to generate larger shapes—Adams builds what becomes the ferocious crescendo of "The Dream of Gold." It breaks off, *fortississimo*, in mid-phrase, as though in frustration.

In "A Dream of Gold" we are in that world of chromaticism whose conquest in "The Anfortas Wound," the middle movement of *Harmonielehre*, was such an important milestone in Adams's development as a composer. As the basis of his harmonic and melodic language, Adams uses an octatonic (eight-note) scale of the type

C - D-flat - E-flat - E-natural - F-sharp - G - A - B-flat.

He points out that this scale, used also by Stravinsky as well as by Bill Evans and other jazz musicians, is flexible to work with, yielding major and minor triads, fifths, and tritones, and being easily harmonized.

In our conversation in June, Adams described "Soledades" as "a long, melancholy landscape." More recently, when he had finished the composition, he elaborated: "It feels like a very serene pastoral giving way to an equally serene scherzo which builds to a crest and then gently drifts down to nothing." The harmonic language is different: it was in this connection that Adams mentioned the modal style of the Sibelius Sixth Symphony. Yet, if at first one is conscious chiefly of the contrast between the two movements of *El Dorado,* the violence that ultimately dominates "A Dream of Gold" and the gentleness of "Soledades," one comes to be no less aware of the connection between them. I found myself reminded of two of Beethoven's late piano sonatas. In the two-movement Opus 111, Beethoven presents a similar pairing of a fierce movement and one that is largely serene, though the proportions are quite different. And in the *Hammerklavier* Sonata, Op. 106, there, too, using completely different proportions, Beethoven writes a tiny scherzo that is a quirky and ironic variant of the craggy first movement. The more I hear *El Dorado* (in its electronic mock-up form—and I have, at the time of writing, not seen a score of the second movement), it seems to me that "Soledades" is a variation of "A Dream of Gold," full of facial and skeletal resemblances, but in a different mood and character, and to different expressive purpose. And it is, after all, the same landscape.

Chamber Symphony (1992)

Sarah Cahill
Lincoln Center's John Adams Festival program book
New York City, 2003

JOHN ADAMS WRITES: "I was sitting in my studio, studying the score to Schoenberg's Chamber Symphony, and as I was doing so I became aware that my seven-year-old son Sam was in the adjacent room watching cartoons (good cartoons, old ones from the '50s). The hyperactive, insistently aggressive and acrobatic scores for the cartoons mixed in my head with the Schoenberg music, itself hyperactive, acrobatic and not a little aggressive, and I realized suddenly how much these two traditions had in common."

In his 1985 *Harmonielehre*, Adams confronted the long shadow cast by Schoenberg over twentieth-century music. The Chamber Symphony is an overt tribute to Schoenberg's own work of the same name, Opus 9, especially its dense counterpoint and rhythmic energy. Adams's composition employs the same instruments as Schoenberg's, with the addition of synthesizer, percussion, trumpet, and trombone. While Schoenberg's work is in one movement, Adams's is divided into three: "Mongrel Airs," "Aria with Walking Bass," and "Roadrunner."

The Chamber Symphony marks a new stylistic era for Adams. It is highly chromatic and continually polyphonic. Each of the fifteen instruments' lines is clearly defined, and each page bustles with hyper-detailed activity. It also demands instrumentalists who, in Adams's words, "are asked to negotiate unreasonably difficult passages and alarmingly fast tempi, often to the inexorable click of the trap set." While speed and virtuosity are certainly present in previous works like *Short Ride in a Fast Machine* and *Fearful Symmetries,* the Chamber Symphony pushes performers with new challenges. The skills of virtuoso ensembles such as the London Sinfonietta, the Schoenberg Ensemble, the Ensemble Modern, and the San Francisco Chamber Players, all of whom performed the Chamber Symphony early on, inspired Adams to write his most difficult music to date.

"Mongrel Airs" opens with a cacophonic eruption, and as a cowbell keeps time, the violin grabs a solo, playing chromatic sixths in rough *pesante* double stops reminiscent of the soldier's fiddle in *L'Histoire du Soldat.* This is one of several small homages to Stravinsky throughout the piece, another one being the bassoon's rapid, staccato descending scales in "Aria with Walking Bass," a nearly direct quote from Stravinsky's Octet. Adams has also cited Milhaud's *La Création du Monde* and Hindemith's *Kleine Kammermusik* as inspirations. These composers were stimulated by the birth of jazz, its raw power and transparent complexity and brilliant solo spots for each instrument. Adams takes those qualities even further, and adds one more element to the mix: cartoon music, summed up best by the meticulously intricate arrangements and antic tempi of Raymond Scott, whose brilliant miniatures show up regularly in cartoons ranging from *Bugs Bunny* to *Ren and Stimpy.*

"Aria with Walking Bass" begins as a slow movement, with a long, expressive trombone melody. Other instruments join, thickening the rhythmic texture, until the slow movement is no longer slow, even though its steady pulse (the "walking bass," ever present except for two brief moments) remains the same. At the end of "Roadrunner" the violin takes the spotlight again with a thorny cadenza. The ever active percussion battery for this piece includes toms, timbales, snare rim, snare, bongos, roto toms, conga, clave, cowbell, woodblock, hi-hat, and tambourine.

Violin Concerto (1993)

Michael Steinberg
San Francisco Symphony program book, January 2000

JOHN ADAMS'S FATHER was a good amateur clarinetist and saxophonist. The clarinet was John's first instrument, too, though he chose to hone his skills to professional level: my first awareness of him was as a member of Sarah Caldwell's opera orchestra in Boston and as an occasional substitute in the Boston Symphony. He was then a student at Harvard. His principal mentor there was Leon Kirchner, for whose teaching, charged with imagination and intellectual vigor, Adams still feels profound gratitude. As a graduation present, his parents gave him John Cage's *Silence,* a collection of lectures and writings of which Jill Johnston said when it appeared in 1962 that "those who read [it] should find it difficult to curl up inside any comfortable box made before picking up the book." It certainly called into question everything that his musical experiences so far stood for. "I don't think my parents knew what they were giving," Adams reflected years later. He found the seductiveness of Cage's reasoning "irresistible," a condition hardly disturbed by his finding the holes in Cage's arguments. Something that particularly stirred him was Cage's emphasis on the importance of sound itself as a physical entity as distinct from the emphasis, standard in teaching and criticism, on the organization of sound.

When he first went to California, Adams was deeply involved with the work of John Cage and some of the younger figures of the then avant-garde, Robert Ashley, Alvin Lucier, and Christian Wolff. During a three-year immersion with electronic music he built his own synthesizer. Paradoxically it was that immersion and his involvement with technical points of tuning that led to what he called his "diatonic conversion. It made me realize the *resonant* power of consonance. There's such a lack of resonance in atonal music with all the upper partials clashing against each other. There's seldom a sense of depth or of sympathetic vibration. The composers that mean the most to me are those whose music is music of sustained resonance." Adams's own purest essay in consonant minimalism is an orchestral work named *Common Tones in Simple Time* (1979), music that still leaves me dazzled with the luster of its sound, enchanted by the purr of its engine, delightfully jolted by its powerful lifts into new harmonies, and happy in its deep calm.

At the time of *Harmonium*, the examples he cited were Beethoven, Sibelius "for sure" (particularly the Seventh Symphony), "the orchestral Wagner," early Stravinsky, Steve Reich. By the time he wrote *Harmonielehre*, he was ready to add early Schoenberg, particularly *Gurrelieder*. But even then, Adams voiced reservations about the relentlessly consonant, low-metabolism way of composing that was then coming to be known as minimalism. In the years since *Common Tones in Simple Time*, Adams has sought—and found—a world of richer harmonic possibilities and has dared ventures into a language "of greater synthesis and ambiguity. The territory...is far more dangerous, but also more fertile, more capable of expressive depth and emotional flexibility." Adams's mature music is a celebration of this stretching, a celebration of event, of wonderfully satisfying, room-filling sonority, of energy born of the force of harmonic movement.

The idea that there should be an Adams violin concerto was born in Jorja Fleezanis's mind on Tuesday evening, March 26, 1985, when she heard John Adams's *Harmonielehre* on the radio. The week before, Edo de Waart and the San Francisco Symphony, where Fleezanis was then associate concertmaster, had given the first performances of that remarkable score. *Harmonielehre* is an exceedingly difficult piece to play, and during the rehearsals, performances, and the recording sessions that followed, Fleezanis had been too busy counting to get a coherent impression of the work. At that time, San Francisco Symphony broadcasts were heard locally on the Tuesday after the previous week's concerts. When Fleezanis had a chance to experience *Harmonielehre* from the outside, she found it a knockout. The moment the broadcast was over, she picked up the telephone, called Adams, and asked him to write her a violin concerto.

Much happened over the following eight years. De Waart, Adams's first champion among major conductors, left San Francisco for Minneapolis. San Francisco was still interested in commissioning the Violin Concerto, but naturally enough, when Fleezanis became concertmaster of the Minnesota Orchestra, San Francisco's plans for an Adams commission changed. (The work Adams wrote for San Francisco instead was *El Dorado*.) De Waart, however, reopened the question of the Violin Concerto at his new post, and eventually a triple commission from the Minnesota Orchestra, the New York City Ballet (for choreography by Peter Martins), and the London Symphony Orchestra was arranged.

On January 7, 1993, at 8:19 p.m., Fleezanis received a fax from Adams with the words "Wir haben es angefangen" (We have begun it) and an A-minor chord about five octaves deep. (Adams had previously told her that the work would be in A minor and had promised it would be "drenchingly beautiful.") In March 1993, by way of a preview, Adams sent Fleezanis the score and tape of his Chamber Symphony, which is full of virtuoso solos for the concertmaster. She got her first look at the Concerto a month later when she visited Adams in Berkeley.

Although January 7, 1993, was the date the first notes went down on paper, Adams had had the Violin Concerto steadily in his mind since completing his second opera, *The Death of Klinghoffer*, and *El Dorado* in 1991. In part, the virtuoso violin writing in the Chamber Symphony, written in 1992, can be seen as the composer's limbering-up exercise for the Concerto. In no way did Adams approach the task lightly; indeed, to begin with, he found it quite intimidating. For one thing, so many composers—Beethoven, Mendelssohn, Schumann, Brahms, Tchaikovsky, Sibelius, Elgar, Stravinsky, Berg, Schoenberg, just to begin a list—had written just one violin concerto. "These," Adams remarks, "tend to be among their greatest works, so unless one is completely historically indifferent, which I can't say I am, one tends to tread lightly."

At the same time, Adams was excited by the challenge: "The violin commands incredible lyric intensity and has a fantastic capacity to deliver a white-hot message." He himself is not a violinist, and for a time he made use of an ingenious device patented by the composer Donald Martino, a T-square that corresponds to a violin's fingerboard, with lines to represent the four strings and with the positions of all the notes marked on those lines.

The Martino T-square is a great help—up to a point. It can help you determine, for example, whether a certain chord can be reached at all by a violinist with the normal quota of four fingers and a thumb. But it is one thing to be able to reach a chord and quite another to play it in the middle of a rapid and active passage. Nor does the T-square help you with the fact that some chords, though theoretically possible, simply do not "sound" and would come across as colorless or feeble. At some point the composer has to come to terms with the violin as it really is.

In this instance, Fleezanis eventually came to replace the T-square, and in so doing, she—and later, Gidon Kremer—became part of the succession of violinist collaborators that began when Ferdinand David worked with Mendelssohn on his concerto. Adams wanted to write a truly violinistic piece. Suggestions, emendations, counter-suggestions flew back and forth by phone and fax between Berkeley and Edina, Minnesota. Sometimes three alternative new versions of a passage would arrive by fax, and Fleezanis would play the various solutions back over the phone, sometimes into Adams's answering machine.

To begin with, Adams had imagined a two-movement concerto lasting a little over twenty minutes, something on the scale of the Stravinsky Concerto. The idea was to have a highly energetic first movement and then a contrasting slow movement, a chaconne, a set of variations over a repeated bass or harmonic pattern. Adams, thinking of Bach's great chaconne for solo violin and the finale of the Brahms Fourth Symphony, imagined a movement that would begin quietly but get "wilder and wilder and more ornate. It was a grand idea, but somehow I never found the right material to justify the form." Musical material always makes its desires known, makes its own laws, and controls its own destiny. Thus the chaconne became, as Adams has said, a more enclosed piece, a kind of dreamy, filmy, almost diaphanous slow movement" in the middle of the work, which, in its final form, has the familiar shape of fast-slow-fast. Partly for that reason, the Concerto also came to be a larger work than Adams had originally foreseen: "I was trying at first to avoid a collision with destiny; nevertheless it came out big." It also turned out to be an important contribution to the repertory: just three years after the premiere, it had entered the repertory of more than a dozen violinists.

The first music we hear is a figuration in the orchestra—eight notes rising, to begin with—whose presence is constant enough to give us a sense of regularity, but whose details keep changing. The solo violin lays a wonderfully free melody across this pattern. "Composed rhapsodizing," Fleezanis calls it, and this sense of freedom, of something being invented on the spot and born out of the very spirit of the violin, the contrast between this and the firm dance floor provided by the orchestra, is characteristic of the Concerto throughout. From time to time a clarinet or some other instrument will step forward with a solo, but essentially the show is in the endlessly inventive and evolving violin part. (As well as endlessly inventive, the violin part is virtually nonstop in all three movements.) It is wave motion enormously magnified; just three or four great surges define the flow of the whole movement. There are occasional changes of speed, and near the end, Adams winds the rhythmic coil tighter by changing from four beats in a measure to just three. This switch occurs in the orchestra; the violin sets up a spicy rhythmic dissonance by staying firmly in four. This friction of three against four is one of the simplest of the cross-rhythms that enliven this Concerto.

With a brilliant passage for the flute, the orchestra makes its exit, and the violin begins a cadenza. After a brief coda at a more spacious tempo and with the solo instrument now muted, the music flows directly into the second movement. This has a title: Chaconne: "Body through which the dream flows," a phrase taken from a poem by Robert Hass. A chaconne is, as Adams puts it, "a highly identifiable musical artifact"—the Pachelbel Canon is probably the most familiar example to most people—and the recognition factor is definitely part of Adams's plan.

Chaconne and passacaglia basses in baroque and earlier music were generally clichés that outlined basic harmonic progressions. Adams's six-measure repeated bass is likewise a cliché (he found it in the article on ground bass in *The New Grove Dictionary of Music and Musicians*): virtually a quotation of the bass Pachelbel used. In Pachelbel's day—and also in 1993 for Adams—the point was to show what fresh things could be done on ground trod so often before. (The literary critic Harry Levin has remarked that quotation, allusion, and collage are of the essence of twentieth-century art.)

But while in baroque music these basses usually stayed at the same pitch and kept their rhythmic shape (as usual, Bach is the exception, at least with respect to constancy of pitch), this bass begins to travel after the third variation. At first the rhythm changes, and the pattern which took six measures to traverse when we first heard it is now expanded to nine. Later it will, for example, be compressed to four. Part of what makes this fresh and delightful is that these augmentations and diminutions, instead of being managed by simple devices such as doubling or halving, involve unusual arithmetic proportions such as 4:5. Adams owes some of these rhythmic ideas to his study of the music of one of the great American eccentrics, Conlon Nancarrow, who died in 1997.

In this movement, too, there is contrast between firmness and freedom (the body and the dream) as the familiar bass is beautifully disturbed by the violin melodies that float and soar freely across it, by changes in meter and harmony, and by the softly shimmering sound of the synthesizers in the orchestra. Something comparable happens in the harmony as well. The bass, at first, outlines the simplest imaginable major-key harmonies, but later, though it always remains recognizable, it moves into other, less familiar modes. (Computer technology now allows a composer to "translate" a melody from major into minor or into any other mode with a single keystroke.) The Chaconne is the movement that underwent the biggest changes in the course of composition. In its original form—and this probably goes back to the stage when Adams thought of it as the finale—the solo violin part was extraordinarily active, all luxuriant tendrils and coils, like something from an Ornette Coleman solo; the revisions allow much more room for expressive lyric melody.

The finale is titled "Toccare." This is an Italian verb meaning both to touch and to play a keyboard instrument—the French *toucher* does similar double duty—and we are more familiar with "toccata," the noun derived from it. In post-baroque music, a toccata is usually a brilliant display piece with a steady rat-tat of sixteenth-notes, and this "Toccare" is a finale in that spirit. Part of Adams's preparation for the writing of the Violin Concerto had involved intense listening to performances of bowed stringed instruments outside the Western classical tradition, such as the work of the extraordinary Indian virtuoso, Dr. L. Subramaniam, and here we find inventive and daring fiddle pyrotechnics on that order. Adams's wife, the photographer Deborah O'Grady, referred to the fast movements of the Chamber Symphony as "caffeine music"—one of the most characteristic features of the Adams-O'-Grady house is the aroma of fresh and strong coffee—and this heady, high-spirited finale is definitely of that ilk. And no nonsense about decaf, either.

Gnarly Buttons (1996)

Sarah Cahill
Lincoln Center's John Adams Festival program book
New York City, 2003

GNARLY BUTTONS'S ECLECTIC INSTRUMENTATION gives the work its distinctive sound. A banjo player doubles on mandolin and guitar. Trombone, English horn, and bassoon are joined by piano, two samplers (playing a variety of sounds including accordion, clarinet, and cow), and strings.

"Gnarly" conjures up both the hands of an aging man and the appreciative accolade of surfer slang. The "buttons," says John Adams, are a subconscious reference to Gertrude Stein's *Tender Buttons*, "but my evoking them here also acknowledges our lives at the end of the twentieth century as being largely given over to pressing buttons of one sort or another. NB: clarinets have rings and keys, not buttons."

"The Perilous Shore" starts with clarinet alone, in an extended solo. This solo's germinating material returns throughout the movement, transformed slightly each time. The clarinet's tune begins with leisurely eighth-notes, and then doubles in speed to sixteenth-notes, then doubles again to 32nd-notes. Monodic nineteenth-century hymns inspired Adams to reinforce the clarinet's line with other instruments, so that they play in unison rather than in harmony.

The meters of "Hoedown" (Mad Cow) sound complex, but really involve only a straightforward alternation between 2/4 and 3/4 time. Along with the soloist, the two dominant instruments here are the mandolin, which strums a slinky tune in unison with the clarinet, and the piano, which softens the clarinet's spiky chromatic passages with soothing E-flat major and A-flat major arpeggios. Listen closely for the cow moo, because it only happens once.

"Put Your Loving Arms Around Me" begins as an aria, a long vocal melody with chordal accompaniment. The clarinet's phrases stretch out operatically, gaining in poignancy. A bassoon takes over the solo line, as the orchestration grows thicker with dissonance and finally splinters into melodic and rhythmic fragments. At the end, the piano plays straight repeated eighth-note triads with the guitar intertwined in a five-beat pattern, while the clarinet returns for one last refrain of its song.

Century Rolls (1996)

Sarah Cahill
Lincoln Center's John Adams Festival program book
New York City, 2003

"THE GERMINATING IDEA BEHIND *Century Rolls* was an experience I had late one night listening to a recording of old piano roll music from the 1920s," writes John Adams. "I was struck in an unexpected way by the fact that, regardless of the performer or the repertoire—be it Gershwin or Rachmaninoff, Jelly Roll Morton, or Paderewski—the technology of the piano roll transformed the music into a realm that could not have been anticipated before what Walter Benjamin called the 'age of mechanical reproduction.' So *Century Rolls*, a concerto requested by my friend, Emanuel Ax, became in part an attempt to recreate that initial response I had received to the sound of the piano as heard via the medium of the piano roll."

Composed four years before the millennium, *Century Rolls* reflects not only on early recording techniques, but on what may have been the last truly popular piano concertos of the twentieth century. Adams never quotes them, but we hear distant echoes of Ravel's two concertos, Gershwin's Concerto in F, Rachmaninoff's Concertos Nos. 2 and 3. It is telling that each of these composers were early advocates of piano rolls as well. But while *Century Rolls* pays affectionate tribute to piano rolls and their pianists, it is firmly anchored in the present tense. One soon realizes that this piece couldn't exist without the music of Duke Ellington, Conlon Nancarrow, and the John Adams of *Grand Pianola Music.*

Century Rolls is a classic concerto in the romantic sense of soloist alternately wrestling with and embracing the orchestra, and it proves to be an even match. The orchestral introduction begins with high delicate rhythms of piccolo and flute, violins, and harp. Layers build in a descending progression, with entrances of strings and winds, until the piano enters on a low F-sharp. The single-line piano part, rhythmically edgy, breaks into syncopated chords, and alternates throughout this movement between a chordal pattern with a speedy swing and Nancarrowesque chromatic passagework.

Century Rolls's first and second movements are separate but linked; one flows seamlessly into the next, the metronomic pulse stays the same, and triplet figures and repeated chords in the piano part echo previous material from the first movement. And yet, we have entered new terrain.

The second movement's punning title, "Manny's Gym," refers both to the athletic workout assigned to Emanuel Ax, and to the *gymnopédie,* a form best known in Satie's three simple slow dances. This is the second *gymnopédie* composed by Adams, the first being the climactic "Aria of the Falling Body" in his opera *The Death of Klinghoffer.* That *gymnopédie* suspended time, and so does this one. It begins serenely, with the piano's left hand doubled by basses and the tune in piccolos, but soon the downbeat is out of kilter, and we sense that perhaps Satie has met Nancarrow somewhere during the age of mechanical reproduction. The piano floats in virtuosic passagework while the winds carry the delicate but still disjointed tune, and finally resumes the *gymnopédie* while the piano riffs in the upper register.

Of the concerto's three movements, it is "Hail Bop" ("so named," explains Adams, "in honor of my misapprehension of the name of the 1995 comet, Hale-Bopp") that particularly conjures up piano rolls, with their patina of mechanical brittleness—Rubinstein complained early on that they made his piano sound like a banjo—the slight but unmistakable distortion of speed, and the aura of the disembodied pianist. There are comical confrontations between Jelly Roll Morton and Paderewski, sudden pauses after which the pianist breaks into a walking bass that wanders aimlessly, cartoonish blurts of the trumpets, and a section where, in Adams's words, "the orchestra seems at the piano's heels like a barking terrier." Nancarrow is very present here—after all, his primary instrument was the player piano, for which he created hundreds of studies. His influence is heard in jutting chromatic triads and with spasmodic lurches of atonal passagework. Ingeniously, Adams evokes a classic swing riff of stride pianists, notating it with tied triplets. Throughout, the huff and puff of the primitive device of air stream propulsion and percussive hammers is almost audible.

Naive and Sentimental Music
A Sentimental Journey (1997–98)

Ingram Marshall
Liner notes for *Naive and Sentimental Music,* Nonesuch, 2002

EXCERPT OF AN E-MAIL from Ingram Marshall to John Adams after a Boston Symphony Orchestra performance of *Naive and Sentimental Music,* February 2001:

> I am beginning to understand *Naive and Sentimental;* rhetorically, or perhaps metaphorically, the first movement is a journey (without a known destination—the trip's the thing); the second movement is the place reached, which turns out to be a timeless dream—a place which is not a place) and the third movement is the return trip (direction and destination known), and I love those "backwards" attacks in the strings—in the latter part of the second movement—as if we were being pulled back through a previous sonic journey.

This large work could be called a symphony by virtue of its three-movement format, but the composer has chosen to call it "music," thus implying a less concrete form. We are dealing here with a kind of music that is both "naive" and "sentimental," words that might be found in the arsenal of a critic determined to shoot down the simplistic and maudlin!

But John Adams in choosing this title was not being coy or even ironic, rather he is using these words in the sense they were used two centuries ago by the German poet Friedrich Schiller, who in his essay "Über naive und sentimentalische Dichtung" ["On Naive and Sentimental Poetry"; 1795] distinguished between two essential types of artistic personalities. The "naive" are the unconscious ones, "for whom art is a natural form of expression, uncompromised by self-analysis or worry over its place in the historical continuum," as Adams wrote in the program note. The sentimental artist, being self-aware, tries to find the lost unity of the naive; he is essentially a searcher, all too aware of his place in history. (Isaiah Berlin wrote succinctly on this Schiller essay in "The Naiveté of Verdi" [1968], from which Adams gets much of his explication.)

One might think of the early minimalist composers of the 1960s as being refreshingly "naive," and thus able to create anew with very basic materials in opposition to the hyper-sentimental serialists, for whom every note and musical gesture had to have a rationale, an historical prerogative. John is often lumped with the minimalists for his early works such as *Shaker Loops* and *Harmonium*, which derived stylistically to some degree from composers such as Reich, but his work of the last fifteen years or so has shown a dramatic shift to a more "sentimental" position—that is to say, a lot more intellectual self-awareness. All this suggests a certain Apollonian/Dionysian push and pull, or, as John has mentioned in the past, the trickster-maverick pieces versus the serious and profound. There are many dichotomies in his music, but as he himself has stated, they can be taken too far.

Quoting again from his program note: "Nowadays all art is in one sense or another self-referential. For gallery goers and concert and theater audiences, 'Statement by the Artist' is a rigorously obeyed prerequisite before the consumption of any new artistic experience. The constant stylistic upheavals in both classical and popular music testify to a painfully acute self-awareness, and the more strident parodists of our time, the Frank Zappas and Jeff

Koonses, express the sentimentalists' outrage at having too much historical debris to wade through."

So the given situation is that we are, like it or not, sentimentalists, and, while we may not easily attain the ideal of the naive, we can at least be aware of it, and perhaps this is the crux of John's stance in this music—a kind of self-awareness of self-awareness.

The naive/sentimental concepts serve only as a starting point for this astonishing and constantly surprising creation; they are basically background considerations. There is the obvious naive/sentimental paradigm in the very opening of the music: it begins with the straightforward strumming of a guitar—accompanied by piano and harp—of some basic chords, over which appears to be a rather simple melody in flutes and oboes, but which has an unruly way of jumping all over the place. As Adams described it, the first movement is an "essay on melody" and is governed by the "naive/sentimental tune, a melody that…floats throughout the…structure like an *idée fixe,* usually accompanied by the strumming of the guitar and harps." He further describes it as a "simple diatonic tune that leaves the nest and ventures out into the wide world like a Dickens child." Throughout this movement this melody weaves, in various instrumental guises, often accompanied by the guitar and its allies. In its peregrinations, the melody finds itself in different harmonic settings, some stranger than others. It is this melodic journey that is the key to the "idea" of this movement, if not the whole work: it's a trip.

Those past works of Adams, especially those cast in large symphonic form, provide a context, perhaps, in which *Naive and Sentimental Music* can be better understood. *Harmonielehre, El Dorado,* the Violin Concerto, and *Century Rolls* are the obvious forebears. Written between 1998 and '99 on commission for the Los Angeles Philharmonic and Esa-Pekka Salonen, who wanted a grand work, it was at the time the most ambitious work outside of the operas. It is that, but it stands apart from these other works; it seems to inhabit a different world, even though it displays many typical Adamsian gestures. Paradoxically, it both summarizes his past work and steps out in new directions. One feels that it is autobiographical, but at the same time, the biographical narrative sur-

renders to a more universal message. This is a music full of dualities.

Its most likely partner is the Violin Concerto, whose first movement exhibits a relentless "hyper-melody" (to use John's phrase).
However, the itinerant melody found here is quite a different thing
as it maintains its basic character—in the Concerto it is endlessly
transformed. Here it hangs on for dear life, for it's on a journey
unsure of its destination; in fact, it gets lost several times.

Listen to the opening and feel the walking pace of the pulsed
chords in the guitar, and hear how a bit later this picks up and
there is a sense of rushing. What starts as an innocent saunter in
the park becomes an urgent journey. Listen also to the way the
melody finds its way into other instruments (like the celli about a
minute and a half in) so that counterpoints are created, and by the
time the violins take it up in a full-throated way, we are running,
no longer sauntering. Soon the running pulse seems to break up
into a series of flurries and the melody loses its identity, or perhaps it is hiding.

The music eventually finds itself in a rather terrifying place
with Scriabinesque trumpets pealing out over full orchestral
sonorities, and then suddenly all is quiet and the familiar flute
melody reappears. So it goes with the chimerical wanderings of
this movement. Another rash and confusing area appears at about
ten minutes, where all sense of direction and tonality seems lost.
We are almost in a world of pure timbre-texture (shades of Ligeti
or early Penderecki?). In the latter half of this movement ["Naive
and Sentimental Music"], the melody often seems completely disembodied from other things going on around it—simultaneities
but no commonalities. Eventually, everything seems to be conspir-
ing towards a perceived end, and there is a kind of goal reached in
the stunning climax of the movement, but it doesn't seem to be a
real destination so much as a final outpouring of ecstasy, almost
Messiaen-like in its brassy exuberance. The music has ended, but
it doesn't feel that the journey has.

The second movement, "Mother of the Man," is referred to by
Adams as "a gloss on Busoni's *Berceuse élégiaque*," the subtitle for
which is *A Cradle Song of the Man at the Coffin of His Mother*.

Some years ago [1989], Adams made an arrangement for chamber orchestra of this haunting lullaby. Those familiar with it will not immediately hear a resemblance, for in a strictly musical sense, there is little. But it is a "gloss," which is to say, a commentary. Leaving the exact relationship to be discovered by future researchers, I would only say that in mood and tone, it is a match, and at that, the Adams commentary goes way beyond its subject.

What it might remind listeners of even more are those pieces he has called *gymnopédies* (after Satie, of course), such as the "Aria of the Falling Body" from *The Death of Klinghoffer,* the "Manny's Gym" movement from *Century Rolls,* and even the Chaconne from the Violin Concerto. These are dreamlike, almost motionless, cyclical essays in suspended animation. Here a drawn-out figure in the high strings, consisting of four notes that outline a triadic harmony, reiterates eternally, accompanied by magical disembodied tones of bowed crotala and vibraphone bars. This creates a limpid landscape over which the guitar eventually appears with a languid melody. (Now its role is reversed from that of the first movement where it provided accompaniment and movement.) Soon it is joined by two bassoons, and a remarkable trio is engaged, although the subtle counterpoint never upsets the delicate ethereal balance.

That this music is a destination, albeit not a known place but a dream, may be a very personal observation, but going with the metaphor of a journey in the first movement, this music has to be the place! Adams in his notes talks about the yin-yang of the Busoni music: "It epitomizes the clash of naive and sentimental, but also summons an archetypal scene, that lies deep in the subconscious of every person, the death of the mother and the...desire to return to the uncorrupted state of infancy." Perhaps the dreamlike quality of this music does represent that same state, but it does not last because the later part of this remarkable movement is an awakening, and a somewhat rude one.

At about 7:45 into the movement the strings begin a series of alternating smooth but abrupt swells from pianissimo to fortissimo, creating a kind of "backwards" sound, an eerie feeling of being drawn back out of this reverie and back into the real world.

This wake-up call becomes rather intense and foreboding; one feels literally dragged upwards to a kind of stasis of high delicate metallic sounds. Then the guitar melody and the triadic four-note theme in the strings reappear, but now it is a waking memory of the dream, not the dream itself.

The sense of journey continues in the last movement ["Chain to the Rhythm"], but it is destination bound; it seems to have a goal. Its sure-footed patterns open up classic Adamsian territory. John writes: "Small fragments of rhythmic cells are moved back and forth among a variety of harmonic areas and, in doing so create a chain of events that culminates...in a fast, virtuoso surge of orchestral energy."

Along the way there are allusions to his own music (*Shaker Loops* near the end) and other composers (the pulsating sixteenth-note clarinet swells near the beginning—Steve Reich?). The chain of rhythms that drives this music leads several times to near de-railments! There are some alarmingly chaotic sections, and at times the neat pulsating patterns grow into grotesque, lumbering giants unsure of their own power; a lot of the trickster composer is at work here. The race towards the very end is breathless, but the ending itself is not grand; it just leaves us hanging onto brazen blasts of the French horns and trombones, as if we were left sus-pended over a precipice.

Naive and Sentimental Music is one of Adams's most personal statements in music. He uses the title's dichotomy as a kind of conceit to create this metaphor of journeying; it allows him to crash around all over the place, mimicking life itself with all its va-garies.

Addendum

If including an e-mail message seems a bit informal or even "chummy" within the confines of a formal CD program note, I should explain that John and I have had a close friendship for many years, stretching back to our "Haight-Ashbury" days in San Francisco in the mid-1970s when we lived in adjacent houses. I have seen his development as a composer close-up, and admired each new piece as it emerged from his pen (or computer!), sometimes up close as it happened, other times after the fact and from a distance. I first got a hint of this particular work in 1997 when John dragged me to a rehearsal of the Los Angeles Philharmonic in Lincoln Center where Esa-Pekka Salonen was running through the Bruckner Fourth Symphony; I was astonished at the power and rightness of the performance and remember saying to John that this was an orchestra that had finally come into its own. It was then that he told me that E-P had asked him for a piece, a "grand" piece (not some diddly little curtain raiser), and I could see that he was truly excited about the prospect of writing something with Brucknerian sweep. John and I had always admired—somewhat secretly—the epic scores of Bruckner, and those of Sibelius as well, not only for their deep brooding qualities, but their paradigms of Nature and amazingly resourceful use of the orchestra and received musical form.

Of course, *Naive and Sentimental Music* would remind no one of either Bruckner or Sibelius, or Mahler for that matter, but Adams has not shirked from the awesome responsibility of composing within that tradition.

One thing that often is revealed in a big Adams piece is a kinship with Nature, not so much in the obvious way of painting an impression of it, but in deeper, more inherent ways. For example, this music seems to be full of dualities—the whole Schiller bipolar idea being at the base of it—and knowing that John composed much of this music at his Northern California retreat in the furthest reaches of Sonoma County in a remarkable natural setting where two ecosystems meet, prompts me to see a parallel. Inland from the foggy coast, about ten miles, John's rustic house lies on the cusp of the deep, brooding, often foggy redwood forest environment where it meets the stunningly dry and often searingly hot coastal range, an area of balding hills with live oaks and golden dried grasses in the summer—almost the polar opposite of the redwood environment. The one is dark and mysterious, a bit scary, but majestic as well; the other is open, bright, and uplifting, and reveals itself more willingly. Yes, landscape can be a very powerful handmaiden in creative human endeavor, and knowing that John has always been responsive to his surroundings (we used to spend quite a bit of time at our respective "huts" in the Sierra Nevada Mountains putting in composing time or just collecting the interest of being there and knowing it would come out in the work later on).

So like *El Dorado* and several other "landscape" pieces, I would count *Naive and Sentimental* as being painted on that canvas of Nature as much as that of literary or philosophical speculation. No one listening to it (despite the extensive use of almglocken!) will ever see mountain meadows or tall majestic redwoods—no, it's not pictorial—but the more I delve into it, the more I hear the connections to the natural world, and that is one of the keys to the piece, I think.

In fact, going back to the metaphor of the music as journey, I can see that much of John's life journey has, indeed, been traversed through a landscape of Nature.

El Niño: A Nativity Oratorio (1999–2000)

Michael Steinberg
Liner notes for *El Niño*, **Nonesuch, 2002**

I SHALL FOREVER BE GRATEFUL that life allowed me to be at the Châtelet Theater in Paris on December 15, 2000, the night of the first performance of *El Niño*. Whether you think of it as the upbeat to the new millennium or the topping of its first year, *El Niño* grandly and movingly symbolized the turning of a huge page. Adams has steadily fulfilled the artist's imperative of growth, and *El Niño* is the summit of his work to date.

If we want a convenient label for *El Niño*, we could call it a Nativity oratorio. The texts—in Spanish, Latin, and English—are taken or adapted from poems by Rosario Castellanos, Gabriela Mistral, Hildegard von Bingen, Sor Juana Inés de la Cruz, Rubén Darío, and Vicente Huidobro, as well as some anonymous verses and passages from the Bible, the New Testament Apocrypha, and The Wakefield Mystery Plays. The music, too, draws from many springs and is nourished by a variety of idioms, from Handel to pop, from court and church to street, but it always sounds unmistakably like John Adams, and it is his distinctive voice we hear.

El Niño is a work that addresses both eye and ear. In Paris, Peter Sellars, to whom Adams dedicated *El Niño*, created a three-tiered spectacle of acting singers (including the chorus), of dancers, and of a film—with occasional glances into the pit and Kent Nagano's vivid presence there. People are not much accustomed to rich artistic nourishment these days, and there were those who found this abundance confusing. I loved it, but I was also glad to be able to go to a second performance only two days later, and sorry I couldn't stay for more.

Peter Sellars not only directed the production, but was an essential partner to John Adams in shaping the work in the first place. The composer's collaborator in several previous projects, including the operas *Nixon in China* and *The Death of Klinghoffer,* Sellars is not just a director of genius, but one of those miraculous non-musicians who understand music more deeply than most of us professionals. Regarding the prodigality of *El Niño,* he put it well: the work, he said, is like one of those multipaneled altarpieces that you cannot possibly take in all at once. To open one wing is necessarily to conceal its verso from view, and the constant traveling and seeking of the eye is part of the experience. The film, the choreography, and the actors' movements also added up to a feast of allusions, particularly to classic depictions in painting and sculpture to such scenes as the Annunciation, the Visitation, and the Rest on the Flight into Egypt. The ear, however, had only one place to go. The essential impulses are in the music, and that essence is preserved on the recording.

The first external impulse for the composition of *El Niño* was a commission from the San Francisco Symphony, with which Adams has had a close association ever since he became Edo de Waart's new-music adviser in the 1978–79 season. San Francisco, at the enthusiastic urging of its former executive director, Peter Pastreich, asked Adams for a work for chorus and orchestra, and at about the same time the Châtelet Theater in Paris proposed that he write an opera for performance there. He saw how he could combine these projects by writing an oratorio that could be staged, and so the practicalities came together. Lincoln Center in New York and London's Barbican Centre came onboard later.

"Scenes from my childhood": Those are the opening words of "Tom Sails Away," a poignantly beautiful song by Charles Ives, a composer—and fellow New Englander—who has meant a lot to John Adams. Woodstock, Vermont, where Adams grew up in the 1950s, is a long way both from Bethlehem and the Hispanic America to which he has transplanted the story; nonetheless, the world of that little New England town is also part of the background or, as Adams himself might put it, the DNA of the captivatingly multifaceted *El Niño.*

The musical part of John Adams's childhood included clarinet lessons with his father and playing in marching bands with him, and an integral part of it was the celebration of Christmas through music, the whole range, from "Jingle Bells" through "Good King Wenceslas" to *Messiah.* Describing all that at a talk about *El Niño* at the San Francisco Performing Arts Library and Museum a month or so before the premiere, Adams had to stop and laugh: "It's all too picturesque, isn't it? Like something dreamed up by a casting director."

However that may be, it is true. "I love *Messiah,*" Adams goes on to say, and it follows quite naturally—and with not the slightest touch of arrogance or suggestion of equivalence—when, with another laugh, he comes out with it: "I wanted to write a *Messiah.*" He never thought that with his "checkered religious background" he would find himself writing a religious work. "I envy people with strong religious belief. Mine is shaky and unformed. I don't know what I'm saying, and one reason for writing *El Niño* was to find out." Digging deep into your own psyche, you learn.

But Adams had also always wanted to write a work about birth, and while *El Niño* is about a specific birth, its subject is more generally the miracle of birth itself. The birth of his daughter Emily in 1984 was an event that changed his life, and the recollection of it still amazes him: "There were four people in the room, and then there were five." For the Western world, the Nativity is, after the myth of the creation of Adam, the most famous of all births, and that, Adams thought, would make it a good pretext or matrix for a contemplation and celebration of birth. (He was startled to discover that his own teenage offspring were less familiar with the details of the Nativity story than he expected.)

The first task was choosing or assembling a text. Adams never intended to offer a straight biblical narrative; rather, he imagined from the beginning that he would follow the plan that appears in various forms in, for example, the Bach *Passions* and *Christmas Oratorio*, in *Messiah* itself, and such twentieth-century works as Britten's *War Requiem* and Bernd Alois Zimmermann's *Requiem for a Young Poet*—a plan that interlards a basic narration with commentary from other sources.

Something else Adams knew early on was that he wanted women's voices clearly heard in a work whose subject was birth: "How can you tell this story in the year 2001 and not have a woman's voice? Seldom in the officially sanctioned stories is there any more than a passing awareness of the misery and pain of labor, of the uncertainty and doubt of pregnancy, or of that mixture of supreme happiness and inexplicable emptiness that follows the moment of birth." All of that can, however, be found in the piercingly eloquent poems by Hispanic women to which Peter Sellars drew Adams's attention when asked to help with the libretto.

The last verbal component to come into focus for Adams was the title. He originally called the work *How Could This Happen?* He had found the phrase in German in a motet by the sixteenth-century Franco-Flemish master Orlande de Lassus, and it comes from an antiphon for Advent. But Adams noticed that people seemed uncertain about the title in conversation, and so he came to the conclusion that there was something not right about: hence the change to *El Niño*. The final title is a signal, too, of the importance of the Hispanic component of the work, an important point for Adams, who delights in living in a polyglot culture and who has said that "the intensity and genuineness of Latin American art and culture is one of the great gifts one receives by living in California." About one-third of *El Niño* is in Spanish. In the film, Sellars underscores the Hispanic element, using a Latino cast, one of striking spiritual radiance as well as physical beauty.

Adams anticipated the comment that his new title would bring the Weather Channel to mind: "The association with storms and violent weather is right. As Sor Juana [Inés de la Cruz, one of the poets represented in the libretto] says, a miracle is not without its alarming force. Christ was referred to as the 'Wind,' a kind of tempest that blows away all that comes in its path and transforms it. Herod knows this. We all know it when a child comes into the world."

Some of the text of *El Niño* will be familiar to you; for example, the words from Saint Luke known as the Magnificat, Mary's response to the Annunciation: "My soul doth magnify the Lord." (The most famous musical setting, in Latin, is Bach's.) Another is a passage from Haggai, a sixth-century [B.C.E.] prophet whose book appears near the end of the Old Testament: "For thus saith the Lord: Yet once, it is a little while, and I will shake the heavens, and the earth, and the sea, and the dry land...." Handel sets it (in slightly different verbal form) in *Messiah*. This is the only instance where Adams goes directly and explicitly head-to-head with his great precursor, although *El Niño* is deeply Handelian in two senses: in the simplicity and directness with which the words convey their message of belief, and in the joy the composer takes in setting English words to music. *El Niño* is, among other things, that rare work, a vocal composition in which you actually hear all the words.

An important part of what gives *El Niño* its distinctive expressive and literary flavor is the presence of many passages from the New Testament Apocrypha. (The Greek word "apocrypha" means "things that are hidden.") This is a gathering of some thirty books that resemble the Gospels, Acts, and Epistles in the New Testament. Many of them were written at about the same time as the New Testament Gospels, but for reasons that range from doubts about their authenticity to accusations of heresy, they have never been accepted as part of the canon. If you want to acquire the New Testament Apocrypha, you have to buy it as a separate book, and you will almost certainly not find it in religious bookstores. Rejected though it may be by the Church, the New Testament Apocrypha is a lively and varied collection. Some of it reads as though written for children or at least for quite a naive audience; other parts are as deeply serious as anything you will find in the canon. The Nativity narratives are often humanly more penetrating than the official ones, and you also find a vein of humor of which there is not a trace in the writings attributed to the four New Testament evangelists. *El Niño*, then, draws on various elements, weaving all together in a dense counterpoint of music, poetry, film, and dance. A lot goes on here. The effect, as Sellars has said, is similar to a many-paneled masterpiece, in which the eye is not sure of exactly where to look.

El Niño is in two parts, and the division between them occurs right after the miraculous birth and the appearance of the Christmas star. The first poem is a medieval English one, "I Sing of a Maiden," sung by the chorus and two countertenors. The music begins with what has become an Adams signature, the steady chugging of a single chord—here D minor—but with the texture quickly becoming more complex as cross-rhythms and dissonant notes are added to the mix. I don't know whether the opening of Beethoven's Ninth, where a D on the bassoon enters to blur the harmony, was a consciously chosen model for Adams, but the effect is similar. As at the beginning of *Harmonium,* the chorus first just reiterates a single syllable—here "may"—and then gradually finds its way into the poem:

> I sing of a maiden,
> A matchless maiden,
> King of all Kings...

A huge crescendo for the orchestra alone propels us into "Hail, Mary, Gracious!," a text taken from one of the mystery plays that made the little Yorkshire town of Wakefield famous in the Middle Ages. Its subject is the Annunciation. The male ensemble of three countertenors takes the part of Gabriel, while the soprano assumes the role of Mary. Taking a cue from Handel, Adams does not lock his three soloists into specific roles: in the very next movement, for example, we will find the mezzo-soprano singing the part of the Virgin. Here Mary's music is in that vein of rapt lyricism that makes Pat Nixon's aria in *Nixon in China* such a lovely moment.

Now we come to the first of *El Niño*'s Spanish texts. In my long listening life, I have often been grateful to composers for introducing me to the works of many wonderful poets: Schubert and

Mahler with Friedrich Rückert, for example, or Schumann with Justinus Kerner, and Britten with Thomas Hardy. I am sure I will not be the only listener for whom *El Niño* will, among other things, mean the first amazed and grateful encounter with the writing of Rosario Castellanos, Sor Juana Inés de la Cruz, Rubén Darío, and Vicente Huidobro. Even in translation it is clear that Castellanos and Sor Juana are among the greatest poets in any language.

Castellanos was born in Mexico City in 1925 and died in a domestic accident in 1974 in Tel Aviv, where she was serving as Mexican ambassador to Israel. She was a writer of enormous range, deeply interested in Mexico's pre-Columbian heritage, but at the same time a thoroughly committed citizen of the mid–twentieth century. Here she is represented by a long poem, impassioned and inward, titled "La anunciación," something to set beside the great Annunciation paintings and, in poetry, Rilke's "Mariä Verkündigung" (The Annunciation to Mary), so powerfully set to music by Paul Hindemith. Adams gives Castellanos's words to the mezzo-soprano, who makes her way through the feast of imagery in strong and varied musical declamation. The orchestra begins delicately and ends in a blaze of string sound.

This expansive song is followed by a chorus on words from Saint Luke, brief, punchy, tight. This is, in fact, the shortest section of *El Niño*.

The next movement, "The Babe Leaped in Her Womb," also draws on the third Gospel, but with a very different sort of text. This sets before us the touching scene of the Visitation, Mary's visit to her cousin Elizabeth. At Mary's greeting, the child in Elizabeth's womb, the child who will grow up to be John the Baptist, leaped in her womb for joy. The three countertenors, with brief help from the chorus, tell the story and sing Elizabeth's jubilant words.

Then, still drawing on Saint Luke, comes the Magnificat, sung by the soprano with support from two of the countertenors and the women of the chorus.

Now the story is continued by the Gospel of James in the New Testament Apocrypha. James, known as the Just, was one of the first leaders of the Christian Church in Jerusalem and died a martyr's death there in about the year 65. Some theologians believe him to have been a cousin of Jesus. A marvelously lively and humanly perceptive writer, he tells the story of Joseph coming home after a long absence to find his sixteen-year-old bride six months pregnant. Reacting in anger and suspicion, not believing her protestations, he can think only like a macho male: What matters is how bad this makes him look. The trio of countertenors sets the scene; the baritone takes the part of Joseph, with the countertenors and the soprano sharing the words of the teenage mother-to-be.

James goes on to tell how an angel appeared to Joseph in a dream, persuading him that "that which is conceived in [Mary's] womb is of the Holy Ghost," and foretelling the circumstances of Jesus' birth "among the animals and beasts of burden, on a cold night, in a strange land, and in a poor resting place." To James's text Adams adds words from Matthew, Isaiah, and one of Martin Luther's Christmas sermons. The baritone changes roles from Joseph to storyteller, and this movement, titled "Joseph's Dream," culminates in a mighty orchestral crescendo that spills directly into the next section.

This is called "Shake the Heavens." It begins with the passage from Haggai I mentioned earlier—"I will shake the heavens, and the earth…"—but moves into another passage from the Gospel of James, describing Mary and Joseph on their way to Bethlehem, Mary both weeping and laughing "because I see two peoples with my eyes, the one weeping and mourning, the other rejoicing and glad." Inevitably, the "shaking" passage alludes to Handel, eighteenth-century virtuoso coloraturas and all. The continuation from James enlists the countertenor trio both to tell the story and to pose Joseph's questions. Soprano and mezzo-soprano join together to give us Mary's replies.

"Se habla de Gabriel" (Speaking of Gabriel) brings us another poem by Rosario Castellanos, one in which she evokes both wryly and powerfully what Adams referred to as "the misery and pain of labor…the uncertainty and doubt of pregnancy or…that mixture of supreme happiness and inexplicable emptiness that follows the

moment of birth." (Gabriel is the name of Castellanos's son.) Soprano and mezzo-soprano bring us the poet's words over a slow-
moving accompaniment.

Without break, the music moves into more words from the
New Testament Apocrypha, partly James, partly the so-called
Latin Infancy Gospel. This is a wondrously moving passage in
which Joseph, in the minutes just before the birth, suddenly realizes that all the world, the heavens, the birds of the air, the workers
on Earth, the sheep and their shepherd, the rivers, the ocean, and
the winds have become totally still, and "the maiden stood looking
intently into heaven." It is the moment when Joseph understands.
Quietly, the baritone evokes this epiphany.

The first part of *El Niño* concludes with a fiery—literally—
poem by Gabriela Mistral (1899–1957), the great Chilean poet
who won the Nobel Prize for Literature in 1945, the first Latin
American writer to be so honored. In swift-moving verse she
evokes the mixed ecstasy and pain of religious revelation, and it is
the chorus, later joined by the countertenor trio and the three
soloists, that gives voice to her words, singing "The Christmas
Star" in Maria Jacketti's translation. Adams conflates Mistral's
verse with rapturous lines, "O quam preciosa" (Oh, how precious),
by the twelfth-century mystic and writer Hildegard von Bingen.
The music descends from the great crest it has reached, and the
last word we hear is "paradisum": "The tender shoot which is the
Virgin's son has opened Paradise."

Sor Juana Inés de la Cruz (1658–1695), whose poem "Pues mi
Dios ha nacido a penar" (Because My Lord Was Born to Suffer)
opens Part II of *El Niño*, has been called Mexico's Tenth Muse and
the Mexican Phoenix. A brilliant writer and intellectual, she was a
nun from her twenty-first year until her death. She learned to read
at three, taught herself Latin before she was in double digits, tried
in vain to have her mother send her to the university in Mexico
City disguised as a boy, and devoted much of her life campaigning
against the notion that women should not be educated. Her poems are recognized as the first truly Mexican ones, as distinct from
traditional Spanish verse written on New World soil. "Pues mi
Dios" is a remarkable, short example of what her mind and ear

could produce. Its text, an artful play of opposites and paradox that speeds up powerfully toward its close, reads like something designed for musical setting; Adams, using the mezzo-soprano and the chorus (all of it at first, then the men only), vividly projects the dialogue while creating a most evocative atmosphere for this extraordinary poem.

Now *El Niño* reverts to the Bible, this time to Matthew's account of Herod's plot to seek out the Child in order, supposedly, to worship him. The setting, over a restless accompaniment, is for baritone and the trio of countertenors.

The commentary on Herod's deceitful plan comes from Isaiah: "Woe Unto Them That Call Evil Good." Again we hear the baritone, this time backed by the full chorus, with the orchestra providing a kind of stride bass.

"And the Star Went Before Them" is Matthew's account of the voyage of the Three Kings, represented here by the three soloists.

Rubén Darío (1867–1916), a Nicaraguan poet, fleshes out the story of Gaspar, Melchior, and Balthasar with reverence, charm, and warmth. The kings are neatly characterized by the three countertenors, and the soprano adds the touching close, bidding the three to be still, for "Love has triumphed and bids you to its feast."

A brief link, "And When They Were Departed," tells how an angel appeared to Joseph in a dream, bidding him to flee to Egypt with his family. The chorus sings the words, which come from Matthew.

"Dawn Air," for the baritone, is part meditation but even more of a love song. The poem is by the Chilean writer Vicente Huidobro (1893–1948), and Adams has set it in the English translation of David Guss.

The next section, another brief one, tells of Herod's Slaughter of the Innocents. The chorus sings the text from Matthew, and the orchestra adds a fierce final punctuation.

"Memorial de Tlatelolco" (Memorial for Tlatelolco), uncompromisingly twentieth century in language and tone, is an enraged lament by Rosario Castellanos. On August 13, 1521, Tlatelolco, now part of Mexico City, was the scene of the last great confrontation between the Aztecs and Cortés and his conquistadors. Casualties were terrible on both sides, but the defeat of the Aztecs was decisive, and the history of modern *mestizo* Mexico begins on that day. On October 2, 1968, Tlatelolco Square was once again the scene of bloodshed. A youth revolt had been brewing that summer, as in so many countries in America and Europe. The first killings by police took place on September 21, with more to follow a few days later. On October 2, in the early evening, some five thousand troops with jeeps, tanks, armored cars, and helicopters attacked the huge crowd of civilians, many of them students, who had filled the square. Mexican police admitted to thirty-two deaths; independent estimates by British journalists set the number at least ten times that amount at the very least. The poet directs her fury not only at the event itself, but also at the subsequent effort to suppress reports of it.

This is the single biggest section of *El Niño*. The soprano abandons her lyric manner and voice to project Castellanos's words in wide-ranging lines of enormous, expressive power. When the poet bitterly tells the reader not to bother looking in the archives "because nothing has been recorded there," the chorus joins in the painful probing of the terrible scene.

Further comment comes from Isaiah—"In the Day of the Great Slaughter"—set as a percussively declamatory chorus.

"Pues está tiritando" (Since Love Is Shivering) again testifies to the extraordinary powers and, no less, the extraordinary originality of Sor Juana Inés de la Cruz. Each stanza brings a new set of contemplations on the power of the four ancient elements, water, earth, air, and fire. The hurling of answers to the repeated question "Who will come to his aid?" brings to mind the powerful antiphonal rhetoric in some of the choruses and arias of Bach's *Saint Matthew Passion*.

Now, as *El Niño* moves into the realm of the quasi-children's tales that give the New Testament Apocrypha part of its special flavor, the expressive climate changes. The story of the infant Jesus facing down the dragons is told by the writer known (a bit disparagingly) as pseudo-Matthew, most probably Matthias, the apostle chosen to take the place of Judas. The setting is for soprano and the ensemble of countertenors.

Pseudo-Matthew is also the source of the tale of the palm tree that, at the bidding of the infant Jesus, bowed down so that Mary might partake of its fruit and which then caused a stream of water to appear to quench the thirst of the Holy Family. The passage is another that exhibits delightfully sharp human perception, and again, I am afraid, at the expense of the blunt Joseph, who might be any modern American *paterfamilias* on a cross-country car trip. Adams combines it with another Castellanos poem, "Una palmera" (A Palm Tree). Here, in a musical setting of touching simplicity, the Spanish verses gradually displace the pseudo-biblical tale. It ends beautifully:

> From the dark land of men
> I've come kneeling to admire you.
> Tall, naked, alone.
> A poem.

The last word we hear, sung softly by the voices of children, accompanied by a single guitar, is "poesía."

John Adams on *El Niño* and Vernacular Elements

Interview by Ken Ueno

This interview was conducted in June 2001, at Ojai, California. That year, the Ojai Festival featured the music of and about Americas, and John Adams was a featured panelist in the U.S./Latin-American dialogue.

Not only are Latin American artists more visible and active in the United States, but also Latin American culture seems to be influencing our most important non–Latin American artists such as you. El Niño exemplifies this synergy between multiple cultures. You did your own translations. Do you speak Spanish?

I'm not entirely fluent, but I have a comfortable reading knowledge and my spoken Spanish is improving by the day. It is easier to learn Spanish here in California than in Massachusetts. I always wanted to become comfortable with Spanish—especially living in California. It's a very logical language,and it's a very vowel-oriented Latin language, like Italian, and I found it just tremendously satisfying to work with.

Were there intrinsic qualities of language that made working with Spanish appealing? How did you adapt the rhythms and qualities of the language to fit your musical style, or vice ersa?

It was a lot easier to set Spanish than it was to set the English texts in *El Niño*. When I set a language, I really want to get a feeling of the spoken flow. I've set a lot of English and still find it hard because of the rhythms of the language, particularly the rhythms of American spoken English, which are so bumpy and tend not to fall into a kind of cadential rhythm.

How did you go about transcribing the natural flow of the rhythms inherent in the Spanish language when you are not a native speaker?
First, I taped a native speaker reading some of the Rosario Castellanos poems, because I have a more authentic sense of the flow.

In composing a work in Spanish for an international audience, were you concerned that Americans in particular might associate the title El Niño with a meteorological phenomenon rather than the Nativity?
I did initially hesitate for that very reason. But then I realized that *El Niño* was an expression of enormous natural power and energy and would therefore to be a good metaphor for the story. Usually when we think of the Nativity story it's almost like a fairy tale—a naive and very sweet story. I wanted to emphasize not only that angelic quality, but also its more serious and potentially violent aspects.

The more violent aspects are certainly evident in the largest single section of the piece, which recounts the Slaughter of the Innocents. The text you use here is the Castellano in which she memorializes the slaughter of students during the 1968 revolt in Tlatelolco Square. The contemporary image of police violence updates, as you said, the violent aspects in the Nativity.
In the United States, we read in newspapers about children being killed in Iraq and attacked in Jerusalem and Kosovo or wherever. Many people have a strange disconnection to violence, which I think comes from overexposure to the news. To read the story of Herod demanding that all the male babies under the age of three be slaughtered seems so unreal that it doesn't have an impact. If I

tried to make it explicitly relevant to current news, with scenes of
Kosovo or Gaza, for example, it probably would have been off-
putting. I thought that this particular event, the massacre of students in 1968, would have a resonance to Americans because it's
very much like Kent State, only far worse. It's the only reference to
a truly contemporary event. Everything else in *El Niño* is sort of
timeless and is not so site-specific.

How did you decide on the texts for El Niño?
    The Spanish text was suggested by Peter Sellars. Castellanos was
completely unknown to me. So was Sor Juana. Like most Americans, I knew only certain well-known names in Latin-American
literature: Carlos Fuentes, Gabriel Garcia Marquez, Pablo Neruda.
I didn't know these women poets. Sor Juana is completely unknown to North Americans. She is a combination of Emily Dickinson and Hildegard von Bingen—a very spiritual figure, but her
work has a truly radical intensity. I think of Olivier Messiaen when
I read her poetry. It's religious, ecstatic, and not very accessible.
You have to work to reach its depth. Her work is vast. In setting
only two of her poems, I felt as though I were spitting into the
ocean. There are thousands of these poems. She was an extraordinary figure.

*When Peter Sellars suggested some of these Spanish texts to you, did
he already have ideas about the piece?*
    No. I came to him with the idea of a Nativity. All my life I have
wanted to compose one. And I think we both wanted to do something out-of-the-ordinary and which had a real intensity to it. And
I certainly wanted to compose something that involved a woman's
point of view. To speak about nativity and pregnancy and the intense emotional world surrounding them, it only seemed right to
find texts by women. As soon as I read Castellanos's poems I knew
that's exactly what I wanted.

*Composers from around the world are increasingly turning to ethno-
graphic resources and popular music, not necessarily in their own
culture. What are your thoughts on this so-called "globalization of*

culture"? To what degree do you feel you are dealing with aspects of culture, especially now having recently completed a major work which draws upon elements from Latin American culture?

You touch on many important issues. The first is the absorption of the vernacular. Throughout my life as a composer I have had extremely strong feelings about this. Part of that goes back to what I felt was a very self-referential sterile environment of the avant-garde, when I was a student in the '60s. New compositions referred to their immediate past, whether it was Schoenberg or Stravinsky or Babbitt writing about Webern or it was Cage writing about Satie. It seemed to be a very small world. I felt it was a world that had no fertility left in it. I grew up in a family of amateur jazz musicians and came of age during the 1960s explosion of rock and roll and rock and jazz. It seemed to me that there was enormous health and fertility in this world of vernacular music, and the world of avant-garde classical music seemed very dead. It seemed to have a very bleak future. So part of my move from the East Coast to California was an expression of that desire to get away from that hegemony and also to embrace a more open attitude towards vernacular elements. Now thirty years later, this has come full circle in minimalism in the music of Steve Reich and John Zorn. We also have pieces like Osvaldo Golijov's *Pasión*, which has an extremely raw and genuine heartfelt vernacular expression. I've been vindicated in my feelings. In fact, I feel almost old-fashioned now. Writing for orchestra makes me a dinosaur compared to some of the younger composers.

Do you think that Golijov's use of Latin American rhythms and vernacular forms is culturally equivalent to your use of rock and roll references?

Yes. I've always felt that my birthright or pedigree as an American was *that* music. I was brought up studying Mozart and classical harmony at the same time as I was playing marching-band music and listening to Benny Goodman and Miles Davis. What struck me as a complete disconnect was how someone like Babbitt speaks of his love for show tunes, but writes compositions that have no relationship to this love. There is no connection between his hobby and his profession. I wanted to create a music, very much like Charles Ives, that reflected my genetic fabric and my genotype.

You have conducted a lot of Ives, often programming pieces that showcase his interest in the vernacular. Another composer you have often conducted is Zappa, who in some ways is a more contemporary Ives.

They're both very complicated composers. I am profoundly dissatisfied in their music at the same time that I am very excited by it. Zappa wanted to be a killer rock guitarist and blow everybody off the stage, and yet at the same time, he wanted to out-Boulez Boulez by writing fiendishly difficult pieces. But he wrote things that were on the margin of unplayability. It's easy for a composer to write in rhythms like 17/21, but I've seen some of the best musicians in the world struggle to execute his scores. The irony is that the end product very often is a letdown. It's just not worth it. These feelings aside, I have to acknowledge that Zappa is an absolute American original, in the way that Mark Twain and H. L. Mencken were. He's phenomenally successful and popular in Europe, where audiences feel that his output really expresses that aspect of American culture that is the antidote to Disney and Spielberg. I also was tremendously inspired by a career like Bernstein's, because I thought that it was a natural expression of being an American composer to be able to work in other genres and not be buttonholed in one.

Your music has always made references to vernacular styles, yet you have no qualms about being labeled a "classical" composer. Does that mean that you are addressing a more specialized audience for your music than the more general demographic that only listen to the vernacular styles?

It's taken me a long time to realize that my audience is small. It will maybe grow a little bit as I grow older and after I'm no longer around. But I sometimes am envious of other composers or crossover composers or pop composers, whatever, that their record sales are in the tens or hundreds of thousands or millions, or a film director I admire, like Scorsese or Woody Allen. They are major figures in our culture, and millions are conversant with their work. They aren't with mine, and they probably never will be. Part of the reason is the complexity of what I do, the result of which is that one has to bring an education to the appreciation of my work.

Why do successful and cultured people find complexity in music difficult to accept, whereas they are more likely to accept complexity when they experience other art forms?

With a difficult piece of painting or sculpture, you can walk away from it. You can decide that's a difficult piece and then walk away until you find another one. Feeling stuck in a concert with a difficult piece can be a very hostile experience. I also think it's the nature of the medium, that complex music or dissonant music (music far more complex and far more dissonant than my own) is essentially very invasive and even aggressive experiences for a lot of people. But in a museum you can see a Damien Hurst cow cut in half and simply can walk away if you are revolted.

A lot of rap and heavy metal is more dissonant than most contemporary American classical music. Why is dissonance more problematic for classical music audiences than pop audiences?

It's also just the sound of classical music. A lot of young Americans hear violins or the sound of an orchestra as simply unrelated to their own experience. But when they hear electric guitars, no matter how harsh it might be, the music relates to their world and their anima. And it doesn't matter whether the orchestra was playing my music or Beethoven, they heard that sound and they associated it with the old days. So it's a complicated challenge. Now I'm being very dark and pessimistic. Of course, there still are relatively large audiences for classical music, and a portion of them are interested in my music, but it's still very small.

Memory Spaces (*On the Transmigration of Souls*) (2002)

David Schiff
The Atlantic, **April 2003**

IT IS AN ODDITY OF OUR CULTURE that more people own David McCullough's book *John Adams* than any CD of music by the most prominent composer today, also named John Adams. Twenty years ago Adams seemed poised to lead contemporary art music out of the wilderness. Since that time his large body of work has bolstered Adams's position as the most influential, technically gifted, and aesthetically ambitious composer of his generation. The vibrant rhythms and dazzling orchestration of *The Chairman Dances* (1985) and *Short Ride in a Fast Machine* (1986) have made them orchestral staples, yet his music is less familiar to the public than the work of George Gershwin, Aaron Copland, or Leonard Bernstein. Even though many composers now cultivate an audience-friendly style, new "serious" music remains nearly as marginal as it was during the heyday of academic atonality.

Adams's symphonic works, which at times sound like Sibelius superimposed on a Eurorock rhythm track, and his two controversial operas, *Nixon in China* (1987) and *The Death of Klinghoffer* (1991), mirror our confused feelings about the function of art music. Indeed, they revel in our ambivalence. But his recent *On the Transmigration of Souls* is a breakthrough. Terrifying and heartrending, it offers reassuring proof that contemporary classical music—too often dismissed out of hand as obscure and unpleasant—has something unique to say to a wide public.

Composers today can get tripped up by contrary expectations. They are told to be mavericks in the hope that quirkiness will lure bright young listeners from alternative rock. But they are also told to make their music accessible and romantic, in order to reach— or at least not repel—the traditional (and older) concertgoer. What sets Adams apart, even more than his technical flair, is his ability to heed these mixed signals with a Whitmanesque desire to embrace contradictions. Adams's music contains multitudes of ideas and moods. It is by turns goofy and grave, spiritual and erotic (sometimes both at once), extravagant and severe, profound and sophomoric. No contemporary music can compete with his for sheer beauty of sound—or, at times, for the power to offend listeners.

I can think of no living composer, and few artists in other media, whose work is more informed by the pleasures and terrors, hopes and disenchantments, of contemporary life. His music makes complex ideas vibrate with troubling energy. And like the greatest music of the past—Bach, Beethoven, Mahler—it can take us beyond those troubles and complexities to states of serenity, wisdom, and peace.

Adams grew up in New England, and while a student at Harvard he played clarinet in the Boston Symphony. After college he went to San Francisco, where he joined the anti-academic scene of minimalists, including Terry Riley (who launched the movement in 1964 with his ecstatically repetitive and tonal *In C*), and Pacific Rim composers, including Lou Harrison, who, while atonal angst ruled on the East Coast, continued to write euphonious, tonal music. In the late 1970s Adams found a way to synthesize the styles of the two coasts, and his music has defied critical pigeonholing ever since. Works such as *Phrygian Gates* (1977), *Shaker Loops* (1978), *Harmonium* (1980), and *Grand Pianola Music* (1982) brought minimalism out of the lofts and into the concert hall. He infused a countercultural style with traditional musical ideas it had previously resisted, recasting the repetitious rhythms and simple harmonies of minimalism as virtuoso vehicles for classical performers. Adams had little use for the conceptual rigor or the emotional coolness of earlier minimalism. In the music of Philip Glass or Steve Reich everything you are going to hear appears in the first few seconds of a piece. The pleasure comes from observing the barely noticeable process of changes to the initial statement. With Adams anything could happen—and did, explosively. His post-minimalism was romantically transcendental, like the music of Liszt.

Adams also gave the symphony orchestra, that nineteenth-century artifact, a twenty-first-century sound. *Harmonium,* a sprawling symphony for chorus and large orchestra, demonstrated Adams's command of orchestral alchemy. By superimposing layers of instrumental oscillations and pulses Adams made the orchestra shimmer in a way not achieved since Ravel. But the symphony gave the orchestra a metallic, post-industrial sound, far from the traditional lush impressionist palette—like going from oil paint to acrylic. The density of sound (Adams writes thousands of notes) and the emphasis on the bright upper register make the live orchestra seem electronically synthesized, as if from a THX sound system.

On the Transmigration of Souls, commissioned by the New York Philharmonic to honor the victims of the 9/11 attacks, is a turning point in Adams's work and, I hope, in American music. Adams has described the piece as "a memory space." It superimposes pre-recorded street sounds and the reading of victims' names by friends and family members, also pre-recorded, on live performances by a children's chorus, an adult chorus, and a large orchestra. This complex twenty-five-minute work takes Adams's high-tech sound into a spiritual realm.

Adams's standing made it inevitable that he would be asked to compose a large-scale, highly publicized response to 9/11. Talk about performance anxiety! The Philharmonic must have been anxious about the outcome, too. A master of rhythm, texture, and color but not a melodist, Adams was unlikely to produce a simple, lyrical piece like Samuel Barber's *Adagio for Strings,* that perfect

American elegy. More worrisome, Adams's reputation had been shadowed by the controversy over *The Death of Klinghoffer,* a treatment of the *Achille Lauro* hijacking that many critics found anti-Semitic. (The opera's Palestinians appear to be noble victims; its Jews seem to have stepped out of an episode of *Seinfeld.*) Soon after 9/11 the Boston Symphony decided to cancel previously scheduled performances of choruses from *Klinghoffer.* Given Adams's leftist, green political positions (not at all exceptional in the East Bay, where he lives), the Philharmonic may have feared that he would exploit the commission to make a political statement. Adams may only have heightened such fears by telling the press that he had many conflicting opinions about 9/11. But then, didn't everyone?

It is not at all obvious how music, or any other art, should respond to catastrophe. Adams's new piece left most critics awed but uncertain of their judgments, and at a loss for words—a loss I felt as I tried to imagine from the reviews what the music was like. Some critics had trouble relating the live to the taped parts of the score; the sound-on-sound texture reminded them, negatively, of movie music. I think the work makes such a powerful impact because of, not in spite of, the "extra-musical" elements; Adams was redefining the relation of music to non-music and of the concert hall to everyday life.

Transmigration does mix sound elements in a way that is unusual in classical music (Steve Reich's *Different Trains* is a precedent) but commonplace in a movie theater. But film sound tracks, of course, do not also feature live performers. Only Adams could have combined these different elements with such imagination and technical skill. Like many of his earlier works, *Transmigration* speaks in a very contemporary idiom (Adams's pieces often begin by laying down a stylized rock groove in the percussion) that is somehow haunted by a ghost of the musical past. In his great 1984–85 symphony *Harmonielehre,* Adams channels Sibelius (Fourth Symphony, 1911) and Mahler (Tenth Symphony, also 1911) in the slow movement, whose title, "The Anfortas Wound," brings the ghost of Wagner to the table. Midway through my first hearing of his recent *Naive and Sentimental Music,* also a monumental symphony, I became aware that, without allusions or quotations, Adams was following the flight plan of Sibelius's Fifth.

In *Transmigration*, Adams has found a new familiar spirit: Charles Ives. In New York on May 7, 1915, the day the *Lusitania* sank, Ives witnessed an episode of communal mourning that prefigured the response to 9/11. People waiting for the elevated train gradually began to sing along with a hurdy-gurdy playing an old hymn. Ives transformed this experience into "From Hanover Square North, at the End of a Tragic Day, the Voice of the People Again Arose"—a great and rarely performed vision of a spiritualized democracy, a community brought together by music at a time of tragedy.

Adams's *Transmigration* builds on Ives's vision. For this occasion Adams needed Ives's example to help depersonalize his music. His earlier work is a very up-to-date post-minimalist kind of romanticism, a deeply personal music that seeks states of ecstasy and transcendence. Like a true romantic, he often found his music in dreams, and in his own spiritual conflicts. The "memory space" of *Transmigration*, however, had to be public, not personal, and Ives—uniquely in the history of music—created imaginary utopian venues, usually by layering different sounds. Adams has the advantage of technology: sound engineering to balance and coordinate the musical and extra-musical elements. Technology also allows him to create a music that is at once visionary and familiar. Transmigration seems more modernistic than earlier Adams: more disjunct and nondirectional, much more dissonant. Yet, without sounding in any way like popular music—as with the bad old modern music, the work has no memorable musical theme or melody—it is more successfully populist. Its sound-over-sound texture connects it to the mass media. We know this ambiance from Ken Burns documentaries, from CNN, from rap music, from the movies. Like Ives but in an entirely new way, Adams extends our sense of music—there is music in the sound bites and the street noises, music in our own state of sensory overload.

Although the opening of the piece seems like a sound collage, Adams does not mingle noises, words, and tones randomly. He sets them in a careful, therapeutic course from the secular to the sacred, leading to a vision of redemption when the sonic chaos converges to form a vast carillon. First we hear only street sounds, as if the walls of the concert hall had been blown away. In place of Adams's usual percussive groove a taped boy's voice repeats the word "missing," a verbal heartbeat that gives the unformed sound of cars and footsteps a rhythmic undertow. The chorus (at first wordless), strings, and harps enter, playing slowly rocking lines that sound like a medieval chant. Are we in the street, a concert hall, or a cathedral? The choral syllables slowly become stammered words and phrases: "re-mem...re-mem...re-member," "you will...you will...you nev..." Noises, words, prayers: for ten minutes the music seems to drift uncertainly and in fragments on memories of Ives's *The Unanswered Question,* in which a distant trumpet poses the eternal question of existence. Over undulating ripples in the woodwinds the children's chorus picks up the gentle rocking lines of the opening with new words that are at once journalism and incantation: "I see buildings, I see water." Without warning the orchestra blasts a sustained chord of anguish, announcing a move to the next level of contemplation. The music becomes simpler. The two choruses repeat the words, now in full sentences, of fathers, mothers, sisters ("The daughter says, 'He was the apple of my father's eye'"), intensifying at the lines "I wanted to dig him out. I know just where he is."

The orchestra again erupts, this time in mounting waves that lead to the long-awaited answer to the question posed by Ives: their voices transformed, transmigrated, into human chimes, the choruses sing out the words "Love" and "Light" over and over, fortissimo. Very gradually the music subsides to the sound-on-sound texture of the opening, but with a new feeling of calm. Orchestra and choruses fade out; a recorded woman's voice, in an unidentifiable accent, repeats the words "I see water and buildings." The street sounds return us to our everyday lives.

In the months that followed the catastrophe, 9/11 became a source more of civic pride than of nationalism. The heroes were policemen and firemen, not soldiers; a mayor, not a president. The names read on television and the short biographies in the *Times* reminded New Yorkers of their diversity and their commonality. In *Transmigration*, Adams breaks down the divide between the high-bourgeois culture that created orchestras like the New York Philharmonic (and the repertory they play) in the nineteenth century and the mass culture that took its place in the twentieth. He has created a music that mirrors and exalts the public wisdom.

John Adams Discusses *On the Transmigration of Souls*

Interview by Daniel Colvard

This interview took place over breakfast on February 9, 2004, at the Europa Café near Carnegie Hall in New York. Adams was in the city for the first of his Zankel Hall conversations, which had taken place the day before with the architect Frank Gehry.

A BBC interview credits you as saying that you felt rescued by the Ives Fourth Symphony after you had been pouring over the online sites [dedicated to the victims of September 11].

That's true. I got this commission, and I frankly didn't want to write it—I hadn't a clue how I could possibly write a piece about September 11. Plus, there was even the aura of opportunism about it: "The composer of *The Death of Klinghoffer* would try to rescue his tarnished reputation"—it was just terrible! I really didn't want to do it, but it was the New York Philharmonic, and it was New Yorkers, people that I deal with on a daily level, and I felt that it was something I had to do...but I really didn't know what to do. So I spent the first month just reading on the Internet, looking for an inspiration, frankly, looking for some material, verbal or visual, or some kind of image that would suggest something. It was like walking around in the dark with a match trying to find something. I found those texts [eventually used in *Transmigration*] and Barbara Haws, the archivist of the New York Philharmonic, showed me some photographs that she'd taken of those little missing persons signs, which I found very powerful. I don't know why the Ives thing came to me, but I thought that Ives, in his most elevated philosophical mode, such as in *The Unanswered Question* or in parts of the Fourth Symphony, [offered] the best model. I didn't think that the Coplandesque brand of sentiment was correct. I often need some kind of model.

An organizational sort of model?

No, just some kind of...of *guardian angel.* For example, a very strange model that's come into my life when working on this new opera about the atomic bomb [*Doctor Atomic*] is Varèse, [who] expresses that postwar angst, and also that fascination with science, with the sound of raw materials. I felt that if I went through this experience with Ives—if he held my hand and I held his hand— that I could come through it okay, and make a piece that was morally honest. Because the one thing that I was really concerned about was that I not write a piece that yanked or tugged the heartstrings. I was disgusted by the way the media had treated 9/11. The first week, the first month was understandable. It was just a shock and horror. And then it turned into a kind of *bathos.* It was an endless repetition of heart-wrenching scenes, constantly reminding us of how much pain we felt, to the point where people didn't feel anymore. They literally didn't feel.

And so you created this space for them to feel again?

That was my attempt. It was kind of an alien experience at Avery Fisher Hall. The hall represents everything that Frank Gehry is trying to get away from. It's too big; it's impersonal; the orchestra feels removed from the audience; and the New York Philharmonic has cultivated a very conservative audience over the years. There were people there who were genuinely moved by the piece. And there were a lot of people who were just irritated to have to sit through this in order to get to the Beethoven Ninth.

Do you see a long performance history for the piece ahead?

It's already been longer than I expected. It's been done in Amsterdam in a very moving performance that I attended, and then I conducted it myself at the Proms. They're held in this enormous Edwardian building called the Royal Albert Hall that seats about five thousand people. The best sort of things that survive these concerts are monster choral and orchestra pieces like Vaughn Williams's *Sea Symphony* or something. I didn't really think that my piece would work in the Proms environment because it was so intimate, but it turned out to be just the opposite. It was very successful and worked very well there.

About the Ives in the piece—there are certainly points, like the trumpet solo, where it's directly alluding to him.

Absolutely. And actually, *The Unanswered Question* is in the piece. When I was in college I took a course in medieval music. I didn't remember much of it, but I remembered that there was something called a parody Mass. They were Masses that were written probably before or during the Renaissance, where composers would either take a melody written by somebody else—or they might even take a folk song—and work that into the Mass. It would be there as a kind of ghost in the background. That's what I did with Ives's *The Unanswered Question*. It's there. It's a ghost in the background, and every once in a while it peeks through this screen of activity. All the voices, and the traffic noise, and the orchestra and the chorus and the children's chorus, and then every once in a while these clouds of event will kind of disperse for a second and you'll just get a glimpse of the Ives *Unanswered Question* as if it's just playing all the way through this piece.

Are the wind parts from The Unanswered Question *preserved?*

No, I don't use the wind parts. It's just the string hymn. And my trumpet solo—it alludes to the Ives, but it's original—[although] it has that minor third at the end, which is the question. And, of course, 9/11 and all the loss of those people and the loss of any people, anywhere in the world, from a sudden violent act *is* an unanswered question.

Do you think of the piece at all—in the way Ives was writing The Unanswered Question—*as experimental?*

I think the *Transmigration of Souls* and *The Dharma at Big Sur* are the two most experimental pieces that I've written since I was a kid. I'm kind of astonished that I did them under such circumstances. These were highly publicized, high-profile pieces. I should have taken the safe route. But if you're going to spend six or eight months writing a piece of that size, you have to just forget about the fact that it's a big public event and lots of critics are going to be there. You just have to write the piece you want to write. And I couldn't have written the *Transmigration of Souls* if I didn't feel the freedom to just do what I wanted to do. *The Dharma at Big Sur* was even more dangerous because there were two elements that were bucking broncos—one was the [just] intonation, and the other was the electric violin, and how to get that to sound right. And they were both failures in the first performance. I was so discouraged. But Frank Gehry said to me yesterday—I sort of mumbled something, an apology backstage about my piece—"Well, I think everybody got the point that it was a work in progress."

But, I hear the piece—and you describe it—as this sort of cathedral. There's so much activity in the music. My first impression, before reading what you had said, was of this sense of spiritual journey: they arrive at the light, and there's a transformation, all this energy.

One of the really trying things about being a creative person is that if you reach a certain level of notoriety, everybody wants you to talk about your work. People say, "Well, what is it? Is it a Mass? Is it a requiem?" I just resisted any of those musical forms. The first time I went into Notre Dame Cathedral was years ago with a friend, the composer Ingram Marshall. I think it was the first time for both of us to be in Paris, and it was a rainy afternoon in November. We walked into Notre Dame, and we sort of went in different directions. What I remember was that there was always sound. Even though they forbid people to talk—they still do. And there're noises. Any large public space with several hundred people walking around is going to have a sort of constant level of ambient noise. At the same time there was some music playing. I can't remember if it was canned music—it might have been an organ. It was something that was very moving. To be in that space itself is intensely moving, because you feel that you're in the midst of many, many souls—not just the people in the building, but all the souls that have been there before. It was an image that I had in my mind when I was composing the piece, that we would be in this space, and that there would be this constant, low-level noise...of humanity. It might be the boy just saying the word "Missing, missing," or people reading names, or traffic sounds, or what life is like. You have to go up to the Alaskan tundra to have total silence. That's what life is like now. I was trying to evoke that in this piece.

You spoke about feeling pressured for explanations of your music....

Yes. Quite a few families came who had lost somebody, and a lot of them did bother to come backstage. I was very moved by that. I thought, "Gee, this must have been really puzzling for these people," because my guess is that 95 percent of all those families who lost somebody probably never listen to classical music, and *for sure* they don't listen to contemporary classical. They've probably never heard the Britten *War Requiem,* or *The Symphony of Psalms,* or something like that. Or the Ives Fourth. So they're invited by the New York Philharmonic, and they hear this piece that's not a simple piece, by any means. It has quarter-tone music in it. It's a hard piece to understand if you're not musically literate, if you don't know the references. I can't even imagine what the experience was like for those people: whether they were just puzzled, whether they were moved. Some of them genuinely were moved. I don't know what about the piece got to them, but something got to them.

None of them who had family members whose names were [included in the piece]...?

Actually, there was one person, David Fontana: I met his wife. Before I wrote the piece, the New York Philharmonic had a luncheon where they invited several people who represented different groups of victims. They were all young women, all of whom had lost either a brother or a husband. One had been extremely active in fighting against putting up another building down there. And there was another who turned out to be the wife of this Brooklyn fireman who had died [David Fontana]. She said, "Oh, let me see your score. I studied bassoon at Juilliard!" And I said, "Well, are you a musician?" And she said, "No, I'm a stand-up comic." So I did a little special thing for her in there where the music comes down, and it's actually my daughter who says, "I love David Fontana." That's a little wink of the eye to that woman.

And your voice is on one of the tracks, isn't it?

That happened as a weird thing. I started by using my voice simply as a sketchpad. My intention was that once I got the piece up and running, I would go back and re-record all those names. I was planning to come to New York and get people with a New York accent. But it morphed into something very strange, because I started recording people that I knew. The little boy is an *extremely* precociously talented composer who was nine at that time. He comes over to my house once a month or so to show me his pieces. I said, "Would you mind reading some of these phrases?" Then I started asking people in my family. I had my daughter read some, and my wife and my son. Then, suddenly, that took on its own emotional core, and it became a very interesting thing. The piece is not about the towers falling, or politics, or who did it, or the violence. It's really just about loss, and about the mother who lost a son, the wife who lost a husband, the daughter who lost a father. So having my family on this sound track suddenly amplified exactly what the piece is about. Then it didn't make sense to take my own voice out. So I went with it.

There's also a close family friend whose voice is at the very end. She has a slight accent. She's actually an Israeli woman. She's the one who says, "I see water and buildings," at the very end—there's a slight accent. What's interesting is that in my research, I discovered that many of the people who had died were foreign-born— that the World Trade Center was actually kind of a mid-level place. By hitting the World Trade Center, the terrorists were hitting people who were just getting going in the finance industry, or they were service employees. There were some people there whose families never even acknowledged them because they were—in our charming terminology—illegal aliens. They were Hispanic people who were working in the kitchen, or guards, elevator repair people: so having a voice with a slight accent in it was very touching to me.

And you just worked them into the piece, as a matter of feeling, in terms of their order of appearance?

I had the traffic sound, and I had several long recordings of people reading names, and then there're some phrases, too, that came off of the missing persons things—I had them as sound files. I didn't loop them, but I put them into a sequencer. I had them in this amazing program called Soft SampleCell. It's a unique hard-drive system that you install onto your computer, and so I had a *huge* library of every single name. I had every single name—I haven't counted up how many names I used—and every phrase, and every bus going by and every traffic sound, and I put them into a sequencer program. I actually made a composition where a voice would come up and be its own little loop. If you listen to just that part without the music, it's an interesting piece in itself. It's like what we called in the old days a text-sound piece. So that's there throughout; it disappears occasionally, and then it comes back on cue. That was the first thing I did. I'm glad I did it that way, because having the voices and the traffic sound: first of all, it was very unique. I'd never heard a piece of music quite like that. It suggested the sort of general tone of the piece—that it would be quiet, but it wouldn't be sort of sticky-sweet and gloomy and reverential. It would have a certain matter-of-fact quality about it. I just love the idea of New Yorkers coming in off of Broadway, walking into the hall and sitting down, and the lights coming down and then the traffic sound coming back up. In that way it was very nice that it was the first piece on the program, because it created this wonderful kind of blur between life and art.

Did you notice if there was excitement or surprise in the audience when all of a sudden the traffic comes up?

I don't know. I sat behind a woman who was just absolutely

hating the piece. She looked over, and I was sitting with Mark [Grey]—we had a big mixing board right in the seats. This woman obviously was a subscription ticket holder, and the first thing she sees was Mark with his ponytail down to his behind. He definitely looks like a sound guy, you know. That put her in a frenzy. And when the music started, she just looked like she was ready to kill somebody.

Do you think computers and the digital sound world we're living in will influence orchestral music?

Of course, it does already. Certainly in my music, in a very subtle way. I use the computer to compose, and it's been an enormous liberation for me. I get more and more agile at it as I work, and so I'm able to experiment in a way that I never could have—or, let's put it this way, it would have been fantastically labor-intensive to do at the piano. And I know other composers who have come up with ideas that they never would have come up with sitting at a piano with pencil and paper. So that's very thrilling. As far as the sound itself, I think that the next big watershed is really going to have to do with sound sources, i.e., loudspeakers. This is what I'm fighting with in a piece like *The Dharma at Big Sur*. I really wanted to write a piece for this amplified violin, because it had an intimacy that was very powerful, but when I got it out in the hall and had the guy plug it through a loudspeaker and try to fill a hall of three thousand people—in order to get that level of intimacy, you had to crank the gain way up, and it just simply became an alien beast next to this orchestra. The two of them just were standing there without any real sense of belonging to each other.

And you're using the sound sources dimension in Transmigration *as well, with the speaker system?*

Yeah, and that was not entirely successful either. It gets better as it goes along. Interestingly, I think that even though the recording lacks the sense of spaciousness, it's far more successful because you can hear the voices in a very intimate way as if someone were breathing or whispering into your ear, but you also hear the orchestra. In the big hall, when you hear *Transmigration of Souls,* you have to make a decision between how loud the voices are going to be and how loud the orchestra and the chorus is, and if the voices are too loud, then you minimize two hundred people on the stage. It's a very tricky, complicated balance. And part of the way that my sound engineer, Mark Grey, tries to deal with that disparity, is that, when he can, he does a little amplification of the orchestra as well—just enough so that the orchestra sound becomes part of the general picture. But it's tricky. And a lot of conductors refuse to do that.

My Father Knew Charles Ives (2003)

Michael Steinberg
San Francisco Symphony program book, April 2003

IN A ZURICH HOSPITAL the day before his death in August 1955, Thomas Mann reported in a letter to his musician son Michael, a violist in the San Francisco Symphony from 1941 until 1950, that he had been reading Alfred Einstein's biography of Mozart. Mann the elder was a Wagnerian through and through for whom music before Beethoven had always been on the fringe, and almost everything he learned in Einstein's book was new to him. "What interested me particularly was that M. had no feeling at all for nature or architecture or objects and places of interest, but always drew stimulation only from music itself and, so to speak, made music out of music, a kind of artistic incest and filtered production—very curious."

I happened to be browsing in Mann's letters around the time I went to visit John Adams to speak with him about this piece of his, and it struck—and amused—me for a moment to think that Mann, at least in principle, would have thoroughly approved of Adams's not at all incestuous and filtered art. I suppose one could say that in his early works—for example, that pure and beautiful essay in extreme or truly minimal minimalism, *Common Tones in Simple Time,* or in the ebullient *Shaker Loops*—Adams was making music out of music; but it seems to me that beginning already in 1980–81 in the first of his many San Francisco Symphony commissions, *Harmonium,* he was composing songs of experience. That bent has remained consistent, as we can hear in his two operas, *Nixon in China* and *The Death of Klinghoffer;* his poignant Whitman piece, *The Wound-Dresser;* his two symphonies (though their titles do not admit this claim), *Harmonielehre* and *Naive and Sentimental Music;* the Nativity oratorio, *El Niño;* and *On the Transmigration of Souls,* the penetrating, disturbing, yet somehow hope-giving piece he wrote for the New York Philharmonic in response to September 11, 2001.

Adams has referred to *My Father Knew Charles Ives* as "a piece of musical autobiography," and as "my own Proustian madeleine, but with a Yankee flavor." When we were together in the Adams kitchen with mugs of tea, I asked whether he had written other pieces he thought of as musical autobiography, a genre that begins with Berlioz's *Symphonie fantastique.* He immediately mentioned the *Grand Pianola Music* of 1982 and then *Gnarly Buttons,* his 1996 concerto for clarinet, that being both his instrument as well as his father's, though the autobiography resides in the echoes of the jazz and swing Adams heard as a boy as much as it does in his memories of learning and mastering the clarinet. It was not long before Adams came to speak both of private events, such as reading Schiller's famous essay that gave him the title of *Naive and Sentimental Music,* to the global ones—mostly horrifying—that have fed into his operas, into *The Wound-Dresser,* and into *On the Transmigration of Souls.* Music, for John Adams, is a way of responding to the world in which he lives, one that both dismays him and gives him deep pleasure. Those who know him and his music will not be surprised that a work now planned is an opera for San Francisco (to be co-produced by Chicago and Amsterdam) whose working title is *Doctor Atomic* and whose central character is J. Robert Oppenheimer.

John Adams's father did not, in fact, know Charles Ives. But Adams sees some similarity between his father and George Edward Ives, the Connecticut bandmaster who was Charles Ives's father and who had a near-mad bent for exploration. Adams also sees his relationship to his father as in many ways similar to

Charles Ives's connection to his. Adams's father, described by John as "a modestly successful businessman" who had wanted to be a painter, played clarinet and saxophone in local big bands and was his son's first clarinet teacher, as well as, in countless other ways, a teacher, mentor, example, and inspiration. John had his first playing experience sitting beside his father and among local worthies such as the town jeweler, garage mechanic, and English teacher, playing in such organizations as the band of the town's mental hospital and the Nevers Second Regimental Band. Both parents were devoted to art and literature, and John was brought up to regard these treasures "as the Holy Grail, the Temple."

The three movements of *My Father Knew Charles Ives* are titled "Concord," "The Lake," and "The Mountain." The closeness to Ives's wondrous *Three Places in New England,* a work Adams has conducted many times in America and Europe, is deliberate. Adams quips—adding that this has already occurred to many people—that another title for his own work might be *Three Places in New England, Only a Little Further North.*

"Concord" is not Concord, Massachusetts, the Concord of the transcendentalists and of Ives's Concord Sonata, but Concord, New Hampshire, the small town, something like forty-one thousand these days, where Adams's parents lived and where he grew up. But "Concord" is a very Ivesian movement, indeed, a true homage. It has a parade, and it quotes not only reveille, but also a little Beethoven duet for clarinet and bassoon that Adams remembers playing as a boy. More important is an effect of layering that Adams absorbed from his many experiences of conducting Ives's Fourth Symphony. There Ives creates the effect of sounds coming from different distances—near, fairly far, and very far, as though the music were being played "in some huge place like an airport hangar." In "Concord," Adams associates these distances with different harmonic languages: the foreground music is the most tonal; the middle ground is "ambivalently tonal"; and the background, almost always *pianissimo,* is "out there," though this is less rigid and methodical than this bare-bones description makes it sound. Sustained harmonies are often lit up by flecks of color that sound the same pitches but in very short notes. You can hear that at the opening, where *pianissimo* strings play an eight-note chord, against which harp, celesta, piano, and various woodwinds set quick dabs of the same notes. The effect of these flecks of color is Ravelian. Adams remarks that, for him, Ives is one of the great impressionists, most perhaps in *Three Places in New England*.

"The Lake" is Lake Winnipesaukee in the center of New Hampshire, some thirty miles north of Concord. Adams's parents met there in 1935 in a dance hall owned for many years by his mother's stepfather. In this tender evocation, you hear tiny fragments of distant jazz, as well as the siren of the *Mount Washington*, the steamboat that plied the lake. The most prominent musical feature is a pair of long, achingly lyric oboe solos designed especially for the San Francisco Symphony's principal oboist, William Bennett.

"The Mountain" is a less specific bit of geographic reminiscence, but certainly the mountain Adams could see behind the family house in Concord plays its part here. Not least, it was surely crucial in turning him into a lifelong mountain-lover. This third movement, which the composer describes as being "less about Ives and more about John Adams," brings the triptych to a quietly meditative close.

The Dharma at Big Sur (2003)

Daniel Colvard

This essay is an abridged version of a chapter from Daniel Colvard's 2004 Dartmouth College thesis *Three Works by John Adams*.

THE DHARMA AT BIG SUR SHOULD NOT BE associated with Jack Kerouac—at least not in the sense that John Adams had originally intended. When Adams first conceived of *The Dharma at Big Sur*, he imagined it becoming an orchestral work with spoken texts, including selections from Kerouac's *The Dharma Bums* and *Big Sur*. Eventually, however, Adams decided to ditch the texts—but not before it was too late to ditch the title as well.

In addition to Jack Kerouac, Adams named two other "guiding deities" in association with *The Dharma at Big Sur*: Californian composers Lou Harrison and Terry Riley. The most obvious connection between *The Dharma at Big Sur* and the music of Riley and Harrison is their use of elements from West, South, and Southeast Asian music. From Indonesian gamelan music, via Harrison, Adams adopted the use of just intonation. From Iran and India, via Riley (as well as by way of recordings by traditional musicians from these places), Adams incorporated sounds and modes largely foreign to Western string instrument performance. He was particularly attracted to the work of Iranian musician Kayhan Kalhor, a composer and performer on the *kamancheh* (a four-stringed spike fiddle that, under various names and in various sizes, is found throughout the region stretching from North Africa to China). Kalhor's recordings feature original compositions that fuse elements of Iranian folk and classical music. Common among the compositions on these recordings is *dastgah,* the system of modally organized suites into which musical items in the Iranian classical repertoire are grouped. Thus, while composing *The Dharma at Big Sur,* Adams was exposed to Asian musical forms and styles both directly (through Kalhor) and indirectly (through Harrison and Riley).

After Kerouac, Harrison, Riley, and Kalhor, violinist Tracy Silverman left his mark on *The Dharma at Big Sur,* and Adams has openly acknowledged Silverman's role in shaping the work's score. Silverman not only factored into Adams's decision to depart from the text and orchestra model he had first imagined, he also participated in the composition of the work's solo part. Silverman and Adams first met in 2003 when Silverman was performing with the Terry Riley All-Stars, a four-piece ensemble led by Riley. The two spoke after the concert, and three months later Adams invited Silverman to be a part of the premiere of *The Dharma at Big Sur.*

In August 2003, Silverman visited Adams at his Berkeley home to improvise over orchestral material Adams had already composed. At first, Silverman and Adams operated on the premise that Adams would compose the violin solo for the majority of the piece and that Silverman would improvise during the final three to five minutes, but after Silverman returned for a second visit to Berkeley two weeks before the work's Los Angeles Philharmonic premiere in October 2003, Adams wrote out the solo part through the work's end. The electric violin solo of *The Dharma at Big Sur,* then, was improvisational in spirit, but fully composed in its final form. In addition, it was composed, for the most part, to complement preexisting orchestral parts. With the electric violin solo and orchestration in place, *The Dharma at Big Sur* took shape. Adams's melding of Asian musical influences, music by Lou Harrison and Terry Riley, and Tracy Silverman's improvisations and idiosyncratic techniques for electric violin resulted in what Silverman has termed a "faux raga." But what exactly is a "faux-raga"?

The Dharma at Big Sur is not an attempt to replicate music of any particular ethnic style. As he readily admits, Adams has not undertaken any serious study of Iranian, Indian, or Indonesian music. Rather, the "faux raga" of *The Dharma at Big Sur* is a "Californication"—to borrow a term from the Red Hot Chili Peppers—of these influences: an intuitive synthesis of Adams's impressions, not of Asian musical forms themselves, and a manifestation of the westward glances taken by Adams and other Californian composers who came before him.

"I planned Dharma as a piece about ambiance," Adams has said, "and then in addition it became a violin concerto." The ambiance that this work seeks to address is one common to contemporary California, a place often associated with the cutting edge of artistic and technological creativity, and a place where sounds and influences from further west—from across the Pacific—are subject to repeated reinvention. Adams recognized this Californian ambiance in the music of Harrison and Riley, and these eclectic, Californian qualities are common to the writing of Jack Kerouac as well. Considering *The Dharma at Big Sur* as a violin concerto, and not simply as an orchestral work, is critical to understanding the interplay of voices found in the piece. John Adams, like Kerouac, Harrison, and Riley before him, manifests his personal synthesis of new and foreign ideas in his art. Ultimately, *The Dharma at Big Sur* is not the expression of a collective Californian experience, but a translation of Adams's own experiences—themselves thoroughly Californian—into music. The electric violin solo plays a similar role, uniting the work's disparate parts and influences. Like Adams or Kerouac, the solo acts as a lone voice, communicating the synthesis of various foreign, patrimonial, and experimental elements found in the work.

Just Intonation

Most of *The Dharma at Big Sur* (with the exception of strings in one passage and the solo electric violin in four other passages) is scored in a just intonation scale based on B. Adams outlined the techniques necessary for playing in just intonation in a note found on the work's title page. In composing for just intonation, he orchestrated for instruments that were sympathetic to this uncommon tuning system, including strings, brass, tuned percussion, and pre-recorded sounds played through samplers. Adams deliberately excluded woodwinds from the score, with the exception of bass clarinets, because the woodwinds' construction works against the micro-tuning necessary to play in just intonation.

Adams readily associates the use of just intonation in *The Dharma at Big Sur* with the work's Californian ambiance, as well as with the music of Lou Harrison (who had begun his own experiments with just intonation some sixty years before). As Adams has said: "Lou Harrison was a strong proponent of unusual tunings, because they brought us close to a universal harmony that incorporated a worldwide scope."

As employed in *The Dharma at Big Sur,* just intonation is more similar than is equal temperament to the tuning systems of traditional Indian and Iranian music. Indian classical music is based on a tonal system known as *svara,* which can be understood as an abstract pitch class rooted on a tonic or reference pitch, with octaves divided into either twenty-two microtones or twelve pitch positions. The tuning system of Iranian classical music is based on Pythagorean whole tones; although it includes a general scale as frame of reference, it has no system tonic. Just intonation, then, has similarities to both Indian and Iranian tuning systems, but the three systems share no single, defining trait. Adams's use of just intonation in *The Dharma at Big Sur* gives the work a mixed—rather than universal—tuning system, and it is intended to introduce non-beating intervals and harmonies to the score. Yet Adams's use of just intonation originates not in an attempt to compose music in the style of any particular ethnic tradition or in a "universal harmony," but instead in the music of Lou Harrison.

Modal Melody

For the most part, *The Dharma at Big Sur* is composed in B major (although it is scored as C major, with B serving as the reference pitch). Within this key Adams explores various melodic modes. This modal orientation contributes to the work's "faux raga" feel (in a true raga, as well as in the raga-inspired music of

Terry Riley, only one melodic mode is used). In its exploration of multiple modes within a single key, *The Dharma at Big Sur* is vaguely similar to Indonesian music, some of which includes modulation between discrete arrangements of scale degrees. Its use of modal melody is most similar, however, to the *dastgah* music of Iran, characterized by its movement between modes (*maqam*). A *dastgah* is comprised of a set of melody models upon which extemporization (*radif*) takes place, any of which can be played during the performance of a given *dastgah*.

The equivalent of mode in Indonesian music (although the music of Indonesia varies so considerably region to region that few musical generalizations can safely apply to the entire country) is *pathet*, a concept that includes a note functioning like a tonic (occurring at important structural positions) and specific arrangements of seven degrees within a scale (only five of which are used at a time). Some Indonesian music allows for movement between different *pathets* within a single piece. Like Adams's experience with Indonesian tuning systems, his known experience with Indonesian *pathet* has been limited and indirect, mediated through the music of Lou Harrison. In September 2003, when *The Dharma at Big Sur* was still being composed, Adams conducted Harrison's *Concerto in Slendro* (1978) in the inaugural concert for Carnegie Hall's Zankel Hall. The violin concerto is inspired by Indonesian scales (*slendro* being a Javanese *pathet* with five named scale degrees) and rhythms. However, the modal melodies of *The Dharma at Big Sur*, unlike the melodies possible within a given *pathet*, use more than five pitch classes and have a definite tonic (B).

The equivalent of mode in Iranian music is a set of pitches called a *maqam*. Each section of an Iranian *dastgah* may present its own *maqam*, and in the introductory section of each *dastgah*, a central or primary *maqam*, along with a characteristic melodic contour (*mayeh*), is identified. Adams has conducted no formal study of Iranian classical music, but listening exhaustively to the music of Kayhan Kalhor has, no doubt, familiarized him with the modal orientation of *dastgah*. *The Dharma at Big Sur*'s opening measures introduce the work's key, primary mode (Dorian, emphasizing C-sharp, D-sharp, F-sharp, and A-sharp), and one of its fundamental melodic shapes (a whole tone step upwards, found at various points of structural importance throughout the work). When the electric violin enters in measure 32, its melodic line follows the same sequence of notes, but they are played in different rhythm and character, unfolding in this mode through measure 65. The beginning of *The Dharma at Big Sur* shares certain similarities with Iranian music, but its opening melody, pregnant with important tonal and motivic information, is not too dissimilar from the first measures of many compositions in the European canon—the opening of Beethoven's Fifth Symphony comes to mind. In measure 66, the electric violin begins playing in B major Phrygian mode, and other instruments support this modulation; sampler 2 plays in E-flat (D-sharp), while a D-sharp is sounded in the tuned gongs. With this transition, the "faux raga" of *The Dharma at Big Sur* begins to define its formal structure.

Form

The piece flows between two movements, one slow and one fast. They unfold through modal and rhythmic transformations, doing so with a sense of timing that can come across as extemporaneous. The form of the work has little in common with Indonesian classical music, yet in its rhythmic development, *The Dharma at Big Sur* exhibits principles common to Indian raga, while in its modal and melodic development, it is more like Iranian *dastgah*.

Form in the music of Indonesian gamelan ensembles—the type of Indonesian music with which Lou Harrison, Adams's source, was most familiar—varies according to region. In Javanese gamelan music, at least two melodic lines must be played simultaneously; in Balinese gamelan music, there may only be a single melodic line. Javanese gamelan music is characterized by its binary or cyclical organization of melodies, which can be repeated indefinitely, and its forms are defined by the lengths of these cycles. Balinese gamelan music is organized according to a succession of cyclical melodies underscored by percussion instruments that mark the ends of these cycles. The form of *The Dharma at Big Sur* is significantly different from either of these Indonesian forms on account of its noncyclical melodic development, even though the work is dominated by a single melodic voice (a quality also found in Balinese gamelan music). The influence of Indonesian gamelan music on its form, however, is negligible, if not entirely absent in the piece.

The overall shape of this "faux raga," at least in its rhythmic development, is far more similar to that of an Indian raga. The performance of a raga typically moves from slow tempo to fast and from unmetered rhythm to fixed meter. The slow/fast division found in *The Dharma at Big Sur* is certainly consistent with the tempo change common in raga performance. And while all of the piece is in metered time, the first movement, particularly its solo part, is composed in free-flowing phrases that extend over the bar lines and blur the perception of meter; its second movement is far more rhythmically oriented, progressing through various rhythmic motifs and underpinned by nearly constant rhythmic pulsation. In the latter, Adams establishes the tempo, which remains constant, according to the delay period of the sampler 1 part. Time is kept electronically, while an improvisation-like solo plays above.

In its modal and melodic variation, *The Dharma at Big Sur* resembles an Iranian *dastgah* suite. Contemporary performances of a *dastgah,* such as those recorded by Kayhan Kalhor, last for roughly thirty minutes (like *The Dharma at Big Sur*), half of which is taken up by composed pieces and half of which includes improvisations based on the opening mode and two or three of the other modes in the *dastgah.* The performance begins with a *daramad,* a piece or melody model introducing the first mode (*maqam*), and then progresses through various other pieces before concluding with a *reng,* an instrumental piece in duple or triple meter in a moderately fast tempo.

Like a *dastgah, The Dharma at Big Sur* begins by establishing its primary mode and melodic shape in the solo part. The piece enters a number of other modes, also established by the solo and supported by changing harmonies in the brass, harp, piano, and sampler parts, and explores other melodic shapes before finally concluding with its original mode and shape. The final notes of the electric violin solo (measures 670–671) are the same as the first two solo notes, but played two octaves higher. The work's second movement, in which the orchestra is significantly more active than in the first movement, is up-tempo and rhythmically driven, and alternates between triple and duple meter. In these ways, *The Dharma at Big Sur* unfolds similarly to a *dastgah*, even if its constituent sections (differentiated by melodic mode, meter, or orchestration) are not deliberately derived from any Iranian melodies or *radif*.

Melody and a Solo Voice

The electric violin solo plays an essential role in establishing the work's fundamental modes and melodies, in driving the work's development, and in synthesizing the ethnic influences and patrimonial sources (Harrison and Riley) found in the work. The use of a solo instrument as the primary melodic voice also simplifies the work's tuning issue: asking a single violinist to play in just intonation is a far more reasonable request than asking the entire string section of a contemporary American orchestra to play collectively in just intonation. Adams uses just intonation to create pure, non-beating harmonies, particularly in the brass writing, but the most significant influence that just intonation seems to have had on *The Dharma at Big Sur* was to make the work melodically oriented. For a composer commonly known for his harmonies and counterpoint, this melodic orientation may mark a new creative departure. It most certainly reflects the melodic orientation of the Asian musical styles that Adams sought to emulate.

The improvisatory feel of certain passages results, at least in part, from the way in which Adams composed the solo: by improvising on a keyboard over the recording of the orchestral part in a MIDI mock-up. A new melody could then be transcribed, which created a scored part that reflects Adams's spontaneous musical response, as informed by his experiences listening to Riley's music, the music of Lou Harrison, and music of various non-Western traditions. The only part of *The Dharma at Big Sur* that deviates from the work's general melodic orientation is the final buildup and climax, the final few minutes of the piece during which Adams had originally intended Silverman to freely improvise over the orchestra's dense counterpoint and driving crescendo.

Thus, *The Dharma at Big* Sur—a work composed for the opening of Los Angeles's much anticipated Disney Hall—draws from the works of California composers Lou Harrison and Terry Riley, who found musical inspiration in sounds from across the Pacific. It also reflects Adams's own westward glance toward the music of West, South, and Southeast Asia, and ties all of these elements together through an unconventional voice: a solo electric violin. Through this unconventional symphonic work—featuring both an amplified soloist and just intonation—John Adams breaks new ground. And although the initial plans that suggested the work's title may have fallen through, *The Dharma at Big Sur* still echoes the voice of Jack Kerouac. The work's solo, its lone voice, projects the experience of an artist coming to terms with Asian ideals—Kerouac's were spiritual, while Adams's are musical—amid the fertile diversity of California.

Coda

But how long will *The Dharma at Big Sur* remain in its current form? Can a composition so influenced by the input of one performer enjoy an extended lifetime in the hands of other soloists? As Adams has recognized, while it works well on paper, this is a problematic piece for the typical symphony orchestra. To date, the work has had mixed success in concert. In the second performance of the work, on March 28, 2004, with the same musicians who played in the work's premiere, Adams asked the orchestra to abandon just intonation and play in equal temperament. The composer's flexibility may help *The Dharma at Big Sur* remain an attractive option for concert programmers and avoid the current fate of works such as those by Harry Partch, whose compositions for experimental instruments in just intonation are infrequently performed.

The second major issue facing Adams as he attempts to make the work viable for performance is the electric violin, which blends poorly with an unamplified symphony and presents challenges that technical concert staff have handled poorly in the work's initial performances (due, in part, to limited rehearsal time). The orchestra and electric violin may sound perfectly balanced in Adams's MIDI mock-ups and in studio recordings, but their textures do not blend as easily in performance.

And how easy will it be for another soloist, or another symphony, to perform *The Dharma at Big Sur* in the future? Future soloists will need a six-string violin; if not that, then a cello, which would require a transcription that Adams has considered making. Silverman has said that the work's solo is entirely Adams's invention, although it may have been inspired by music on Silverman's recorded albums and the improvisations Silverman played while working on the piece at Adams's home. The unique qualities of Silverman's electric violin, however, are significant to the work's expressive effect. The electronic effects that Silverman has used while performing the piece—flange, delay, chorus—as well as Silverman's use of multiphonics, are carefully marked in Silverman's personal copy of the solo part, but are found nowhere in the work's score. Perhaps they should be. Or perhaps these finer points will be handed down only as expressive gestures used in one soloist's interpretation of the score. Regardless, to avoid becoming an installation piece, *The Dharma at Big Sur* may have to change. If it does, some of the elements that made this work so groundbreaking for Adams may be lost in the process, though the exquisite, highly personalized synthesis found in the original score will remain.

John Adams on *Doctor Atomic*

Interview by Thomas May

This interview took place in February 2005 as Adams was still engaged in the composition of *Doctor Atomic*.

Describe the time frame for Doctor Atomic *as a project.*

The idea for an opera about J. Robert Oppenheimer and the creation of the first atomic bomb was suggested to me by Pamela Rosenberg, the general director of the San Francisco Opera [between 2001 and 2005]. I think we first talked about it in the late winter or early spring of 2002. I didn't start work on the opera until January of 2004. I finished the full score in June of 2005, so that means I wrote the entire opera in less than eighteen months. I find that rather shocking—an opera of that size composed in less than two years. It's longer and more complex than any of my previous stage works. There are 550 pages of full score. Both *Nixon* and *Klinghoffer* were each twenty-four months from start to finish.

How about El Niño?

I wrote *El Niño* in a year. It was extremely intense to do it in such a short time, though. I wrote *El Niño* the same way I wrote the two previous operas, by which I mean that I composed the whole work first by just doing the vocal parts with a very rudimentary piano score. And then I went back and orchestrated it. With *Doctor*

Atomic I went straight to fully orchestrated score. The piano version, necessary for stage rehearsals, was done by a gifted composer and arranger in New York, Scott Eyerly. I did not envy him, having to make some kind of sense of my very detailed orchestrations. In the 1980s and 1990s several other large works—*Harmonium, Nixon in China, The Death of Klinghoffer,* and the Violin Concerto—were arranged for piano by John McGinn, an amazingly talented arranger (and composer) who started doing piano reductions of my scores when he was a freshman in college. These are no small feats. When I look at Wagner scores, I wonder who did the grunt work of reducing those richly orchestrated scores down to two-hand piano music. We know that part of Alban Berg's slavish relationship to his teacher, Schoenberg, included having to make a piano reduction of Schoenberg's *Gurrelieder,* one of the most gigantic musical compositions ever written.

How are you approaching the libretto for Doctor Atomic *since Alice Goodman decided to withdraw from the project? You had such an incredible chemistry going with Alice in the earlier operas.*

Alice and my chemistry was, well...only a chemist could describe that! We had major disputes, even some hard feelings with the two operas [*Nixon in China* and *The Death of Klinghoffer*]. I think some of it had to do with the fact that she was a literary person working in what's fundamentally a musical world, opera, always feeling that her value was never quite appreciated. Parts of the *Nixon* libretto were never set to music, something that puzzled and probably annoyed her. I hope she'll publish the whole original version someday. I don't think she has any idea how much her work is beloved by people who know the opera. Enough time has passed for people to realize what a great libretto *Nixon in China* is. *Klinghoffer* is equally wonderful, but it's a more difficult, less immediately accessible text, and like much great poetry, it requires contemplation and effort to appreciate. Making these operas was a collaboration that couldn't have happened without Peter Sellars. In addition to suggesting the stories, Peter, with his perennial optimism and good humor, often prevented us from self-destructing [laughing].

In Klinghoffer, *part of the excellence of that libretto comes from how Alice transmogrified factual text material. How does that compare with what Peter Sellars has done in compiling sources for* Doctor Atomic?

What Alice did both with *Nixon in China* and with *The Death of Klinghoffer*—what all three of us did, in fact—was to read extensively, absorbing everything, particularly personal, firsthand accounts. In the case of *Nixon in China,* the reading covered everything from articles about Pat Nixon in *Ladies' Home Journal* and similar middle-brow magazines to biographies of Madame Mao and Chairman Mao's poetry. I remember reading several books on the Cultural Revolution, one by Harrison Salisbury about the Long March, and rereading Fan Shen, a book about communal life in revolutionary China that I'd first encountered at Harvard in a course taught by Ezra Vogel, the great China scholar. And, of course, Alice dutifully plowed through *Six Crises* by Nixon and *The White House Years* by Kissinger. (That was a sacrifice I was unwilling to make!) All this reading was in the spirit of things, because Mao himself was a habitual reader. The famous meeting between the two world leaders took place in a library, the chairman's personal library. I love Alice's putting the comment in Mao's mouth, speaking to Nixon: "*Six Crises* isn't a bad book." And this is followed by Chou en Lai lamenting, "He reads too much." This is the kind of wit and sly reference to history that you just don't get in your standard opera libretto.

In the case of *Klinghoffer,* Alice did something even more extraordinary: she read a translation of the memoirs of the captain of the *Achille Lauro,* the Italian cruise liner that was hijacked. These memoirs were never published in English, so we had to get someone to translate them for us. I've since lost my copy of it— that's a shame, because it's really a precious document. I remember reading his memoirs after I'd composed the opera and being amazed at how Alice had poeticized the inner musings of this ship captain, making him into a Conradian storyteller.

In 2002, nearly twenty years after the actual hijkacking, there was a production of *The Death of Klinghoffer* in Torino, Italy, and the captain, Gerardo de Rosa I think his name is, came to one of the performances. I wasn't there, but an Italian friend of mine who was in the audience told me that the cast invited him onto the stage after the performance. He spoke a bit to the audience, saying that the opera literally made him shiver because it brought back the exact emotions he had felt during the hijacking. I thought that was really a compliment to the opera: at least for him, the text and music had achieved a level of verisimilitude that equaled his deepest memories of the event.

In the case of Doctor Atomic, *is a similar principle of "found poetry" at work?*

The texts for *El Niño* and *Doctor Atomic* were both created by arranging pre-existing texts. In the case of *El Niño,* Peter and I decided on a group of poems, biblical excerpts, and other texts, all having to do with the Nativity but spanning a huge historical period, from the Old Testament through the Apocrypha, English "miracle plays," and Martin Luther up to twentieth-century writers like Rosario Castellanos, the great Mexican poet and novelist. Then Peter made a narrative sequence from them that I set it to music. All the Hispanic voices in the piece were Peter's discoveries, largely the result of his knowing several Mexican poets living in Los Angeles. To me, they were all completely new names.

Doctor Atomic was more extensive and much more of a challenge because we were dealing with information from all sorts of sources: firsthand accounts, memoirs, journalistic narratives, declassified government documents, and, in one case, a detailed description of the construction of the plutonium sphere I'd found on an Internet site, and which I set for women's chorus. And then, of course, there was the poetry, verses that Oppenheimer, an immensely literate individual, loved: Baudelaire, Donne, the *Bhagavad Gita.* Peter introduced me to the work of Muriel Rukeyser, a socially committed poet who lived at the same time as Oppenheimer and whose work expresses that special tone of wartime consciousness so powerfully.

It's wonderful what Peter does: he reads voluminously. When I visited him in his tiny bungalow in Venice, California, I noticed he had an entire wall devoted to books on the Los Alamos story and about Oppenheimer. I thought I'd assembled a pretty deep collection on the subject, but Peter's was three times as large. I took a peek at random into his collection, and every book was marked profusely with Peter's pencil notations. He'd read everything! That's the way he is with all the works that he takes on, whether it's *Tristan und Isolde* or Artaud or *Idomeneo* or Euripides. He's the deepest, most thoughtful, and most reactive reader I've ever met.

El Niño is more like a fairy tale, an oratorio, and because of that one doesn't really require active theatrical dialogue. I was worried about how this method of libretto creation would work for *Doctor Atomic*. In an opera you need that personal interaction, clashes of will, strong emotions, anger, discord, love, hate—the whole gamut of human intercourse. The last thing we would want would be something historically accurate but emotionally frozen, like a Victorian oratorio or some such thing. But, in fact, he did a brilliant job of solving that challenge. I think that the dialogue in *Doctor Atomic,* particularly in the first act, virtually crackles with the high energy of human interaction. It's every bit as involving and as realistic as anything I've seen in any other opera libretto.

You talked earlier about your reading habits in terms of a general aesthetic. What specific things have fed into this project? For example, there's that famous book by Richard Rhodes....

That was the first book I read: *The Making of the Atomic Bomb,* a very influential book, and far more than a mere description of the bomb. It is, in fact, a history of physics in the first half of the twentieth century. I read the Rhodes book and its sequel, *Dark Star,* which is less about science and more about the Cold War, thermonuclear weapons, and Soviet-American espionage. I've read a collection of Oppenheimer's letters. When some people see this opera and hear Oppenheimer singing Baudelaire, the *Bhagavad Gita,* and a John Donne sonnet, they're likely to think that its creators are being much too arty. But, in fact, if you read about Oppenheimer and read his own letters, you see that he was quite possibly the most cultured scientist who ever lived—more so than Newton or Einstein or Niels Bohr. He did, indeed, quote the Sanskrit poetry (which he read in the original!), and he and his wife Kitty had little coded signals to each other that were based on Baudelaire lines or some such text. When he was a seventeen-year-old undergraduate at Harvard, he and his roommates would have sonnet-writing contests. So it's appropriate, and no stretch of the imagination, that in this opera Oppenheimer would express his deepest thoughts in great poetry.

There are passages from the letters, too?

No, I didn't use any of Oppenheimer's letters, but at the end of the first act I set John Donne's sonnet, "Batter my heart, three-personed God," as a soliloquy for Oppenheimer. He is alone—a rare moment of solitude for him—and feels a very deep dissonance within himself over the fact that here he is bringing forth this terrible weapon, something that is going to introduce an unknowable amount of pain and destruction into the world. The Donne sonnet, which Oppenheimer later said prompted him to name the test site Trinity, is a poem of almost unbearable self-awareness, an agonistic struggle between good and evil, darkness and light.

[John Donne: Holy Sonnet No. 14

Batter my heart, three-personed God, for you
As yet but knock, breathe, shine, and seek to mend;
That I may rise, and stand, o'erthrow me, and bend
Your force to break, blow, burn, and make me new.
I, like an usurped town, to another due,
Labour to admit you, but Oh, to no end.
Reason, your viceroy in me, me should defend,
But is captived, and proves weak or untrue.
Yet dearly I love you, and would be loved fain,
But am betrothed unto your enemy:
Divorce me, untie or break that knot again,
Take me to you, imprison me, for I,
Except you enthrall me, never shall be free,
Nor ever chaste, except you ravish me.]

The poet speaks as one whose soul, "like an usurped town," has been taken captive by dark forces—the dark "shadow" of his own self. The real God must come forth and batter him and break him and bend him and destroy him, and make him whole and new again. It's a very profound moment in the opera. Later, after I'd set this sonnet to music, I read in a new biography of Oppenheimer, *American Prometheus,* how Oppenheimer went into a deep depression after the initial euphoria of the bomb's success wore off.

But you don't cover that in Doctor Atomic—*it ends with the Trinity?*

Yes, that's right. It ends with the Trinity test. We'd originally planned an epilogue, a setting of a declassified transcript of a phone conversation between General Groves and an army doctor about two weeks after the Hiroshima and Nagasaki explosions. It's clear from this phone conversation that General Groves considered all the stories about horrible death from radiation as nothing more than Japanese propaganda. He, like many others in the government, refused to believe that radiation could cause such horrible forms of painful suffering and death. He was, as we'd say today, in major denial. People were only just beginning to realize the horrific nature of a nuclear attack.

What was the first musical impulse you had for the opera?

I thought about the art, music, and films that emerged out of the immediate postwar period—in the late '40s and early '50s— and how it expressed a chilling awareness of man's ability to destroy himself. Science-fiction movies started appearing, and a typical plot would involve a nuclear explosion in the desert—in Nevada perhaps. This would result in some disturbing phenomenon, something frightening and threatening. Nature would go awry, or a monster would appear. And, of course, the truth is, some of the physicists working on the bomb in Los Alamos were not 100 percent certain that their invention wouldn't ignite the entire Earth's atmosphere.

So I had several ideas. One was to evoke science-fiction movie music, which was one of the reasons why I decided to call it *Doctor Atomic*—I wanted to give that sense of science fiction, plus, of course, the backdoor reference to [Thomas Mann's] *Doctor Faus-*

tus, a book which comes from the same postwar era. But, actually, the first really strong musical idea came to me when I thought about Varèse—a work like *Déserts,* which suggests to me a post–nuclear holocaust landscape. That was my first inspiration, and I went with those ideas—Varèse and science-fiction music. You can hear it in the very opening bars of music. This comes after one of several *musique concrète* preludes that are interwoven into the operatic structure.

You're well-known for your ability to bend natural rhythm so beautifully. And you've become so much more experienced now in word setting, through your previous operas and with El Niño, *setting Spanish texts for that. Has there been any significant change for* Doctor Atomic *in terms of how you deal with prosody, etcetera?*

I don't think so. I'm a little more aware of trying to make the lines more fluid and more enjoyable to sing. It's hard to set English—especially just plain flat-out prose like "He said that I should go over and tell that to Oppenheimer" or something like that. I notice when I'm composing that I can get distracted and lose track of the necessity to make good vocal lines. Another temptation I have, shared by many other composers, alas, is to write too high for the men. I have to go back and be very careful about the vocal lines so that they're not only beautiful, but also that they don't always lie in a zone that's exhausting for both singer and listener.

I think I really made a major breakthrough in my vocal writing in *El Niño.* It has vocal lines that are much more beautiful than those in *Klinghoffer* and *Nixon.* I've been to operas when, upon leaving the theater, I have no memory whatsoever of the singing—other than that it was just people barking at each other for three hours. I remember seeing a recent production [June 2004] in San Francisco of [Busoni's] *Dr. Faustus:* it just seemed to be people shouting at each other the whole opera. Singing is something that should be beautiful, I think—especially if you have great singers like the ones I write for—Sanford Sylvan, James Maddalena, Dawn Upshaw, Lorraine Hunt Lieberson, Gerald Finley, and others of that level. That's why I try to think of Mozart as often as possible.

You've spoken earlier about landscape in your music. How much landscape is present here?

I've used some sound effects that will come up on loudspeakers—weather sounds mostly, rain, thunder, wind. It's very eerie when you hear it—both eerie and mysteriously beautiful, just the sound of rain, for example. On the night before the scheduled test, on the 15th to 16th of July 1945 when they were getting ready to detonate the first plutonium bomb, a tremendous electrical storm came out of nowhere. It was completely unseasonal and fearsomely dangerous, as the bomb had already been hoisted up on scaffolding, ready to detonate. You'd be hard put to deny that there's something mythic and portentous about a storm of this magnitude suddenly appearing right as the world's first atomic bomb was about to explode.

One of the things I came across in the course of reading about nuclear energy was a homely little analogy, perhaps a bit oversimplified, but nevertheless very vivid: it expresses how much energy is involved in keeping an atom stable. If you imagine that there is roughly enough energy binding the atoms in a glass of water to power the *Queen Mary* across the Atlantic and back, you can get an idea of the forces involved. That is an astonishing thing. It expresses how vast is the amount of energy in a very small amount of mass. And if all of that mass can be liberated into pure energy, think of how much power is unleashed. You've seen these pictures of a thermonuclear explosion, or even just the bomb that was detonated at Trinity? That plutonium explosion had the force of a hurricane and for a moment approximated the heat of the sun. And it was nothing more than a very small mass that caused it, a plutonium sphere the size of a grapefruit. Even that sphere itself was not entirely solid—it was packed with tamper. So the actual material that fissioned was very small. The understanding of that interchangeable relationship between energy and matter, $E=mc^2$, is what revolutionized twentieth-century thinking and what made the bomb possible.

Are there any trickster elements in this opera? Any need for comic relief?

These scientists and their wives all found ways to unwind, but life was undeniably difficult. The men all worked six days a week, and the wives who were not themselves scientists were either given very menial jobs or were just left to cope with the primitive living conditions. Remember that Los Alamos was almost entirely created by the army slapping together rickety housing with poor plumbing and only a single wood-burning stove. They were very young people, remember, mostly in their twenties and thirties. I read accounts of life on the mesa. Everyone was cooped up and under guard by army MPs. Most unwound with big parties on the weekend. Heavy drinking, practical joking, and doubtless for those fortunate enough, plenty of sex. But this is basically a male story: Oppie and General Groves were the "elders," and Oppie himself was only in his early forties. Teller and most of the other people were in their thirties and even twenties. So, by and large, you have to imagine the sound of men, male energy, male thinking, male voices, the violence that this male energy is going to produce. The two women in the cast—Kitty Oppenheimer and her Tewa Indian maid, Pasqualita—almost by default become prophetic voices, in contrast to the men and their science. Do you know the term *das Ewig-Weibliche*?

The end of Faust?

That's right. The "eternal feminine," sort of a German equivalent to "Gaia knowledge." The phrase *das Ewig-Weibliche* appears at the very end of Goethe's *Faust Part II*. In *Doctor Atomic*, Kitty Oppenheimer assumes the role of eternal feminine, a Cassandra, channeling human history in her long soliloquies. She carries a deep moral awareness of the consequences of what is being done there on the mesa, an awareness that apparently only came to the men much later.

Of course, women were not allowed on the actual test site at Alamogordo; they were not even supposed to know what their husbands were doing. There's something very symbolic about that as well: as much as to say, "You can't know. I just want you here in my bed when I get home."

Kitty has her own Brangäne, a female soul mate, in the Tewa

maid Pasqualita. A lot of what Pasqualita sings verges on the incomprehensible—poetry by Muriel Rukeyser that has vague references to some tribal past, some prehistoric consciousness, with a hint of land being corrupted and a people being destroyed. The poetry is ambiguous here, and that's a strange and mysterious quality. There's a line of Kitty that says, "To the farthest west, the sea and the striped country/and deep in the camps among the wounded cities."

Of course, you know it's 1945, and "camps" makes one think of concentration camps. But then just before we have the image "striped country." Anyone can have his own reaction to the mysterious "striped country," but for me it evokes the Southwest, the canyons and their rock formations. And "striped" also made Peter think of the striped uniforms that concentration camp prisoners were made to wear. Poetry like that is very nonlinear, purely imagistic, skirting the irrational, but it's immensely evocative.

The role of mythology in your stage work is intriguing: the way the specific is related to the universal. I've always thought that the rubric "CNN opera" was such a misnomer because it's such an obvious thing to say, but that's not what it's about—it ignores how the specific becomes the mythic. I know you've pointed out that the Faust legend doesn't have so much resonance for Americans. But I was thinking in pop culture perhaps it does: We do have the whole Robert Johnson story of a pact with the devil. In August Wilson's Ma Rainey's Black Bottom, *one of his huge anecdotes is about a guy who sells his soul to the devil.*

It's going to take another few decades for the whole "CNN opera" reference to be laid finally to rest. It's a pain in the butt, but its cuteness will eventually have no meaning. Nor do I particularly like it when people use the term "political," as in "Mr. Adams is fond of political themes for his stage works." All life is political. Does one say the same thing about Mozart or Verdi, who wrote operas about the struggle of one person's will against another's?

I didn't want *Doctor Atomic* to be launched as an "American Faust," which was Pamela Rosenberg's original idea. I think she understands now why I resisted having the opera come into the world with that baggage. First of all, I don't see a close analogy here. These physicists working overtime to build the bomb thought they were in a race to protect us against the Nazis. They had reliable information to think that the Germans were working on their own nuclear bomb. Imagine if Hitler actually had such a weapon to hurl at the English or even at us. I don't see anything Faustian about that endeavor at all: I think it was a heroic race to save civilization.

And then suddenly the war is over in Europe. The Japanese are seriously sending out peace feelers through diplomatic channels. There was an unmistakable change of mood among the Japanese, and the U.S. government knew this. The only sticking point was FDR's buzzword "unconditional surrender," which Truman inherited. It wasn't clear what we meant by that. The only requirement the Japanese had was that the emperor would not be humiliated and that he would continue to reign, no matter how symbolically, after the surrender. But the terrible irony was that the Japanese diplomats had chosen the Russians, the worst of all possible diplomatic channels, to launch a peace initiative. Stalin already had plans to declare war on Japan, and had even announced to the Allies that he would do so on August 15, 1945. That would give him a right to join in the spoils, possibly even seizing Manchuria. The Americans knew this, and they were very anxious to bring the war to an immediate end, as well as make a big noise to blow back the Russians. I think our using the bomb was a foregone conclusion. There was a terrible kind of inevitability about it, a juggernaut, part strategic, part political, and part determination to put to use this weapon just to show to the world who was boss.

The scientists at Los Alamos suddenly realized that the government's position was "Okay, we've let you make your invention and explode it, now thank you very much, we'll take it now." It was just dawning on these young physicists that their invention was going to be used on civilians. It was James Conant, the chemist and president of Harvard, who proposed dropping the bomb on a civilian population in order to make the greatest psychological impact. We have the minutes of the meeting in Washington, where the targets were selected by a blue-ribbon panel of experts. Oppenheimer attended that meeting, too. It was not just the U.S. military who were responsible for the decision of how and when to drop these two bombs, but intellectuals like Conant and Oppenheimer as well.

So maybe it doesn't work, then, if we think of the individual scientist genius as the Faust, but it might be a military-industrial complex kind of thing that becomes more Faustian....

It's really hard to say, because I think that when a full-out, no-holds-barred war is under way—as World War II was—the goal lines are changed, and people's attitudes are very different. I read a book several years before I even thought about doing this opera— *With the Old Breed,* by Eugene Sledge. He was a young guy from the backcountry of Alabama who enlisted in the marines and went to fight as a grunt, an infantry marine, in three of the worst battles of the Pacific. After the war he wrote a book about his experience. His book is, in my mind, one of the great works of literature about war and should be placed up there with Tolstoy and *All Quiet on the Western Front.* Eugene Sledge gives us an absolutely unflinching description of what mortal combat is like, how extreme the act of killing is, and how utterly dehumanizing battle is. Not even the most graphic moments in films like *The Thin Red Line* or *Saving Private Ryan* can begin to approximate what Sledge's book reveals.

With the Old Breed affected me immeasurably, because I realized that the human species undergoes a profound change in combat, almost a systemic chemical change. And this may be why when soldiers return home they rarely are able to regain their former equilibrium. When a war is no longer a glitzy, strategic run of victories, like the beginning of the Civil War for the Confederacy or the beginning of the present Iraq war for the U.S., and instead it becomes a stalemate of attrition, soldiers think and behave differently. By 1945 the war had devolved into a matter of killing—kill or be killed. There was little room for niceties. And the notion that this bomb may be used to kill civilians, as well as military targets, tended not to come up in conversations. As we saw from the European bombings by both sides, civilians by now had become military targets. There was no distinction.

What the Americans wanted to do with Japan was make the quickest and most profound impact on the population, do it as fast as possible, and get it over with. What they were apparently unwilling to do was consider the possibility of a negotiated settlement, which I think is tragic. Politicians felt anything less than total victory would not play well back home. After three years of reading about this, I am convinced that the bomb didn't have to be used. As Oppenheimer said in later years, nuclear weapons will only be used by aggressors against populations that are already terminally weakened. And that was certainly the case with Japan.

Then you can also say—and this is an unknowable thing, but also human nature—that if the bomb had not been used by us then and there, it inevitably would have been used by someone, if not by us, then by the Russians later on. It's just like one of those terrible Greek myths of self-discovery: the weapon is there, we built it, and somebody is going to use it, just to see what it's like.

Whereas in the earlier works, there is a tendency perhaps to move from the very specific out into a kind of mythological universal, with El Niño *it's the reverse, in a way. You're taking the myth, a folktale, and you use certain specificities like the Massacre of the Innocents vis-à-vis the 1968 student massacre, and so you get this wonderful interplay between the specific and the mythic. Where does* Doctor Atomic *stand in that spectrum for you?*

Doctor Atomic is more like *The Death of Klinghoffer* in that it's about a real historic event that immediately took on mythic meaning. *El Niño* is, of course, one of the most familiar of all myths in Western culture. It was particularly pleasurable to assemble those texts to give a new shading to a well-known narrative and not have to worry about making sure the audience knew the plotline.

The *Klinghoffer* story had the benefit of being what we might call "contemporary mythology," an event that did, indeed, occur during our lifetime, but which immediately spun out of control, shedding its specifics to become a symbol for something larger and more abstract. As I learned all too well, the story continues to arouse extremely violent emotions and elicits heated and conflicting opinions. I've had to absorb reactions from listeners who admire almost all of my work, but when it comes to *Klinghoffer* they can't find enough words to express their revulsion.

One could think of a spectrum in your music from the reexamination of nineteenth-century romanticism in Harmonielehre *or* Naive and Sentimental Music *to the rigorous language of the Violin Concerto. How would you sort of classify the idiom in* Doctor Atomic?

I'm still so close to it, still involved in its creation and prefer not to characterize it in any way. It's coming out very fluidly, and largely without my analyzing it. I think I'd rather not do so: it would be like when you go to a great restaurant and then make the mistake of walking through the kitchen to get to the restroom— and you come back having lost your appetite. I think I'd rather not look in the kitchen here, but for the moment just enjoy what's on my plate.

You mentioned science-fiction movie music as one element that became a springboard. Is there anything in a more structural or even generic sense that did that? The way the Passions *are a backdrop to* Klinghoffer?

No, I don't think so. I did set the John Donne sonnet in a way that has an archaic feel to it. It's in D minor and has a harmonic profile suggesting a slow, solemn classical chaconne. But that's the only moment in the whole opera where there's an "artifact," and I think it's entirely appropriate given the audacity of bringing poetry of that level onto the test site of an atomic bomb, as Oppenheimer did. I think the tone of my setting amplifies Oppenheimer's enormous historical awareness.

How do you compose with this kind of pressure—the time pressure and publicity? Even before its premiere in Houston in 1987, Nixon in China *had become a major media event. What is it like now, trying to write a work like this with so much public attention?*

I actually don't feel that there's as much public attention building up for *Doctor Atomic* as there was with *Nixon*. Maybe I'm more insulated from it. Or maybe the attention now, at least among the critics, is more like "Well, can they pull it off one more time?"

Remember that in 1987 an opera drawn from recent historical events was a brash and novel idea. People couldn't imagine what an opera named *Nixon in China* would be like! There was huge curiosity. Nixon was still alive. Everyone wanted to know "Did Nixon see it?" (He didn't attend a performance, but Leonard Garment, his lawyer during the Watergate crisis, told us that Nixon was obsessively interested in everything written about him, so there's every reason to presume he saw the *Great Performances* telecast from Houston.) Also, in 1987 minimalism as a musical style was still quite controversial. In the intervening eighteen years there's been a boomlet in newly commissioned operas resulting in lots of competition for attention among audiences and the press. Opera companies small and large are commissioning and performing new works regularly now. That's a good thing, although I think there's too much attention paid to premieres and not enough to establishing a repertory.

Does that make you more optimistic than you were a few years ago about where classical music is in our culture?

Well, I fear becoming a kind of Hamlet about the fate of contemporary classical music. The warning signs of its demise as a living art form are all over the place. Yet I persist in thinking that there are some aspects of the human record on this planet that can't be satisfied by popular music alone, no matter how sophisticated it may be. I was powerfully affected, for example, by the fact that, in the weeks right after September 11, many people needed classical music for access to a part of themselves that other forms of music were powerless to satisfy.

As far as the many new operas being composed now, I haven't heard a lot of them. They might be good, but my sense is that we're not experiencing some incredible moment in musical history, one that's giving birth to a host of great new, meaningful operas. I'm very grateful that there is interest and that people want to commission artists. That's an undeniably healthy environment, even if it turns out that only a couple of lasting works resulted. Certainly the scene for commissioning new work is infinitely better than it was thirty years ago, when almost no major composer in this country had an opera commission. But the test is whether people want to have an opera come back after a hiatus of a couple of years—whether an opera, once it's written, has "legs."

What about this idea of controversy that seems to have unintentionally attended so many of your works? How does that affect your sense of the social responsibility of an artist?

Well, some people say I design these controversies! Social responsibility—that's an interesting area on which Peter and I don't always agree. He believes deeply in the social responsibility of art and artists, and I've noticed often that the music that he talks about most enthusiastically is music which he can construe as having a social message. I am uncertain about what kind of a dynamic exists between encountering a work of art and then transferring that experience into social action. For sure, an artwork's aesthetic value has nothing to do with its social import. Some of the most earnest works of art, works of undeniable sincerity, are perfectly awful as art. What appeals to me in subjects like the Nixon-Mao meeting, or the *Achille Lauro* incident, or the atomic bomb, is their power as archetypes, their ability to summon up in a few choice symbols the collective psyche of our time. I'm not interested in lecturing my audience, teaching a social parable in the manner of a Brecht *Lehrstück*.

What has been really wonderful about knowing Peter for over twenty years is being reaffirmed in the notion that art is a serious matter—that even comedy should be done always on the highest level. What both of us deplore is art as a commodity. That's why I'm disgusted and appalled by looking at the marketing that goes on, for example, in the classical music industry. The worst aspects of mass marketing have been appropriated to "sell" classical music to an otherwise sophisticated music public, as we witness regularly when your major institutions send out their glossy brochures full of maxed-out adjectives and ridiculous claims.

The "democratizing" of art, particularly in the hands of Americans, has resulted in a deadening repetition of the same familiar "products": endless Beethoven festivals, Mahler cycles, traveling art shows, tacky "theme" programs, and the personality cult of big-name artists and performers. This creates a hectic, market-driven environment in the "nonprofit" world, where the big institutions behave like vacuum cleaners sucking up all the available funding, leaving only crumbs for small community or radical art. And those out-of-the-way "fringe" organizations, of course, are where the seeds for real creativity take place.

So if music as an art may not function so well as a measure of social change or consciousness, how about on the individual level, changing somebody's life? Is a work of music actually able to transform somebody's life?

Yes, but I think it's a cumulative thing. Art is so vast a human activity that it's really foolish to try to sum up its meaning. Nevertheless, I think it's probably right to say that art sensitizes us in the deepest of ways. I like to listen to baseball games on the radio. It's fun and puts me in an agreeable mood. But my deeper self tends to go to sleep, as if I'd hit the "pause" button on my psyche. That's fine for a time, but it's no comparison to what goes on in my inner self when I listen to a Bartók quartet or the *Well-Tempered Clavier*, or when I watch a Bergman film.

Certainly a person can be very sensitive to other human beings' feelings and not be an artistic person. And, conversely, you can have highly sensitized aesthetes who are nevertheless rude, self-absorbed, and unfeeling people. But art, even in its baser forms, speaks to the better part of ourselves. That's why everyone has a need for it, even if they think they don't.

I think that a lifetime of being exposed to art, and particularly making art, makes for a fuller person. Certainly, if you have children and you give them training in the arts—theater and painting, poetry and music—they grow up to be more interesting and more fulfilled and especially more sensitive individuals.

PART THREE

Collaborators and Interpreters

Creating Contexts: Peter Sellars on Working with Adams

Interview by Thomas May

Without doubt one of the most intriguing operatic partnerships of our time has been the decades-long collaboration between John Adams and the stage director Peter Sellars. From the fateful moment in the early 1980s when Sellars planted the idea for *Nixon in China* with a composer utterly reluctant about the prospects for opera, they have joined forces with the poets Alice Goodman and June Jordan and, in their most recent stage works, in a dialogue with poets from the past, as well as with the choreographers Mark Morris and Lucinda Childs. As with the other great pairings in opera history, the secret of their chemistry is as irreducible to a simple formula as it is rare. Peter Sellars took time from a frantic schedule in the final weeks before *Doctor Atomic*'s world premiere to look back over the relationship and to share his insights about why he has responded so deeply to Adams's music. The following interview was conducted by Thomas May in September 2005.

You were essentially responsible for getting John Adams involved in writing opera in the first place. How did you first become aware of his music?

I met John at the Monadnock Music Festival in New Hampshire [in the early 1980s], where I was staging Haydn's *Armida*. I had set it in the Vietnam War [as a story] about a reluctant soldier destroying a forest and what defoliation meant—which Haydn, of course, powerfully pictures. I was reading the Henry Kissinger memoirs to prepare [chuckles] and had just come back from China, where I had seen my first *quanshu* opera (although I didn't really know that's what I was seeing at the time). I was fascinated with Mao and was discussing the yenan form lectures with James Bolle (the head of the Monadnock Festival). Monadnock was a place where we could talk about art in the mountains, in this kind of retreat, and it had an amazing program of a different concert basically every night in all these little town halls. There was a mix of obscure classical music and contemporary music. Among the composers passing through were Elliott Carter and John Adams. John's music was something that Ivan Tcherepnin had introduced me to at Harvard. And I had become interested in the range of music John was introducing at the New and Unusual Music Festival in San Francisco. I was looking forward to meeting John and hearing *Shaker Loops* as it was played that summer. It was thrilling, because here was music that was genuinely dramatic. *Shaker Loops* builds up these incredible sweeps of tension and then goes into astonishing release and then adrenaline-inspired visionary states: that is absolutely what you hope for in theater. I realized that this is theater music, which has the ability to build and sustain tension. It also struck me that way exactly because of the tonalities involved. Through these the piece goes back into an interesting moral zone. Just like Haydn was showing the forest being destroyed harmonically, John's harmonic language actually took you into areas of right and wrong, where not just anything goes. That was very powerful because drama is *always* about a moral imperative. There is a right action and wrong action—or there are actions that are doomed to be both simultaneously.

That's fascinating when you think of Adams's earlier roots: he was being typed as a minimalist, but he had emerged from the experimental music scene, with its Cagean chance, in San Francisco. That seemed to have its own theatrical element, in the sense of performance art.

John Cage really changed my life, and I have nothing but the deepest love and admiration for his work, which informs my own to this day. It's not that Cage—or Schoenberg, for that matter—is "immoral." But [setting aside] this Buddhist possibility or atonality, it's interesting that the return to Western harmony in a kind of tonal language actually allows the other big thing I was working on, which was Bach. His language, which depicts spiritual struggle, is based on a harmonic understanding—you reach certain points that resonate so deeply in a human being. There truly is nothing like it.

I had heard other music of John [Adams] before coming to Monadnock, but because *Shaker Loops* was played that summer it made this deep impression at that moment. Because I was working on this Vietnam stuff and had just come back from China and wanted to deal with Mao and the Kissinger memoirs, I asked him what he thought of an opera about Nixon in China. His reaction was, politely, "No." I think he really believed I was not serious. About a year later he called back to see if I was still interested. You never know when the right moment is, but we're always planting seeds.

Did you have any idea of how the chemistry would turn out at that point?

No. I hugely admired Alice Goodman, who had written some long-form poetry that I got to know when we were in college together. I thought it should go to the next level as a libretto. With John and Alice, there was an exciting energy setting out. It was a question of doing something serious that cut into the heart of these major American images and at the same time had the possibility of humor, horror, and liberation—as in a Hitchcock movie. I was certainly obsessed with Hitchcock at the time. At the time I was in Washington [as newly appointed director of the mid-1980s American National Theater]. I had gotten material out of the National Archives and vividly remember when we spent several days of sessions at the library of the Kennedy Center. The material itself was exciting. We had such a good time shaping the thing because we put in everything you ever wanted to put into an opera. I was obsessed with the complete history of Western opera in the first two acts and then, in the third act, moving into a new place. As Mozart reimagined what opera could be by inventing the ensemble, [we wanted] to reinvent the ensemble on our terms and find the basis of equality and exchange—which is, of course, what we're looking for globally in our generation.

And even while all this was going on, the idea of the Klinghoffer *opera had already sprung up as a joint project?*

I wouldn't be surprised. There was a very vivid set of issues in the years after Israel's invasion of Lebanon [in 1982]. It was difficult to find a way to speak of these issues in the United States. Opera provides a way which is not just propaganda. It creates something that is layered, multivocal, and intricate and doesn't just produce flat statements. And at that point it seemed so urgent. The other thing that was important for me was constantly to make operas about Americans: it's *Nixon* in China. *The Death of Klinghoffer* deals with Palestinians, but is about Americans in the middle of the situation, through the Klinghoffer family. For me it was important constantly to work as American artists and as Americans and not in a tradition of opera based on exoticism, writing about pearl fishers and so on. We wanted to create a way in which one of the key questions becomes "What are we doing in the middle of this?"

All the more reason why the label "CNN opera," which so irks Adams, is, indeed, a misnomer?

I don't even see how you could get that, when the opera itself is a million miles away from anything you would ever see on CNN! [chuckles] One of the most important reasons to do these operas was to say precisely that we *aren't* getting the actual history of our times. We are used to the media feeding frenzy, with the rush to judgment and the rush for the scoop, and then it all gets dropped. In the Age of Information we are strangely *underinformed* about what is going on and what is at stake—exactly because there's a historical blank for so many Americans. The way journalism has evolved, context is not reported very deeply. [As artists] we have to make a structure which is context rich. Opera is able to go inside to a place where the headlines aren't going. The classic thing with Greek theater is that it's not, say in *Oedipus Rex,* about what does an exploding eyeball look like, but about *why* someone would dig out their own eyes. Whether it's about suicide bombers or 9/11 or any of these events that have happened to America, the question that is not allowed to be asked to this day is "Why would people do this?" That's the question, of course, that drama asks. Exactly to find what was not in the news, what was *missing* from the news: that's why we worked in this genre.

It seems you're really interested in the dialectic between context or historical situation and issue and some kind of universal resonance that lingers on, as in Greek tragedy?

What happens in opera is that it exists across time. John's musical language isn't just contemporary. It moves back across and through time. And Alice's language isn't just contemporary: it's also biblical and the metaphysical poets and the 1940s and '50s. We're trying *not* to say, "This is the morning's headline," but to give a longtime picture, to show that these events have roots going way back and have cycles. What we can do with this form of opera and drama is also to invite the ancestors into the room and deepen and extend the borders of the conversation. The question is, How do you create, in a poetic atmosphere, a place where you [deal with] not only what you just said, but what is behind it and what is its aspiration in the future? Strangely, America is able to have created itself as a country out of an economic revolt against an occupying army. The most bizarre, perverse twist is how in the twentieth-century America was able to come out as the oppressor against every popular democracy movement: just because the question, What are these people hoping to achieve? was never allowed to be asked. I think that's why Beethoven wrote music: it's about aspiration and this struggle for freedom. And it's in John Adams's *Grand Pianola Music,* for example. John has this Beethoven streak that is unabashedly about these issues, yet always in a context that doesn't let them become these flat statements but insists that they have a deeper resonance and that they are contextually very complex.

You're certainly no stranger to controversy, but as we witness the Klinghoffer *controversy evolving through the years, did that feel different in kind or somehow unique for you?*

There are many struggles and occupations in the world today, but the occupation of the West Bank is *the* tinderbox which has sparked violence all over the world. So, yes, it's a unique situation and has created a range of aftereffects and other conflicts. The virulence which even the *mention* of it creates shows you're dealing with something unbelievably painful, tortured, and provocative. It is to this moment what has the world on the threshold of World War III. But we're in such denial of why we are involved in a situation which for the Arab world is an egregious and absolutely unbearable miscarriage of justice. We all have to find ways to talk about it and really discuss it in meaningful ways, rather than name-calling and hate speech.

It's well-known that you're very passionate about activist art, art as social action. But is it fair to say that Adams has a different stance from your approach?

I think deeply we're probably coming from very closely aligned perspectives. Exactly what art *doesn't* do is pretend to answer anything. What it does is to bring things up in a way that the questions must be asked and debated: to me that's what democracy is about. Democracy is the creation of and ability to sustain an environment where even difficult things can be talked about without inflicting further damage, in an atmosphere where all sides can be heard, as Alice Goodman likes to say, "as eloquently as possible," and where the structure itself is large enough to contain all the voices. The heart of the operatic form is *simultaneity,* where all these things are held in contingency. You have to recognize everything as part of a larger interlocking structure. That has incredible social and political implications.

The other thing to emphasize is opera's inclusiveness. It is inclusive of *all* the art forms. The idea of finding a common ground and collaborative space in which people of differing points of view, understandings, and expertise can literally share the space is what it means. So we have Alice Goodman and [choreographer]

Mark Morris and John Adams all sharing a space. The presence of Mark Morris in those first two collaborations [*Nixon* and *Klinghoffer*] is really crucial. These operas are not just reflections; they are also about action. Dance is the most direct action. It's no accident that John is the most choreographed contemporary composer, because his work *is* music of action, as well as contemplation. The rhythmic impulse and physical motor under way in John's music is another thing that lifts it from university-composed academic art music into a field of thought and action in the world. That worldly imagery of John's music, coupled with its otherworldly, transcendental side, generates the tension that makes these pieces have long lives.

I'd like to look at the vernacular that is a part of Adams's music and how the vernacular plays into your own work. It seems this becomes particularly prominent in El Niño—*and then there's the Native American vernacular in* Doctor Atomic. *From your point of view, how does Adams bring this about musically in these stage works? Is it something you both discuss?*

I don't think of it as a self-conscious or appropriative gesture. They all come from John's actual universe. Mao and Jerry Lee Lewis are already going at it in the second scene of *Nixon in China*. All of our lives *do* have all of these elements and connections, and obviously we're in the presence of an incredible interplay of cultural traditions and evolving languages. The way culture works is never "pure"—everything is cross-pollinating all the time. That is the energy of our period, which is by definition multicultural and multileveled, where everything comes from a surprising place.

Nixon in China, for example, has no overt Chinese reference in it musically, but sets up a world which you regard as Chinese—in some amazing way that goes beyond *The Mikado*. [laughs] Instead of using a kind of musical orientalism, it's quite the opposite: what is the *shared* world here? One of the most important things about John's music is that it's not a colonialist viewpoint tapping into someone else's music. It presents the texture of a world we are actually sharing, in which this interpenetration of influence and aspiration from all sides is creating something that is itself a new culture.

On a pragmatic, dramaturgical level, how do you work out the relationships of these layerings? I'm thinking, for example, of the element of the film in El Niño, *which was criticized for creating a distracting overlay. Do you have some sort of process for negotiating this with Adams?*

First of all, the idea that music critics are writing about opera is just too bad, because they're missing three-quarters of the form and its potential. What is most important is almost never written about by the people who have the eyes and ears and larger sense of what is under way. Most music critics are literally blind and have no background—I'd say they write about Verdi with the same blinders. That a music critic is distracted is just bizarre to me. The very thing that is opening the art form to the future for a new generation is what they're attacking.

As far as negotiating with John, these pieces survive both of us. They'll go on to be whatever they are and whatever people find in them. They all survive my initial productions of them and will obviously go on to many other forms and versions. You have to allow your children to go out into the world—they're not going to stay at home forever. John and I talk a lot, we're friends, we have a lot of things that interest us in common. And, of course, it's normal to have differences. I'm just so excited to work with John, to be in the room with June Jordan [the late librettist of *I Was Looking at the Ceiling and Then I Saw the Sky*]. I'm so thrilled by the content of these pieces that do demand attention and that you deeply want to talk about and bring out into the world in a form that begins to offer them their due. I don't mean this in the sense of self-importance or grandeur, but as necessity. For me it's not a leisure activity, but something so urgent at this moment in the world, that these things are spoken in public and that voices are raised and spirits are lifted—that steps are taken, onstage by dancers and in the world by human beings. The driving force of all this is sheer necessity, the sense that something is missing from the world and that this piece goes one step toward supplying it.

What was the driving force behind El Niño? *Previously, you had been the one to come to John with these ideas for stage works.*

Nothing at all prepared me for John saying he wanted to do the birth of Jesus! [laughs] It was the last thing I would have imagined after the previous work we had done. Meanwhile, in those years I had begun working very closely with artists in East Los Angeles, making shows that were both in Spanish and English: with the poet Gloria Alvarez, the painter Gronk, and the painter Yreina Cervantes (whose work profoundly influenced *El Niño* and is on the cover of the record). For me it's an ongoing commitment to do works in both Spanish and English that reflect the cultural and demographic realities of the state of California.

Moving on to Doctor Atomic, *you're right in the middle of a process where you and Adams are about to unveil this new creation to the public. What's your sense at this point of where the opera stands in Adams's body of work?* El Niño *was such an extraordinary step forward. What are you feeling about* Doctor Atomic *in terms of his artistic evolution?*

The beauty of *El Niño* was John's discovery of early music—Hildegard and so on—and the unfettered voice, and singers he could write for. He knew Dawn [Upshaw] and Lorraine [Hunt-Lieberson] and had heard Willard [White] on Simon Rattle's *Porgy* recording. So it's the first piece that is vocally driven, where the vocal line is determining everything else. Before, John wrote these instrumental structures which the voices fit into, [finding] their place in the puzzle. With *El Niño* it's the voice that is leading. It becomes Sibelian, or it becomes baroque in the sense that the voice is moving into flights of improvisation, declamation, declaration, and self-liberation. The orchestra is creating a context for that and has to be responsive. It's a new, interesting performance problem—it's no longer really modern music, but is part of a history of music that is improvisatory and has a kind of liberty as its heart and soul. How you get all those sixteenth-notes to also line up becomes a genuinely tricky performance problem. [chuckles] We're now in that phase where John is writing music that in many cases startles interpreters of his early work. You need an inner freedom in performance for his later music.

There have, of course, been signs of this rhapsodic path before: the Violin Concerto and, recently, the incredible *Dharma at Big Sur*. It's an incredibly important piece—John's first complete *California* piece, where the final traces of the East Coast and Leon Kirchner are gone. It is the open road in California: artistically, spiritually, socially. John took the occasion of the opening for the new Disney Hall and this meeting with Frank Gehry—he took this question of California and what kind of culture are we trying to create for the next generation so deeply. *The Dharma at Big Sur* is a profound breakthrough piece. Parts you can recognize have been coming for a while, of course, but it [shows] John in a state of such rhapsodic depth of emotion and then just soaring.

With *Doctor Atomic*, initially when we were working on it, John was concerned that it be entertaining and lighter, that the subject not create something just doom laden. Then as he began working on it, the entertainment fell away and he literally reached for *Götterdämmerung*, which he studied last summer. Not that Wagner was new for him: there's pure Wagner in Act II, Scene ii, of *Nixon in China*. John's always had this streak. Ironically, I was also in the middle of working on Wagner, because I had been collaborating on *Tristan* during this same period with Bill Viola and Esa-Pekka Salonen. I grew up on Stravinsky and his conversation books and accepted them as gospel: Stravinsky was good, and Wagner was evil. [laughs] Stravinsky's dance-oriented, spring-loaded rhythmic energy was real music.

What's amazing about where John went with *Doctor Atomic* is that he's written the *Götterdämmerung* for our time. For Wagner, the end of the world was a myth, an image. For us, it's a reality that we're living with every minute. The minutes don't exist in some Wagnerian pre-history of archetypal unconscious. They are actually, minute by minute, second by second, the pulse of our existence: we are living right next to and surrounded by our own complete annihilation. So John's music has a kind of urgency not in *Götterdämmerung*. But what Wagner also does is that the orchestra knows more than the characters. The characters are making their claims, and the orchestra is telling you *otherwise,* or is providing a seedbed of history and emotional layering that lets you know that those words mean so much more than anyone uttering them is even aware of.

Listen to this Wagnerian harmony—with its dense, dark tubas and contrabassoons, the basses on an endless tremolo, and these horns emerging from the dark woods of moral nightmare. What John did harmonically is to take that murky morality and to process that through his own particular Schoenberg language to give you the moral conflict of the twentieth century *and* to have all those languages meet and be inseparable from the rhythmic energy and moral acuity of Igor Stravinsky. Here are the two things I grew up with as opposite camps—you were either with or against Stravinsky or Wagner, with Stravinsky or Schoenberg. John has had these languages meet profoundly in this piece and has taken everything which was impossible and brought them all under the same roof.

Breaking Taboos (Portrait of Alice Goodman)

Rupert Christiansen
Opera magazine, May 2003

I DIDN'T KNOW WHAT TO MAKE of Alice Goodman's librettos for John Adams's *Nixon in China* and *The Death of Klinghoffer* when I first heard—and then read—them. They don't offer a simple onward dramatic thrust or immediate clarity; A does not lead straight to B, and I was thrown by their indirection, as well as their poetic ambition. There are highly-wrought literary texts: Goodman's diction isn't as flowery as Boito's, or as psychologically sophisticated as Hofmannsthal's, but it is clearly influenced by the tradition, embodied in the poetry of T. S. Eliot, of using verse as a medium for philosophical meditation. And as I have gradually discovered over the past decade, the intrinsic beauty and wisdom of these librettos is matched by their rare musicality.

Nothing demonstrates this latter element more forcefully than Nixon's "News" aria in Act I of *Nixon in China,* in which the words bounce like tennis balls off the orchestral syncopations; or the haunted, edgily contrapuntal chorus which opens Act II of *The Death of Klinghoffer* and relates the biblical story of Hagar walking through the wilderness:

Every few miles she stopped to rinse her mouth
And give the child her breast. She was like one
Who walks across a room in a shuttered house
Naked and unwatched.

Here the stark poignancy of the imagery and diction seems to melt into Adams's setting. No, you won't necessarily hear every syllable in performance, but you may feel, as I do, a deeper sense of words and music at one with each other's meaning—and it is that quality, not immediate 100 percent audibility, which makes a first-rate libretto.

Adams and Goodman are now at work on the third part of what has evolved into a trilogy dealing with some of the deepest dilemmas of post–World War II America—its subject being the case of Robert Oppenheimer, the nuclear scientist whose Communist associations brought him into disrepute. *Doctor Atomic* (a provisional title, which Goodman doesn't much like) is scheduled for a premiere in San Francisco during the 2005–06 season. If it proves as successful as *Nixon* and *Klinghoffer,* then Adams and Goodman will surely come to rank as one of the great creative partnerships in operatic history. [After a year of contemplating a libretto, Alice Goodman withdrew from the project for personal reasons; the final libretto was compiled from preexisting texts by Peter Sellars.]

Alice Goodman is American-born and a graduate of Harvard University. Married to the poet Geoffrey Hill, she lives in Worcestershire, where she works as a curate in the Church of England. Her deep love and wide knowledge of opera was first imbibed, she relates, through repeated reading of *Kobbé,* and her father "who had a friend in the claque at the old Met and a huge collection of 78s—Caruso, Gigli, Ponselle, Galli-Curci—which I listened to throughout my childhood." She is a woman of high intellectual caliber, enormous charm, and strong personality: if her relationship with Adams—and with the third creative party in these operas, the director Peter Sellars—has at times been fraught, that is because she passionately believes that the librettist is rather more than a servant to the composer.

"Writing a libretto is such an odd skill—nobody and nothing can train or help you. It is simply a matter of striking in. People seem to think that you have to distinguish between singable and unsingable words, but you only have to sing a few hymns to realize that good word-setting has very little to do with the right vowels or consonants. One sings doctrine and meaning, not syllables. Anything is 'singable.'

"The composer is initially dependent on your words—the music can't start until they are provided, and therefore the first job of a librettist is simply to inspire the composer; communicating with an audience is the second job. When an opera is being written, it's *prima le parole*; when an audience hears it, it's *prima la musica*. But I've never felt that my words have been subsumed into John's music; they coexist."

It was all Peter Sellars's idea: he and Goodman had been friends at Harvard, where he'd much admired her poetry. But in 1984 she was much engaged with a thesis on the Elizabethan writer Thomas Nashe at Cambridge University, when Sellars phoned to ask her "whether I'd like to write a libretto in rhymed couplets for a piece commissioned by Houston Grand Opera. I had never heard of John Adams, but I was very taken with the title and the notion of *Nixon in China,* and accepted on the condition that it would pay me as much as my research fellowship. Then I listened to a tape of John's choral piece *Harmonium*—and at first I thought, 'Oh, no, I don't like this. What has he done to Dickinson's and Donne's words?' Then I fell for the sheer vulgarity of *Grand Pianola Music,* and felt happier. But it must be the first time in history when a composer and librettist completely unknown to each other entered into a marriage arranged by a director!

"About a year later, John, Peter, and I met to trawl through a lot of archive material and worked out a skeleton—what would happen, what the voices would be. We fought over the tone: Peter wanted something satirical of Nixon, which didn't interest me. John was in 'wait and see' mode. David Gockley, who runs Houston Grand Opera, tried to persuade Peter to get rid of me and hire Doris Lessing instead. But that passed.

"Then I went home and sat in Cambridge University Library

and read very deeply in the field—a lot about Mao, nutty books about Nixon, but nothing published after 1972, when the China visit actually took place. I made an exception for Kissinger's 1977 memoirs: he's the only character I ended up disliking, and it's fitting that he's a *buffo* bass. Madame Mao? Well, she's the Queen of Night, isn't she?

"I tried not to imagine what John would do with what I was writing. Which was just as well, because what he actually produced was so different from what I couldn't stop myself imagining—I soon realized that words could counterpoint rather than harmonize with the music. We set it scene by scene, working chronologically by mail, and on the whole John accepted what I gave him. Occasionally, he would say, 'I need an inch or so removed here,' or, 'I can't get my four-wheel musical drive up the rocky track of your libretto,' and I'd write back and say, 'Please give it a try, I can't think of any other way to put it.' Bypassing Peter became a sort of game. Choruses were cut, arias inserted. There was a lot of violent disagreement. Some of it was resolved, some wasn't, but I think that the remaining tensions became a strength of the piece.

"*Nixon* is now remembered as having been a great success from the start. But it wasn't—just look at the reviews. Our great good fortune was having six co-producers, which meant that it had several chances to ride the bumps and establish itself. But we knew that it was good, and we knew that whatever we wrote next would suffer in reaction."

Work on *The Death of Klinghoffer* started before *Nixon in China* had even been given its premiere in 1987. "The idea came in New York in 1986, when parts of *Nixon* were being played through during a work-in-progress weekend. Somebody asked what we would do next. Peter said, 'Klinghoffers Tod.' I don't know if it was premeditated. Everyone thought he was joking, in rather bad taste." (The cruise ship *Achille Lauro* had been hijacked in the Mediterranean by PLO terrorists in 1985, and a crippled Jewish-American tourist, Leon Klinghoffer, has been murdered as a result.) "But John and I knew at once that it was a brilliant idea. Like Nixon, it was so compact. The trouble with so many politico-historical operas is that they take way too long a time span—you can't do the whole life of Malcolm X and make it cohere dramatically.

"Today, I look back and wish that I'd made the *Klinghoffer* libretto even shorter. Peter had originally wanted a second half, dealing with the media circus which followed the end of the hijack. We chucked that. And Peter also wanted it to be much more pro-Palestinian than it is—he kept saying, 'Don't call the boys terrorists.' He had specific books he wanted me to read and use—particularly something by someone he knew. I absolutely refused. As background, I read the Koran, the Book of Lamentations, the Psalms, Brecht, and a lot of Spanish poetry of the Renaissance, where Arab and Christian cultures meet—that comes through in Omar's martyrdom aria. The British dancing girl in Act II is based on my very smart stepdaughter.

"Is *Klinghoffer* an opera? Borderline: perhaps it's more a semi-secular oratorio, though, contrary to what many critics have suggested, the Bach *Passion*s were never my model—they may have been John's. I imagined it as resembling a tympanum above a cathedral door, where all the saints and angels are displayed in tableau, and for the figure of the Captain, I thought of the narrators in some of Conrad's fictions—eloquent, but not completely knowing. Rather a bore, in fact."

The collaboration proved rockier than it had been over *Nixon,* partly because of the additional input of the choreographer Mark Morris. "Three is a good unstable number: four splits into two and two. I split off with Mark, against John and Peter. John and I got quite vicious with each other towards the end—I was working very slowly and faxing John sheet by sheet, which, to say the least, wasn't ideal. John was making cuts without consulting me. By the first night in Brussels, we were scarcely speaking to each other—I remember he pushed my onstage at the curtain call ahead of my cue, and I hissed 'dickhead' back at him. It was that bad."

The premiere took place in March 1991. The Gulf War had ended days earlier—had it still been in progress, the performance would have been postponed, such were the political sensitivities. Rehearsals had taken place in a secret location. "People thought we might be a bomb target—as I recall, there were armed police outside the theater. But although the first reviews said some extremely negative things about the horrible libretto and the frigid music, there were no complaints about a pro-terrorist slant."

Like *Nixon, Klinghoffer* was a complicated co-production. (Controversially, Glyndebourne withdrew from the deal, and in Britain the opera has only ever been staged in concert form. Although the management claimed that George Tsypin's enormous set couldn't be made to fit the Glyndebourne stage, Goodman believes that this was an excuse and that pressure from donors was the real reason.) Yet after the initial run of performances in Belgium, France, and the U.S., and a recording, it looked as though *Klinghoffer* wasn't going to "take," despite much tweaking and the radical cut of a ten-minute prologic scene in Act I, set in a generic suburban living room—"John came to hate the music, and it wasn't dramatically essential. But one day it will probably resurface."

Meanwhile, *The Death of Klinghoffer* has proved resilient, not least because its topicality has become more rather than less urgent, and a new cinematic version will surely give it a further lease on life. Its genesis was a concert at the Barbican in 1999, where Adams was conducting some choruses from the opera. In the audience, moved by the power and beauty of what she heard, was a television filmmaker named Penny Woolcock, who had directed two brilliant exercises in working-class realism, *Tina Goes Shopping* and *Tina Takes a Break*. Woolcock, a great music lover, was casting around for a new departure. She fantasized that the opera might make a film, shot naturalistically onboard ship. To her amazement, the idea became reality: Jan Younghusband at Channel Four boldly commissioned the project on a budget of nearly £2 million, and shooting took place last spring. The result looks set to break new ground in the televising of opera and will develop the trend, led by Phyllida Lloyd's film of *Gloriana* and Margaret Williams's of *Owen Wingrave,* of treating the drama cinematically and using locations, as well as undubbed recording of the voices.

Goodman is very excited about the film. She admits that she didn't much like Sellars's austere, stylized, and audience-unfriendly original production and thinks that neorealism may be just what the piece requires—both she and Adams have always hankered after "the Bermuda-shorts production." Regrettably, but inevitably, there are some major cuts—selected for the chop by Woolcock, not Goodman—and one of the score's highlights, the previously mentioned "Hagar" chorus, had been eliminated.

On September 11, 2001, Adams was in an Abbey Road studio conducting the orchestral sound track recording when the news of the attacks on the World Trade Center and the Pentagon broke. It was an extraordinarily terrible moment. But within hours everyone involved was convinced that the best response was to carry on. In the autumn *The Death of Klinghoffer* was dragged further into controversy when the Boston Symphony Orchestra decided to cancel a performance of some of the choruses on the grounds of "sensitivity," and Richard Taruskin wrote a long article in the *New York Times* supportive of this covert form of censorship, proposing that *Klinghoffer* "romanticizes the perpetrators of deadly violence" and regards "in vastly unequal terms" the sufferings of the Jews and Palestinians.

This followed some harsh words written in the May 2001 issue of *Opera* by Andrew Clark, in the course of an altogether unfavorable review of Tony Palmer's production of the opera in Helsinki: "What sticks in the gullet," wrote Clark, "is [Sellars's, Adams's, and Goodman's] very impartiality, their refusal to point the finger, their espousal of the politically correct view that everyone has rights, as if they were trying to generate some phony moral debate. In fact, they were cashing in on an event of recent notoriety for their own narrow commercial/artistic purposes, while loftily proclaiming that all art is 'religious.'" Following a concert performance of the complete work at the Barbican, *Opera*'s editorial of February 2002 deemed Goodman's libretto "desperately naive," echoing Clark's sentiments and agreeing with Taruskin's view that "now more than ever, *Klinghoffer* is best left unperformed."

Goodman is unmoved. "When Taruskin's critique came out, my husband had just had a serious heart attack, and I couldn't be bothered with it. When I finally got round to reading it, I felt it was bilious, and although the hatred was fresh, the arguments were all too familiar. I don't wholly disagree with him about the necessity of censorship in certain circumstances, but not here. His idea that in the aria of the falling body [Klinghoffer's dying meditation] I am implying that the only good Jew is a dead Jew is not just a bad reading of what I wrote, but a case, I believe, of pathological Jewish self-hatred on Taruskin's part." ("Only after death does the familiar American middle-class Jew join the glamorously exotic Palestinians in mythic timelessness" are Taruskin's precise words.)

"I think what upset a lot of people was that the libretto violates certain taboos, common to all minority groups, such as the taboo on washing one's dirty linen outside the community. People didn't like the way that I presented Klinghoffer as an ordinary, touchy, vulgar bourgeois—there's this Jewish fantasy that our heroes and our victims are always either highly cultured or pious. Well, some of us can be very vulgar—we aren't all Nathan the Wise. And we have behaved very badly towards the Palestinians, they have justifiable grievances, and we and they are very, very much alike—temperamentally, culturally, in family dynamics, and in ultimate origin. At which point I should add that by origin, upbringing, and education I am a Jew. I'm Jewish by nearly every definition. I converted to Christianity between writing the choruses and arias for *Klinghoffer*."

The accusation that she has sentimentalized the terrorists puzzles her. "I can only say that I learnt from a book, T. W. Baldwin's *William Shakspere's Small Latine and Lesse Greeke*, that the Elizabethan grammar school used as a rhetorical exercise the technique of taking both sides of a case and presenting them both as fully and forcibly as you could. That's what Shakespeare does with *Macbeth* or *Coriolanus*, and that's my procedure, too. But it's perfectly clear in the context that "Rambo" [who utters the shocking line "Whenever poor men are gathered they can find Jews getting fat"] is an evil thug."

After *Klinghoffer* first came out, Goodman believed that she would never work in opera again. "It was altogether a very bruising experience. John went off to write the Violin Concerto, and after a bit, I went to theological college—that, I thought, would be that. I knew the operas were good, but for several years I couldn't bear to listen to them. The relationship between John and me was not good. I was much pricklier than I am now; John appears to be mellow, but he's very often a bundle of nerves. We're very different, and our working relationship functions because we live so far away from each other.

"About five years ago, he sent me a copy of the big CD compilation of his music, John's *Earbox,* and I listened to it with great pleasure. We got in touch again, and agreed that we would collaborate on his Nativity oratorio *El Niño.* In the end, my daughter became ill, and I had to withdraw. But I was very happy with the texts he wound up using—many of them ones we'd talked about. It has taken us fifteen years to truly know and like each other."

Now they're warming up to *Doctor Atomic.* "I'm still reading and researching," Goodman says. "I have written very little recently, and hope I can still do it. I think e-mail will help our communication. Anyway, I embark on the thing older and, I hope, a little wiser."

Robert Spano on Conducting the Music of Adams

Interview by Thomas May

Robert Spano, music director of the Atlanta Symphony, has been a leading advocate of contemporary American music since his days at the helm of the Brooklyn Philharmonic. He is one of the leading interpreters of Adams's music today. The following interview was conducted by Thomas May in April 2005.

While you were music director of the Brooklyn Philharmonic Orchestra, you became well-known for your thematically oriented programs, mixing new works with classic repertory. How did the music of John Adams work in that context?

I began programming John on concerts as soon as I started conducting. I had even done *Shaker Loops* when I was teaching at Oberlin and continued paying attention to everything he was writing. In a sense, John's music always enjoyed its own focus [at the Brooklyn Philharmonic], because we did both *Nixon in China* [in December 1999 as part of the Brooklyn Academy of Music's Next Wave Festival] and *The Death of Klinghoffer* [in December 2003]. *Nixon* was officially a "semi-staged" production, but it was theatrically satisfying nevertheless. And *Klinghoffer* we did as a full production. As far as parts [of a larger program], we did, for example, *Harmonielehre* in a different way. We did it in conjunction with the Berio *Sinfonia* and Elliott Carter's "Allegro Scorrevole" [final movement of his *Symphonia*, in a November 1998 program]. The idea there was actually to look at new things juxtaposed with each other. And we did *The Chairman Dances* from *Nixon* on another program that was primarily new music.

You've conducted the huge orchestral and operatic works of Adams. From that experience, how would you characterize the overall challenges in conducting his music?

What I've found amazing is that the challenges are different with each piece. This is one of the things that I admire so much about John's music: his perpetual exploration. He's a polymath. I find that I'm differently challenged and engaged with every piece of his that I do. Conducting *Nixon* was nothing like conducting *Klinghoffer; El Niño* was nothing like doing *Harmonielehre*. The Violin Concerto and the Chamber Symphony are each completely different stories. The obvious challenges [in general] are often rhythmically based, but even that is presented in different ways. The rhythmic challenges of *Nixon* are quite unlike those in the Chamber Symphony, for example. In *Harmonielehre* or *Klinghoffer,* the challenge is to shape the largest picture of the piece, so that it takes on an architectural life. On the other hand, the Chamber Symphony is constructed in such a way that [the big picture] takes care of itself, but there are tremendous amounts of detail to take care of, with shifts in focus.

Your conducting style itself has been described as "muscular" and "fierce." Is there a way in which that personal approach is conducive to Adams's own style?

I had an immediate affinity for his music as a teenager. In those days I was a composer and was always listening to new things. When *Harmonielehre* appeared, suddenly there was this unimaginable thing in my musical universe—it was a revelation and I felt liberated. Here was music that made sense to me on a grand symphonic scale and that had tremendous tonal organization and was unabashedly tuneful. It was so expanding for me, when I had been listening to Stockhausen and Berio and Ligeti (even Crumb—I was pretty broad in my tastes) all the time. And as I've continued to pay such close attention to his music I continue to have that affinity.

But I think that one of the fascinating things about Adams's style is his stylistic variety. And yet I always think it sounds like John's music. That's true of other great musical figures, like Stravinsky. They share a similar kind of ability to engage so many languages and styles and yet retain an identity. It feels very unforced and un-self-conscious to me—John's individuality seems to come naturally. I think that's why he's so successful at dealing with all these styles. It reminds me of a line of Cocteau: "An original artist cannot help but be original; therefore he need only copy."

As a conductor, what's the primary thing you bring to Adams's music. I think of the dictum of your mentor Max Rudolf, that the conductor's primary role is to be the listener, to bring attention to the music. How does that relate to what you contribute as a conductor when you're interpreting a piece of Adams?

I think I approach his music the way I approach everything. The nice thing with doing John's music is that often he's able to be around my doing it, so I can get feedback and greater understanding of what he's interested in hearing. To me, that's one of the great pleasures of doing music by living composers: to be able to work with them. (Mozart hasn't been answering my calls.) It's the same attitude for me, with the added benefit of the living presence, of trying to get inside the composer's sound world, inside their aesthetic, their interests, their sense of beauty. As a performer, maybe that's why I have such an affinity for John's music. He seems to be able to engage so many different things. And that's what I try to do as a performer: I try to engage all these composers and find my way into their world. Without intention I end up being there, too, but I don't strive to imprint something of myself on these things. I just think it's inevitable than everyone does.

Do you have an example of working on an Adams piece where something changed?

There was an experience recently when he was in Atlanta for the local premiere of *El Niño* [in May 2003]. John was able to attend rehearsals. I remember there was a movement where my perception of its character was slightly "to the left" of what he had in mind. John's such a verbally expressive person as well. He described what he was looking for so precisely that I could see exactly what he wanted in a way that I had not. So I was able to adjust on a very subtle level. It wasn't a question of changing tempo or something basic, but one of the real mood and character of the section.

You come at this music as a composer yourself. Does that influence how you take one of these scores apart in analyzing them?

I think that I tend to study scores as a composer, even though I end up conducting them. My interest in how they're put together, what structures they take, what set of values is at work: I approach that as a composer. Any given piece expresses certain musical interests above others. *Klinghoffer*, for example, explores a world of expressivity that's not absent from *Nixon in China*, but occupies a different place in the hierarchy of musical interest. The kinds of rhythmic games and drives and structures that John creates in *Nixon* don't play the same role in *Klinghoffer* at all. So there's a different musical interest on his part in each case. I try to understand how that's achieved and study it as a composer. The better understanding I have of a piece intrinsically, the better I'm going to be able to conduct it.

You mentioned finishing the Atlanta Symphony season in 2003 with El Niño. *That work has been compared with another hugely successful choral work, the Golijov* Pasión, *which you've also conducted. The comparisons tend to look at what's perceived as a kind of neo-religious, folk sensibility. Do you think there are common threads?*

I hear the two pieces as so completely different, it's hard to see what would connect them. But looking at the tremendous audience response brings one thought to mind. When something is authentic and has its own power because of the sincerity and directness of the creative mind that gave it voice, people respond.

Perhaps that's what these works have in common, however differently I view them as pieces. Ultimately they're both successful pieces with a wide audience because they [exhibit] some need to say what they're saying. They're not pieces written just to write a piece, but rather because something was boiling over in the creator in both cases. I trust in that. I see that as a characteristic of all great music.

You've had two main Klinghoffer *experiences as a conductor: there was the controversial 2001 cancellation of the choruses with Boston, which you were scheduled to conduct, as well as the Brooklyn Academy of Music revival you conducted in 2003. In a nutshell, what is your experience?*

I think the Boston cancellation was an incredibly emotional time, it was so soon after 9/11. We were planning just a snippet of *Klinghoffer:* three choruses, not the whole thing. Two members of the chorus (that I'm aware of) had relatives die on those planes. It felt very wrong to try to appreciate those pieces in that environment, for many reasons. As for the cancellation, it wasn't my decision to make entirely, but I was complicit. My feeling was that the work shouldn't be judged with all kinds of prejudice. There was no way to appreciate those choruses at that time for what they are. It also seemed wrong to me not to be doing the entire work if you want to try to evaluate it. The opera became a subject of argument that, to my mind, has nothing at all to do with the work. The media frenzy about the cancellation was endless. To me the work is about humanity's capacity to be inhumane and about how our hatreds can blind us. My fear was to do three choruses from that work in an isolated way, so soon after an incident that had many people incapable of finding any objective point of view…It was so wonderful when we did it in Brooklyn. It was long enough away in time that people who weren't going [to stick to] entrenched views about it could perceive the work on its merits.

Were there surprises for you in the audience's response to the 2003 Brooklyn performances?

I wasn't surprised but gratified that so many people in the audience got it and were clearly moved. That's how I see the opera, what it's meant to do. I end up viewing it not as political but as personal, because I think the opera forces me to examine what prejudices or hatreds or entrenched viewpoints I might be living with internally. It takes on a different charged meaning because it's Israelis and Palestinians specifically in that work. But the issue is actually one that I have to grapple with in my own self—as I think any sentient being needs to.

You've conducted so much of Adams's music by now. Does that give you a sense of hierarchy, of what pieces might be more enduring than others?

I'm glad you asked that, because you made me realize something I'd never thought about: they're all so damn good; they all shouldn't be that good! When I think of just the pieces I've performed—let alone what I haven't—I'd be hard-pressed to say which is a better piece: I'm trying to evaluate them on their own terms. I think of *Slonimsky's Earbox,* just twelve minutes but so strong—it is what it is. Certainly *Naive and Sentimental Music* or *Harmonielehre* are operating on a much grander scale, but they have a different mission to fulfill, a different set of expectations.

For all the differences you've pointed out, is there a common denominator, shared even among the opera and concert works you've conducted?

I think of John as an architectural composer. Even in the operas he creates tableaux; they don't have a lot of dramatic enactment, they have dramatic situations that are relatively static except for the musical unfolding. John's music makes me think of big blocks that are actually very vibrant within themselves but very clear. They're related to each other, but you know when you've left zone A and moved into zone B. Maybe that's something he learned from his minimalist days. What is dramatic is that when you're in panel B it's a very different experience from what was going on when you're in panel A. In my musical world Adams has become as important as Bach, Mozart, Sibelius, Tchaikovsky. He doesn't have to die for me to give him that place.

John Adams on Conducting Ives

Interview by Ingram Marshall

The following is excerpted from a longer interview conducted by Ingram Marshall for the Oral History of American Music project at Yale University. The interview took place on August 12, 1999, in the Sierra Nevada Mountains, California.

John, I know you've been doing a lot of conducting in recent years. As long as I've known you, you've always conducted, but it seems to have picked up a lot professionally in the last decade or so. I know you're presently getting ready to conduct the Ives Fourth Symphony *with the Ensemble Modern. I'm wondering what is the relationship between your conducting and your composing? Big question.*

I think I did my first conducting when I was in high school. It was a small community orchestra in Concord, New Hampshire, that was sponsored by the New Hampshire State Hospital. I played in the orchestra with my father, and they performed several pieces of mine when I was—oh, I don't know—fourteen, fifteen years old, and I also conducted them. I was interested in conducting from a very early age. It must have been some means in which music could be expressed choreographically or in some sort of Dalcrozian sense because I remember even as early as the age of four or five, listening to records with my parents and conducting with my mother's knitting needle, I think it was!

I don't know where the model of a conductor came from, because this was Woodstock, Vermont, and we didn't have television then, and I don't know when I had ever seen anybody actually conduct. But then I became entranced with Leonard Bernstein when I was a little kid, and I did watch him on television.

But it's been a kind of a yang activity to the yin activity of composing. Composing, of course, is a very introverted process. It's very internal and, I suppose one could say, it's very subjective. Conducting is just the opposite. It's a very extroverted activity. It requires fast, practical solutions to problems that often have more to do with personalities than they have to do with actual musical issues. And it takes me out of the very private, introverted world of creative activity and takes me into just the opposite world.

As painful a transition as it is—and it always is very painful—it's painful to return back to composing; it's painful to leave it and go out into the world—as painful as it is, it's still, I think, a very healthy one for me. I couldn't imagine being one and not the other. It's given me a lot of insight into personalities, like Mahler, for example, or Wagner or Berlioz or Stravinsky, all of whom were very active performers but, obviously, very important composers.

I think it was a couple of months ago I was talking to you when you talked about studying the Ives Fourth Symphony, and it was really a bear for you. You couldn't figure it out. You said: "I don't understand this symphony, and I really don't like it." I am quoting you. "I wish I didn't have to do this." Your view seems to have changed from the last time I asked you about it. What has been going on with that?

Part of that was just frustration and, I suppose, resentment that I had to basically stop composing this summer, partly to devote myself to learning this piece. The Ives Fourth is really the *Finnegans Wake* of music. It is such an imponderable behemoth of mysterious detail, and the condition that Ives left the piece in and the present condition of the parts and the scores and the confusion over what Ives really meant—it requires that one take up vows, as if one were going into a monastery, and learn this piece. It's just not a piece that you pick up a month before the first rehearsal and learn. It's something you have to live with for a long time.

And, of course, I've conducted a lot of Ives in the past five or ten years, so it seemed right that I should do this piece. But I think when I first approached the Fourth Symphony, I experienced irritation over it because so much of the internal detail is, on the one hand, extraordinarily difficult and unreasonable, basically on a rhythmic level, and yet this detail is obliterated in performance because of the acoustical nature of the orchestration. It's very hard to know how much of that is due to naive assumptions on Ives's part. He was an immensely, enormously sophisticated musician who nevertheless never heard his orchestral works done in proper performance. I think he heard one performance of *Three Places in New England,* and God knows what that sounded like on very little rehearsal. And there was no tradition for performing music of this level of difficulty when Ives was still composing.

So one wonders if, had he been a practical composer like Stravinsky, for example, who did hear *The Rite of Spring* or did hear *Petrouchka* hundreds of times and was able to tweak it, would Ives have changed his mind; or philosophically would he have said: No, that's the way I conceived the piece, and if you don't hear these groupings of nine inside of four inside of three in the second violin part—it's like a town meeting, where everybody has his say. So I had to overcome this. Of course, this is a problem that exists in a lot of his orchestral pieces. But the Fourth Symphony is particularly a problematic piece.

In the course of this, I've also come to see this work as really one of the great masterpieces of music. It's a very puzzling work because, as I was saying to you the other day, when you get to the end of the Fourth Symphony, the final moments that are just sublime beyond belief—you get the feeling that you've slogged up this mountain and you suddenly reach the summit, and the Milky Way is overhead, and you hear "Nearer, My God, to Thee" hummed by the chorus off in the distance—you feel like you should be at the end of a symphony that's at least ninety minutes long or two hours long, like the longest Mahler symphony.

And yet the timescale of this piece is very mysterious. It's really only thirty-three, thirty-five minutes long, and you're left wondering if Ives actually made somewhat of a miscalculation in terms of how long in terms of just pure clock time it would take to get to this moment. But, again, it's a work in which information is so compacted that time functions in a very different way.

Maybe one could see it as a culmination of almost a life's work.
Oh, there's no doubt about it.

It is a late work.
It's his *summa,* and it is really his final work. He contemplated, of course, the *Universe Symphony* and other pieces, but it's the only one that was left near completion. I've been trying to figure out some of these inner rhythmic activities, which are simply inaudible in performance, and they're also unrealizable in their precision—triplets that are piled up against triplets but that are staggered by a half a beat, for example, in the second movement.

At a pretty fast tempo?
Yes, and even if you've got the world's greatest orchestra and unlimited rehearsal time, the simple acoustical problems of having a brass section that's fifty or a hundred feet away from the podium—it's almost impossible to realize. But I've entered a lot of it into MIDI, which has been an interesting and amusing and revealing experience because there you can actually hear what Ives intended.

One of my revelations has been that now I understand why Nancarrow went to the player piano because I'm sure Nancarrow was very informed by these Ives rhythmic experiments and realized that the only way to really achieve that was through a kind of mechanical representation.

Right, the MIDI of his day.
Yes, exactly.

As long as we're on the topic of American music, I know you've also performed some transcriptions of Nancarrow done by—
Yvar Mikhashoff.

Yes. I remember hearing those with you conducting the Ensemble Modern?

And they were very effective, I thought. Again, it raises that thing about here was a genius who could figure things out in his studio atmosphere, and perhaps it's fitting that someone else should enlarge it somewhat. With the Ives it's almost the opposite: You're going back and figuring out what he did by tinkering with it on a MIDI system. You can get the most minute subdivisions of rhythms and things.

That's actually true. The other thing about the Fourth Symphony that's often neglected is that in some way it's a piano piece that's been expanded to gigantic size by the addition of this monstrous orchestra, but the solo piano plays throughout, except in the fugue movement, and the fugue, of course, is a piece from an earlier part of Ives's creative life. But the other three movements essentially are an orchestral elaboration of this individual piano part. It's an extraordinary piece of music on every level: rhythmic, harmonic, structural.

What I love about Ives and I particularly love about this symphony is that it's fundamentally a spiritually optimistic work. What strikes me about this is that the works written in Europe at this time were so bathed in pessimism—I feel that in the common comparison between the last movement of the Ives Fourth and the last movement of *Das Lied von der Erde*, they both kind of fade out into twinkling outer space, but that the Mahler is one of deep, Schopenhauerian resignation and pessimism, and the Ives is just the opposite. It's a kind of New England transcendental optimism.

For me, this is a tremendously meaningful thing because it defines a spiritual difference between the Eastern and Western hemispheres, and I think that, although a lot of American composers have been ridiculed and belittled in Europe for many years, as being naïve or optimistic or simplistic, I think in a sense what makes American music very powerful now—and this includes jazz and ethnic music, as well as American classical music—is there is a fundamental optimism about it—whether it's Cage or Gershwin or Copland.

I never would have thought of Cage as an optimistic composer, but now that you mention it, yes, I could see that.

There is a fundamental optimism in Cage [laughs], even if it's the tossing of coins. There's this faith that—

It'll all come out.
Yes, that there's some kind of mystical organizational principle behind it which will have value.

It's interesting to me that you're doing this Ives Fourth with a Central European ensemble and going all over Germany. It must be fantastic that they are doing this because it requires hiring a chorus and—
This is called the Ensemble Modern Orchestra. It's only brought together once a year. The core is this marvelous ensemble, the Ensemble Modern, which although based in Frankfurt is a very international ensemble. There are several Australians, French, a lot of English, and a couple of American performers in it. They're all in their mid-twenties to mid-thirties, so they're an ideal group to be doing a difficult program like this with.

Probably a lot better than doing it with a traditional orchestra—if you walk into the Berlin Philharmonic with the Ives Fourth, you might encounter difficulties. I don't know.
I think that it really depends a great deal on the conductor. I've come to believe that conducting is 90 percent charisma. Most good conductors have technique to burn these days. Any conductor who's under the age of fifty usually has enormous technical apparatus, but an orchestra will respond when they're inspired. If you have an Esa-Pekka Salonen or a Simon Rattle or a Michael Tilson Thomas standing in front of the orchestra, they tend to believe what the conductor's mission is, and they will give. I have a recording by Michael Tilson Thomas of the Ives Fourth done with the Chicago Symphony. It's a miraculous recording in terms of the love and the sensitivity and the respect given to this score. That obviously emanates from the musicians' respect for the conductor.

But if you were to bring a hack in or a journeyman conductor in front of the same performers, chances are you just wouldn't get an inspired, devoted performance.

Just to shift gears a little bit now, when you work on a new piece like the Ives Fourth—new for you—or any composer, for that matter, is there any direct connection with your own composing? Can you remember, say, any situation where having learned a piece by another composer, you found it creeping into some work of your own, perhaps not directly but collaterally?

Oh, yes, absolutely. I would say the classic case of what happened to me was getting involved in the Nancarrow arrangements that this same group, Ensemble Modern, asked me to come and conduct. I felt that Yvar Mikhashoff's arrangements of the Nancarrow were not simply orchestrations; they were a revivifying of the music because I have very mixed feelings about what Nancarrow's music sounds like on player piano. I find it very tiring after a while. But Mikhashoff's orchestrations turn them into something far more creative, I think, than Nancarrow ever imagined.

It was a tremendous inspiration to me because it was rhythmically complex and yet, at the same time, it was very colorful and, most important, it was very accessible. I thought, "Well, this is remarkable." This is music that is based on an American vernacular (I'm speaking of Nancarrow here), whether it be blues or ragtime. There's one study which is a Benny Goodman big-band riffing, and there's another one that's based on flamenco ideas. I feel that's very important. This has always been a major point to my own musical life, is that I think classical music needs to have a close, symbiotic relationship with vernacular music; and if it doesn't, it becomes very solipsistic and very self-referential.

I thought that the Nancarrow—and I feel this way about Ives, by the way—that their relationship with vernacular is so strong that it makes the music healthy. Pardon me if I sound a little touchy-feely here, but I think that there's a fundamental sense of health in music that is close to the vernacular, whether it's *The Rite of Spring* or Brahms's gypsy movements or Mozart's arias in *Figaro*. There's this kind of a musical health to them. That's what I took from Nancarrow, as well as the sense of complexity that, at the same time, had an accessibility to it.

Emanuel Ax on Performing Adams's Piano Concerto

Interview by Thomas May

During his tour with Yefim Bronfman in spring 2005 playing piano four-hands music (including *The Rite of Spring* in a reduction for two pianos), Emanuel Ax stopped to share his thoughts on a work of Adams of which he is the leading representative, the piano concerto *Century Rolls*. Ax, against an incongruous backdrop of endlessly cheery Muzak in a hotel restaurant, described his relation to the piece. The interview was conducted in March 2005 by Thomas May.

Since you're so well-known for your interpretations of the classical and romantic repertory, what kind of risk were you taking when you commissioned a new concerto from John Adams?

I didn't think of it as a risk at all. John was the first composer I met and got friendly with, really early in his career, maybe the late 1970s. I was doing concerts with the Saint Louis Symphony with Leonard Slatkin, and there was a chamber concert. I heard him conduct of *Shaker Loops*. I thought it was an amazing piece and felt completely in love with it. At the time I didn't know much about new music. And then I met John, who was there for the weekend. I had an incredible sympathy toward him. And my first real experience playing [living composers] was *Tristan* of Hans

Werner Henze, in the early '90s. So a couple years later I was in Cleveland. The topic came up that they'd love to commission a piece involving me. Christoph [von Dohnányi, then music director of the Cleveland Orchestra] asked who I had in mind, and I said, "John Adams." It was such a natural choice, since I already knew him. They said they already had him writing a piece, and I asked them to make it a piano concerto. So it was a natural, pretty simple process.

Did you see the score in process along the way?

John is very correct and pretty much on time. So I got it in one piece, although he had sent me a couple of questions along the way, asking whether this or that can be done. When I got the piece, of course it was the piano part. I didn't know what to make of it: there were so many little notes! Lots of eighth-notes, I noticed, thinking that's not so fast. But when I saw his tempo I realized all of it was fast. But I couldn't figure out what was going on from seeing only the piano part. John sent me a computer tape. One of the scary things is that the computer doesn't play wrong notes. [laughs] It was very intimidating.

So I started practicing and began to realize that it's a kind of mosaic. It's like in Italy, where you have these little pieces of tile and they're all designs of this or that, and every tile means something—but only in the total picture. My part is like one of the tiles, or maybe a lot of the tiles. Other players are other tiles. When they add up it presents this amazing picture of, in a way, a romantic piano concerto. The first movement has this long line—it starts out almost like a chamber piece—and gets bigger and bigger, and then there's a huge climax. There are hints of Gershwin and Tchaikovsky—I don't mean direct quotes but in the way you play—and then it all comes back down to that chamber thing. It's like a big arch.

Adams talks about inspiration from the mechanical player piano at the turn of the century. What was it like coming to this kind of work especially given the natural, poetic warmth that's the signature of your style?

I knew the piece wouldn't be an updated Chopin concerto because I knew something of his music. It was an incredible discovery of having good rhythm. Most classical pianists—myself at the head of the list, don't necessarily have such good rhythm. We're always thinking about line and harmony but we don't necessarily have a good feel for inexorable pulse. This is why with pieces like the *Pulcinella* reduction [for piano and cello] of Stravinsky—which I worked on with Yo-Yo this week—I had a hard time just being accurate, not rushing, not slowing down. It's incredible discipline that really helps you with everything. There's so much to think about for a pianist: line, harmony, the way that one note relates to the next, because the sound decays, so we have to think about connecting things; sometimes rhythm takes a backseat. So I practiced with a metronome, which I've been doing ever since. I'm realizing that you need to put rhythm into the hierarchy that you're working out.

What was initial performance like?

There were difficulties in terms of balance. John scores heavily, and it didn't always come out with the prominence he wanted for piano. He's changed some of the scoring since. The first entrance of the piano part was down low and hard to cut through. On the recording there's no issue, but in concert hall there's sometimes a problem. We even used some amplification. I have no problem with that: there's nothing that you intrinsically improve by saying I have more muscles.

Looking at the piece itself in detail: what do you make of John's use of the classical three-movement form?

I think fast-slow-fast works well—I wouldn't restrict it to classical concerto form. Anytime you went to a Sinatra concert you'd get an upbeat song, a slow ballad, and a fast song to finish up. It's a natural progression—it's necessarily related to standard concerto in that sense. I think John wanted to write a concerto that had connections to the early twentieth century: Ravel, Gershwin, Rachmaninoff, all stuff that was there. It's very intimidating to write a piano concerto because you're faced with this weight of

274 • The John Adams Reader

history. I think that's a bigger problem than the instrument itself. There are all these monuments of pianistic culture. Beethoven, of course, but even in the twentieth century there have been so many great concertos. In our time as well: the twentieth century produced so many great concertos I think John has been careful about writing for piano. This was his first real big foray after a long time. He'd done *Phryian Gates* [back in the '70s]. This piece posed a really big challenge.

How did Adams solve that problem if he didn't just update Chopin Piano Concerto or write an anti-concerto?

He really did try, for me, to combine this idea of a big-scale thing (emotionally speaking) with putting it together out of the little things that he's used to doing. He's been going that way generally. *Harmonielehre* is in a way the same kind of piece. I love it: You have these big sweeps, but they're all put together like this [gestures with his hands], these little pieces of mosaic. If you were to identify his style, I think that combination is perhaps unique to him: that romantic sensibility combined with…not minimalism, that's such a loaded word by now, but this idea of little motifs that are repeated.

I was at a program once with *Century Rolls* and Bruckner's Sixth Symphony, and I thought that was really good programming. If anybody is a nineteenth-century "minimalist," it's Bruckner. Another inventive program was when the Cleveland Orchestra took it [the concerto] to New York—it was the Ives Fourth, intermission, then *Century Rolls* and *Ameriques* of Varèse. I thought that was fabulous.

Adams speaks of very concrete images that occurred to him as he was writing: for example, in the "Hale-Bop" movement, he had an image of the Road Runner being chased. Did you develop your personal images about the texture of the piece?

The third movement is probably the most overtly jazzy, but at the same time there are these sudden attacks. [Gestures and hums staccato passage] I have two images: one was of deconstruction. You get everything that came in the first movement that was filled in: now he's taking things out, and all you're left with are the accents. [hums again] There's a piece like that—if it's not too silly a comparison—by Berio, the *Sequenza* for Trombone. There's a place in it where the trombone is doing all kinds of gestures but only sounding certain notes. It's very theatrical and wonderful . Another image I think of is jabs to the nose in a boxing match. It's an exciting, thrilling movement. And, of course, I'm also very proud that I have a movement named after me ["Manny's Gym"]. John just said he hoped I'd be pleased by the name of the second movement, and I felt so honored. Now there are other people playing the piece, and they have to play "Manny's Gym"! It's a kind of *gymnopédie*. It's in three, but the tune is a little bit off, like a slow Erroll Garner tune. I used to have these Erroll Garner records where I'd listen to his amazing quality of being able to go off with his right hand and his left hand doing two different things and then meeting up six bars later perfectly in sync. There's something of that in the movement. It's very beautiful writing.

How has your interpretation changed in the decade since you've been playing Century Rolls?

I'm just more solid with it. It's a very complicated piece, so the more I play it, the more aware I am of everything going on around me. At first you're so focused on what you are doing that the stuff going on around you is almost a distraction. The more I get to know the piece, the more I can interact, play like a piece of chamber music: actually playing off the violins or flute. If we went on tour with this piece I think the orchestra would become almost like a combo, being able to connect with each other in the group. That's one of the great things about John's music. The more you work on it, the more rewards there are. You don't get bored with it. It's like connections in Brahms: it takes a long time to connect all these little things that are going on between people.

Dawn Upshaw on Singing in *El Niño*

Interview by Thomas May

The extraordinarily versatile soprano Dawn Upshaw is the best possible advocate for new music by virtue of her honest and deeply felt interpretations. Her role singing the solo soprano part in *El Niño* was an integral part of the work's reception. The following interview was conducted by Thomas May in March 2005.

How significant has John Adams's music been in your career?

Before my involvement with *El Niño*—which was a life-changing experience for me—it didn't play such a big role. Earlier I had done his arrangements of Ives songs [on the Nonesuch CD *American Elegies*], as well as Pat Nixon's aria from *Nixon in China* [on the Nonesuch CD *The World So Wide*]. But *El Niño* was the first project where I worked with John, and we had a fair amount of correspondence, especially the summer before the world premiere [in December 2000 in Paris]. Most of that concerned the big "Memorial" scene in Part II of *El Niño*.

What was the impetus behind the collaboration in El Niño *in the first place?*

I had, of course, worked previously with Peter Sellars quite a lot. So I knew from that experience what it meant to him to be involved in creating something with John. I could tell this new collaboration would be something powerful for me, since I share enough with Peter in terms of my outlook on life and the way that I work. But it went way beyond that for me. It was such a powerful experience that I now think of John and his music as playing an integral part of my musical life and growth. You live for moments like that.

It was a real epiphany for you as an artist?

It happened in the middle of a time when I was starting to stretch myself more. It's uncanny how well John understood what I might be able to do but hadn't attempted yet in performance. An example is the "Memorial de Tlatelolco" I just mentioned. There's a real fierce, angry quality to parts of it that I don't think people who know my voice easily associate with me. I wonder what John had been thinking of from my earlier work—perhaps *The Rake's Progress?*—to push me in this way. It surprised and even exhilarated me to see the possibilities John enabled here. It's incredibly demanding vocally but also emotionally. John wrote that in the music too—not just by way of the vocal line, but by the response in the orchestra and chorus so there could be a reciprocal response that feeds what I am doing. While I was working on *El Niño* I went nuts and listened to a lot of his music. At that time, I felt *El Niño* was taking a big step, especially in terms of vocal writing—it showed an even greater depth of understanding of the possibilities for the voice. *El Niño* is a real sacred experience for me: I was frequently moved to tears throughout the performances, not even necessarily knowing why. Not that it never happened to me before; but it happened more consistently with this piece than with any other.

Was there an unusual amount of collaboration with John Adams himself during the preparation process?

When you're looking at a new piece of music, you don't really know what you might be capable of. In the "Memorial," for instance, which makes tremendous demands of stamina, I remember telling John I needed a break about three-quarters of the way through. This is the point where there are oboe solos and the chorus sings while I'm resting. Eventually I join the oboe line for its final phrase. Originally John paired my line with the oboe's entire solo and I didn't have a break. Having John write for me specifically for the very first time in *El Niño* maybe made me a little more cautious in conveying this kind of concern to him. He was almost too cautious himself in responding. So he took those phrases out.

When we performed the work the second time around, I suddenly felt I was capable of the original phrasing and wanted to put those pieces back in—it felt natural, given the agony and crying of the character in the poem. I began to see that maybe there was even a necessity for [the way he had originally written the vocal part]. We discussed it, but John had gotten used to his change, so at least in that run I didn't end up going back to his original idea. I still think of bringing it up again.

How did the collaboration with Peter Sellars work? How does El Niño *represent the Sellars aesthetic?*

First, there's the personalization and working with specific individuals, pulling out of them something very intimate and personal. I can understand Peter's excitement and interest in such personal stories that are expressed in the different texts used in *El Niño.* The different voices that we hear from are typical of Peter's way of thinking. There have been responses that criticize, for example, his use of video montage. Some of my friends and colleagues had mixed reactions to that aspect of the production. But Peter has a greater perception of what's going on around him than just about anyone I know: he's an artist who tries to make us see what is already there.

There's also the issue of form. I don't feel it's an opera, but there is more of a story line from beginning to end—a connection from one movement to next that I feel is more dramatic than "oratorio" suggests. The form leads to a certain kind of physicality of expression and gestures. Peter's world uses this physicality onstage in a way that seems to speak very purely and honestly, as in the early music I've done with him: the [staged] Bach Cantatas, for instance, and Handel's *Theodora. El Niño* seems to have more in common with those collaborations than with some of the more contemporary operatic things I've done with Peter, such as *The Rake's Progress* or Kaija Saariaho's *L'amour de loin*. To me, Peter connects *El Niño* to this earlier world in the way he chooses to orchestrate us physically.

Do you sense anything unique in how John Adams sets these texts?

I think it's very natural. Look at the *Magnificat*—besides being beautiful and exhilarating, it is set so well. Where there is stress or a word that he wants to highlight, it's very clear by way of rhythm or range and pitch—he shapes things so clearly. The *Magnificat* involves huge leaps, and I found singing it one of the most gratifying things I've ever done. With those big leaps, I feel as though I'm using every part of my being. It's much better than stretching! You dig down deep at the bottom of these intervals and then reach up to the heights. And therefore it expresses the ecstasy of joy almost as in a sport where you give it your complete all. When I finished a performance, I'd be totally exhausted but totally exhilarated.

You almost become unconscious of the challenges involved. How does El Niño *compare with other challenges from your extensive experience in contemporary music?*

What I love about the work is how it's all spread out for me. The *Magnificat* is the first big piece, and then come all the intimate parts with the countertenors and mezzo. All of that is interspersed with the "Christmas Star" to end the first part. [Singing this] always made me feel like I would almost lose my breath because of the amazement of the moment. The whole thing meanwhile is also building up to the "Memorial." It's hard work, but by the end of the evening I felt spent only in the sense of knowing I had used all of myself. The technical difficulties are interwoven with the emotional ones—that's the sign of a masterpiece.

From your perspective, what did audiences gain from those first encounters with El Niño?

Peter talked about this being similar to one of those amazing altarpieces where you flip open one door and there is suddenly a whole new world and, for a moment, you lose sight of what was on the back side of that door. I think that when we are confronted with something new that is being said to us in a language that we're not quite familiar with yet—musical or visual—it takes some time for us to see certain things to be able to absorb them. I recall a strength of response from those original audiences which showed that people were changed in some way by what they heard and saw.

Did you feel any similarities to the experience you've had working with the music of Osvaldo Golijov, whose Pasión según San Marco *has been compared in terms of its spiritual concerns—or other contemporary composers for that matter?*

I feel so lucky to be working on pieces with composers who have found true, honest voices within themselves—that truth is what every creative artist is looking for. What ties these artists together is knowing who they are and what they have to offer all of us—they're going on journeys, too, and their music is always changing. Of course, what's fascinating, too, are the differences. I hear John's music as something very large-scale that is slowly unfolding, slowly shedding light on certain things around me. It's a totally different experience from other people's music for me. This is music with immensity and power, music that is very sure of itself in most ways. That's not to say there isn't vulnerability—for example, the duet "Se Habla de Gabriel" with the mezzo can be quite vulnerable. But it's a kind of music that is very sure-footed.

PART FOUR

Critical Reception

Early Works

Edward Rothstein
The New Republic, December 2, 1985

"MEISTER ECKHARDT AND QUACKIE" is the rather whimsical title John Adams gives to the last movement of his newest composition—*Harmonielehre*—which I heard at the Contemporary Music Festival at Tanglewood last summer and which has just been released on a Nonesuch recording (9 79115-1 F). "Quackie" is Mr. Adams's baby daughter; Meister Eckhardt the renowned medieval mystic; and Mr. Adams the newest sensation on the contemporary music scene. Five recordings of his music have been released in the last year—possibly a unique achievement for a living composer. He has been in residence at the San Francisco Symphony; his music is widely performed, widely cheered. And his vision? Well, the composer's explanatory note to this movement is revealing: "Quackie, who is still too young to walk, rides upon Meister Eckhardt's shoulders as they glide among the heavenly bodies. Quackie whispers the secret of grace into Meister Eckhardt's ear."

Musically, it turns out, the secret of grace is a syrupy melody played by the strings while winds and percussion repetitively tinkle in a tireless patter as if illustrating innocence with images of bewinged fairies. The vision of "heavenly bodies" glides to a percussive climax, full of fortissimo blasts, beating of drums, and vulgar brass exclamations—as mannered and tonal and familiar as the rest of the work. At Tanglewood, the audience was on its feet, ecstatic at the music's winning fantasy. But even if this music could give an authentic thrill, what had *Harmonielehre* to do with Eckhardt? Or with Schoenberg's masterful text on harmony? Very little. Eckhardt is mentioned just for the mystical connection, and as for Schoenberg: "I'm not trying to teach anyone harmony," the composer said in the program notes. "This is the culmination—so far—of my teaching myself about harmony."

But harmony is much beside the point. Mr. Adams, now thirty-eight years old, has an M.A. from Harvard. His musical interests, soon after graduation, turned to minimalism, that contemporary style which has less to do with harmony than with repetition and variation of simple rhythmic and melodic patterns. Unlike Steve Reich, with whom his music is often associated, Mr. Adams's ambition seems to have been to combine the Eastern meditative attentiveness apparently demanded by minimalist music with the Western European notions of drama and narrative. The result has been seen by some as indicating the future of minimalism: out of its roots in the 1960s counterculture, out of a fascination with pattern and meditation and ecstatic contemplation, would supposedly come works that would merge—dialectically, so to speak—with the great nineteenth-century tradition of high art.

Instead, Mr. Adams's unique combination of bad taste and bad faith has undermined both traditions. What he has succeeded in doing, curiously enough, is to at least temporarily unite their audiences. Contemporary music has generally not found a way into the hearts of listeners devoted to the nineteenth century. Minimalist music has found an audience, but it is, as has been made clear again and again, an audience whose aesthetic roots are in the 1960s. John Adams's sole accomplishment is to join the minimalist audience with the mainstream, offering condescendingly accessible works that speak to both.

Eagerness for just such a reunion of audiences must lie behind the exaggerated acclaim that has welcomed Mr. Adams, for there are few other ways to account for it. *Shaker Loops* (1978)—recorded in its orchestral version by Edo de Waart leading the San Francisco Symphony (Philips 412214-1)—is meant, for example, to be a punning invocation of both the devotion of the Shakers and the shaking of trills, the loops of taped repetitions and the loops of return to origins. Its traditionally minimalist repetitions are mixed with almost treacly harmonic gestures. It can even seem parodistic; the interest is not in subtle shifts of phase, as in Mr. Reich's music, or in insistent lyricism, as in Philip Glass's work, but in invocations of various musical manners—romantic melody, oriental devotion, Mahleresque climax. What is aimed for here is Effect, and all stops are pulled to get it; what is achieved is so unprincipled that the result can seem, despite his intentions, a form of aesthetic nihilism. But *Grand Pianola Music* (1982)—recorded by Ransom Wilson conducting Solisti New York (EMI/Angel DS-37345)—is apparently meant to be that meaningless. There are two pianos playing slightly out of phase to give a hint of pianola sound. There is wind music Nelson Riddle might have used, singers chanting "Nah, Nah, Nah," piano patter up and down the keyboards, and a final movement that, far from being humorous, becomes grotesque—a tonal "romantic" melody breaking through the patter like a kitschy anthem, all in the cause of great applause.

It would be tempting, given the mixture of parody and serious-ness, of kitsch and sentiment, to call this music a variety of post-modern camp, but that would be giving it too clear an intention. Mr. Adams is very sincere. How else account for the pious endless patter of *Light Over Water* (1983) (New Albion 005), a *Symphony for Brass and Synthesizers*, originally written as accompaniment for Lucinda Childs's choreography? And in *Harmonium* (1981)—recorded on ECM 25012-1—Mr. Adams goes so far as to set po-ems by John Donne and Emily Dickinson, which indicate, like his other programmatic intentions, hardly a moment's thought be-yond the most elementary. The Donne poem, *Negative Love*, is ex-quisitely paradoxical, an attempt to define something by its inverse image; the setting ploddingly moves from climax to cli-max, the text unaffected and unilluminated by the minimal ges-tures. Similarly, the climactic cymbal crash in the first movement of *Harmonielehre* suggests more a coming scream and fall of a body, à la Hitchcock, than the resolution of a musical drama concisely and appropriately worked out; it is effect, pure and simple, ineffective without context.

Mr. Adams is not without talent. It can be heard in those quiet, meditative, atmospheric moments that appear, here and there, even in his latest opus, when all drive for drama has ceased and the composer is content; no bad ideas are heard, because no ideas are heard. But elsewhere the music monotonously repeats the same pattern, one that would not be inappropriately called the "choo-choo" gesture: it imitates the approach of a rather large freight train over the tracks, building to a weighty climax of rumbling cars and finally receding in the distance, leaving some relief in its wake. A roller coaster might also be an appropriate image. Mr. Adams is the Steven Spielberg of minimalism. One wonders what he will do with his next project, a full-length opera called *Nixon in China*.

I think, though, that Mr. Adams is important far beyond his achievements: he marks, in a peculiar way, the end of minimalism. That musical style has served its function and its audience. Not without its felicitous achievements, it has given the fundamentally anti-intellectual counterculture a system for "serious" music; it has refocused attention on music as a creator of a "state of consciousness" in the listener; it has made simple demands on the listener and repaid him with simple pleasures. Philip Glass's *Satyagraha* and Steve Reich's early works were its apotheoses. Mr. Adams marks its demise.

What Mr. Adams has done is to use minimalism as just a tool in his grab bag of clichés, a cover for an absence of thought, a gesture toward the avant-garde in music that is fundamentally directionless. The minimal style hasn't even enough power to stay vital, scarcely a generation after it came into being. It started with Terry Riley, Mr. Reich, and Mr. Glass, attending to the realm of the spirit; it ends with Mr. Adams's Quackie alternately whispering and shouting presumed revelations into our ears.

Mischief (*Grand Pianola Music*)

Alan Rich
LA Weekly, July 30, 2004

IN THE MATTER OF TOGETHERNESS programmed in Heaven, try this for a night at the Hollywood Bowl: Beethoven's "Emperor" Concerto, with its roistering, rolling E-flat piano arpeggios before intermission; John Adams's *Grand Pianola Music,* with its roistering, rolling E-flat piano arpeggios after.

The Beethoven, soberly but accurately played by Andreas Hae-fliger, with Ilan Volkov conducting the Philharmonic, drew a fair ovation from the paltry (5,500 out of 18,000) crowd. The Adams, with Gloria Cheng and Joanne Pearce Martin at the two pianos, drew the expected pitter-patter of applause with a few half-hearted boos. My memories of previous hearings of that work include a roof-raising chorus of cheers at the world premiere (San Francisco, 1982) and an equal volume of boos (New York, a year later). Maybe the warm summer air dampened reaction this time.

Those earlier outpourings—San Francisco pride of ownership versus New York xenophobia—were easily understood twnty years ago. The lingering hostility, considering the heights that Adams's music has attained since then, is more troubling today. Adams created his *Grand Pianola Music*—mischievously, he has stated—as a respite, even a lark, after the ferocious self-declaration of *Harmonium,* his astounding choral work commissioned by the San Francisco Symphony and still refulgent in the repertory. *Pianola* rattles on, at some length to be sure but congenially, with nothing more on its mind than a quest to reach E-flat. It arrives via a constant nibbling and ultimately lands with a gigantic, Beethovenian *whoosh*—worthy not of the "Emperor" Concerto perhaps, but at least of some upper-echelon bad piece like, say, the 'Triple" Concerto.

Adams has gone further, in directions not easy to predict at the time of the *Pianola* premiere, yet you can't just dismiss this as an apprentice work. The exuberance that carries it forward to that climactic cataract remains inbred in his musical language. Works of even longer duration and even more discursive content—the *Naive and Sentimental Music*, for one—rely on just that fund of ferocity to carry an audience around the bends and the upgrades. Years after *Pianola*, when *Nixon in China* had established Adams's predominance among practitioners of his time, he said of the earlier work that "it's the most thorough piece about who I am musically. It has a real streak of vulgarity about it, full of the vernacular of the American musical experience." With a name like John Adams, what else would you expect?

My neighbors in the next box at the Bowl, whom I've gotten to know over the years in all but name—they give me cookies and stuff—loved all the E-flat adventures in the "Emperor" Concerto, but were reduced to groans and moans as soon as Adams's equally pretty music began. "Oh, my God," said the woman next to me, as trombone and tuba propounded a long-held dominant seventh chord, perhaps a little more insistently scored than it would have been in Beethoven, but the same chord nevertheless. Fear stalks the land, and a name out of the new-music galaxy—Adams, Cage, perhaps even Salonen—can strike terror. There's still work to be done.

Nixon in China

Edward Rothstein
The New Republic, January 4, 1988

THE TWISTS AND TURNS of the contemporary musical "avant-garde" will someday require a chronicler all their own, but I am sure that the opera *Nixon in China*—which opened at the Houston Grand Opera, played at the Brooklyn Academy of Music (where I saw it), and will now proceed to the Kennedy Center, the Netherlands Opera, and the Los Angeles Music Center Opera—will deserve a separate chapter. As these hosts and sponsors, past and future, attest, the "avant-garde" is now big business, and so deserves mention only in quotation marks. The contemporary avant-gardist need not fight the mainstream: he need only claim to.

Nixon in China has all the credentials needed to certify centrality. It was conceived and directed by Peter Sellars, composed by John Adams, conducted by Edo de Waart with a libretto by Alice Goodman, choreographed by Mark Morris. I expected Adams's music to be a calculated mixture of kitsch and facile allusion. I expected Sellars's direction to swerve between hauntingly brilliant and quixotically willful. I expected the opera as a whole to be an extension of the minimalist operatic style and countercultural imagery pioneered by Philip Glass and Robert Wilson. I expected all this—and was surprised. For *Nixon in China* isn't even coherent enough to arouse such mixed reactions.

And if this much-hyped, much-prepped, much-attended work so thwarted even a skeptic's expectations, something quite unusual must be taking place. How could the intermission crowds be stifling yawns (and they were when I went) when this was an opera that promised everything—not only the avant-garde in music and theater, but the avant-garde in politics too, dramatic figures of mythic importance: Richard Nixon and Mao Zedong? This was a work that, in Sellars's original conception, was to be a recounting of the former president's trip to China in February 1972. It was to turn that event into a primal meeting of cultures. Its six scenes recount the landing of the Nixons in Beijing, the meeting with Mao, the first banquet in the Great Hall of the People, a tour Mrs. Nixon takes to a pig farm and a glass factory, a performance of Mme Mao's ballet at the Beijing opera, and a last introspective night in Beijing.

If Glass's *Satyagraha* was a heroic opera about Gandhi, in which each scene about his life had a counterpart in the 1960s counterculture, *Nixon in China* apparently was to be a sort of sequel, the meeting of the counterculture's demonic villains (Richard Nixon and Henry Kissinger) with some of its heroes (Mao and Chou Enlai and the Chinese people). The minimalist music of Adams—more vulgar and more pompous than anything Glass has written—would presumably be used to heighten the contrasts between East and West, to show how, if in *Satyagraha* the East could be an inspiration to the West, here the East could at the very least outclass the West.

To a certain extent, the opera follows this map quite precisely. Henry Kissinger is sung by Thomas Hammons, his bespectacled head tilted forward, his chins pressed against his chest, looking like a college professor turned derelict—a buffoonish villain. During the final introspective scene in which the characters dream of their hopeful pasts, his only role is to go to the bathroom. Kissinger also boasts to Mao of assigning the chairman's books at Harvard, and seems altogether less swift than Nixon; his music is bumptious, vulgar, intemperate. Finally, during the opera's fantastical ballet when the visiting Americans are shown Mme Mao's agitprop work, *The Red Detachment of Women*, Kissinger appears as a character in the ballet—a villainous overlord, leering and leching, whip in hand, pressing his body against a bound, innocent peasant, singing: "When the first cut!—Come on you slut!—/Scored her brown skin/I started in,/Man upon hen!"

Nixon—finely sung by James Maddalena—seems to have a bit of the buffoonish villain about him as well. When his plane is shown landing outside Beijing, the music becomes positively heroic, bombastic, as fakely grand as only Adams could make it. Nixon walking out of the plane received guffaws from the audience just for the tilt of his head and the wave of his hand. He is obviously a fool abroad—and at sea too, when meeting Mao, whose book-lined shelves and gnomic comments are supported by the cool, imitative melodies of three secretaries (known informally during rehearsals as the Maoettes). In case anyone misses the point, Adams gives Nixon a sort of self-important stuttering musical style, when not being overtly nostalgic (touched with musical hints of Glenn Miller).

These may sound like the ingredients for a strident, satiric polemic—a revival and celebration of the political lusts of the counterculture. But there were other ambitions at work. At least one was expressed by the librettist, Goodman, who insisted that the opera be a "heroic" opera, not a satire; the text was written in near-rhyming couplets. The idea may have been to append to these political figurines some deeper nuance and complication, the grandeur of this meeting of cultures.

But the execution of such high ambition was also fraught with complication if not contradiction. With poetic grandeur, Nixon calls himself "An old cold warrior/Piloting towards an unknown shore/Through shoals"—a proud vision undercut as he undresses, giving his clothes to Pat, who is standing dutifully nearby. Pat herself (sung by Carolann Page) begins a scene in cutesy sentiment ("I treat each day/Like Christmas"), just as she is about to be portrayed as a sensitive observer of Chinese culture. But the most telling ambiguities occur later in the opera, when it is clear that there really is no dramatic structure to the work at all, so uncertain is it about its subject and its purpose.

For in the phantasmagorical ballet scene, in which Kissinger demonically appears as representative of the Evil the Communists overturned, Pat Nixon runs onstage, later assisted by Dick himself, to help the poor victims of his oppression. And then, after the opera dutifully shows the victory of the revolution and the People's Army, Mme Mao (Trudy Ellen Craney) herself holds aloft the Little Red Book and passionately sings as the dancers turn violent, bashing each other's heads in the name of the Cultural Revolution.

What is happening here? What are we to make of her hysterical shrieking about "the book," the brutality of the Cultural Revolution, the villainy of Henry K., the intercession of Pat, and then, in the final scene of the opera, the two couples—Mao and Madame, Dick and Pat—each engaged in sentimental reminiscence and embrace? It is as if the opera's principal creators had decided against a political cartoon but then had no idea of where to go, and so resorted to touching on every possible permutation of interpretation without ever settling on any. Nothing depends on, or grows out of, anything else.

Some explanation of all this is found in Goodman's program notes, which muse about the characters' disillusion and motivation in this "heroic opera"; each character, she asserts, is meant to be as "eloquent as possible." Thus, Nixon is occasionally fleshed out with human longing and nostalgia, American innocence and thrust; Mao takes on some earthly shadows as he speaks his knowing ironies. (Even Kissinger, I assume the thinking goes, must be somewhat human; he has to use a toilet.) I am not sure where Goodman would have gone with this material on her own, but I am sure that what is left is much less than eloquent. There is evidence of many hands at work in this opera, each fussing with the work of the other—opera by committee. Goodman hardly keeps it a secret:

> There are places where the music goes against the grain of the libretto, and places where the staging goes against the grain of both. My Nixon is not quite the same character as John Adams's Nixon, and they both differ slightly from Peter Sellars's Nixon, not to mention James Maddalena's. My view

of the Cultural Revolution is not the same as theirs, and theirs are not the same.

She calls the collaboration "polyphonic," but the result is more polymorphously perverse. Anything goes, characters shift under our eyes, the heroes turn villainous, the villains turn sentimental, and all the issues of revolution and reformation, of ideals and power, are discarded with postmodernist distaste for distinction. It's a Chinese brunch, all courses offered.

By the end, the Nixons become somewhat sympathetic characters (a shock for anyone who wants the comfort of cartoons) and the Chinese somewhat confused by the forces of history. But this is just another perspective thrown in, not a dramatic resolution or revelation. The opera depends on lyrical talk during the long last scene, as if it has lost the will to dramatize what it is saying; it can't take the dissolution of its own cliches seriously enough. That would undercut the very notion of doing an opera that appealed to the "avant-garde."

By contrast, Kissinger, in the first volume of his memoirs, actually presents a portrait of Mao that could well be the focus of a contemporary *Boris Godunov*. He was a man who summoned his guests suddenly and without warning, and lived as mysteriously as the emperors he disdained. He projected such "raw, concentrated will-power" that Kissinger is as awed by this "colossus" (a word used without irony), "that great, demonic, prescient, overwhelming personality," as by Mao's lucid, elliptical conversation. "It was as if one were dealing with a figure from another world who occasionally lifted a corner of the shroud that veils the future, permitting a glimpse but never the entire vision that he alone has seen." One sentence Kissinger hears makes its way into the opera's libretto in altered form. Nixon said that the chairman's writings "moved a nation and have changed the world," and Mao replied, "I have not been able to change it. I have only been able to change a few places in the vicinity of Beijing."

This declaration, treated in offhand fashion in the opera, is taken by Kissinger as central: the modest claim of a man whose life had been devoted to overturning the entire structure of his society. "In its matter-of-fact resignation it underlined the revolutionary dilemma." For what began in revolution congealed into regimentation, a "fate that so cruelly mocked the suffering and meaning of a lifetime of struggle." Hence, Kissinger writes, came the cycles of frenzied campaigns to continue the revolution, destroying the country, killing millions, overturning institutions, purging the Party—tragic cycles, which, Kissinger hints, no one understood better than the chairman himself.

The Kissinger who wrote in this way was no mere overlord or dissolute professor; the Mao he describes hardly resembles the man who appears through the haze of confusion and contradiction in this dull, dissipated opera. To have taken such a perspective into account would have meant discarding the received political and aesthetic worlds, and attempting a work that was not postmodern but tragic, not "avant-garde" but avant-garde.

Nixon in China

Tim Page
Newsday, March 28, 1988

RICHARD M. NIXON, the thirty-seventh president of the United States and the first to resign the position, returned to Washington Saturday night, transmogrified into myth.

Nixon in China, an opera by John Adams and Alice Goodman, was commissioned by the Houston Grand Opera, the Brooklyn Academy of Music, and the John F. Kennedy Center for the Performing Arts. Houston presented the premiere last October, and then *Nixon* ran in Brooklyn for a week or two last December. Finally, Saturday night, the opera came to Washington, where it will play through April 3.

And so *Nixon* is suddenly the hottest ticket in town. The Saturday night performance was sold out, and the roster of dignitaries in the audience was said to include some dozen congressmen, three senators, and Justice Sandra Day O'Connor, as well as several journalists who accompanied Nixon on his visit to China in 1972.

The reviews of *Nixon in China* have generally been mixed, and this one will be no exception. But there was an obvious extra-operatic interest to the Saturday night performance. For the presenter was not a Sun Belt organization like the Houston Grand Opera, distinguished but provincial, nor an off-the- beaten-track sanctuary for the avant-garde like the Brooklyn Academy of Music. This was the Kennedy Center—the citadel of official culture in our nation's capital, a vast marble edifice that (in one of the evening's many ironies) stands right next door to the Watergate complex.

But the opera is about "Nixon in China," not "All The President's Men," and it contains no prefiguration of the scandal that would eventually drive Nixon from the White House. Its subject is the Nixon/Kissinger visit to China in 1972 that ultimately led to full diplomatic ties between countries which had hitherto been implacable enemies.

Nixon in China is, for the most part, a generous, enthusiastic celebration of what John Reed might have called "Six Days That Changed the World," at its best in depiction of formal ceremonies, and at its worst in the pseudo-philosophizing that informs some of the soliloquies. There is a bright, crackling energy to the entire first act, which depicts the American arrival in China (a stylized pasteboard airplane drops from the sky) and the initial toasts between wary but eager former combatants.

Act II is markedly less successful. If there was a triumph in China, victory belonged to Henry Kissinger, as well as to Nixon. To treat the president evenhandedly and then transform the secretary of state into a venal, jibbering, opportunistic buffoon is to lower the level of discourse considerably.

There have been some changes since the New York production. What was once an extremely long second act has been bisected, so that there is a welcome intermission before the meditative finale, now Act III. James Maddalena, who doesn't really look all that much like Nixon yet evokes his presence with uncanny acuity, has softened his characterization somewhat, making the president more sympathetic than he seemed in New York. The Peter Sellars production remains innovative and often beautiful, much more successful than his revisionist versions of standard masterpieces. The cast also included Trudy Ellen Craney, Sanford Sylvan, John Duykers, Carolann Page, and Thomas Hammons, all uniformly excellent. John DeMain's conducting was skilled and purposeful.

After the opera, we adjourned to the Kennedy Center Terrace. Several journalists who accompanied Nixon to China were there, wearing red roses in their lapels as a mark of honor.

How well did *Nixon in China* reflect the events of 1972? "Well, the plane was the same," Mel Elfin, then a bureau chief for *Newsweek*, now the editor, special reports, of *U.S. News & World Report*, said. "And I think the lead dancer in the ballet might have done a couple of steps that were similar to the dance we saw in China. And Mao's red book was the same." Did he like the opera? "It was, uh, 'interesting,' as they say."

Tom Jarriel, a correspondent for ABC News, was more enthusiastic. "I thought it was terrific musical theater, in the same way the visit was terrific political theater," he said. "It brought it all back."

And the central figure? Richard Nixon has not seen the opera, nor has there been any indication that he ever will. But it will be televised shortly, and a new compact disc recording is due soon from Nonesuch, so it is not inconceivable that Nixon may privately watch and perhaps enjoy this flawed, engaging, poetic recreation of one of his finest moments.

THE *KLINGHOFFER* CONTROVERSY

The following seven selections are concerned with a work that has beyond question generated the most intense series of controversies within John Adams's career. His second opera, *The Death of Klinghoffer*, caused outrage from the moment of its premiere in 1991. Its dramatization of an actual terrorist incident from 1985 touched political and emotional nerves to such an extent that discussion of the opera's artistic significance was eclipsed. Indeed, the cancellation of several planned productions imposed a de facto censorship. Following 9/11, the debate around *The Death of Klinghoffer* renewed in intensity when the Boston Symphony decided not to perform choruses from the opera that had been scheduled for a concert program. A series of op-ed pieces brought John Adams's name before a public that normally doesn't listen to contemporary classical music. The critical reception of *The Death of Klinghoffer* has, as a result, been remarkably polarized.

These selections survey the entire spectrum of the controversy. Bernd Feuchtner's "The *Klinghoffer* Debate" summarizes the issues perceived to be at stake and considers each phase of the opera's reception. John Rockwell's review of the world premiere in Brussells reports on the European perspective; Edward Rothstein lambasts the work on the occasion of its American premiere. The pieces by Mark Swed and Alex Ross reflect on the significance of the Boston Symphony's *Klinghoffer* cancellation in the wake of 9/11. In that context, Richard Taruskin framed the debate with a widely circulated denunciation of the opera in a Sunday *New York Times* Arts and Leisure article, "Music's Dangers and the Case for Control." Taking the *Klinghoffer* case as a starting point, Taruskin considers the larger significance of the impulse to censorship. Finally, Alan Rich writes about Peggy Woolcock's film version of *The Death of Klinghoffer*.

The *Klinghoffer* Debate

Bernd Feuchtner

This essay is a slightly abridged version of an article originally published in German in *Opernwelt Jahrbuch 2004*; translated by Thomas May.

WE'RE ACCUSTOMED TO SEEING HEATED DEBATE about how an opera is staged—but how often does it really happen nowadays that the debate centers around a particular opera by itself? John Adams's *The Death of Klinghoffer* presents a rare case. If the European world premiere in 1991 was relatively inconspicuous, the verdict in the United States quickly centered on a single issue: Is this an anti-Semitic opera? As a result, the work was hardly produced at all in America. The events of September 11 reheated the debate, since performances related to the work were canceled in the aftermath, while the composer protested against this reaction. The *New York Times* published a major article by a renowned musicologist essentially recommending a ban on the opera. On that fateful September day, Adams himself was preparing the sound track for the film version of his opera by Penny Woolcock. Subsequently shown at film festivals and on various TV channels, the film led to further outcry. But instead of becoming recognized as *the* opera of our time, *Klinghoffer* remains superficially known by the headline "terrorist opera." That is the issue around which the entire debate has become focused in the United States.

Beauty Tells the Truth: America in Search of Cultural Self-Understanding

At the end of the first act of his opera *The Death of Klinghoffer*, Adams made a note: "11 December 1990." Five years had passed since the hijacking of the *Achille Lauro* by Palestinian terrorists and the murder of its wheelchair-bound passenger Leon Klinghoffer. The first scene of Act II was completed by New Year's. But in the second scene, in the middle of Marilyn Klinghoffer's dialogue (she doesn't yet know that her husband has been shot), another real-life event caused Adams to record yet another date with the words "the sufferers": "16 January 1991, 4 a.m., War..." When the composer finished his score on February 12, 1991, the Gulf War was in full swing and the United States was heading into an adventure, the dimensions of which it did not yet fathom. And by the world premiere on March 29 in Brussels, the war was over, having just ended the week before. It's hard to think of another opera that's so completely enmeshed in actual politics as *The Death of Klinghoffer*.

Politics also quickly caught up with the opera. After the premiere, Manuela Hoelterhoff suggested in the *Wall Street Journal* that the opera transformed the senseless murder of a disabled elderly Jew in a wheelchair into a cold meditation about meaning and myth, life and death—and all this "without a penny of subsidy from the PLO." In her opinion the entire incident was just "a further example of the blind brutalizing rage of Muslim roughhands." She called director Peter Sellars's preface in the program book both morally disgusting and culturally pretentious. Following the American premiere at the Brooklyn Academy of Music, Edward Rothstein wrote in the *New York Times* that the opera assumes Jews and Palestinians are in equal measure the victims of a mutual hatred. He accused the opera of being "morally tawdry." Yet others accused the creators of Zionism. The result was that the opera's co-producers, Los Angeles Opera and the Glyndebourne Festival, refused to stage it. Performances in San Francisco were picketed by Jewish protesters, while many American opera houses didn't dare to undertake a production. The piece was forgotten. Yet the wake of September 11 made it clear that, a full decade later, the wound was still fresh.

The Boston Cancellation: Classical Music Should Console

In November 2001, the Boston Symphony Orchestra canceled performances of the *Klinghoffer* choruses scheduled for a concert program. Several chorus members were said to have difficulties with the "Chorus of the Exiled Palestinians." It was proposed that Adams's *Harmonium* be performed instead. The composer refused, saying he had no problem with the cancellation in itself (he had also accepted the cancellation of a London performance of *Short Ride in a Fast Machine* after Lady Diana's death in a car accident). But to go along with substituting *Harmonium*, Adams felt, would indicate agreement with the prejudices in circulation about his opera. For Adams, this was a serious, humane work that did not advocate rage and violence but rather compassion and understanding. He was thus especially indignant at the reason Boston gave him: "Moments like these remind us of the consolation that classical music can provide." "*Klinghoffer* certainly belongs to a riskier category," Adams wrote back. "This makes it all the clearer to me once again how all the fuss over 'great music' imposes the status of museum culture on classical music." Concerts, in his opinion, should instead pose at least as great a challenge as the Museum of Contemporary Art or *Angels in America*. He couldn't understand how one could consider the music lovers of Boston so timid that they would be unable to bear these choruses.

The major newspapers supported the composer in detailed articles. Anthony Tommasini quoted John Kerry in the *New York Times*, who a few days after September 11 had said: "The American people have not really tried to understand why so many Muslims hate us"—and that this is exactly what John Adams and his co-creators were trying to do. In the *New Yorker* Alex Ross scoffed at how the Boston Symphony replaced the *Klinghoffer* choruses with Copland's First Symphony. Mark Swed, writing in the *Los Angeles Times*, also suggested that Copland's First is anything but a harmless work. He reminded us of how a contemporary critic had compared its "squalling" scherzo to the shrieks of "a bewildered banshee which by some twist of locale has found itself at the Wailing Wall."

In fact, in October Swed had written a longer article describing how he had listened to his copy of the *Klinghoffer* CD the day after the September 11 attacks. The basis for the opera, he observed, was a history that had been playing out since 1985. Swed declared, "*Klinghoffer* is exactly the work of art we now need" and concluded his article with a challenge to Los Angeles to perform the opera. But a few days later an article that changed everything was published.

Richard Taruskin: It's Time to Learn from the Taliban
On December 9, 2001, the highly influential Arts and Leisure weekend section of the *New York Times* published a lengthy article titled "Music's Dangers and the Case for Control." Accompanying the article was a woodcut illustration of an ancient musician with his fingers nailed to his flute. That was precisely the intention of the author Richard Taruskin, a renowned music scholar: to impose a ban of silence on *The Death of Klinghoffer*. (As a professor at the University of California in Berkeley, he is, so to speak, a neighbor of the composer.)

The Death of Klinghoffer ("the notoriously controversial opera"), in Taruskin's view, both stages the murder of an American Jew by Palestinian terrorists and interprets this re-enactment. Taruskin reviews and passes judgment on the journalists who had supported the opera. He then returns to his chief claim: "If terrorism…is to be defeated, world public opinion has to be turned decisively against it."

He believes that the authors had themselves implicitly revealed such a romanticizing attitude in light of the fact that they deleted the middle scene of the prologue "for American consumption" (here he incidentally mistakes Paris for Lyon as the city where the second European premiere was given, a slip curiously out of keeping for such a meticulous writer). This is the scene in which suburban neighbors gossip about the Klinghoffers' upcoming cruise to the accompaniment of stale pop music. This portrait of materialistic American Jews, with its allegedly trivializing music, is thus contrasted with the mythically elevated Palestinians. (In fact, the creators excised this theatrical scene because it interrupted the two choruses and they wanted to bring the work closer in character to an oratorio).

Taruskin believes that the original version was meant to cater to the favorite prejudices of the Europeans: anti-American, anti-Semitic, anti-bourgeois. Moreover, he claims, such prejudices were hardly removed from the revised version, as is clear from the music itself.

Taruskin advocates control over such a work—but to avoid emulating the Taliban, it should, above all, be a matter of self-control. The Boston Symphony did so in an exemplary way, Taruskin says. Taruskins concludes: "Censorship is always deplorable, but the exercise of forbearance can be noble."

A "Witch Hunt" and a Bit of Background

A stunned Adams remarked: "It makes the row over Robert Mapplethorpe's pictures look like a little divertissement. Not long ago our attorney general, John Ashcroft, said that anyone who questioned his policies on civil rights after September 11 was aiding terrorists; what Taruskin said was the aesthetic version of that. If there is an aesthetic viewpoint that does not agree with his, it should not be heard. I find that very disturbing indeed." Regarding the Boston cancellation that had served as the occasion for Taruskin's article, Adams had begun to believe that it had been "an overblown affair, and possibly one I contributed to."

Gregory Freidin, a professor of Slavics at Stanford University who is familiar from personal experience with the era of Stalin, Khrushchev, and Brezhnev (he also translated the memoirs of Kruschev into English), responded to Taruskin's article with a letter to the editor that the *New York Times* did not print. He expressed shock that Taruskin was positioning himself in a lineage with Plato, Goebbels, Tolstoy, Stalin, and the Taliban when it's a matter of telling artists that they are not free. The great history of Western art tells us precisely the opposite—that the task of artists is to examine their contemporaries' belief systems and to subject them to self-examination and critical thinking. For no other calling (neither science nor politics) is allowed a similar degree of independence: "This is the essential task of art in our civilization." Freidin shares this idea with Kant, who described art as the free play of the cognitive abilities, free from all dependency on inherited values.

"Where would our Western culture be without art?" September 11, too, should remind us of this free play of cognitive abilities: "In the free world listeners do not need to be protected by latter-day Platonists, whether bureaucrats or academics. It suffices that they can boo music of Debussy or Diagilev's Ballets Russes and that they feel free to do it again and again."

The journalist Martin Kettle published an article titled "The Witch Hunt" in the *Guardian* on December 15. At the beginning he quotes the famous phrase of Talleyrand that "treason is all a question of dates." He compares the situation of the composer with that of the artist in the McCarthy era and finds it paradoxical that the figure judged to be "the most American of our composers" should be perceived as anti-American. Indeed, the music of John Adams had changed in recent years. If pieces such as 1985's *Harmonielehre*, with its strong reference to Schoenberg's manual of the same name and Mahler's Tenth Symphony, had a European touch, he was turning increasingly to American sources. He himself had declared in an interview in 1995 that he was just going through a strongly American phase.

But it seemed that *Klinghoffer* was finished, once and for all, as far as America was concerned.

John Adams and September 11

But how did John Adams himself experience September 11, 2001? At the time he was in London rehearsing with the London Symphony Orchestra for the sound track to a BBC film of *The Death of Klinghoffer*, the first British production. An Adams Festival had been planned for that winter at the Barbican Center, where Leonard Slatkin was scheduled to conduct *Klinghoffer*. At the time they were working on the scene in which Marilyn Klinghoffer thinks that the hijacking has ended without violence and that her husband is being taken care of in the sick bay. She learns instead that he had been murdered and reacts with an aria that expresses first her shock and then her anger, only to culminate in complete hopelessness and desolation. During a break Adams went to the lobby telephone, where he saw a group of people bunched up in front of a TV screen. He saw the images of the jets crashing into the towers and thought that under these conditions there was no way to go on with the recording. "But the opposite happened. Whole sections—the soloists, the chorus, the orchestra—seemed to live through an existential experience. When we played through the sound track in Abbey Road, I read the corresponding text of Alice Goodman to the chorus and orchestra before each scene. Her smart and insightful words corresponded exactly to the mood of everyone, and I have to admit that everyone in the room listened with complete concentration."

In an interview with the Web magazine andante.com [conducted by Elena Park] (also cited by Taruskin), Adams emphasized yet again what the death of Leon Klinghoffer meant for him: "*The Death of Klinghoffer* treats the murder of Leon Klinghoffer as the tragic event it was. In that sense I saw him very much as a sacrificial victim, and his murder was not all that different from the crucifixion that is at the heart of the Bach *Passions*. Both Jesus and Leon Klinghoffer were killed because they represented something that was suspect and hated. But the opera doesn't simply stop here; it also gives voice to the other side. We look into the minds and souls of the Palestinians and see what might have driven them to produce a generation of young men easily willing to give up their lives to make their grievances known."

And the composer expressed himself very precisely about how an artist should react to the terrorist danger: "We have to remember that the goal of a terrorist is to disrupt and destroy the internal fabric of a society…. People in the art world or the theater world, people who read novels and go to see provocative new films expect to be challenged, and even on occasion to be upset. But classical music consumers are being typecast as the most timid and emotionally fragile of all audiences."

In January 2002 the London Adams Festival took place. It was a giant success, and the concert performances of *Klinghoffer* were the hot ticket. On the same weekend there was also a concert version in Ferrara. Afterward a man ran to the stage and gave a little speech. It turned out that this was the actual captain of the *Achille Lauro*. He declared that the opera told the truth about the event in a deeper sense.

Brooklyn Academy: Beauty for a Sick World

The Death of Klinghoffer was more or less blacklisted in America following the Taruskin article. But in December 2003, twelve years after the American premiere, the Brooklyn Academy of Music presented a semi-staged performance under Robert Spano. The critics Anthony Tommasini, John von Rhein, and Mark Swed used this as an occasion to stake out positions. Tommasini wrote that, "for what it's worth," his companion, a young Israeli psychiatrist and ex-soldier, observed that Palestinians probably wouldn't tote M-16 rifles (as the singers did onstage), but he found the opera "humane, perceptive, and engrossing." Whatever conclusion you draw, said Tommasini, "this ambitious and deeply felt work deserves to be heard and debated."

John von Rhein lamented that Chicago Lyric Opera had rejected the work, not least of all since the media had mischaracterized the piece through the headline Singing Terrorists. He agreed with Adams's opinion that certain works of art must be unpleasant in order to lead us to a better understanding of who we are and what our responsibility for each other is and found the music to be like spiritual balm over troubled water. Beauty, it suggested, is possible even in a world of sickening hatefulness and clashing ideologies. Von Rhein praised the representation of the well-meaning Captain who is duped by the terrorists and of the ordinary people who unwittingly find themselves in a situation out of a horror film. His conclusion: "*Klinghoffer* is precisely the kind of art that the world needs to work through these awful conditions."

Mark Swed was not so moved by the performance itself and was more interested in comparing Adams's work with older operas in which Judaism was a theme (*La Juive* of Halévy and *Benveuto Cellini* of Berlioz were at that time playing at the Met). An anti-Semitic remark in *Cellini* had simply been eliminated from the Met titles, while *La Juive* was perceived in the Paris of its time as a protest against anti-Semitism. Swed found the treatment of this theme in *Klinghoffer* to be far more sensitive. The end of his piece quoted audience members who characterized the opera as too undramatic and distant and wondered what all the fuss had been about.

Penny Woolcock Joins the Debate: From Oratorio to Action Film

The undiminished volatility of John Adams's second opera was yet again proved when a film version was released. Penny Woolcock had become known as a film director through her realistic TV films for Channel Four (*Tina Goes Shopping*). These focused on the lives of the working class in Northern England. Previously Woolcock had had no involvement with opera, but she became fascinated when she heard the *Klinghoffer* choruses, and she determined to film the opera: not to direct a new film based on it, but simply to film the opera itself—in her own style. The result therefore was quite unlike Peter Sellars's original production. As though he had wanted to conceal the explosive nature of the theme, Sellars (who, in fact, conceived the original idea for the opera) erected an abstract steel scaffolding on the stage. On and around this the chorus ran and dancers rushed. The action scenes (such as that prologue scene, later cut, involving the Klinghoffers' neighbors) were arranged to take place around this, giving them the effect of foreign bodies. Only the poster and the title page of the program book hinted at a political statement, in that they depicted oil wells in the desert—and by implication American interests in this conflict.

But Penny Woolcock's version doesn't shy away at all from political themes. The two choruses of the prelude, which represent the myths that collide in the political conflict, are performed against powerful accompanying images. During the first chorus we see a Palestinian family being evicted from its house by Jewish settlers. The husband had been a concentration camp survivor, as we see from his tattoo. The children of the evicted Palestinians grow up to be terrorists, while the man who evicted them will become a victim of the terrorists as an old man onboard the *Achille Lauro* and be forced to relive his trauma as a prisoner. Accompanying the "Chorus of Exiled Jews" is historical footage of the arrival of Jewish refugees from Europe who hope for a new homeland.

All of this, of course, circumscribes a hugely controversial minefield. An unending series of historical investigations seeks to prove the opposite of each of the stories told, claiming that everything was in reality completely different. But neither an opera nor a film can pretend to offer a historically correct representation. The first two choruses present myths that both groups cherish— therefore we see them represented according to the respective truths of each myth. And, as a result, they aren't mutually compatible. What's essential is the irreconcilable contradiction involved. The "Hagar" chorus at the beginning of the second act recounts the origin shared by Jews and Arabs and represents the associated myth of the hostile brothers (Abraham sends Hagar together with her firstborn son, Ishamel, into the wilderness after his wife bears him Isaac—yet God announces that he will also make a people out of Isaac). This is cut from the film.

For the scenes on the *Achille Lauro,* Woolcock hired an authentic cruise ship traveling from Cyprus to Malta and back—following September 11, prices had fallen drastically. Even so the production ended up costing some £1.9 million—more than any comparable project before. Only realistic action scenes are played onboard the ship—the way in which the director interweaves these into the opera's structure is masterly. John Adams wrote little "bridge passages" to fit a couple of adjustments. His minimalist music here works to its best effect; and with it those very traits that go beyond minimalism—utilizing the complete arsenal of historically available music—prevail.

The sound track was made in the studio, but the singers also sang live on the ship and were recorded via hidden microphones. Behind the cameraman an assistant conductor stood to coach the singers to the playback track. After this, the live recordings were mixed with the tape—the effect is of lip-synching in a way that has scarcely been seen before in opera films (at most, perhaps, in the films of Peter Weigl). Together with the wonderfully imaginative representation of convincing singers, this gives the film the texture of realism that characterizes Woolcock's style. On TV it's as if the hostages and their hijackers are living through the real-life escalation of the Middle East conflict that was taking place in March 2002.

As in the world premiere, Sanford Sylvan is Leon Klinghoffer. He brings tremendous vitality and warmth to the title hero—who is not really the main character in what is, in fact, a complex en-semble. He is a typical American tourist who looks forward to pleasure, but is also a loving husband. And he lets loose in a raging speech against "Rambo" as the latter bullies him (ironically, he's played by baritone Leighton Melrose, an American Jew who lost a friend in the collapse of the World Trade Center). The baritone Tom Randle plays the terrorist Molqi with the brio of an actor in a thriller, while the Egyptian baritone Kamel Boutros convincingly represents the dreamy Mamoud—he philosophizes during his ex-change with the Captain, yet is not any more dissuaded from his willingness to use violence. The youngest hijacker, Omar, is played by a male, but is sung offstage by Susan Bickley, which allows for leaps between present and past. For Woolcock, in general, every-thing that's one-dimensional seems much too boring.

Christopher Maltman endows the Captain with great authen-ticity and also sings with utmost urgency. Sometimes he looks into the camera like a child who has been caught doing something es-pecially bad, but then he suddenly becomes the commander in charge once again who thinks he can control the situation. What really crushes him is not the terrorists, who prove resistant to his attempts to mediate, but Marilyn Klinghoffer. Mezzo-soprano Yvonne Howard gives us a widow who gains an unexpected di-mension when the Captain relates the grim news to her. Mamoud, having been arrested, has just left after pressing his good luck charm into the Captain's hand. "You shook his hand!" she says to the Captain accusingly, rejecting his attempt to console her. Yvonne Howard's theatrical achievement is poignant. She also ap-pears at the film's beginning, in a silent scene, when she spits in the face of one of the terrorists in a lineup. This is one of the director's inventions—she uses it to generate tension in a film-savvy way that she could not have accomplished with the two choruses of the prologue alone.

As Mark Swed expressed it in the *Los Angeles Times*, this scene seems to say, right from the start, that "terrible history has led to terrible deeds. There is no forgiveness." Swed was again the first in the United States to write about the BBC film of *Klinghoffer*. The English broadcast on Channel Four was in May 2003. He had already seen the film at the San Francisco International Film Festival in April, during the same week, in fact, that Abu Abbas (the mastermind of the hijacking) was captured by American troops in Baghdad.

Justin Davidson wrote in *Newsday* that the film reveals *Klinghoffer* to be a highly political opera—even if the composer stated it was only a question of hatred and the killing that resulted and that this was no different from what happens in a Verdi opera: "Verdi, too, after all, was a political composer." The plot in Woolcock's version seemed to him less like a *Passion* and much more like a new *Iliad* about how violence keeps on spiraling. Davidson accuses the opera of taking a position: "When you characterize an act of violence as the by-product of historical forces, you remove individual responsibility—as in the case of Abbu Abbas. And when you compare the defense of Israel to the SS, you're certainly not taking a neutral position."

On May 13 the film was shown in New York's Walter Reade Theater as part of a Lincoln Center Adams Festival. Edward Rothstein wrote a polemic against it in the *New York Times* under the headline Images of Evil's Flowering Disagree about Its Roots. He compared the opera to the popular Fox Channel series *24,* in which the hero regularly "races the clock" to rid the world of terrorists, preventing their murderous deeds and avoiding catastrophes. While he concedes that the opera is clearly more serious than the series, in the aftermath of September 11 *Klinghoffer* strikes Rothstein as even worse than it did before. For it perceives the roots of terrorism to be in the behavior of Israelis, thereby implying that the Jews behave like Nazis. The theory that injustice is the cause of terrorism is, however, fallacious, for terrorism, Rothstein says, feeds off "religious delusion," cultivates hatred, and has totalitarian ambitions. The film avoids depicting such complexity.

Charles Michener in the *New York Observer* argued, in contrast, that Rothstein's imputation starkly exaggerated this alleged equation of Jews with Nazis. The film, says Michener, if anything, redeems the opera from any limiting anti-Semitism. What's more: opera is no history lesson, and the artistic intention of the creators becomes even clearer in the film.

Feelings also ran high on the Internet after PBS decided against broadcasting the Woolcock film. The online news forum Opera-L had one member writing this about Rothstein's article: "In case there's any question at all: I include John Adams on my list of 'artists' that I go out of my way to avoid. Of course, that's the topic here. I'm wearing a fireproof suit." On the same day, May 13, someone else wrote that he was disgusted with any kind of separatism: whether of a party, a tribe, a group—the phrase "those people" made his blood boil. Therefore he defended Adams against the charge that he relies on all-too-obvious and politically correct perspectives. And he describes how profoundly he was shocked by the portrait of the young Omar, who is ready to throw away his life because he is so full of hate: "I will never fully understand how someone arrives at such a point....[and this] is as deep a tragedy as the loss of Mr. Klinghoffer's life.... What we humans do to each other!" This process of humanizing the conflict is what constitutes the opera's quality: "I'm grateful to Mr. Adams, Ms. Goodman, and Ms. Woolcock for giving some of us something to chew on, something to wrestle with, and something—which one way or another—has the power to impact our lives, move us and make us think."

New York Magazine, on June 2, 2003, contained Peter G. Davis's ultimate slashing: "Leaving politics aside for the moment, what strikes me as most offensive about the work is its sheer ineptitude. Every important composer is entitled to write a stinker now and then, but Adams has surely produced a lulu with *The Death of Klinghoffer.* Goodman's libretto is worse than naive—it fails on just about every level. Her character portraits are cold and bloodless, the larger vision is prosy and constipated, and her self-conscious literary tone has the musty odor of a vanity-press poetry journal. No wonder Adams seems baffled trying to find music for this miserable text. All he has managed to produce is a hopelessly meandering, tensionless score that sounds like the most vapid New Age pap." Was it a coincidence that at just the same time John Adams won the Pulitzer Prize for his *On the Transmigration of Souls?* Written the previous year as official memorial music for the victims of September 11, Adams here intelligently avoided all the sentimentality one might have expected from a work commissioned for this kind of occasion, instead producing a reflective, moving piece of good music.

Once again advocates and opponents faced each other with no hope of reconciliation—just as in American politics, which the *Klinghoffer* debate seemed to mirror precisely. Only one opinion remained unsolicited: that of everyday operagoers. As before, they were considered incapable of deciding for themselves what to think and feel. *The Death of Klinghoffer* remains absent from American opera house programs. The financial risk would, of course, be too big if an angered patron should demand their subsidy be returned—and when there's doubt, patrons with deep pockets tend not to be on the side of material that grapples with the causes of an entrenched conflict. At any rate, the DVD release of the Woolcock film opens the way to a democratization of the debate. Now anyone can create a complete picture from the text and music for themselves and subsequently arrive at their own interpretation.

From an Episode of Terrorism
Adams's *Death of Klinghoffer*

John Rockwell
The New York Times, March 21, 1991

LIKE *NIXON IN CHINA* but in more incendiary fashion, *The Death of Klinghoffer* transmutes contemporary history into operatic poetry. Unlike the earlier work by the team of John Adams, composer; Alice Goodman, librettist; Peter Sellars, director; and Mark Morris, choreographer, the new opera, which received its world premiere Tuesday night at the Théâtre Royal de la Monnaie, has problems that need refinement. But the potential for eventual triumph is there.

The premiere attracted enormous attention. The audience was overflowing with critics—they filled the foyer for an intermission reception, glowering at one another suspiciously—from seemingly every corner of the Western world and, perhaps, the Middle Eastern world as well. And the work is guaranteed a wider public, since it was co-commissioned by five other opera companies. After seven performances here through April 2, it will travel over the next year to Lyons, France; Brooklyn (the American premiere is scheduled for September 5 at the Brooklyn Academy of Music); Los Angeles; San Francisco; and Glyndebourne, England (or London under Glyndebourne auspices).

The subject of *The Death of Klinghoffer* is the seizure of the Italian cruise ship *Achille Lauro* in October 1985 by four Palestinian terrorists and the murder of a wheelchair-bound American Jew, Leon Klinghoffer.

The hatreds of Jews and Palestinians surface here and there, sometimes violently. But the opera as a whole, laid out in two acts of approximately eighty minutes each, deliberately cools passions into meditations from afar.

The action, which alternates choruses and solo declamations, sets the events into a cosmic context inspired by Greek tragedy, Bach's *Passions*, and large-scale dance-dramas of the Orient. The chorus sings of ancient injustices in biblical imagery, of night and sand and heat, while the narratives combine recollection, interpretation, and, only occasionally, present-tense immediacy.

In his music, sympathetically conducted Tuesday night by Kent Nagano, Mr. Adams has long since transcended Steve Reich–style minimalist mannerisms. Such devices remain, but they are incorporated into a fabric that also encompasses neo-romantic lyricism and sometimes pointed harmonic acerbity. The solo narrations, like those of most modern operas, cede principal melodic interest to the instruments. But they possess an introspective beauty of their own, particularly when enunciated by such sensitive singers as James Maddalena (the Captain), Sanford Sylvan (Klinghoffer), and Sheila Nadler (Marilyn Klinghoffer).

More unusual in Mr. Adams's score is his blend of conventional and electronic instruments and the amplification of all the singers and instruments, with microphones and loudspeakers embedded in the set and the balances constantly modified by the sound engineer, Jonathan Deans. At its best, this creates fascinating new sound-colors and invests the climaxes with powerful energy. At its worst, it muddles and harshens the texture.

After all the expectations, the actual production took a considerable time to gather momentum. The prologue and first act are predominantly contemplative, except for a more animated, if claustrophobically staged and mushily enunciated, scene of everyday life with the Klinghoffers' friends in New Jersey. What was intended as meditative and dreamy turns static and dreary.

Everything looked and sounded unsure, from the cluttered constructivism of George Tsypin's unit set, steel girders and pipes ascending on high, to James F. Ingalls's glaring lighting to Dunya Ramicova's stubbornly workaday costumes.

Mr. Sellars, his head as usual buzzing with half-realized ideas, sought to reinforce the deliberate obfuscation of identity in Ms. Goodman's text, in which the laments of the Palestinians and Jews sound poignantly alike. But the result, in the first act, too often reduced everything to a faceless bustle.

Mr. Morris's choreography looked incongruously formalistic: neat little rows of dancers doing their balletic turns with little sense of emotional connection to the drama.

Mr. Adams's music, too, stuck too long in a bland lyrical mode, with the Monnaie chorus struggling but failing to articulate the English words clearly and the stage bereft of supertitles. Ms. Goodman reportedly opposes the use of titles, but their absence meant that her beautiful words were simply lost. If the first act was meant as lowering clouds, there were too many clouds and they lowered too long.

The second act, however, restored one's faith in this team's creative capabilities—especially everything from Scene ii, itself subtitled "The Death of Klinghoffer," to the opera's end. Here, everything cohered into powerful drama. The use of rock-style concert projections, expanding every intimate expression on the protagonists' faces, enhanced the already vivid acting of Mr. Sylvan and of Eugene Perry and Thomas Hammons as two of the terrorists. (Other singers, like nearly all the principals taking two roles each, were Stephanie Friedman, Thomas Young, and Janice Felty.)

Most of the soloists' words, more than those of the chorus, came across clearly and movingly. The use of dancer-doubles by Mr. Morris and Mr. Sellars (where the work of one stopped and the other began was vague, to the production's benefit) became suddenly potent, as did Mr. Sellars's use of ritualized gesture and movement. The opera attained its finest depths of feeling in the two final scenes for Mrs. Klinghoffer—the first in which she heartbreakingly doesn't yet know that her husband has been shot and the second a bitter denunciation of what she sees as the Captain's complicity—and Klinghoffer's farewell, an astonishing "Aria of the Falling Body" set in the score as a *gymnopédie*, or slow, hypnotic dance.

All is hardly lost for the first act, leaving the hope that the entire opera can succeed as potently as its final scenes. The joint commissioning process may form a progression akin to workshop development, with the production and perhaps even the score undergoing tightening and focusing along the way. Last night's premiere brought warm, friendly but curiously curtailed applause. In a more pointed production, that applause could turn into ovations.

Seeking Symmetry Between Palestinians and Jews

Edward Rothstein
The New York Times, September 7, 1991

ALL THROUGH THURSDAY NIGHT's New York premiere of the much-awaited *Death of Klinghoffer*, one knew exactly what the creators wanted a listener to think:

Setting the story of the 1985 Palestinian hijacking of a luxury cruise ship and the killing of a wheelchair-bound American Jew not on an ocean liner but in an Erector Set of scaffolding and ramps would treat yesterday's newspaper reports as mythic, ritualistic repetitions of timeless struggles.

Telling the story in highly stylized language (by Alice Goodman) and music (by John Adams), using formalized gestures developed by Peter Sellars, having Mark Morris choreograph his dancers with hyperbolic poses and frenetic movements would raise audiences' reactions above knee-jerk notions.

Using choruses that seemed to stand outside the plot and having the same singers play multiple roles of terrorists and Jews would undo all preconceptions of identity. The Palestinians and the Jews would be shown as symmetrical victims of each other's hatreds. Like the principals' previous opera, *Nixon in China*, the work would be beyond politics. "On the 'politically correct' scale, we don't even register," boasted its director, Mr. Sellars, last spring when the work was unveiled in Belgium.

That, at any rate, was what the work wanted us to feel and think; it was also the kind of reaction its premiere sometimes inspired.

But in actuality the performance, at the Brooklyn Academy of Music (four more performances are scheduled, starting tonight), was something else entirely.

Though expertly conducted by Kent Nagano and well sung by the cast (particularly James Maddalena and Sanford Sylvan), Mr. Adams's music has a seriously limited range. He creates languid but ominous murmurings of ostinato figures, frenetic pulsings of rising pitches that indicate approaching climaxes, and poplike riffs used for mockery and irony. That is about it; the music is either atmospheric or emotionally elementary, while the text is set in so unmusical a fashion that the surtitles are required to decipher it.

But the music is just a sign of deeper problems. Consider just the prologue. It begins with the cast arrayed onstage in contemporary street clothes (worn by every character throughout the work). The women sing a "Chorus of Exiled Palestinians": "My father's house was razed/In nineteen forty-eight" reads Alice Goodman's libretto, "When the Israelis passed/Over our street."

The accompanying orchestra pulses delicately, the vocal lines elegiac, ornamented at times in nearly Arabic fashion. The men then join in a description of the resulting destruction in a crescendo until by the end of the chorus the singers are spitting out their words *fortissimo*, the orchestra churning as singers threaten that stones will now break the Israelis' teeth.

This empathetic evocation of the intifada suddenly comes to an end as a family gathers on a couch and chair on a raised platform in midstage. They are the Rumor family, Jewish friends of the Klinghoffers. Mr. Rumor sits crankily with a television remote control in hand, squabbling with his missus over the tourist items she picks up every time they travel. She berates him for spending so much time on the toilet overseas, and also manages to suggest to her son that he check out Myrt Epstein's daughters. The music burbles along like a theme song from a 1950s television show, raising its voice along with the family's. In the midst of this bourgeois fricasee, Mrs. Rumor spots an item in the newspaper about Yasir Arafat, the Palestinian leader, and is outraged.

Then begins, as if on cue, the languorous chant of the "Chorus of Exiled Jews," a set piece that is a sort of tourist's recollection of devotional sentiment about the Promised Land, mentioning sights like military barracks, the Western Wall, movie houses picketed by Hasidim, the Dome of the Rock, and a goat in an orchard. The words have no historical weight, though the Daughter of Zion poetically (and tendentiously) informs her tourist visitors: "I am an old woman. I thought you were dead."

The work continues to give seemingly historical resonance to Palestinian wounds. There is even an extended narrative dance of Hagar and her son exiled by Abraham, wandering in the desert and giving birth, in the biblical account, to the Arab people. The plot doesn't gentrify the terrorists' acts, but their victims continue to be little more than variations of the offensive Rumors: narrow in their focus and vision, singing primarily about their physical condition, revealing the simple-minded historical blindness that the avant-garde has long attributed to the bourgeoisie. Even Marilyn Klinghoffer's final aria is just a display of purely individual pain that leaves one cold. Who could tell from this work just what the Jewish side really is—a sort of touristy attachment to an ancient land?

All this would not matter if the opera did not go out of its way to lay claim to historical insight and sensitivity. It might even have worked without such wisdom. But *The Death of Klinghoffer* is constructed not out of traditional narrative, but out of poetic monologues, meditations, and musings, creating an extraordinary challenge for the text in evoking character and ideas.

The libretto, though, is not up to the challenge. Even when the protagonists' faces are projected on a giant television screen, they remain distant figures, remote from either sympathy or horror. The text seems almost casually random in its use of imagery and portentous statement. Ideas are undeveloped, cryptic passages are chanted, mixed metaphors created, references left unclear. When this miscellany is combined with Mr. Adams's film-scorish impressionism, the result is a monochromatic stage show that relies on the audience to bring along the appropriate sentiments.

Klinghoffer, with all these failings, is the product of expert international packaging. Its $1 million cost is being shared by the international opera houses at which the work is being presented. The reasons are clear: it seemed to promise a revivification of contemporary opera, sensitive treatment of controversial subjects, new audiences for an increasingly dour international cultural scene. And despite the lukewarm reaction the work seemed to receive on Thursday night, the companies may yet see a return on their investment.

But the work itself turned out to be more about its intended reception than about its subject, more a matter of pitch than substance. Without historical insight, without profound revelation of character, without the advertised symmetry, without even a coherent libretto and convincing score, *The Death of Klinghoffer* becomes simply another monument to an avant-garde that is repeating old political and aesthetic gestures while acting as if it is daringly breaking new ground.

Seeking Answers in an Opera

Mark Swed
Los Angeles Times, October 7, 2001

SERIOUS TIMES CALL FOR SERIOUS ART, and classical music has responded. Beauty is balm, and the fervent beauty of Samuel Barber's *Adagio for Strings*, for instance, has served us well in concert after concert as a national song of lamentation.

Bach, Mozart, Beethoven, and Brahms nurse nervous uncertainty. Their wonderfully rational music, whether it seeks to represent spiritual grandeur or simple elegance, offers us respite from the anxiety of a chaotic world.

But however valuable the soothing of wounded psyches may be, art can accomplish more. On September 12, preferring answers and understanding to comfort, I put on the CD of *The Death of Klinghoffer,* John Adams's opera about terrorists and their victims. Its characters are based on the Palestinians who hijacked the Italian cruise ship *Achille Lauro* in 1985 and on the crew and passengers they held hostage.

Opera is often called the most irrational art form. It places us directly inside its characters' minds and hearts through compelling music, often causing us to enjoy the company of characters we might normally dislike. Adams's opera requires that we think the unthinkable.

As a profoundly disturbing meditation on the tragic death of an innocent man, *Klinghoffer* hardly supports or apologizes for terrorism. But it does require, in the way that only opera can, that we identify with the emotions that drive actions we despise. And by presenting the terrorist act from all points of view, it becomes not just a study in suffering, a painting in the simple strokes of the banality of evil, but a wrenching panoramic expression of the complex interaction of motives and actions, all against a background of the biblical imperatives that both enliven the Middle East and tear it apart.

Although paid little attention in the past few years, *Klinghoffer* can tell us a lot about why the world is the way it is today, and our neglect of it, it is now clear, has been to our detriment.

The *Achille Lauro* hijacking riveted the world. The terrorists shot and killed Leon Klinghoffer, a sixty-nine-year-old American Jew who used a wheelchair, and then they announced that they had thrown his body overboard.

When Adams began his opera, the image of Klinghoffer falling from the ship in his wheelchair was still fresh, and the times were charged. In the notes accompanying the Nonesuch recording, Michael Steinberg writes that Adams began it in 1989 while "the United States was lavishly supporting Saddam Hussein" and "completed it on February 12, 1991, while we were dropping 'smart bombs' down Baghdad ventilator shafts."

The premiere was held under tight security in Brussels one week after the end of the Gulf War. Controversy was inevitable, and the critical response included accusations of namby-pamby evenhandedness, of craven opportunism, and of exploiting personal tragedy.

At one extreme, the opera was called a Zionist plot; at the other, Adams, director Peter Sellars, and librettist Alice Goodman were denounced for being unashamedly pro-Palestinian. Goodman received death threats. The U.S. premiere at the Brooklyn Academy of Music later in 1991 was picketed by Jewish protesters. "Give me a break!" a woman sitting next to me at BAM loudly exclaimed in response to nearly every Palestinian remark onstage.

There were certainly those who recognized in the opera a rare insight into the most troubling and destructive political and cultural division of our age. But it was an opera ahead of its time, and it wasn't long before timid companies dropped *The Death of Klinghoffer* like a hot potato. San Francisco Opera mounted the Sellars production in 1992, but Los Angeles Opera and the Glyndebourne Festival Opera, both part of the consortium of *Klinghoffer* commissioners, never did.

In a curious twist of fate, a renewed surge of interest in the opera has already begun in Europe. In February, the Finnish National Opera mounted a production by the British TV director Tony Palmer. Concert performances were scheduled in Amsterdam later this month and in London next January. Meanwhile, an avant-garde British stage and film director, Penny Woolcock, decided to make a film of the opera for British TV. On September 11, as the airliners were flying into the World Trade Center and the Pentagon, Adams was in London rehearsing the singers in *Klinghoffer* for a sound track recording for that film. Neither he nor any of the other artists wanted to comment.

In the wake of September 11, *Klinghoffer* shocks with inescapable, prescient power, even in an almost silly aria, a bit of mild comic relief sung by a passenger, a character called British Dancing Girl. She is accompanied by a snappy minimalist version of '60s bubble-gum rock as she distinguishes between two of the terrorists—the dreamy, poetic Omar, who "kept us in ciggies the whole time" and the brutal "Rambo," who slaps the hostages around. Actually, she observes, men like that aren't capable of much:

> You watch out for the type
> Who looks as if he wouldn't fight
> If he were paid

Because the music is cute, the observation doesn't immediately sink in. Now, look again at the seemingly soft, shy face of Osama bin Laden in the photographs.

Klinghoffer, I was also reminded by a fresh listening, is one of the most beautiful operas written in my lifetime. But the beauty— in the music, the words, the memories, the images—doesn't always illuminate what we want it to.

The opera opens with a chorus of exiled Palestinians who sing:

> My father's house was razed
> In nineteen forty-eight
> When the Israelis passed
> Over our street.

That house was a place of sacred hospitality, idyllic, and the music draws you in through simple sketchy melody that becomes ever more enticingly elaborate, like an Arabic chant. The images are sensual: On a hot day, coolness rises like a wave from a pure well, and one practically tastes it in the refreshing pulsing of the orchestra. But as the pulse increases, the feeling of rapt nostalgia mutates into rage, an electrifying, exhilarating climax with a shocking sentiment:

> Let the supplanter look
> Upon his work. Our faith
> Will take the stones he broke
> And break his teeth.

That sucker punch is thrown repeatedly in *Klinghoffer*. Late at night on the ship, a terrorist, Mamoud, tunes into Arab radio stations and hears songs of his youth. Sad laments of parted lovers magically travel over the water, his own operatic singing matching the eloquence of melismatic Arab music. But again, almost imperceptibly, his nostalgia turns to memories of childhood, exploding metal, closing the eyes on the head of a decapitated brother.

Once we begin to share the characters' dreams, to feel their motivations, we become aware of the startling power of opera. No one protested two melodramatic television movies about the *Achille Lauro* hijacking, one starring Karl Malden, another with Burt Lancaster. The terrorists were comic-book villains. Tension was undercut by commercial breaks. But in *The Death of Klinghoffer*, Mamoud is flesh and blood, one of those characters into whose dreams we are drawn without choice. And so the woman next to me at BAM offered her "Give me a break" refrain as if it were a mantra to ward off evil.

Still, the opera does not side with the terrorists. Nor is it ultimately evenhanded, not after we've endured Klinghoffer's death and witnessed the unassuagable rage of his widow, Marilyn.

The death itself is one of the most moving in the history of an art form that would be nothing without dying. After Klinghoffer's body is thrown off the ship, his soul sings a very slow, time-stop aria as it falls through the water in a timeless journey to another world. The fall, staged by Sellars (whose idea the opera was) with choreographer Mark Morris, is a dance between Klinghoffer and his body: a dancer slowly drags the singer across stage on a flowing white shroud.

The opera ends with the ship captain offering his condolences to Marilyn Klinghoffer. He is a weak, vacillating character, and she won't have it. She sees through him, just as her husband had eloquently debunked the terrorists' claims of righteousness in an earlier aria. She is not eloquent. She is beyond words, beyond any affirmation of life, left with pure, raw emotion. Her last words are "I wanted to die."

And yet one does not leave the opera house devastated. It is the audience's difficult role to sort through the contradictions and conflicts *Klinghoffer* raises, but Adams and Goodman offer help by turning to the model of Bach's *Passion*s, those penetrating tellings of the death of the Christ, from several points of view.

Like Bach, Adams and Goodman frame the central drama in grand choruses of ocean and desert, day and night, anger and fear, full of biblical allusions that place us in the seat of civilization. After Marilyn Klinghoffer sings her terrible last words, there is one more chance for beauty in haunting counter melodies from a background chorus and a solo oboe. In them, we hear her sorrow against a larger context. Her tears are reminiscent of those of Mary in the *Passion*s, and Klinghoffer's death comes to seem almost Christ-like, suggesting that there is a greater good to be gained from all this.

That alone explains why *Klinghoffer* is exactly the work of art we now need. Not surprisingly, no company in America has indicated an intention to present *Klinghoffer* as a vehicle in which to examine the international situation. In Europe, however, the show will go on, with precisely that in mind. Jan Zekveld, presenter of *Klinghoffer* in Amsterdam in two weeks, said that he never had the slightest doubt about going ahead with the performance by the Netherlands Radio Orchestra at the Concertgebouw. "I think the piece has a very strong message to all human beings," he said by phone from Holland. "It is a great work of art, and I am absolutely convinced that the message can't be misunderstood."

Channel Four, the London network producing *Klinghoffer* for television, has also confirmed that it will proceed as planned. The filming is on schedule for February, on a cruise ship in the Mediterranean; the broadcast is set for 2003. A concert performance of *Klinghoffer* at the Barbican Centre in January will be conducted by Leonard Slatkin as part of a weekend Adams festival in London sponsored by the BBC Orchestra. In all three cases, the attitude in Europe seems to be that John Adams is a great American composer; *Klinghoffer* is one of his most important works; and it has a resonance for our time that no other opera can possibly equal.

That American opera companies shy away from *Klinghoffer* is part of their tendency to avoid controversy altogether. Unlike their European counterparts, they rely on private, and to a large extent corporate, support. Understandably, they have wanted a piece of the late '90s economic boom and have sought to serve complacent corporate culture with "safe" contemporary operas, based on already accepted works in the literary canon: André Previn's *A Streetcar Named Desire*, William Bolcom's *A View From the Bridge*, and John Harbison's *Great Gatsby*. Jake Heggie's *Dead Man Walking*, based on an unflinching look at crime and punishment, might have bucked the trend, but saccharine music turned it into a sentimental, feel-good opera.

As opera houses have forgotten or avoided Adams's opera, so the rest of us have conveniently forgotten about the story of Leon Klinghoffer and its aftermath. The investigation in 1985 quickly identified Palestinian Abul Abbas as the mastermind of the *Achille Lauro* takeover. After slipping through the hands of the Italians, who arrested the hijackers, Abbas found protection in Iraq. In a memoir, *A Spy for All Seasons*, Duane Claridge, then head of CIA counterterrorism, tells of traveling to Baghdad in 1986 to exchange U.S. satellite intelligence for custody of Abbas. The Iraqis got their intelligence but then reneged on turning over the terrorist.

Abbas has since publicly apologized for the death of Klinghoffer, which he says was not intended. As part of negotiations between the Israelis and the Palestinians, he was permitted to move to Gaza City, where he openly heads the Palestinian Liberation Front and has close ties to Yasser Arafat. A lawsuit brought by Leon Klinghoffer's daughters (their mother died of cancer) against the Palestinian Liberation Organization was settled for an undisclosed amount in U.S. District Court in Manhattan in 1997 after twelve years of litigation.

Now, of course, everything to do with terrorism has extraordinary resonance. And *Klinghoffer* demands the American stage. Of all American companies, Los Angeles Opera is in the best position to now offer *Klinghoffer*, especially given that its new principal conductor, Kent Nagano, conducted the opera's premiere in Brussels. That it has attempted to brush this work under the rug has been a blight on the company's reputation over the years. At a moment when bravery is so prized, Los Angeles Opera has an exceptional opportunity to demonstrate real artistic courage. But will it or any other American opera company dare to participate in the deepest way art can in these grave and troubling issues?

Dept. of Raw Nerves:
Hijack Opera Scuttled

Alex Ross
The New Yorker, **November 19, 2001**

THE COMPOSER JOHN ADAMS, who made his name with *Nixon in China*, is accustomed to getting entangled with current events. He did not protest a few years ago when a London performance of his piece *Short Ride in a Fast Machine* was canceled in the wake of Princess Diana's death. He spoke up last week, however, after the Boston Symphony called off performances of three choruses from his opera *The Death of Klinghoffer*, which tells of the hijacking of the *Achille Lauro*, in 1985. "I was told that Boston audiences were too 'fragile' to encounter my music at this time," Adams said, from his home in Berkeley. "Meanwhile, I noticed that Seiji Ozawa, their music director, was here in San Francisco, conducting a crazy symphony by Berlioz that ends with a graphic execution and a manic descent into hell."

As artists struggle to come to terms with the new reality, Adams's opera radiates a mesmerizing prophetic power. The opera infuriated some listeners at the time of its premiere, in 1991, because the librettist, Alice Goodman, let the terrorists speak for themselves. Certain passages, steeped in the Koran, now read like intelligence reports that went unheeded. "My soul is all violence," one of the Palestinian hijackers says. "My heart will break if I do not walk in Paradise within two days." On September 11th, Adams was in London, supervising a new recording of the score, which will be used in a forthcoming film version. At the moment the planes struck the World Trade Center, Yvonne Howard, in the role of Marilyn Klinghoffer, was rehearsing the climactic aria in which the widow unleashes her rage and grief. "If a hundred people were murdered and their blood flowed in the wake of this ship like oil," she sings, "only then would the world intervene."

You might think that an orchestra would seize the opportunity to present such acutely relevant material. But Mark Volpe, the Boston's managing director, was quick to give reasons for the cancellation. In the *Klinghoffer* choruses, the orchestra was to have been joined by the Tanglewood Festival Chorus, one of whose members had lost her husband, Ted Hennessy, in the attacks. He was aboard Flight 11, which flew into the north tower of the World Trade Center. "After singing in the memorial service for Ted," Volpe said, "a few members of the chorus came to me, wondering how, exactly, we were going to approach this." Ozawa raised the same issue and asked Volpe to talk to Robert Spano, who was to conduct. Spano agreed that there was a problem. "For me, it simply wasn't fair to the work to present a few excerpts out of context so soon after the attacks," the conductor said. "Before you pick the scab, you have to let it heal."

John Oliver, the conductor of the Tanglewood Festival Chorus, had been looking forward to the *Klinghoffer* performance, but he understood the management's decision. "The opera opens with a 'Chorus of Exiled Palestinians,'" he told me. "It is a mysterious, beautiful piece that contains some very violent language. There is a line about breaking the invaders' teeth with stones. As a performer, in order to get that across, you have to summon up a certain bloodthirstiness. Right now it's a lot to ask, considering what one of our most beloved singers has been through."

Adams was not swayed by these arguments. "I grieve for this woman's lost companion and for all victims of the attacks," he said. "But my opera is not a work of anger and violence. It strives for compassion and understanding." Adams was especially irritated that a letter he received from the Boston Symphony contained the following sentence: "It's at moments like these that we are reminded how great music can provide solace and comfort." He said, "*Klinghoffer* was clearly in some other, more risky category. It made me realize once again how the obsession with 'great' music is reducing classical music to the status of a museum culture."

In place of the *Klinghoffer* choruses, Boston audiences will hear Aaron Copland's First Symphony, a now unobjectionable work that caused some controversy in its day. In 1925, on the occasion of the premiere, the conductor Walter Damrosch said of Copland, "In five years he will be ready to commit murder." Letting the audience judge for itself, he played the music anyway.

Music's Dangers and the Case for Control

Richard Taruskin
The New York Times, December 9, 2001

AND ON TOP OF EVERYTHING ELSE, the Taliban hate music, too. In an interview in October with Nicholas Wroe, a columnist for the British newspaper the *Guardian,* John Baily, an ethnomusicologist on the faculty of Goldsmiths College, London, gave the details. After taking power in 1996, the Islamic fundamentalists who ruled most of Afghanistan undertook search-and-destroy missions in which musical instruments and cassette players were seized and burned in public pyres. Wooden poles were festooned with great ribbons of confiscated audio- and videotape as a reminder of the ban, imposed in keeping with a maxim attributed to the prophet Muhammad warning "those who listen to music and songs in this world" that "on the Day of Judgment molten lead will be poured into their ears."

Musicians caught in the act were beaten with their instruments and imprisoned for as many as forty days. The interdiction on professional music-making closed off yet another avenue to women's participation in public life. The only sounds on the Taliban-dominated radio that Western ears would recognize as musical were those of ritual chanting (something quite distinct from "music," both conceptually and linguistically, in Islamic thought, as in many of the world's cultures).

So what else is new? Utopians, puritans, and totalitarians have always sought to regulate music, if not forbid it outright. Ayatollah Ruhollah Khomeini, probably the Taliban's immediate model, banned it from Iranian radio and television in 1979, because its effects, he said, were like those of opium, "stupefying persons listening to it and making their brains inactive and frivolous."

But our own "Western" tradition is just as full of suspicion toward music, much of it religious. In the fourth century, Saint Augustine confessed that as a result of his sensuous enjoyment of the melodies he heard in church, "I have become a problem unto myself." In the twelfth, John of Salisbury complained that the spectacular music sung in the Paris Cathedral of Notre Dame could "more easily occasion titillation between the legs than a sense of devotion in the brain." Protestant reformers in England and Switzerland seized and burned books containing "popish ditties" with Talibanish zeal. Somewhat later, the Orthodox patriarch of Moscow ordered bonfires of musical instruments, thought to be avatars of paganism.

Religious distrust of music often arises out of distrust of its conduits, especially when female. Saint John Chrysostom, the great Father of the Greek Orthodox Church, complained that when marriages were solemnized, "dancing, and cymbals and flutes, and shameful words and songs from the lips of painted girls" were introduced, and with them "all the Devil's great heap of garbage." Near the beginning of my career as a college music teacher, a young Hasidic man in fringes and gabardines approached me on the first day of class to inform me that he was willing to take my course, but that he would sit near the door, and I was to warn him whenever I would play a record that contained the sound of a woman's voice so that he could slip into the hall and avoid it. (Don't do me any favors, I replied.)

Secular thinkers have been no less leery of music. In a famous passage from Plato's *Republic*, Socrates advocates banning most of the musical modes or scales, "because more than anything else rhythm and harmony find their way to the inmost soul and take strongest hold upon it, bringing with them and imparting grace, if one is rightly trained, and otherwise the contrary." If Plato were writing today (or less euphemistically), he might have put body in place of soul. For surely it is the all but irresistible kinesthetic response that music evokes that makes it such a potent influence on behavior, thence on morals and belief.

That is what sets music off from literature and painting, and attracts the special attention of censors despite its relative abstractness, which might seem to exempt it from the need for political policing. Tolstoy compared its effects to those of hypnosis, linking right up with Ayatollah Khomeini's strictures. And it can only be a similar discomfort about music's affinity with our grosser animal nature that led so many musical modernists to put so much squeamish distance between their cerebral art and viscerally engaging popular culture.

In any case, Plato's mingled awe and suspicion of music's uncanny power over our minds and bodies have echoed through the ages wherever governments have tried to harness music to uphold the public order (or at least keep music from disrupting it). They found the greatest resonance in those twentieth-century totalitarian states that tried to turn the arts into a delivery system for political propaganda. Here is how one of Plato's heirs, Joseph Goebbels, retorted to the conductor Wilhelm Furtwängler's plea for moderation in implementing Nazi arts policies:

"Art, in an absolute sense, as liberal democracy knows it, has no right to exist. Any attempt to further such an art could, in the end, cause a people to lose its inner relationship to art and the artist to isolate himself from the moving forces of his time, shut in the airless chambers of 'art for art's sake.' Art must be good but, beyond that, conscious of its responsibility, competent, close to the people and combative in spirit."

The same kind of pronouncements and policy directives emanated from the Soviets, nominally the Nazis' enemies. Awful memories of the 1948 show trials convened by Andrei Zhdanov, Stalin's de facto cultural commissar, at which the leading Soviet composers (among them Prokofiev and Shostakovich) were humiliated for their "formalist" misdeeds, feed the current mania for vindicating the same composers, absurdly, as dissidents. The similarity of Nazi and Soviet views on the arts is only one reason political classifications nowadays tend to group the old far right and far left together, in opposition to the "liberal democracy" that appeared, until September 11, to have beaten all of its opponents into submission.

That is probably why the Taliban's ban on musical performances, while in no way an unusual historical event (and not even really news), has suddenly drawn so much comment. It symbolizes the survival of impulses we might naively have thought discredited for good and all—as dead, in their way, as smallpox, with whose revival we are also unexpectedly threatened in these unsettled times.

Anything that conjures up both Nazis and Soviets, and now the Taliban, can have few friends in contemporary Western society. As Mayor Giuliani found out before he became our hero, hardly anything a politician can do will elicit a more dependable outcry across the political spectrum than a move in the direction of arts censorship, even if it threatens no direct intervention in the affairs of artists but only the withholding of municipal largesse from institutions (like the Brooklyn Museum of Art) that support them. There is near unanimity in the West today that when it comes to the arts, laissez-faire (coupled, perhaps illogically, with handouts) is the way to go.

But who takes art more seriously? Those who want it left alone or those who want to regulate it? Moreover, the laissez-faire position entails some serious denials. Some say that art is inherently uplifting (if it is really art). Others say that art is inherently transgressive (if it is really art). The words in parentheses, designed to discourage counterexamples and make refutation impossible, merely empty the statements of real meaning. Does such a defense really show a commitment to the value of art or merely an unwillingness to think about it?

And what about public opinion, which sometimes demands abstentions from the performance or exhibit of artworks? Is that just another censorship tribunal?

The musical test case par excellence has always been the taboo on Wagner performances in Israel. Breaching it makes headlines, as the conductor Daniel Barenboim knows very well. He did it last summer to a great din of public protest and righteous indignation. But those who defended Mr. Barenboim's provocation often failed to distinguish between voluntary abstinence out of consideration for people's feelings and a mandated imposition on people's rights.

It was only a social contract that Mr. Barenboim defied, but he seemed to want credit for defying a ban. His act implied that the feelings of Holocaust survivors had been coddled long enough and that continuing to honor them was both an intolerable infringement on his career and an insult to artistic greatness. To agree with him, one had to stretch the definition of censorship way beyond that associated with Nazis, Soviets, and Islamic fundamentalists, into moral terrain usually associated with forbearance or discretion or mutual respect.

Now the issue has been joined again, even more pointedly and painfully, in the aftermath of the September 11 terrorist attacks. Announcing that it preferred "to err on the side of being sensitive," the management of the Boston Symphony Orchestra recently canceled its scheduled performances of choruses from *The Death of Klinghoffer*, the notoriously controversial opera—masterminded by the director Peter Sellars, with a libretto by the poet Alice Goodman and a score by John Adams—that re-enacts and comments on the murder of an American Jew by Palestinian terrorists aboard the cruise ship *Achille Lauro* in the fall of 1985.

For thus showing forbearance and discretion, the Boston Symphony has taken some pies in the face. In an exceptionally vulgar rant that appeared in the *San Francisco Chronicle*, the arts columnist David Wiegand, enraged at what he perceived as a slight to Mr. Adams (a Bay Area luminary), wrote, "There is something deeply wrong when a nation galvanizes its forces, its men and women, its determination and its resolve, to preserve the right of the yahoos at the Boston Symphony Orchestra to decide to spare its listeners something that might challenge them or make them think." What nation had done this? And why shouldn't people be spared reminders of recent personal pain when they attend a concert?

A month earlier, Mark Swed, the chief music critic for the *Los Angeles Times,* had expressed a similar opinion, only slightly more decorously, when he boasted that, "preferring answers and understanding to comfort," he had listened to the Nonesuch recording of *Klinghoffer* the day after the World Trade Center had collapsed. But whence this quaintly macho impulse to despise comfort (women's work?) and even deny it haughtily to sufferers? And whence the idea of seeking answers and understanding in an opera peopled by wholly fictional terrorists and semifictionalized victims, rather than in more relevant sources of information?

Anthony Tommasini, in the *New York Times,* endorsed Mr. Adams's contention that his opera offers "the sad solace of truth." What truth? *The Death of Klinghoffer* trades in the tritest undergraduate fantasies. If the events of September 11 could not jar some artists and critics out of their habit of romantically idealizing criminals, then nothing will. But isn't it time for artists and critics to grow up with the rest of us, now that the unthinkable has occurred?

If terrorism—specifically, the commission or advocacy of deliberate acts of deadly violence directed randomly at the innocent—is to be defeated, world public opinion has to be turned decisively against it. The only way to do that is to focus resolutely on the acts rather than their claimed (or conjectured) motivations, and to characterize all such acts, whatever their motivation, as crimes. This means no longer romanticizing terrorists as Robin Hoods and no longer idealizing their deeds as rough poetic justice. If we indulge such notions when we happen to agree or sympathize with the aims, then we have forfeited the moral ground from which any such acts can be convincingly condemned.

Does *The Death of Klinghoffer* romanticize the perpetrators of deadly violence toward the innocent? Its creators tacitly acknowledged that it did, when they revised the opera for American consumption after its European premieres in Brussels and Paris. In its original version, the opening "Chorus of Exiled Palestinians" was followed not by a balancing "Chorus of Exiled Jews," but by a scene, now dropped from the score, that showed the Klinghoffers' suburban neighbors gossiping merrily about their impending cruise ("The dollar's up. Good news for the Klinghoffers") to an accompaniment of hackneyed pop-style music.

That contrast set the vastly unequal terms on which the conflict of Palestinians and Jews would be perceived throughout the opera. The portrayal of suffering Palestinians in the musical language of myth and ritual was immediately juxtaposed with a musically trivial portrayal of contented, materialistic American Jews. The paired characterizations could not help linking up with lines sung later by "Rambo," one of the fictional terrorists, who (right before the murder) wrathfully dismisses Leon Klinghoffer's protest at his treatment with the accusation that "wherever poor men are gathered you can find Jews getting fat."

Is it unfair to discuss a version of the opera that has been withdrawn from publication and remains unrecorded? It would have been, except that Mr. Adams, throwing his own pie at the Boston Symphony in an interview published recently on the Andante.com Web site, saw fit to point out that the opera "has never seemed particularly shocking to audiences in Europe." He was playing the shame game, trying to make the Boston cancellation look provincial. But when one takes into account that the version European audiences saw in 1991 catered to so many of their favorite prejudices—anti-American, anti-Semitic, anti-bourgeois—the shame would seem rather to go the other way.

Nor have these prejudices been erased from the opera in its revised form. The libretto commits many notorious breaches of evenhandedness, but the greatest one is to be found in Mr. Adams's music. In his interview, the composer repeats the oft drawn comparison between the operatic Leon Klinghoffer and the "sacrificial victim" who is "at the heart of the Bach *Passions*." But his music, precisely insofar as it relies on Bach's example, undermines the facile analogy.

In the *Saint Matthew Passion*, Bach accompanies the words of Jesus with an aureole of violins and violas that sets him off as numinous, the way a halo would do in a painting. There is a comparable effect in *Klinghoffer*: long, quiet, drawn-out tones in the highest violin register (occasionally spelled by electronic synthesizers or high oboe tones). They recall not only the Bachian aureole, but also effects of limitless expanse in time or space, familiar from many romantic scores. (An example is the beginning of Borodin's *In the Steppes of Central Asia.*) These numinous, "timeless" tones accompany virtually all the utterances of the choral Palestinians or the terrorists, beginning with the opening chorus.

They underscore the words spoken by the fictitious terrorist Molqui [sic]: "We are not criminals and we are not vandals, but men of ideals." Together with an exotically "oriental" obbligato bassoon, they accompany the fictitious terrorist Mamoud's endearing reverie about his favorite love songs. They add resonance to the fictitious terrorist Omar's impassioned yearnings for a martyr's afterlife; and they also appear when the ship's captain tries to mediate between the terrorists and the victims.

They do not accompany the victims, except in the allegorical "Aria of the Falling Body," sung by the slain Klinghoffer's remains as they are tossed overboard by the terrorists. Only after death does the familiar American middle-class Jew join the glamorously exotic Palestinians in mythic timelessness. Only as his body falls lifeless is his music exalted to a comparably romanticized spiritual dimension.

Why should we want to hear this music now? Is it an edifying challenge, as Mr. Wiegand and Mr. Tommasini contend? Does it give us answers that we should prefer, with Mr. Swed, to comfort? Or does it express a reprehensible contempt for the real-life victims of its imagined "men of ideals," all too easily transferable to the victims who perished on September 11?

In a fine recent essay, the literary critic and queer theorist Jonathan Dollimore writes that "to take art seriously—to recognize its potential—must be to recognize that there might be reasonable grounds for wanting to control it." Where should control come from? Unless we are willing to trust the Taliban, it has to come from within. What is called for is self-control. That is what the Boston Symphony laudably exercised; and I hope that musicians who play to Israeli audiences will resume exercising it. There is no need to shove Wagner in the faces of Holocaust survivors in Israel and no need to torment people stunned by previously unimaginable horrors with offensive "challenges" like *The Death of Klinghoffer.*

Censorship is always deplorable, but the exercise of forbearance can be noble. Not to be able to distinguish the noble from the deplorable is morally obtuse. In the wake of September 11, we might want, finally, to get beyond sentimental complacency about art. Art is not blameless. Art can inflict harm. The Taliban know that. It's about time we learned.

Born Again (Film of *The Death of Klinghoffer*)

Alan Rich

LA Weekly, November 10, 2003

THE DEATH OF KLINGHOFFER is again before us, insistent, moving, inescapable. Nobody of consequence has ever challenged the intense *musical* power of John Adams's opera; within a different dramatic context, absent the outcries of Palestinian terrorists stating so compellingly the basis of their hatreds, of their belief that "America is one big Jew," this opera of 1991 would be everywhere recognized as a dramatic score of foremost quality. Yet the work survives in an aura of hatred. Michael Steinberg's program note for the original Nonesuch recording of the opera struck an ironically prophetic note: "On whichever day you read these words," he wrote concerning the tragedy of Leon Klinghoffer, "there will be a new installment in the morning paper."

Now *Klinghoffer* has been reborn, in a version which, beyond all previous stagings—and certainly beyond all carefully unstaged concert renditions—creates the best possible context for the work's greatness. Another irony: Adams and the British filmmaker Penny Woolcock were creating this version in London when the news of 9/11 broke; it took only a moment's hesitation before the decision was made to continue. The result, which played at last year's Sundance Festival, is now available on a DVD issued by Decca.

The film offers the strengths of *Klinghoffer*, by more and by less. "By more" is the fact that the score has been drastically reworked; dramatic reordering has occasioned musical reordering as well, and the results are stunning. Much use has been made of news footage; a Palestinian sings of his family's being dispossessed by new Jewish settlers in 1948, and there are shots to support his words. The passengers aboard the hijacked cruise ship sing of their sufferings of generations past, and shots of Nazi pogroms are intercut. "By less" is a minor deprivation: the opera has been shorn of twenty shearable minutes.

More to the point, the action of the opera itself has been moved onto a plane of reality removed from Peter Sellars's original, somewhat idealized conception. The murder of the wheelchair-ridden Leon Klinghoffer actually takes place center stage—not offstage, as in Sellars—and then his final tragic invocation, "May the Lord God and His creation," is sung by his murdered body as it slowly descends through clear Mediterranean waters. Once again, as with the opera since its creation, the eloquent Sanford Sylvan inhabits the personage of the good, tragic Klinghoffer fiber by fiber; no less powerful is the steel-and-granite Marilyn Klinghoffer of Yvonne Howard. Adams himself conducts.

Stunning opera-making, stunning movie-making; I am tempted to regard this remarkable piece of silvery plastic as a major forward step in the dissemination of an artistic commodity through the popular media. The fluidity—the easy transition between the reality of trapped, innocent people on a cruise ship in the hands of equally confused captors and the social forces that have brought them to this point; the transitions, as well, between these people at this point in their lives, and the state of their lives yesterday and the week before—is an element wedded to film. It is brilliantly managed here.

At the end there is nearly an hour's worth of auxiliary material, every word of it relevant to the matter at hand with filmmaker and composer especially inflamed by the splendor of the work they have created. Most moving also are the words of librettist Alice

Goodman, whose life has been most drastically changed by the fate of Klinghoffer, the citizen and the opera. A "nice Jewish girl from Chicago" in 1991 (with the enormous triumph of the Adams/Sellars *Nixon in China* to rest upon), she has assumed the brunt of the reproach leveled at *Klinghoffer*'s controversial message and stands by her words. Whether because or despite, she has in that time abandoned Judaism and now preaches at an Anglican church in London, to a largely Palestinian congregation. She comes off the video as someone you'd love to meet, and someone you have to believe.

Something To Say (Violin Concerto)

Alan Rich
LA Weekly, **November 9, 2004**

JOHN ADAMS'S VIOLIN CONCERTO swept through the cheering Disney Hall crowd last weekend like the fingers of a perfect massage. There is no show-off piece quite like this; memories of sloe-eyed moppets fiddling away at their Wieniawski and Bruch, of overaged adolescents jiggling fingers at windup Mendelssohn piano concertos (and drawing windup "bravos" from uncomprehending crowds) vanish in its path. Adams's Concerto is harder to play than any of the above, but you get the constant impression that it is there on the stage to tell us something about itself. What that might be you have to guess; the tone of Leila Josefowicz's performance last Friday—with excellent support, by the way, in the debut of guest-conductor Mikko Franck, Finnish, blond, and in his twenties (sound familiar?)—told me different things about the work from what I learn from the Gidon Kremer recording on Nonesuch.

Adams's own description of his concerto in a program note—"a throwback to traditional means of discourse and syntax"—is quite beside the point. The amazement in this work is the intensity of the discourse, which overrides matters of syntax. I know of few other works, concerto or any other genre, in which the argument among elements is carried through so powerfully and with greater conviction among the arguing parties. Violin and orchestra slither past one another from the get-go; the first movement seems a single breath. Then there is a pause, then further discourse of overpowering sadness, brought on by soft harmonies from a synthesizer. Finally comes a new level of chaos, wherein soloist and orchestra have at each other nonstop, broken into once when the orchestra calls for rescue from something sounding like the final dance of Stravinsky's *Sacre du Printemps*. The end is no ending at all, merely a stop as though the battle has just moved to another planet out of earshot.

I could have this scenario all wrong, of course; it's interesting that the New York City Ballet was one of the co-commissioners of the work. It would be fascinating to conceive someone else's choreography but difficult to imagine the concertmaster of a ballet orchestra with the chops to manage such a killer solo part. Josefowicz had the chops the other night, as she did at London's Barbican, when I heard her play the work in 2002 during a glowing weekend of all-Adams. In the Kremer recording I hear a higher level of ferocity, and, perhaps, a deeper emotion during the impassioned slow movement. That the work engages the mind and the fingers of two such remarkable contemporary musicians is commentary enough on the quality of the work.

I Was Looking at the Ceiling and Then I Saw the Sky

Sarah Cahill
East Bay Express, May 19, 1995

NO ONE HAS FIGURED OUT exactly what to call the new collaborative venture between composer John Adams, poet June Jordan, and director Peter Sellars. Since it opened for previews on May 3, it's been referred to as "that new opera/music theater/musical performance whatever" or "John Adams's latest um...uh...thing." Its resistance to pigeonholing might work to its advantage. This is a youthful, exuberant creation that will get fans of classical opera and of MTV to commingle in the theater. After the world premiere of *Ceiling...Sky* last week, I watched a TV biography of choreographer Agnes de Mille, who recalled that audiences of *Oklahoma!* often told her they hated ballet, so they couldn't believe that it was ballet they had such a good time watching in *Oklahoma!* Similarly, *Ceiling...Sky* is so entertaining that you forget it's "opera" and "poetry," those loftiest of lofty art forms. This may be a piece with a profound message, imaginative direction, and complex, sophisticated music, but you still come out of the theater humming the tunes.

I Was Looking at the Ceiling and Then I Saw the Sky—the title is a quote from an LA resident describing the moment her house collapsed in the earthquake—follows the stories of seven young characters as they deal with hot topics like immigration, racism, birth control, and natural disasters. Love is at the core of the work, in many guises: the surging lust of the young preacher David; love against all odds between the Salvadoran undocumented immigrant mother Consuelo and the black reformed gang leader Dewain; the empathy of Rick, a Vietnamese lawyer; TV crime reporter Tiffany's obsession for Mike, a white cop; Mike's own confused sexuality; the deep yearning of Leila, who works in a family planning clinic. Their stories are told through a fluid, seamless sequence of twenty-two songs, during which Mike arrests Dewain for stealing two bottles of beer, Leila and David go to bed and feel the earth move, and Tiffany's love life takes an unexpected twist. Very few props enter the bare stage. The only sets involve dramatic banners of vivid graffiti, painted by twenty California graffiti artists to introduce each song. Violent, immediate, richly detailed, and technically dazzling, these paintings reinforce the action and set up each scene.

While Alice Goodman, librettist for Adams's and Sellars's *The Death of Klinghoffer* and *Nixon in China*, wrote highly stylized poetry in rhymed pentameter peppered with curiosities like "bituminous" and "manumitted," Jordan's work is, as the title of her UC Berkeley class suggests, "Poetry for the People." We hear street talk, slang, and the clipped rhythms of American speech. Of course, there are moments of great poetry, but they don't depend on archaisms or arcane vocabulary (although Goodman's librettos are tremendous achievements).

Adams's musical response to Jordan's libretto sounds, if anything, more natural and fluent than the music/text relationships of *Klinghoffer* and *Nixon*. He has always shown an unusual respect for language, keeping its everyday rhythms intact. (You have only to compare his setting of the title song, in which the phrasing of *I Was Looking at the Ceiling and Then I Saw the Sky* precisely matches its spoken counterpart, with the work of his colleague Philip Glass who, for his theater piece *Hydrogen Jukebox*, chopped up the expansive exhalations of Allen Ginsberg's poems into distorted bits of syllables, obliterating all sense of Ginsberg's voice in the process). It's as if Adams took Jordan's text and spoke it over and over until he found the natural cadences and melodic contours of each phrase, and then composed the music to fit. This is true of each song from Rick's virtuosic discourse in his legal defense of Dewain, "Your Honor My Client He's a Young Black Man," in which the last three words are hammered out with punchy emphasis, to the gentle lyricism of Leila's solo "Alone," where she sings "I want to be somebody's straight-up number one" with a lift and pause on "up," just as one would speak it. The music also underscores dramatic tension at crucial points: when Dewain and Consuelo argue, for instance, the music thickens with dissonance and accelerates. Even at its most amplified, the music never overwhelms, thanks in part to each singer's handheld microphone.

On the surface, Adams's mixture of pop, jazz, gospel, blues, funk, and other idioms may seem like a radical departure from his work for the concert hall. It is, in fact, a logical extension of his music to date, which has always been rooted in the vernacular. From the opening bars, in which one pitch generates layers of shimmering ostinato patterns, Adams's own compositional voice predominates. In "Your Honor My Client" and in other songs, we hear the playful contrapuntal density of his 1992 Chamber Symphony, each instrument given its own independent line punctuated by offbeat thumps of percussion. Consuelo's touching solo "Donde Estas?" with its poignant, glassy guitar riffs, recalls the wistful pedal steel guitar soliloquy from Adams's "Disappointment Lake," on his 1993 all-MIDI album *Hoodoo Zephyr*. We even hear a brief hint of his 1973 *Christian Zeal and Activity*, when a disturbing saxophone line insinuates itself to build tension, in "Terrible in the Middle," a confrontation between Tiffany and Mike. Strangely, moments in Jordan's text even recall *Klinghoffer*: the line "Obviously this is not a good night," Tiffany's massive understatement in the face of personal and seismological calamity, echoes the moment in *Klinghoffer* when the terrorist Mamoud sings the ironic line "As things stand now, this will not be an easy day."

Ceiling…Sky belongs to no category but its own, yet resonates with its roots in opera and musicals. You can find conscious or un-conscious references to everything from *Don Giovanni*'s "Cata-logue Aria," when Leila taunts David with a list of his conquests' names, to *Hair*, with a symmetrical pairing of men's and women's ensembles singing about the wonders of sex. In the latter, "Song About the Bad Boys and the News," the three singers team up for an angelic hymn and then break into a no-holds-barred paean— fusing Motown, gospel, a stride bass, and polyrhythms—to the male body. (Jordan seems to have a thing about fish and flowers: the women describe the penis as "the flower, the fish, and the bone" in this song, and later Dewain recounts the earthquake as "a miracle of fish and flowers.") The men's fabulously filthy "Song About the Sweet Majority of the World" is a hip-grinding hilari-ous gem with a sexy slow groove and Hammond organ–like funk progressions. But if in *Ceiling...Sky* we hear echoes of various genres, the music is both warmly familiar and also entirely origi-nal.

The eclectic group of eight musicians performing as the Paul Dresher Ensemble contributes enormously to Adams's score, which demands some improvisation. Since the ensemble includes both outstanding improvisers and classically trained musicians, the music reflects their combined skills. For instance, pianist Phil Aaberg pounds out a rousing gospel piano solo for David's Baptist preaching, and keyboardist Dred Scott gives us a screaming wild solo right after the earthquake (which, by the way, is ingeniously rendered by a remarkably small group of instruments).

Each of *Ceiling...Sky*'s seven cast members gets a moment to shine. Jesse Means II whips the audience into a frenzy as the charismatic preacher David, kissing audience members and shouting out the Gospel as he races across the stage. Kennya J. Ramsey, the powerhouse Acid Queen in the recent tour of *Tommy*, gives Leila a dimension of soulfulness in her solo "Alone." Welly Yang, in Rick's "Your Honor My Client," projects energy and charisma, articulating with beautifully choreographed hand ges-tures. Sophia Salguero, playing Consuelo, reveals the range of her agile soprano in "Donde Estas" when she slips down a slow de-scending chromatic scale. Harold Perrineau Jr. exudes extraordinary vitality and feline grace in Dewain's "Solo in Sunlight," in which he basks in his newfound freedom from jail. Kaitlin Hopkins as Tiffany and Michael Ness as Mike transform their characters: we see them first as unappealing people with racist proclivities, but finally they become sympathetic and multidimensional.

There will, of course, be detractors. Later, in a record store, I overheard an Asian woman vehemently object to Rick's attraction to Tiffany, since she has just told him to get back on a boat. Why should Rick have anything to do with her? In front of me, two audience members wished for more foreshadowing of Mike's latent homosexuality, and an elderly woman wondered aloud why the women's ensemble about men was so much more graphic than the men's about women. It's fitting that the piece premiered in Berkeley, which is simultaneously one of the most tolerant towns in the country and a place where people stick to their little factions and ridicule any conflicting points of view. While the final message of *Ceiling…Sky*—that we can overcome our differences and celebrate the unifying force of love—may be simplistic, it is conveyed with such passion and optimism that we may just begin to believe it.

Adams, Sellars Think Smaller in New Opera (*I Was Looking at the Ceiling and Then I Saw the Sky*)

Richard Dyer
The Boston Globe, July 23, 1995

I WAS LOOKING AT THE CEILING AND THEN I SAW THE SKY, the new opera by composer John Adams, poet June Jordan, and stage director Peter Sellars, is so significant in what it attempts that one wishes it were better than it is, so successful in all kinds of peripheral ways one wishes the essential part of it were any good at all.

Ceiling/Sky opened in Berkeley in May, then moved on to Montreal before achieving its New York premiere in the "American Visionaries" series in Lincoln Center's Serious Fun! Festival a week ago. Now, like its predecessors, it goes on the festival circuit, with performances scheduled for Hamburg, Paris, Edinburgh, and Helsinki; no doubt, CD and video are in the works as well.

Ceiling/Sky moves away from the operatic dimensions and pretensions of the Adams/Sellars works that preceded it, *Nixon in China* and *Klinghoffer*. Most performances of *Klinghoffer* were sold out, but the wrong kind of controversy swirled around it—political, rather than artistic or sexual. Opera companies became afraid to touch it, and several years of work went down the drain.

Adams has not failed to note what happened, and why, nor has he failed to note the durability of practical, small-scale operas on unexceptionable themes. (The Britten estate is thriving.) So *Ceiling/Sky* calls for a cast of seven and an orchestra of eight, and the scenic demands are modest; its theatrical ancestors are not so much the small-scale Britten operas as the Brecht/Weill *Kleine Mahagonny* and *Threepenny Opera* and Marc Blitzstein's *The Cradle Will Rock*. Its musical progenitors include *Porgy and Bess*, *West Side Story*, and pop concept albums like *Abbey Road*, *Tommy*, and *John Wesley Harding*.

The unexceptionable theme Sellars and Adams presented to June Jordan is love. To dramatize it, the collaborators brainstormed a catalogue of young characters—all of them twenty-five or under—living in contemporary California. Jordan calls her text, which has been published by Scribner, an "earthquake/romance," and the title comes from something a woman said after her house collapsed in the 1994 earthquake in Los Angeles. The cast includes an undocumented-immigrant mother from El Salvador; a gang leader trying to go straight; a black Baptist minister; a family-planning counselor in an abortion clinic; a Vietnamese-American Legal Aid attorney; a white "TV crime-as-news reporter"; and a community-activist cop who isn't about to "teach baseball to queers."

The opera is a suite of a couple dozen songs in various popular styles from various eras in Adams's lifetime—jazz, blues, gospel, and rap. The composer's ear is for all the popular music of his forty-seven years rather than for what people twenty-five or younger are actually listening to. The songs link the characters in elaborately contrived ways and generate a plot of sorts: Dewain, the gang leader, steals two bottles of malt liquor (Colt 45) for his girlfriend, Consuelo, and all the pent-up rage of society comes down on him; Jean Valjean has stepped out of the long run of "Les Miz" to rob a convenience store.

The point is that all these characters have been held in, pent up, put down by some sort of ceiling American society has erected over them, until they realize love can set them free; it takes a Richter-scale upheaval to bring them to this realization. The psychological process is sometimes improbable and in one instance utterly ridiculous. After the earthquake, Tiffany, the soulless television reporter, finds herself without electricity, water, windows, clothes, and even her indispensable security blanket, the videocam that reduces reality to something she can deal with. Mike, the cop, has struggled across the rubble of the city to reach her.

This is the seismic moment she chooses to ask him if he's gay. A New York audience twenty-five years after Stonewall laughed out loud; Jordan and Sellars had all but hired a skywriter to out Mike before he figured anything out for himself.

Jordan's language has a deceptive simplicity going for it, and a sophisticated sense of urban rhythm; she knows how to release an emotional tug quite directly. But she apparently has no ability to create a compellingly complex character or a convincing dramatic situation. In "Kleine Mahagonny," Brecht dispensed with conventional storytelling; Jordan falls back upon it, and that's fatal—conventional storytelling would demand that she tell the story better, and release more implications.

If these characters had been depicted satirically, they would be politically incorrect and offend the right-thinking audience the work is addressed to. Because *Ceiling/Sky* preaches to the converted. Depict these people sentimentally (even Puccini would have shied away from Consuelo, the perpetually pregnant immigrant), and we are supposed to find them believable, moving, and uplifting. But sentiment on this scale is implausible as truth and impossible as art. The characters are merely clichés, and the family-planning counselor doesn't even make it to that level.

In some ultimate sense, therefore, these representatives of our society are being patronized by the highly articulate, prize-winning, much-lauded artists who are giving voice to these "voiceless" figures. One remembers that Virgil Thomson thought that *Porgy and Bess* shouldn't have been written at all, for comparable reasons; he found *Porgy* indecent.

Adams does continue to spring surprises. The music is full of the perpetual motion you would expect, but also of a color and life you might not, and it is much dodgier in its strategies than its pop-culture models. A few of the pieces even have breakout potential, and not just the songs about sex for the women ("Song About the Bad Boys and the News") and the men ("Song About the Sweet Majority Population of the World"). He has found ways to make electronic instruments sound both beautiful and musical. He has also learned a lot about how to put words to music: He sets Jordan's text with far greater ease, sophistication, and experience than he brought to Alice Goodman's librettos for the earlier operas. He has found a way to make popular-musical idioms even more sophisticated and challenging. What he has not found a way to do is use them to bring shading, depth, complexity, and feeling to these people.

Sellars's production represents a step back for him, and that is good. This is not a big-budget, high-tech effort that only a major opera company could possibly afford—it returns to the notebook immediacy of his early student productions at Harvard, or Handel's *Saul* with the Cantata Singers. For the first time in years, Sellars is working with a cast of young performers unknown to the public. And as usual, he has assembled a first-class group of theatrical collaborators.

The set is a group of drops, painted by California street and graffiti artists (Acme, Anger, Angst, Axis, and Bash begin the alphabetical list). There are no props. Dunya Ramicova's costumes are, as usual, colorful and theatrically stunning representations of the thing itself. The lighting design by James F. Ingalls is primary and primally effective. The conductor, Grant Gershon, presides over singing and playing of precision, discipline, and conviction. And the sound design by Francois Bergeron is simply the best electrification of a stage show this writer has ever encountered. The sound is powerful but never painful; it never distorts; and you can always tell who is singing what. (This cannot be claimed on behalf of, for example, *Sunset Boulevard.*)

Sellars has trouble staging the dramatic actions because the material is so weak (the scene in the abortion clinic wouldn't fly even on a soap opera), but no contemporary stage director, or choreographer, has a quicker eye for body language and the multiplicity of messages it sends, or a more secure sense of how to create theatrical patterns out of it. Sellars can motivate performers to impossible things, and there is always something to watch in *Ceiling/Sky*, even when you'd rather not.

The young cast is pretty terrific. Although most of them lack classical musical training, they have have mastered the complexity of Adams's rhythms and intervals and make them come out sounding utterly natural. The appealingly fragile soprano of Sophia Salguero takes quite a beating in Consuelo's music. The best voice belongs to Michael Christopher Ness as Mike. It must have delighted Sellars to find a singer named Ness to cast as a cop and to know that this insecurely macho character would be por- trayed by a performer who had appeared as Curly in *Oklahoma!*— and looks the part. The gospel-music vaultings of Darius De Haas's voice are spectacular, and Harold Perrineau Jr. is breathtak- ing in movement and body language as the reformed gang leader. Welly Yang is agile in both voice and gesture as the volatile Viet- namese-American attorney. Kennya J. Ramsey and Kaitlin Hop- kins are talented performers struggling with roles that are badly conceived, or hardly conceived at all.

Nixon in China and *Klinghoffer* gradually transformed an artifi- cial video image into a convincing human reality. The characters in *I Was Looking at the Ceiling and Then I Saw the Sky* remain throughout the multicultural poster children we meet in the opening chorus and ensemble. This piece was meant to be a major statement on behalf of the young and the future; all of the work that went into it was dedicated and some of it was very good work. The saddest thing about the disappointing sum of all its parts is that the ceiling above these young people is one that Adams, Jor- dan, and Sellars have securely installed, and the sky is only graffiti art.

Adams's Twentieth Century Rolls— and Rocks (*Century Rolls*)

Mark Swed
Los Angeles Times, **February 5, 2001**

JOHN ADAMS'S SIGNIFICANCE in the twenty-first century can hardly be known at this early date. But what he means to us here and now proved interesting to think about Saturday night at the Dorothy Chandler Pavilion, where the Bay Area composer was on hand to conduct the Los Angeles Philharmonic in two of his works.

Century Rolls (a piano concerto) and "The Nixon Tapes" (excerpts from the opera *Nixon in China*) take fond, almost nostalgic looks back at specific moments or aspects of the twentieth century that are embedded in our daily lives. That's a big task for music, but a doable one. And for anyone searching for what differentiates new classical music from the popular culture, this is a good place to begin. Pop music's immediacy speaks in a common tongue to and about the moment. New classical music has a larger view of the past and a fancier language. But when it works as well as Adams's music does, its freshness feels permanent.

The inspiration for *Century Rolls*, Adams told the audience before the performance (the second of three over the weekend), was his love for three jazz-flavored piano concertos, by Gershwin,

Ravel, and Copland, from the 1920s. Like Ravel's, his concerto has a soft, meltingly lyrical center. Like all three, it has a clanking, swinging final movement, which Adams titles "Hail Bop," having, at one time, amusingly mistaken the comet's name. But what takes this engaging half-hour concerto out of the past is its celebration of the machine in music.

The sound we know of the Jazz Age is mechanical reproduction, either the phonograph, or in the case of what interested Adams, the player piano, with its bright metallic clatter. Later in the century, the player piano became the focus of a renegade American-born composer working in Mexico City. Punching his own piano rolls, Conlon Nancarrow discovered exciting new ways of complicating rhythm that has had a profound effect on composers, Adams among them.

Also at the time of those jazz concertos Adams admires, it seemed that modernists everywhere were infected by what literary critic Hugh Kenner called "the mechanic muse." Today, the heartbeat of much popular music is, of course, the rhythm machine. Minimalism, one of the dominant styles in late twentieth century music, was once described as broken-record music.

Century Rolls puts a very human face on all this mechanization. It was written for a warm, substantive pianist, Emanuel Ax. And although he is most at home in the nineteenth century—Ax is one of our most outstanding Chopin pianists—he has an impish sense of adventure. In *Century Rolls*, Adams can be merciless, forcing Ax into mechanical rhythmic grooves, but the machine is full of delightful kinks that send it off into unpredictable, and often surprisingly effusive, directions.

The long first movement reminds me of an elaborate Buster Keaton chase scene—you never know what Ax is going to run into next. The slow movement, "Manny's Gym," is a fanciful takeoff on Satie's *Gymnopédies*. "Hail Bop" is a riot of catchy rhythms, complex enough to sound almost inscrutable, thrilling enough to bring roars of approval from a large and enthusiastic crowd. Ax performs the concerto often and is a consummate virtuoso. He still seems a little worried about some of the mechanical passages, but that only adds to the attractiveness and humanity of his playing.

Nixon in China celebrates a moment in history less for its political implications than for its cultural and profoundly human ones. It examines the clash of East and West, but it does so by looking deeply into the characters who held radically opposing views that still divide our world today. The marvelous portraits in *Nixon in China* are of leaders who, when faced with a culture they didn't understand, were forced to examine their own insecurities. No documentary can show you what it might have felt like to be Dick or Pat or Mao at that time, but through Adams's music and Alice Goodman's words the cultural struggle becomes personalized and newly comprehensible.

A couple of years ago, Adams assembled three different sets of excerpts from the opera under the general title "The Nixon Tapes" in hopes of generating a new interest in the 1987 opera, which, having lost its novelty, had been languishing. The parts he chose for the LA Philharmonic performance included the opening scene of the opera, in which Nixon steps off Air Force One and sings with that special Nixonian blend of glee and paranoia about being on the news and part of history. The suite concluded with the first Chinese banquet and toasts by Chinese Premier Chou En-lai and Nixon. The middle section was Pat Nixon's touching aria from the second act.

The performance was a suggestion, but only that, of what this important opera has to offer. James Maddalena, who created the title role, has unnervingly absorbed Nixon's physical mannerisms. Susan Narucki made a bright and sympathetic Pat. William Sharp, however, was less successful at capturing Chou's wise nobility. John Ames took the small role of Kissinger. Adams subtly amplifies solo singers and the chorus (the confident Los Angeles Master Chorale), but the balances between singers and orchestra were never convincing (an opera company has more time and resources to work out those mechanical problems).

Nor is Adams the most convincing conductor of his music. He is capable on the podium and a winning presence. He knows exactly what he wants, and he is careful and precise with difficult rhythms. He clearly seems to enjoy performing, and he seems to have an easy relationship with the orchestra and audience. Everybody likes him.

But as performances of his music by Kent Nagano, Esa-Pekka Salonen, and Michael Tilson Thomas have demonstrated, there can be more nuance, more punch, more expression to his music than he brings out. Still, the personal relationship that the orchestra and audience have forged with Adams has a value that goes beyond specific performances: It helps get the music in our collective bloodstreams, where it belongs.

Bigger Proves Better in Adams's Grandiose World (*Naive and Sentimental Music*)

Mark Swed
Los Angeles Times, **February 22, 1999**

JOHN ADAMS'S MASSIVE *Naive and Sentimental Music*, which was given its world premiere by the Los Angeles Philharmonic on Friday night in the Dorothy Chandler Pavilion, is not what it first seems. Compelling, original, and assured, it is music hardly representative of its title, at least in the modern sense of naive or sentimental. And although it's Adams's most ambitious orchestral score, it does not represent a stylistic breakthrough, as have a number of his other major scores (the orchestral *Harmonielehre* and the Violin Concerto or the operas *Nixon in China* and *The Death of Klinghoffer*).

Pluck just about any phrase from the forty-eight minutes of *Naive and Sentimental Music*, and it will sound familiar. The use of the big orchestra as a lumbering machine that huffs and puffs during breathtaking liftoff, the employment of endless melodies that weave with winsome unpredictability for minutes on end, the chugging rhythms, and the dazzling instrumental colors are all known footprints of America's most admired orchestral composer. It is, as Adams's music has been before, jazzy and melancholy.

But, a heavier ship, its takeoffs are more gravity-defying; its melodies, more winsome; its colors, more dazzling; its jazz, jazzier; its rhythmic energy, more obsessive; its melancholy, more devastating; its surprises, more surprising. Everything is bigger and better.

Size, this huge canvas seems to be saying, in the popular parlance, matters. And to some extent it does. Size draws us in, makes us feel part of something grand. The first movement culminates with a magnificent onrush of sound and energy. The third movement ends the work with pealing bells and joyful annunciatory horns, the rushing of strings and winds. These are awe-inspiring vistas that no small music could produce.

Still, like the best epics, *Naive and Sentimental Music* is ultimately personal, intimate. We need to place ourselves within the vast universe and among the masses, and it is in the epic in which individual stories peek through the onrush of history that we can do so. The grandeur of Adams's sonic panorama, then, is an inflating of sensation, not of sentiment.

The title, more than the music, needs explanation. Adams has hoped to revive the German poet Friedrich Schiller's notions of naive and sentimental from two hundred years ago. For Schiller the naive poet was intuitive, at one with nature, whereas the sentimental poet consciously inserted himself in society and in history.

Adams has fought that battle with himself over the years. Earlier works divided between an intentionally trickster persona and a more despondent one. By now the musical schizophrenia is healed.

Stylistically, too, *Naive and Sentimental Music* is a grand, healthy synthesis. Our ending century runs all through it—Scriabin's ecstatic trumpet here, the stuttering swells of Steve Reich's winds there; the soberly quiet open strings of Copland here, the brash big-band sound of Ellington there. The angular rhythms of Stravinsky's Hollywood period, an expressionistic scream of anguish from Mahler's Vienna, and groovy strummed guitar chords from the summer of love all happily cohabit.

An enormous amount of activity occurs throughout the three movements and their tens of thousands of notes, but the musical argument is remarkably clear, especially for a composer who is known to meander. Liquid, syncopated melody, never predictable, never resolving, but immediately appreciable, journeys through a first-movement adventure. The second movement, inspired by a Busoni berceuse, takes its character from luminous open strings, the ringing of bells (cowbells and temple bells), and the slicing shimmer of a bowed vibraphone. Through it is a touching amplified guitar solo. The third movement has a minimalist core, repeated motives accruing and discarding notes one at a time, a rush of rhythm, a bedazzlement of orchestration.

The work, a symphony in all but name, is dedicated to Esa-Pekka Salonen, who conducted its premiere with an arresting sense of command. For all the music's immediacy, it is a huge challenge for conductor and orchestra, and Friday there were first-night jitters. It had a shaky launch with flaccid guitar and uncertain flutes and oboes. But with thrilling control, Salonen righted what appeared to be an eminent crash, and the performance ultimately achieved the music's magnificence.

The audience responded with thunder. This is music people want to hear and should hear. The Philharmonic, though, has been too stingy: only three performances instead of the four for most subscription programs, and it is not part of this summer's Hollywood Bowl schedule.

But the concert, itself, was a happy occasion. The tone for Adams was curiously but illuminatingly set by a titillating, alert performance of Hadyn's Symphony No. 7 ("Le Midi"), a score that anticipated the modern symphony, thus book-ending Adams's post-symphony symphony. It also included Heinrich Schiff's gripping performance of Schumann's strange, loopy, romantically excessive Cello Concerto.

Rebirth of a Savior in *El Niño*

Mark Swed
Los Angeles Times, January 13, 2001

JOHN ADAMS has been a bold maker of music theater. And with Peter Sellars to egg him on in the operas *Nixon in China* and *The Death of Klinghoffer*, Adams has looked hard and deep into the human psyche and culture, how and why we all have such a difficult time communicating with one another. The Northridge earthquake, in *I Was Looking at the Ceiling and Then I Saw the Sky*, is the symbol for a society—in this case Los Angeles—shook up by its diverse and not-yet-integrated cultural mix.

With *El Niño*, which had its first performance in Paris last month as an opera and was given its North American premiere Thursday night at Davies Symphony Hall by the San Francisco Symphony as a semi-staged oratorio, Adams and Sellars now confront the birth of Christ. At this millennial moment, they tell an old story in a new way. They use modern, multimedia means. Sellars shot a silent film, with eloquent and harsh images of LA street life, which runs through the entire performance. There are three principal vocal soloists, three countertenors with smaller parts, and three dancers. All are in costume (casual clothes and barefoot), and all enact their roles. The texts come from the Bible, Gnostic sources, the Wakefield Mystery Plays, several Latin American poets, and fashionable medieval composer-mystic Hildegard von Bingen.

But what is truly modern and new about *El Niño* is its message: that the way to unite a divisive world is to look at the birth of Christ not as a religious miracle but a biological one. Birth itself, Adams and Sellars suggest, invests spiritual power in every individual.

The other miracle of *El Niño* is the music. Adams's model for his two-part and nearly two-hour work was Handel's *Messiah*, with which it shares a mosaic-like approach to narrative and room for contemplation on the meaning of events. But given Adams's much broader selection of texts, which range over two thousand years, his music must be an even greater unifying force than Handel's—and so it proves to be. This is Adams's most powerful and affecting and sublimely assured music. Though *El Niño* is a vocal work, its soul is in the orchestra, which creates a sort of ocean of sound in which all the elements of the oratorio live. It is often roiling and forceful, always eager for a magnificent climax—the play on words in the title, which means both "the Christ child" and a phenomenon of nature, is intentional. (And indeed, the oratorio blew into town on the crest of an El Niño-sized storm.) The orchestra, its sound rich and complex (with a glittery integration of electronic instruments), was also a conduit for deep and emotional song, as well as a comforting cushion for the singers.

Those singers were America's finest—Dawn Upshaw, Lorraine Hunt Lieberson, and Willard White. None was assigned specific characters. Sometimes Upshaw and Hunt Lieberson portrayed Mary, and White made a strikingly angry and confused Joseph. Meanwhile, the countertenors (Daniel Bubeck, Brian Cummings, and Steven Rickards) and the dancers (Daniela Graca, Nora Kimball, and Michael Schumacher) interacted in ever changing roles.

Not that all of the texts are theatrically specific. Rather they dwell on what it feels like to be a mother, to be a father, to comprehend a miracle in ancient times and in modern times. The two longest and most difficult poems, both by twentieth-century Mexican writer Rosario Castellanos and sung in Spanish, were set to haunting, inner-directed music, and sung with amazing intensity by Upshaw and Hunt Lieberson.

As in his last large piece, the orchestral composition *Naive and*

Sentimental Music, which was given its premiere by the Los Angeles Philharmonic two years ago, Adams seemed to put everything
he knows into his score. Echoes of *Nixon, Klinghoffer,* and *Ceil-
ing/Sky* were everywhere. But there is also a musical freshness to *El
Niño*—its tunes are catchier, its rhythms spikier, its exuberance
more thrilling, its complexities more integrated than anything
that has preceded it. The application of big-band jazz, of a rock
bass line, of some slashing strings straight out of a Hitchcock
sound track never sounded self-conscious or like parody, but
rather like bits of an older culture still useful for a new one.

Kent Nagano conducted, as he had the premiere in Paris. The
chorus was that of the San Francisco Symphony. And one of the
pleasures of hearing these musicians perform Adams was that they
were speaking their own language. He represents the Bay Area,
and they have played and sung his music more often than anyone
else. The performance, on every level, was superb.

Still, *El Niño* is more than music. Not everyone in the audience,
it was clear at intermission and afterward, wanted theater to in-
vade the concert hall. Sellars's film brought its own emotional sensibility, showing the sufferings of police and homeless alike. The
staging diverted attention among the poetic text (projected under
the film), complex music, acting, dancing, and an intricate interaction of stage and screen movement. It is a total experience—
confusing, overwhelming but also, in its multiple parts, liberating.
It allows nothing to be taken for granted, which is, after all, the
whole point of a miracle.

Washed in the Sound of Souls in Transit (*On the Transmigration of Souls*)

Anthony Tommasini
The New York Times, September 21, 2002

IT'S UNDERSTANDABLE THAT so far most American composers of note have avoided writing works that deal with September 11. The event is still too close, too immense. But the need to come to terms with it artistically, at least in some manner, is also real. So give John Adams credit for trying. Mr. Adams's *On the Transmigration of Souls*, commissioned by the New York Philharmonic and Lincoln Center's Great Performers series, received its premiere on Thursday night at the first subscription concert of the Philharmonic's season, conducted by Lorin Maazel in his second appearance as the orchestra's music director.

Mr. Adams is reticent about calling this work a musical composition. His intent, as he wrote in the program note, was to create a "memory space" where "you can go and be alone with your thoughts and emotions." He wanted to make the concert hall something akin to a great cathedral, where you feel in the presence of generations of souls even as you are surrounded by other people: whispered voices, children whimpering, shoes scuffling on the stone floor.

Mr. Adams uses taped sounds of the city as a faint aural backdrop for the work: cars swooshing by, brakes squealing, fleeting laughter. To this recording he added the names of victims, read in mantralike manner by his various friends and family members. After the taped sounds establish the mood, the orchestra enters, first the strings playing tender parallel chords, then increasingly agitated rustlings in the woodwinds and nervous stirrings in the brass.

The text the double chorus sings is a collection of short phrases taken from missing-person posters and memorials in the vicinity of ground zero, sensitively assembled by Mr. Adams. Single words like "Missing" and "Remember," and poignant phrases like "He used to call me every day…" are turned into repetitive musical motives. This could have easily come across as mawkish. But Mr. Adams's restraint gives tragic stature to plain, intoned phrases like "My brother…" Rhythmically, the music is intentionally static. Even rippling minimalist patterns that come and go seldom disrupt the overall meditative state. Though the chorus sings some wafting lines, Mr. Adams essentially avoids melody as well. The richness and solemnity of this music come primarily from its harmony, a subtle mix of sturdy tonality and anxious, stacked-up orchestra chords spiked with shards of dissonance.

Tension builds as the work unfolds, climaxing in a prolonged passage that seems an attempt to depict the work's title. For Mr. Adams, transmigration happens to the souls of those left behind to grapple with loss as well, as to the souls of those moving from life to death.

The music crests and swells and turns on itself; piercing dissonances make you wince, like the aural equivalent of staring into glaring light. Finally, the chorus sings almost hysterical repetitions of the word "light" as the orchestra music dissolves, breaking into squiggles, remnants, and sputtering sounds. It's as good a guess as any at what the transmigration process must be.

Some listeners may find Mr. Adams's material to be insufficiently involving on a purely musical level. But this atypical concert work asks you to put aside typical expectations. And there is real musical method to its structure, for thirty minutes passed by almost too quickly.

Though in recent interviews Mr. Maazel has emphasized the central importance to the Philharmonic of the standard repertory, contemporary works like this one may make the best use of his keen technical skills.

With just two rehearsals he pulled off a raptly beautiful account of a complex score, with the Philharmonic joined by the New York Choral Artists (Joseph Flummerfelt, director) and the Brooklyn Youth Chorus (Dianne Berkun, director).

The Art of 9/11

Arthur C. Danto
The Nation, **September 23, 2002**

> Recall that after Schubert's death, his brother cut some of Schubert's scores into small pieces, and gave each piece, consisting of a few bars, to his favorite pupils. And this act, as a sign of piety, is just as understandable as the different one of keeping the scores untouched, accessible to no one. And if Schubert's brother had burned the scores, that, too, would be understandable as an act of piety.
>
> —Ludwig Wittgenstein

ANNOUNCEMENTS HAVE BEGUN TO COME IN of exhibitions of art dedicated to the memory of 9/11. One of them, to be called *Elegy*, had a September 3 opening at the Viridian Gallery in Chelsea, and its card in particular caught my eye. It displays a photograph by someone named N'Cognita, which embodies a mood of elegy with a remarkable specificity. It is a view down an unmistakable but anonymous New York street, taken in sharp perspective, with the buildings, most of their details obliterated, silhouetted darkly against an orange and lavender sky. They are vintage tenements, of the kind we all know, with heavy cornices and water towers, and the melancholy of the image is heightened by the absence of towers at the end of the street.

"We" refers, of course, to New Yorkers, for whom the view of emptiness at the ends of streets and avenues has been the nagging reminder of what we had more or less taken for granted as always there. No one loved the towers as much as everyone missed them—but it was not so much the erasure of the landmarks that tore at the heart as it was the inerasable memory of how they fell. That memory, however, belonged to the whole world, to viewers everywhere, who kept seeing, over and over, as in a nightmare, the planes, the black smoke, the flames, the falling bodies, unforgettable against the brilliant blue Manhattan sky. But it is the rubbed-out skyline, framed by the distinctive New York buildings, that is the constant reminder for those who lived the experience by being in New York when it happened, and whose visual habits keep it vivid through being thwarted. I was recently in Berlin, and I was struck by how my friends there keep seeing the absence of the Wall, drawing my attention to blanknesses that I, as an outsider, would otherwise never see as such. Those blanknesses now define the soul of Berlin, as these define that of New York.

I somewhat resist the idea of the anniversary, but at the same time acknowledge a deep wisdom in the way an anniversary marks a symbolic ending. The art that belonged to the experience of September 11 now constitutes a body of work that differs from the art that will undertake to memorialize it. The difference in part is this: One need not have shared the experience to memorialize it. The Vietnam Veterans Memorial was designed by Maya Lin with supreme memorialist intuition, though she had no experience of the Vietnam conflict, having been too young when it tore the nation to bits, nor had she lost anyone who meant something to her in the war. But the art I have in mind could only have come from having experienced the event. Jan Scruggs, the infantryman who made it his mission to bring a Vietnam memorial into being, titled his book *To Heal a Nation*. That is what memorials should do, hateful as the events memorialized may be. That is the function of elegies as well. They use art as a means of transforming pain into beauty.

That already began, on September 11 itself, with the moving, extemporaneous shrines that appeared spontaneously all over New York, and became inseparable from the experience, so much so that, appropriate as they were at the time, it would be a bad idea to re-create one as a memorial, say in a vitrine. There is nothing about Maya Lin's masterpiece that itself belongs to the event, the way, say, a helicopter would, or a mortar that had actually been used there—though the artist Robert Irwin once told me that sometimes a cannon on a lawn can be exactly the right solution, and I think I understand why. It is the grass that makes it right, which builds an image of peace into the emblem of war: "Green grows the grass on the infantry/at Malplaquet and Waterloo." I thought that artists could have done nothing better than the anonymous shrine-makers, who knew intuitively that the shrines should consist in flags, flowers, candles, scraps of poetry or prayer, and photographs. But I have since thought about some of the things artists, in fact, did at the time, which came from the same impulse as the shrines—and this work has a certain interest through the ways it, like the shrines, caught something of the experience it responded to.

An artist I am close to wrote me, some weeks after the event, "I am fine, though it is hard to think about what kind of work to make at this point, other than decorative, escapist, or abstract. I suppose I'll explore one or all of these things." The work for which she is deservedly famous is so different from what it now occurred to her to explore, that it seemed clear to me that she was seeking something with the symbolic weight that the shrines had had, as signs and acts of what Wittgenstein speaks of as piety. A very deep piece of art history remains to be written about what New York artists did in those months when we thought or talked about nothing else, and the enormity of our shared experience flooded consciousness fully.

I single out "New York artists" mainly because I have the sense that the intensity of the experience depended very greatly upon whether one was here or elsewhere. A former student, at the time teaching in California, told me that he felt "impotent" in being away. He realized that so far as helping clear the rubble, search for bodies, bring in the supplies, he would have been redundant. The city had all the help it needed. But he felt, having lived and studied here for several years, that he had been injured in a way someone who was not a New Yorker had not been—and he felt the need to be here to share the grief. Not being here was internal to his impotence, if that makes sense, not that it would have made the slightest practical difference whether he were here or not. And I think being here meant that this grief was palpable, that it was like something one breathed. One mark of that feeling was the way everyone became very considerate of everyone else, as if each of us was due a measure of moral sympathy. The kind of art that began to be made was another mark, special to the feeling.

Lucio Pozzi, a performance artist who really cannot properly be described quite that narrowly, tells how a European friend, who managed to get a call through, said, "At this point one cannot carry on making art." Pozzi answered, "Today I have painted a little watercolor, and I shall paint another one tomorrow." He had painted a copy in watercolor of a watercolor of his own, from a photograph of it in one of his catalogues. It is of yellow fields. He did this three times. On the following day, he stood outside his downtown studio and photographed the smoke as it lay in the street where his studio is located. He took several shots quite rapidly, just seconds apart, and turned the images into Xeroxes, which he stapled together into pamphlets, to be mailed to friends. Someone might have thought the pictures so alike that they could have been the same shot, reproduced ten or twelve times. I have seen such sets of images used in psychological experiments, mainly to demonstrate how pigeons, whose visual acuity is far sharper than ours, are able to distinguish between pictures that humans tell apart only with great difficulty. In my view, the images did two things: They showed what everyone downtown would have recognized as how their streets looked, and they did this with the zero degree of art. The other thing was to show how it felt to be there, engulfed in a cloud of sadness that would not lift.

I was struck by the fact that as with the photographs, Pozzi's watercolors looked alike. If I were to curate a show about how New York artists responded to 9/11, I would certainly include his series of photographs, and all three copies of the watercolor. And I would include several of the watercolors I mentioned in an earlier column, by Audrey Flack, who felt the despair of impotence my student spoke of, and went out to Montauk to paint the sunlight on fishing boats. Audrey does monumental sculptures. I have greatly admired her immense figures of powerful females, for the feminist symbolism of course, but also for their masterful execution. She had been at work on a new colossus, intended to stand in the water off Queens. It was to have been of Queen Catherine of Braganza, after whom the borough of Queens was named. It was a brilliant concept, brilliantly executed, and Audrey modeled two airplanes, one for each of Catherine's pockets, standing for the borough's two airports. The reason the work was never completed belongs to the unedifying story of racial politics, but I mention her colossi here for the vivid contrast they point to between her sculptural ambitions and the water-and-sunlight aquarelles that met her needs after the terrible event. They are not in the least monumental. They are daringly ordinary, like skillful enough paintings by a conventional watercolorist, with nothing on her mind except to register how the world looked. The real world needed to be affirmed, and these are perfect examples for the art history of 9/11.

Had Queen Catherine stood, like the Statue of Liberty, when 9/11 took place, the two airplanes would certainly have been read as portents. But I cannot imagine airplanes in my 9/11 show. Tom Kotek, a graduate student in fine arts at Hunter College, told me how he and some fellow students visited an art school somewhere in New England not long after the event. They saw a work consisting of some cardboard towers and a toy plastic airplane. Wittgenstein tells of ways of expressing grief symbolically that we all understand and accept, even if it would not have occurred to us to do things that way. But there are certainly ways that would strike us as wrong or odd. Kotek and his friends thought that the installation they saw was not at all like something they would have made, having been in New York when it happened, and still tasting the grief. In fact, none of them had done anything they would consider 9/11 art yet, and weren't sure they would. There was nothing exactly wrong about the little plastic-and-paper crash-site. It was the kind of thing that might naturally have occurred to artists who had not been in New York, and were given an assignment. But genuine 9/11 art, as my examples suggest, had to find ways of embodying the feeling rather than depicting the event, and is inevitably oblique. An artist I spoke to who happened to have been in Australia on 9/11 showed a drawing she had done of the Sydney Opera House. Her thought was that the terrorists would have taken out the most important building in whatever city they struck. So the Sydney Opera House symbolized the World Trade Center towers, like a substitution in the language of a dream. But I cannot imagine a 9/11 New York artist drawing the great opera house as a way of conveying what it felt like to have lived through the event.

I have been gathering ideas for my imagined 9/11 show, and asking artists whether they have done anything in particular that might be included if I were to have gone forward with it. Here are a few more examples of what I consider true 9/11 art.

I spoke with Robert Zakanitch a week or so after 9/11, and he told me he was painting lace. Readers may recall an essay I devoted to an ensemble of huge paintings by Zakanitch a few years ago, which he called the *Big Bungalow Suite*. He had made his first reputation as an abstract expressionist, but like many, including Audrey Flack, felt that he wanted to produce something more meaningful, having to do with life. He became part of a movement in the late 1970s called "pattern and decoration"—"P and D"— which attracted a number of artists disaffected with mainstream art. *Big Bungalow Suite* refers to the wallpaper and slipcover designs of his *Mitteleuropa* grandmother's house in New Jersey, where his family worked in factories. He associated that profusion of decorative motifs with the comforting femininity present in what was a sanctuary for him. Lace made a lot of sense, given this background, even if he might have painted lace if 9/11 had not happened. But it had a particular meaning for him because 9/11 *had* happened.

The sculptor Ursula von Rydingsvard was born to peasant parents in a labor camp in Germany, and her work is an effort to create a world she never really knew. Her immense wooden sculptures refer to a primitive form of life in primordial worlds. One of her main forms is that of the bowl—she did a huge bowl for her last show at the Neuberger Museum, in Purchase, New

York, which was eighteen feet across. They are made of milled cedar beams, stacked, glued, and shaped with power tools. They feel as if they were made with giants in mind. Interestingly, von Rydingsvard sometimes carves lace. But her first work after 9/11 was a crisscross, fencelike structure that she titled *mama, build me a fence!* A fence, like lace, is, as Wittgenstein would say, understandable.

The idea of an edge or a boundary also suggested itself to Mary Miss, whose studio is situated just north of ground zero. Miss is sometimes referred to as a "land artist," and her work is public through and through. Her most recent installation is a kind of "acupunctural" transformation of the Union Square subway station: Various points and fixtures throughout the space have been neatly painted a uniform red. She and her assistants conceived the idea of a "moving perimeter" around ground zero, which would in the course of the work take on the form of a wreath—and, indeed, the title of the piece is *A Wreath for Ground Zero*. It would have the form of a figure eight, with reference to the two linked areas where the towers stood, or of the infinity sign, symbolizing the "endless knot" of mourners. The "wreath" would allow visual access to the site as the rebuilding took place, and it would also "make a place for the flowers, flags, candles and notes that have appeared throughout the city." Miss's idea got the backing of various public arts agencies, but inevitably ran into resistance with the bureaucracy and business interests of the city. One bureaucrat rudely asked who the hell she thought she was, coming forward like that when there were so many who had just as great a right as she. Her response was that everyone should be called to come forward with their ideas. Nothing immediate came of her project, but on her Web page she has issued a call for ideas, in a way modeled on the shrines that appeared everywhere, for memorial sites throughout the city, recognizing that New York as a whole was and is a mourning site. We should all be memorial artists.

I would certainly want to include in my exhibition an example of a post-9/11 shrine (attributing it, perhaps, to N'Onymous). But I might also include some art that somehow belongs to the experience, but only, in a way, after the fact. Let me explain. There is an artist-in-residence program sponsored by the Lower Manhattan Cultural Council, which had used the ninety-second floor in tower one as studio space. The artists, whose work had been destroyed (and one of whom was killed), were given a chance to show their work at a special exhibition given by the New Museum of Contemporary Art after 9/11. I had the sense that many of them were in a way continuing what they had been doing during their residency, which is certainly the sort of thing many New York artists did, however deeply affected they were by the circumstances. A lot of the best artists I know would either have continued along their trajectories or simply stopped working. As part of his residency in 1999, however, Stephen Vitiello, impressed by the silence within the tower in contrast to the vitality of the city outside, placed two contact microphones against the glass to record external sounds. He called these "World Trade Center Recordings," and one of them, *Winds After Hurricane Floyd, 1999—2001,* was included in the Whitney Biennial of 2002. It became a very affecting work, in part because of the metaphor that powerful and destructive winds generate, in part because of the fact that no such sounds will ever again be made. And in part because the sounds are the noises of a building far more vulnerable than it looked, or than the interior silences due to the thick glass walls would have led one to suppose. Like all the 9/11 art in my imagined exhibition, it tells us something profound about art, and about ourselves.

I have not made an especially systematic effort to track down further examples of 9/11 art. I really lack the curatorial impulse. And it would be a very strange exhibition were it all brought together, since the work would have very little in common other than the experience that occasioned it. I don't think 9/11 art will stop being made just because the anniversary is at hand. Who knows when an experience will need to be expressed in art? But because of the conditions on its authenticity, it will differ from memorial art, which must be public and take on the responsibility of putting the event at a distance, and must negotiate the controversies such memorials generate. The 9/11 art was private and personal, and dealt with the mitigation of grief.

Symphony Premieres Adams's Splendid *Ives*

Joshua Kosman
San Francisco Chronicle, May 2, 2003

JOHN ADAMS HAS PROVIDED San Francisco Symphony audiences with some powerful musical experiences over the years, but nothing to compare with the rich emotional splendor of his latest opus, which received its world premiere Wednesday night in Davies Symphony Hall with Michael Tilson Thomas conducting.

My Father Knew Charles Ives, a funny, rueful, and heartbreakingly beautiful musical memoir, melds Adams's personal history with that of American concert music in one easy and daring artistic stroke, and it was the highlight of a program that also featured the welcome return of violinist Hilary Hahn. This is a capacious and detailed thirty-minute orchestral essay by our nation's most important composer working at the height of his creative powers.

And this, one suspects, is just the beginning. *My Father*, which Thomas and the Symphony will take on their European tour this month, is the first of four Symphony commissions that Adams has signed up for over the next ten years—in addition to the opera about J. Robert Oppenheimer and the making of the atomic bomb that is in the works for San Francisco Opera.

All this comes at a time when Adams, at fifty-six, seems to be exploring new paths with renewed artistic vigor. Although *My Father* is unmistakably the work of the composer of *Harmonielehre, Nixon in China, El Niño,* and the recent Pulitzer-winning *On the Transmigration of Souls,* it also charts new directions for Adams's rhythmic language and use of the orchestra.

The title, though not literally true, couldn't possibly be more apt—in fact, a musical archaeologist knowing only the score could probably reconstruct the title with near certainty. Over the course of three movements, Adams revisits his past (musical and purely biographical) through the lens of Ives's retrospective vein.

The Ives references are most explicit in the first movement, "Concord" (though suggestive of Ives's piano sonata of the same name, the title refers to Adams's New Hampshire hometown). After a haunting, lyrical trumpet solo (delivered with stunning grace by Glenn Fischthal) that tips its hat to Ives's *Unanswered Question,* Adams begins a collage of New England musical life.

Just as in Ives's memory pieces, snippets of marches, and hymn tunes parade across the stage, colliding with one another and with other musical fragments—reveille, or a Beethoven duet that the young Adams played as a beginning clarinet student.

The movement is exciting and breathlessly funny, but the complexities go deeper. By invoking Ives's sonic pastiches (particularly those of the Fourth Symphony), Adams has extended the nostalgia by an extra layer, summoning not only his own boyhood musical memories, but—for the majority of listeners who have never witnessed a New England town band—also our communal memories of Ives's memories.

Even more unforgettable is the second movement, "The Lake," which re-creates the waterside dance hall where the composer's parents first met (that Tristram Shandy–ish detail is helpful but not essential for the movement's emotional impact).

Like the first movement, this one opens with the piece's distinctive textural backdrop: shimmering, slow-moving string harmonies punctuated by blurry twitterings from the woodwinds and percussion, like sonic fireflies on a long-ago summer evening. And then, as if from across the water, come the strains of old-time dance music, exemplifying, in Noel Coward's phrase, the potency of cheap music.

The piano, playing with just enough rhythmic freedom to cast a scrim of memory over the proceedings, delivers a series of slow, ruminative chords (Peter Grunberg voiced them gorgeously), while the brass, their Harmon mutes in place, punch out gentle, tightly spaced harmonies. The entire movement creates a tone of wistful elegance, reminiscent of the last act of *Nixon in China* and that opera's dapper offshoot, *The Chairman Dances.*

Having settled up with Ives and his father, Adams turns inward in the final movement, "The Mountain." The tone here is less unified, as the composer cycles through diverse strains, but the effect is no less telling.

Another trumpet solo begins things, harking back to the piece's opening measures, and there are passages of craggy assertiveness à la Carl Ruggles and a brief, wild rhythmic gallop before the music comes to a contemplative close.

Thomas and the orchestra gave a fervent, rhythmically vibrant reading, even if it was clear that it will take them a few more performances to get the piece fully under their belts. No worries on that score—this is a major addition to the orchestral repertoire and will be with us for a long time.

History's Unholy Trinity
(*Doctor Atomic*)

Justin Davidson
Newsday, October 3, 2005

THE SECOND ACT OF JOHN ADAMS'S new opera, *Doctor Atomic*, takes place during one of history's most unquiet nights. In the lightning-streaked predawn of July 16, 1945, the scientists who devised the first atomic bomb wonder if testing it might ignite the heavens and consume the Earth.

"I can find no reason to believe that the test shot will touch off the destruction of the world," is how Edward Teller puts it in the libretto that director Peter Sellars has drawn from archival sources.

The suspense is both attenuated and ratcheted up by knowing how the opera will end: not with self-inflicted apocalypse, but with that possibility becoming forever a part of human existence. One of the achievements of *Doctor Atomic* is that it absorbs the compressed anxieties of the era deeply into the music's own flesh.

A montage of sounds runs through the score: alarms, screams, strange metallic grindings, scratchy tunes poking through radio static. In the orchestra, the tension jumps from tectonic timpani rumbles to dry staccato sprints in the strings to gelid woodwind chords. Occasionally, Adams's score rises to a raging shout, and at other times it relaxes into arias of consolatory beauty. But it never ceases to quiver.

The countdown lurches toward that man-made dawn, changing tempo and tone. It comes as short horn blasts, or inexorable chimes, or bows tapped percussively on the strings, or a frenzied tremolo. The pulse grinds faster, then slows and picks up speed again, becoming the fitful rhythm of destiny and dream.

Doctor Atomic had its world premiere at the San Francisco Opera on Saturday, and our fragile, threatened planet is a little richer for it. Rumors of the work's scheduled progress across the country over the next few years—Chicago next season, the Metropolitan Opera a season or two after that—suggest that it will have a future that eludes most new operas.

Adams is America's pre-eminent composer, so the work might have had a brief half-life even if he had not fashioned such a dark and riveting masterwork. But he did, and since the theme will never become dated, perhaps it will slouch into the operatic repertoire, and stay.

The tight score contains the full panoply of Adamsian techniques and moods: the agitated hyperactivity of his Chamber Symphony, the dense, billowing orchestration of *Naive and Sentimental Music*, the Violin Concerto's stately lyricism above churning harmonic seas, the serenely tragic mode of the opera *The Death of Klinghoffer*.

Just getting through the thing is a titanic project, yet conductor Donald Runnicles led a brilliantly intense performance that betrayed no discomfort with novelty.

The "Doctor" is a Strangelove with a conscience, however faulty: J. Robert Oppenheimer, the cultivated, slender, chain-smoking scientist who directed the Manhattan Project in a business suit and a fedora. He is as sharply sketched a Faustian character as any in the operatic literature, and the excellent baritone Gerald Finley sang the role with tormented nobility.

Oppenheimer steps back and forth across the line that separates the laboratory from his private life. Among the grim, isolated people laboring on the "gadget," he speaks in clipped, stilted assertions, trying to force a moral quandary into becoming a technical problem. Alone or with his wife, Kitty, emotions are expressed in verse.

The passion of the physicist is a setting of John Donne's "Batter my heart, three-person'd God," the plea for redemption that gave the test bomb site its name: Trinity. Here, the rattling of fate falls away, and the music reaches a clearing of pure loveliness. Donne's lines are set to a series of falling sighs reminiscent of the music of another Elizabethan, John Dowland, a composer of divine laments.

The other men are mostly figures of bluster or doubt: the irascible Teller, Gen. Leslie Groves, who berates a meteorologist for the weather, and the young scientist Robert Wilson, gripped by spasms of regret. Though the bomb was a male affair, it is Kitty Oppenheimer who supplies much of the opera's soul, as well as soprano relief. She opens Act II with a soaring setting of Muriel Rukeyser's "Easter Eve, 1945," a vision of a phoenix planet regenerating out of the atomic ash. Kristine Jepson made it a tour de force of poignancy.

Doctor Atomic is very much a Peter Sellars show. He assembled the libretto and directed the mesmerizing, spare production, in which luminous abstraction rubs against cinematic realism, Dunya Ramicova's period costumes against Lucinda Childs's choreography. The main prop is the bomb, a clumsy metal ball wrapped in wires and suspended like an idol, humanity's pride and nightmare.

Adams and Sellars show us its seductive horror, the painful dilemma that no amount of hindsight can assuage. "Lord," Oppenheimer sings in the final seconds of the pre-atomic age, "these affairs are hard on the heart."

Learning To Love the Bomb (*Doctor Atomic*)

Alan Rich
LA Weekly, October 14, 2005

LIKE THE EXPLOSIVE "GADGET" that forms its centerpiece, *Doctor Atomic* casts a blinding light upon the gloomy musical landscape. Suddenly there is something new and famous in classical music: an American opera, no less—not a rewrite of a movie script this time (as is contemporary practice among lesser souls), but a work of serious, attention-grabbing artistic stature. And if you thought that John Adams might have been flirting with trouble by orchestrating Richard Nixon, Henry Kissinger, and Palestinian terrorists onto his operatic stages in the recent past, consider that his latest foray, into lands once held sacred by the likes of Mozart and Verdi, terminates in a sound and a stage effect that could very well be meant to stand in for the end of the world—depicted, need I further inform you, in the brilliant, imaginative orchestral language that happens to be one of Adams's specialties.

It was appropriate, of course, for the San Francisco Opera to involve itself in a work about the conception and birth of the atomic bomb, much of whose planning took place in nearby Berkeley, where Adams himself now resides. The notion of commissioning and putting forward an opera on this level of enterprise, furthermore, is exactly the mind-set that made Pamela Rosenberg such a strong choice to head the company four years ago. San Francisco's operagoers, alas, were not yet ready to countenance such strength. A leadership that had begun nobly with Messaien's *Saint-François* and ended memorably with *Doctor Atomic* (and embraced along the way two Handel operas in modern-dress productions, German imports that I could learn to live without) will not be soon stricken from San Francisco's memory book.

Doctor Atomic teeters precariously on the needlepoint of time, June and July, 1945, on the eve of the Bomb's first test—in New Mexico at Manhattan Project HQ in Los Alamos and at the detonation site at Alamagordo two hundred miles to the south. Assembled around this moment of crisis are the scientists J. Robert Oppenheimer and Edward Teller and their idealistic acolytes, facing off against the hard-nose military project command. Ideals and moralities do battle. Germany has surrendered; the question resounds: why develop so deadly a weapon merely against Japan, who is virtually defeated anyhow? Voices offstage sound further dissonant counterpoints: a letter from physicist Leo Szilard implores scientists to petition President Truman against using the bomb; word comes that Enrico Fermi is taking bets that the A-test will destroy the world's entire atmosphere in a chain reaction. Closer to home, an unseasonal electrical storm threatens to set off the trial bomb (or "Gadget," as it is known) ahead of schedule. "I demand a signed weather forecast," General Leslie Groves blusters at the post meteorologist, "and if you are wrong I will hang you." Interesting operatic material this, beside which Adams's *Nixon in China* might pass for *La Traviata* redux.

This Is How It Ends

I wrote some months ago, in a different context, that the words of Peter Sellars cry out for musical setting. Here we are, then; Sellars's libretto for *Doctor Atomic* constitutes a poetic and rhetorical foundation that endows its dark life even beyond musical considerations. Much of his text derives from military and scientific notes and from conversational scribblings possibly fished out of wastebaskets—chit-chat, for example, about General Groves's dieting problems. For leavening there are the human sidelights: family life among the Oppenheimers, with alcoholic Kitty drawing solace from Muriel Rukeyser poetry, Robert lost in lines from John Donne. Pasqualita, their Navajo nanny, croons her own visions. From these discordant fragments, personages take shape in the dimly lit desert landscape—and that is the genius of Sellars's words. Subtle, anticipatory moments nudge the alert observer. One of the scientists mentions Hiroshima among possible Japanese target cities, and Adams's orchestra gives off a meaningful groan. At the final curtain, as a chorus down front cries out its anticipation of humanity's oncoming agony, and the words of a single Japanese woman sound above the multitude.

Measured against its time and place—a major Hiroshima anniversary year, widely honored in literature and conferences, nowhere more assiduously than in and around the Bay Area where so much of the thinking began—it might be easy to set down *Doctor Atomic* as a work of ambitious opportunism. Adams, as with his 9/11-inspired, Pulitzer-honored *On the Transmigration of Souls,* has no problems in transforming contemporary headlines into important, large-scale musical designs. The wonder of *Doctor Atomic,* overriding the timelessness of its subject matter and the intelligence in the way it has been set forth, is the deep penetration of Adams's music into the troubled souls of his characters. More than in any large-scale work of his to date, I get the sense here of extraordinary mastery over a vast spread of expressive technique, and the intelligence to summon its variety at the proper moment. This is operatic writing in the grandest sense, the more so for it being entirely of its own time—and ours.

Pamela Rosenberg speaks of the opera as the last in a series she has produced in the shadow of the Faust legend. In the *Doctor Atomic* of Adams/Sellars, I detect more of Wagner's *Parsifal* and, in the troubled genius/mystic/hero, the tortured martyr of Amfortas himself. "Batter my heart, three-person'd God," cries Oppenheimer at the shattering first-act curtain under the Bomb's menacing shadow, in the words of John Donne that had given the Bomb project the subtitle Trinity, "for I never shall be free, nor ever chaste, except you ravish me." Later in atomic history Oppenheimer will feel the thrust of the betrayer's spear, as Edward Teller leads the inquisition against him that will bleed him of his stature among scientists. But that is matter for another opera, another time.

At San Francisco's Opera House, where I attended the third and fourth performances of *Doctor Atomic* last weekend, Donald Runnicles led bone-chilling performances of Adams's many-edged music, before not-quite-sell-out audiences. Gerald Finley is Oppenheimer; Kristine Jepson has the underwritten and arguably superfluous role of Kitty; Richard Paul Fink is Teller; and the real star, the Bomb itself, hangs over the production like some evil-eyed monster from the deep about to swallow us all. The marvelous abstractions of Lucinda Childs's choreography take us back to her work in *Einstein on the Beach,* and that seems exactly right. The work needed to be heard twice; I find it the brainiest, the most challenging of Adams's large-scale stage works, the one least subject to easy solutions. Even the final explosion, which everyone in the theater knows is coming, turns up in Adams's music and Sellars's staging as a splendid and imaginative backward thought. Since there are four performances left this coming week, I will say no more.

Aspects of John Adams's Music: Floating Elegies and Music Boxes

Renaud Machart

The following is an excerpt from *John Adams*, published by Actes-Sud in 2004; translated by Thomas May, with assistance by the author.

Floating Elegies

Thy song expands my numb'd embonded spirit, thou freest, launchest me, Floating and basking upon heaven's lake.

—Walt Whitman

"TWO THINGS PARTICULARLY EXCITED ME about John's music," observes Simon Rattle in the booklet accompanying *Earbox*, the 10-CD compilation of music by Adams Nonesuch issued in 1999. "One was that it always seemed to be moving forward in space, that I would imagine while listening to it that I was in a light aircraft flying rather fast, close to the ground. The other thing is that, in almost all of his best pieces, there's a mixture of ecstasy and sadness—the catharsis at the end of *Harmonium,* or the still, sad, personal last act of *Nixon in China,* or the middle movement of the Violin Concerto. It has an immense sadness and depth at the center of it."

These observations by the conductor Rattle, a friend of the composer, underscore two essential dimensions in the work of John Adams: the notion of a space rich with possibility and an elegiac sensibility that almost constantly underscore it (with the exception of several virtuoso, boisterously energized pieces that seem to function rather like sonic "palate cleansers" for the composer, coming between two profoundly solemn works).

This elegiac sensibility affects a good deal of twentieth-century American music. The obvious archetype behind this trend is a mythic work by Charles Ives: *The Unanswered Question*, composed in 1908. This piece is an enigmatic elegy that features a questioning and meditative distant solo trumpet. The trumpet hovers above an almost static layer of strings, overshadowed by increasingly agitated interruptions from a quartet of flutes. One is easily reminded of another well-known elegiac composition of the twentieth century: *Quiet City*, an atmospheric piece of stage music that Aaron Copland composed in 1939. It, too, features a solo trumpet and an English horn, accompanied by strings.

The prominence, in both works, of an elegiac and meditative trumpet part links the two to Walt Whitman's moving poem "The Mystic Trumpeter," published in *Leaves of Grass:*

> Hark, some wild trumpeter, some strange musician,
> Hovering unseen in air, vibrated capricious tunes to-night.
> I hear thee, trumpeter, listening alert I catch thy notes,
> Now pouring, whirling like a tempest round me,
> Now low, subdued, now in the distance lost.

As Aaron Copland observed, "I cannot take credit for what a few reviewers called my affinity to Whitman's 'mystic trumpeter' or Ives' persistent soloist in *The Unanswered Question*. My trumpet player was simply an attempt to mirror the troubled main character, David Mellnikoff, of Irwin Shaw's play" (quoted in Vivian Perlis, *Copland, 1900 through 1942*).

It is, however, impossible not to notice traces of this trumpeter in the work of John Adams, who has expressed his deep admiration for Whitman by setting his words to music in *The Wound-*

Dresser. In Adams, the trumpeter is, if not mystical in character, then at least elegiac. The most immediately striking example is the pair of fanfares Adams wrote in 1985 and 1986, respectively: *Tromba lontana* and *Short Ride in a Fast Machine*. In their respective ways, each fanfare seems to illustrate the characteristics expressed by Whitman in the verses quoted above.

The trumpet (or the bugle, with its duskier, more melancholy sound) plays a central role in many of the works of John Adams; it emerges from the orchestra in oft-elongated, melancholy strains. In *My Father Knew Charles Ives* (2003), the instrument intervenes in the first and third movements like a distant memory—filtered through a dream—of *The Unanswered Question*. It is present in the second movement of *Harmonielehre* (1984–1985), in *On the Transmigration of Souls* (2002), and in the cantata *The Wound-Dresser* (1988), where the part, played by a piccolo trumpet, is taut and quite dramatic in keeping with Whitman's anguished text. In the second part of *El Dorado* (1991), a bugle almost exactly quotes the patterns of shifting notes from *Tromba lontana*, etc.

Further along in Whitman's poem "The Mystic Trumpeter" occur some lines that seem to be a poetic counterpart to the mercurial elegies of which John Adams is a master:

> Thy song expands my numb'd embonded spirit, thou freest,
>   launchest me,
> Floating and basking upon heaven's lake.

Among these examples of "floating elegies" in Adams's music, so reminiscent of the most beautiful moments from the opera *The Death of Klinghoffer,* are the "Ocean Chorus" or the "Aria of the Falling Body," where the slackening chromatic descent represents the inevitable sinking of the victim's body in the ocean's depths. Equally reminiscent of these depths is the text from the Offertory in the Requiem, where the prayer is for deliverance de profundo lacu). Consider, too, Mamoud's very beautiful aria "Now It Is Night," with its dreamy arabesques for obbligato bassoon swirling in the night air. Many other occasions in Adams's music engage our attention in a similar way: the unearthly, watery chaconne of the Violin Concerto, where "the violin floats like a disembodied spirit above the orchestral tissue" (in the composer's own phrase); the central movement of *Century Rolls* (forming, like the Violin Concerto's slow movement and the "Aria of the Falling Body," a third sort of Adamsian *gymnopédie*); the two solo piano works from 1977, *Phrygian Gates* and *China Gates*; *Common Tones in Simple Time*; the central movement of *Shaker Loops*; and some of the studies in *Hoodoo Zephyr* (where the artificial space is extremely fluid and mobile).

In his recent works—notably *On the Transmigration of Souls* and *My Father Knew Charles Ives*—Adams evokes atmospheres characterized by a sense of free-floating numbing melancholy. "The Lake"—the second movement of *My Father Knew Charles Ives*—seems to transcribe into sound the liquid movements of an underwater garden: wandering figures of ethereal woodwinds, sinuous as seaweed, result in a hazy texture of weightlessness. These spare wind figures swim in a watery space of sustained strings mingled with the shimmering waves of various sounds contributed from celesta, piano, harp, and small percussion. Similar atmospheres (which also color the score of *On the Transmigration of Souls*) had been tried out by Charles Ives, for example in "The Housatonic at Stockbridge" (from *Three Places in New England*) or "An Elegy to Our Forefathers" (from the Second Orchestral Set)—one of those elegies that Adams will seem to take to its extremes.

The cantata *The Wound-Dresser* (written in 1988 to another poem of Walt Whitman) is an early example, as is the mysterious (and almost disturbing) slow movement of *Naive and Sentimental Music* (1997–1998)—which seems in its own way to revisit the diatonic and "open" spirit of the beginning of Copland's *Appalachian Spring* (1943–44). It includes an electric guitar solo that is the musical cousin of the electric violin part in *The Dharma at Big Sur* (2003). This movement, titled "Mother of the Man," is paradoxically the least "fetal" and "amniotic" of Adams's elegies: by contrast, its texture is almost desert-like and lunar.

Eros Piano (1989)—included by Adams on his Nonesuch

recording *American Elegies*—uses a scintillating, jigsaw-like, highly chromatic language, one which seems more than ever to pay homage to French music (Debussy and Messiaen). Actually, the direct source of his inspiration here is *Riverrun* (1984), a work likewise for piano and orchestra by the Japanese composer Toru Takemitsu (1930–1996). Adams had been struck by this piece on first hearing it.

The extremely refined music of Takemitsu is made of proliferating patterns, fluid textures sometimes seized by climatic accidents (such as winds, clouds, or flocks of birds). This music also suggests some French touches distinctly modeled after Debussy, Ravel, and Messiaen. All of these qualities aroused in Adams a desire to immerse himself in someone else's *musical body*. Listening to *Eros Piano* and *Riverrun* in close succession reveals one of the most beautiful examples of musical twin compositions. In *Eros Piano*, the harmonic imprint of Adams is practically unrecognizable.

Finally, consider one of the rare early compositions of John Adams still available on disc and from publishers: *Christian Zeal and Activity*, a piece for instrumental ensemble and magnetic tape (1973). This is an almost immobile elegy based on a Protestant hymn that partakes simultaneously of a "blank" neo-Palestrinian style and a Mahlerian lament, harking back to the static strings from *The Unanswered Question*. Charles Ives's piece remains decidedly fundamental for American modernism, one that Adams will evoke again in the slow section of *Slonimsky's Earbox* (1996) and in the first and third movements of *My Father Knew Charles Ives* (2003).

Music Boxes

With György Ligeti, John Adams shares a propensity for machine gadgetry and its tendency sometimes to go haywire. Ligeti once mentioned in an interview from 1978 that "recalcitrant machinery, unmanageable automata have always fascinated me." Among the "machines" that spin out of control is minimalism, since Ligeti, indeed, subjects it to a sardonic critique with "*a touch of irony*" in the second of his *Three Pieces for Two Pianos*, titled

"Self-Portrait with Reich and Riley (and Chopin in the Background)." In the case of Adams, his works from the period 1991 to 1996 (from the Chamber Symphony up to *Scratchband*) teem with traits of uncontrollable mechanisms which are restrained or diverted, and which sometimes end up falling apart like toys that work a little too well, so that kids grow bored and toss them aside. It's credible that, just as with Ligeti, these works were conceived with a strong dose of irony (one thinks of how *Fearful Symmetries* or *Grand Pianola Music* play with a façade of false grandeur so as to make fun of the slickly oiled mechanisms of "pure" minimalism).

For, indeed, a large part of the Adams catalogue involves a critique—or rather interpretation—of minimalism. The creator of *Shaker Loops* has been accused of "corrupting the purity" of minimalism. Evidence of a taste for playfulness can be seen in the very term "earbox," the generic title Adams chose for the retrospective box set of his work Nonesuch released in 1999 and, indeed, for his own Web site (www.earbox.com). Such a sound box—call it a "music box,"—is at one and the same time a toolbox, a reservoir of gestures, a conservatory for the memory, and a place for experimentation. Perhaps the most striking application of this playful spirit can be found in *John's Book of Alleged Dances* (1994), a wide-ranging collection of studies that encompass watchlike precision, as well as the strange allure of corny old tunes, all the while accompanied by a pre-recorded percussion track (i.e., a rhythmic sampler). The sense of a kind of musical toy box implicit in this work is even more evident in the fact that the performers can play all or just part of the score in an undetermined order.

Lollapalooza (1995) is a short and formidably difficult rhythmic piece. It is based on the progressive decentering of a syncopated theme (which has a hint of boogie-woogie). Through the accumulation of rhythmic layers, this theme progresses toward its own deconstruction, ending in a final dissolution: the winds literally skitter away with piercing sixteenth-notes in triplets, leaving in their wake a thunderous, denuded texture of brass and timpani. This process, whereby material that is as persistent as a churning motor dissolves away, can be found in *The Chairman Dances*

(1985), a piece composed as a study while the opera *Nixon in China* was in progress. By the end of *The Chairman Dances*, nothing from this faux fox-trot survives except for a rhythmic residue; the pace slackens as the piece runs its course, like a mechanical spring that has completely wound down. The ending of *Common Tones in Simple Time* (1979) similarly spotlights the residue of the material it started out with; in this case it's not a matter of rhythm but of harmony as we hear, in the woodwinds, the natural harmonics of the notes played.

The Chamber Symphony (1992), particularly its third movement, is like a rhythmic robot spinning out of control. But the robot is conceived as one with extremely complex workings, comparable to a "salad spinner" (to use Adams's own expression). Its gyrations are a crazed whirligig mixing snippets of the Chamber Symphony (Op. 9) of Arnold Schoenberg (Adams was immersed in studying that work when he wrote his own chamber symphony) with music from the cartoons his son was watching in the next room. It's an astonishing tossed salad, at once one of the most entertaining of Adams's works (besides being one of the most frequently recorded) and one of his most complex in terms of its scoring and polyphonic thinking, the whole piece decked out in cleverly trashy hues.

Written the year following, the Violin Concerto (1993)—which has already entered into the repertoire and has been performed by famous violinists from Gidon Kremer to Vadim Repin—is replete with virtuosic patterns. The relatively abstract and playful writing of the first movement emphasizes those trademark "stairlike" scales of John Adams which are one of the implements found so plentifully in his musical "toolbox." But the true "cog" of this concerto occurs in the second movement, a chaconne (i.e., a composition based on repetition of the bass line). The movement, subtitled "Body Through Which the Dream Flows," gives the impression of a mercurial, ethereal fluidity, blunting what might otherwise be all too easily perceived as a dogged formal juggernaut, robotic in its persistence. The finale is unbridled and virtuosic in the manner of the Chamber Symphony's last movement: again we experience scalar movement (with its hints of a "stairway") and the motoric drive of incessant sixteenth-notes. The title of this movement, "Toccare," implies that this piece is really about one thing only: *playing*, in every sense of the word.

Road Movies (1995), one of John Adams's rare forays into chamber music, also reverts to the genre of toccata with regard to its two fast movements. This is a "fragile" piece which, in order to sound as good as possible, needs its performers to be engaged with full force and ready to *swing* (the third movement is, after all, sub-titled "40% Swing"). A similar spirit of toccata that "swings" is the short piano piece *American Berserk*, written in 2001 and pre-miered by Garrick Ohlsson at Carnegie Hall on February 25, 2002. Wildly off-center, the piece lives up to its title in suggesting what could almost be termed a mental derailment.

Hallelujah Junction, a piece for two pianos written in 1996 and premiered in April 1998, is one of Adams's insolent and "inde-cent" works. Its tone even tempts one to borrow the expression *style casquette sur l'oreille*, which Francis Poulenc used to charac-terize his sassy, oh-so-Parisian pieces. The melodic and harmonic material of *Hallelujah Junction* is intentionally lean and "minimal" but is ingeniously "decked out" in the course of some fifteen min-utes by means of rhythmic "decenterings" (which, incidentally, re-quire absolute precision in order to render the deliberate effect of playing "out of sync"), *caches*, or masks, and shifted perspective (who is playing what?). After a series of asymmetrical alternating chords rein in the first section of the piece, Adams creates the sen-sation of an adagio. Yet this is really only a slowing down of the machine—the very same machine that boldly takes over in the last pages, leading to an extraordinary effect of calculated disorder, as if it had been "written to be played badly" (a fitting phrase, which I borrow from the pianist Jean-Claude Pennetier, as reported by my colleague Alain Lompech, in regard to certain features of Poulenc's piano writing). It's a formidably synchronized joust for two pianists, rather like those perversely limping *pas de deux* with which certain ballet companies, indeed, have already started to in-terpret this scene (particularly the Royal Danish Ballet in 2001, followed by the New York City Ballet in 2002, in a choreography by Peter Martins). The Danish choreographer had already used seven Adams works, including *The Chairman Dances,* the Violin Concerto, *Fearful Symmetries,* and *Guide to Strange Places*). If *Hallelujah Junction* seems to return to the more "minimalist" endeavors like *Phrygian Gates* and *China Gates* (the two pieces for solo piano from 1977), its markedly staccato features—rather like an eccentric toccata—equally bring to mind the refined honky-tonk of Conlon Nancarrow, whose rhythmic studies for player piano (pianola music, indeed!) betray an alarming complexity.

John Adams proceeds to make a more objective reference to the player piano, or rather, its punched paper music rolls, in another work written in the same year, *Century Rolls* (1996). The first movement (untitled) of this concerto for piano and orchestra is a sort of toccata whose sunlit tonalities and volubility are reminiscent of the texture of Steve Reich's *Music for 18 Musicians.* But, as usual, Adams doesn't let this fine machine—which seems guided by "the sort of electronic pulsation of a pacemaker"—tranquilly follow its course. Starting with the moment the piano enters, rhythmic disturbances intrude and the movement hurtles down its course exuding a sense of "instability" and an energy that evokes the composers of other famous piano concertos, Ravel and Prokofiev.

Despite its subtitle *Manny's Gym*—which references both Erik Satie's *Gymnopédies* and the physical calisthenics of "Manny" (i.e., Emanuel Ax, the original performer to whom *Century Rolls* was dedicated)—the second movement, by virtue of its atmosphere, recalls the Adagio of Ravel's Concerto in G more than the two Satie *Gymnopédies* that Debussy orchestrated in an unearthly, fluid style. The third movement ends with a veritable boogie-woogie which looks back as much to the rhythmic mania of Nancarrow as to Jelly Roll Morton. A recollection of the finale of the Chamber Symphony percolates to the surface, and the unbridled movement comes to a close in a sort of controlled and suddenly interrupted chaos (stopping with a *cut* very much in keeping with the idea of "mechanical roll").

The very same year as *Century Rolls,* in 1996, Adams wrote *Slonimsky's Earbox.* This is a virtuoso composition inspired by what is for Adams a key work by the musicologist, conductor, and historian Nicolas Slonimsky (1895–1995), *The Thesaurus of Scales and Melodic Patterns,* published in New York in the year Adams was born (1947). Slonimsky's book draws an inventory of numerous scalar formulas and melodic motifs. The explosive beginning of Adams's orchestral version of this "study abounding in virtuosity" makes direct reference to Stravinsky's *Song of the Nightingale* (1916–17) and to his use of modal scales in that work. Written with a mind-boggling richness of detail, *Slonimsky's Earbox* seems to be a kind of preparatory study for the great triptych *Naive and Sentimental Music* (1997–98). Attentive listeners will moreover notice that in the calmer sections of the two works there are shared features (sustained and "swollen" chords)—and, in the case of *Slonimsky's Earbox,* a short sample from Ives's *The Unanswered Question* played by the strings. *Naive and Sentimental Music* will come to mark the peak but also the limit of an ultra-complex kind of writing confined to "art for art's sake" that Adams will continue to expound and integrate in a more organic manner in later compositions, notably *El Niño* (1999–2000), a pivotal and extremely important work which opens on to the new century.

"Rumor Scene" from *The Death of Klinghoffer*

Alice Goodman

The following scene was originally part of the Prologue to *The Death of Klinghoffer*, occurring between the "Chorus of Exiled Palestinians" and the "Chorus of Exiled Jews." It was cut after the opera premiered in Brussels in March 1991.

A living room in New Jersey, carpeted in ivory. There is a pastel-colored "Jackson Pollock" hanging over the ivory couch. A number of family photographs in golden frames are arranged on various surfaces according to their importance. On the glass coffee-table Architectural Digest, Art in America, the New Yorker, the New York Times Sunday Magazine, the New York Times Book Review, the New York Times, the New Republic, *and* Time *have been fanned out neatly. Mr. Rumor's recliner has the best view of the entertainment center. He is semi-reclined, flipping from channel to channel by remote control, with the sound off. Jonathan Rumor, thirty years old, relaxes on the couch eating cold spaghetti. Mrs. Rumor walks in carrying a tray of coffee things which she puts down on the coffee-table.*

ALMA
Jonathan, you should be ashamed.

JONATHAN
Hi, Mom.

ALMA
We naturally assumed
You came for lunch. You call that lunch?

JONATHAN
Mother!

HARRY
    Look at him. What a mensch.

ALMA
    Reagan? That asshole?

JONATHAN
    Guess who I
Bumped into at the gallery.
Dana. She says she'll bring the wine.

ALMA
Can she drink wine?

HARRY
    There's Evian
In the refrigerator.

JONATHAN
    Steve
Is crawling backwards.

ALMA
   God, I love
That child!

JONATHAN
   Check out the paper bag
Next to the stove. I got some egg-
Plant. You now, little tiny ones.

ALMA
Remember those Italians,
Carlo and Silvia, on the cruise?

JONATHAN
Melanzanine.

HARRY
   Would you please
Not mention that man's name again?

ALMA
I liked him.

JONATHAN
   Ho ho ho.

HARRY
   Someone
Pass me the Times.

ALMA
   The Klinghoffers
Will never manage all the stairs,
Those little ladders! Marilyn
Is so brave. She's a saint.

JONATHAN
  Hang on.
He had the stroke.

HARRY
  The dollar's up.

JONATHAN
Good news for the Klinghoffers.

HARRY
  Hope
All the logistics get worked out.

JONATHAN
Oh, Marilyn will see to that.
Friday Manhattans by the pool,
Saturday Eretz Yisroel.

ALMA
Yes, go ahead and laugh. Are you
Familiar with these people? No.
Maybe to you they seem grotesque,
Your parents' stupid friends. But ask
Yourself, "When I am seventy
Will I be glamorous? Will I
Be awe-inspiring?" Huh! If you're
A decent man like Klinghoffer
I'll have no reason to complain.
Now, who wants coffee?

HARRY
  My caffeine
Fix for the afternoon! Hooray!

JONATHAN
How old—no thanks Dad—will you be?
Ninety? A hundred?

ALMA
   I won't die.

JONATHAN
I said no thanks.

ALMA
   Until I'm good
And ready.

JONATHAN
   Was this coffee brewed
In that machine from Istanbul?

ALMA
No—one from Harrods Winter Sale.
We only used that Turkish thing
Once, and it made it much too strong.

HARRY
Sort of metallic. It's somewhere.
Still in its box.

ALMA
   I'm not so sure.
I may have given it away—

JONATHAN
You gave that thing to charity?

ALMA
—Last winter there were all those showers.

HARRY
This house is full of souvenirs;
Coffee pots, tea sets, little cups
For drinking sake. Tourist traps
And sweatshops on five continents
Turn the stuff out. Your mother haunts
The markets when we go ashore,
Looking—

ALMA
   We all know where you are
While this is going on.

HARRY
   —For some
Hideous relic to bring home.
Out rush the natives at first sight
Of her enormous summer hat
Rubbing their hands.

ALMA
   You spent the day
Parked in the one clean restroom—

HARRY
   They
Have made their fortunes! And my wife—

ALMA
—In all of Athens. There were half
A dozen angry guys outside.

HARRY
—Has vanished in the sweaty crowd
Waving her pocketbook.

ALMA
   He'd fought
His way in—

HARRY
   God in heaven! What—

ALMA
And I watched him—

HARRY
   —Must she endure—

ALMA
—Fight to get back to the fresh air.

HARRY
—Buying her piece of the Old World.

JONATHAN
You loved that cruise. There were those cold
Buffets at midnight when the cooks
Surprised themselves; you walked the decks
Carrying gold-rimmed china plates,
Half-shadowed by the swinging lights,
Until the waiters went below
And the band scraped their chairs and blew
A couple of wrong notes—then what?
Women felt chilly, wished they'd bought
A sweater, and imagined it
Lying across the stateroom bed.

JONATHAN
So, the last of your friends retired.
And so you followed your friends down,
When the Mediterranean
Had swallowed Dad's cigar.

ALMA
  You ought
To be more serious about
Your social life.

HARRY
  Did you pick up
My suit?

JONATHAN
  The man had shut the shop.
A family emergency.

HARRY
The cat ate the canary.

JONATHAN
  Try
On Monday.

ALMA
  Listen, Jonathan,
I want you to feel free—

JONATHAN
  I can
Hear something. Is your chicken done?

ALMA
—To introduce your friends to us.

HARRY
The chicken, Alma.

JONATHAN
　Let me guess.
Myrt Epstein has a daughter.

ALMA
　Two;
Two lovely, lovely girls.

HARRY
　I'll go
And take it out, okay?

JONATHAN
　Look. Mom.
You know I've got a bar exam.

HARRY
I'll put those peapods on to boil.

ALMA
I'll do it. Don't get up. They're vile!

JONATHAN
Who's vile?

HARRY
　Just about everyone.
This time I think she's got a bone
To pick with Arafat.

JONATHAN
　You should
Fold the paper so she can't read
The headlines.

ALMA
    What's the matter with
You anyway? I'm sick to death
Of reading about misery.
It's never-ending. God knows why
I still get angry, but I do.
You wash your hands and go on through.

Synopsis: *I Was Looking at the Ceiling and Then I Saw the Sky*

John Adams

CHARACTERS

Dewain: A young Black man. Today he's feeling especially fine because he's out of jail and on his way to see his girlfriend Consuelo, the mother of his little baby girl. Dewain's brushes with the law have been pretty minor stuff, and after this most recent lockup he's determined to clean up his act and get his life back on the right track.

David: In his late twenties, the minister of the neighborhood African-American Baptist church. Always smiling, smooth-talking, confident, handsome. He doesn't hesitate to enjoy the favors of the more attractive women in his congregation. But no matter how hard he tries, he can't seem to make those charms work on:

Leila: A Black graduate student, now employed in a local Planned Parenthood clinic, where she's laboring, sometimes in near desperation, to counsel young kids of all ethnic backgrounds about birth control. Among her clients is:

Consuelo: An undocumented immigrant mother from EL Salvador, where the father of her fourteen-year-old boy was murdered by the death squads. Now living in Los Angeles, she ekes out a hand-to-mouth existence, an "illegal alien," whose only bright spot in her life is her love for Dewain, the father of her second child.

Mike: A White rookie cop in the Los Angeles Police Department. He hasn't yet developed the cynicism and abrupt bearing that will be expected of him by his co-workers. In fact, he's something of an activist, viewing his job as away of helping to turn the neighborhood around and getting the kids on his beat out of gangs and off drugs. He's even worked with Dewain to develop a neighborhood boys' basketball league. But his inner conflicts, both social and sexual, are making his life an unbearable mass of contradictions, not the least of which is his relationship with:

Tiffany: Prim, pert, airbrushed anchorwoman for a local TV station. With her matching purse, shoes, and business suit she's the model of televised perfection. Tiffany is a consummate professional. And her career is on course for even bigger things. The best part of her job, though, is those hours when she rides around with Mike in his police car, watching him patrol the neighborhood and do occasional busts on its in habitants, all of which she captures on camera for her weekly "crime-as-entertainment" show.

Rick: Born In LA of parents who were Vietnamese "boat people," he's just finished law school and is working as a public defender. Like Mike, he hasn't lost his sense of idealism and still believes in the ability of the law to change things for the better. He's spent his last dollar on a snazzy Brooks Brothers suit (which he can ill afford) so that he can look good in court. Rick is about to receive a hard lesson in how the legal system really works.

ACT I
Ensemble—I Was Looking at the Ceiling and Then I Saw the Sky
The band sets the mood. It's a sunny morning on a street in LA. A

sequence of cameos by each of the cast puts his or her dilemma into play.

A Sermon on Romance

David, the preacher, uses all his golden-throated pulpit virtuosity to sweet-talk Leila into submission. Glory Hallelujah! He's never seen anything as divine as this supreme model of womanhood, shaped by the loving hands of our Creator—not since this morning, anyway. But Leila's no dope. She doesn't want to end up as just another name on his long list of "converts."

Consuelo's Dream

For Consuelo, a flashback to her first love in EL Salvador. A knock on the door. Terror of foreboding. But it's not the soldiers. It's her lover, a hunted man, come to see her in the deep, dark, luminous silence of the mountain night.

Mike's Song About Arresting a Particular Individual

"Spread your legs! Both hands on the car!" Mike performs a textbook arrest, and he does it for the camera, explaining every detail of the procedure so that Tiffany can air it on her television news show. He's trying to look tough, but, in fact, he's intensely uncomfortable because it's Dewain he's having to rough up.

Tiffany's Solo

"How far can I go in a car (driven by a cop)?" Obviously she'd go a lot further if Mike would only loosen up and stop being Dudley Do-right. Riding around late at night in the passenger seat of his squad car, Tiffany can barely control herself. She wants Mike so badly that it's causing her to lose her professional decorum. Why won't he give her even the smallest sign?

Song About the On-Site Altercation

There've been some strange goings-on in the neighborhood. Consuelo's son is missing. It seems "the authorities" have taken him to a juvenile detention center, and if she goes there to claim him she will be arrested and deported. Dewain hears about this and rushes home. On his way, being Dewain, he decides to pick up a few bottles of beer to help himself think more clearly. But there's a long line at the convenience store and he's in a rush, so he slips out without paying. Bad luck, Dewain! It just happens that Mike and Tiffany are there with the TV crew, and they capture the whole incident on videotape. Dewain is charged only with a misdemeanor, but his fury at being harassed and his anxiousness about Consuelo cause him to explode in a tirade of name-calling. Mike is now in a terrible spot. He realizes he's on camera and must look like he's in charge of the situation, but no one will behave. Leila in particular is incensed by this intrusion into her community. Mike draws his gun, and Dewain ends up handcuffed and charged with threatening an officer, a felony. Tiffany is thrilled.

Song About the Bad Boys and the News
A break in the action while the three girls, Leila, Consuelo, and Tiffany, forget about their troubles and apostrophize the glories of the opposite gender.

Your Honor My Client He's a Young Black Man
Rick, our young public defender, has his big moment in court, making a case for dropping the ridiculous charges against Dewain. The stakes are high, because Dewain's felony is his third, and this means a long, life-destroying mandatory prison term if he is convicted. Rick is just young enough to believe that reason will prevail in a court of law. "Your Honor my client…his petty mistake…two bottles of beer and his life's now at stake!"

Leila's Song: Alone (Again or at Last)
Leila is a real grown-up, and her pains are grown-up pains as well. She wants the real thing from David.

ACT II
Three Weeks and Still I'm Outta My Mind
David, our much admired and sought-after preacher and moral guidepost of the community, has finally succeeded in getting Leila alone. Where? In the church, of course. It's late at night, and no

one else is in the building. He makes his big pitch to her: "I gotta get my disc to match your drive!" She protests, but in the end she manages to convince herself that he really means what he says.

Crushed by the Rock I Been Standing On
No sooner are David and Leila locked in an embrace than the earthquake happens, causing the walls of the church's sanctuary to crumble and bringing the ceiling down on the two lovers. They are plunged into darkness, dust, and debris. Leila is crushed by a fallen pillar, and David holds her dying body in his arms. Only now are his eyes opened by the truth of her love. The rock he'd been standing on—the church, his God—has now suddenly collapsed on him, and, as he holds Leila's nearly lifeless body in his arms, he begs God for just one more chance.

Dewain's Song of Liberation and Surprise
The earthquake has affected everyone. Tiffany finally realizes what Mike has been unable to admit to himself—that he's gay and that his love for her can never go beyond the platonic stage. She now turns her energies on a very relieved and delighted Rick, who has been dazzled by her since cross-examining her on the witness stand. Meanwhile Dewain sits alone in his prison cell. With the earthquake having knocked down all the walls around him, he is free to walk out. No one will stop him. But his grasp of his own situation far transcends the moment. "It doesn't matter where I put my head to bed. I'm here! I am the way I will be free!"

¡Este País! This Country!
Consuelo finds Dewain in his prison room and begs him to escape, to go back with her to El Salvador: "This Country! It doesn't want you and it doesn't want me!" But Dewain knows that running away isn't the answer.

One Last Look at the Angel in Your Eyes
A song of parting for Consuelo and Dewain. In the place of bitterness or sadness they find only a deep appreciation for the love that's sprung between them.

Finale

A slow, gentle passacaglia for all the characters, each singing his or her signature motif in a polyphonic web. Then follows a burst of daylight as the ceiling above yields to the sky beyond.

Synopsis: *Doctor Atomic*

John Adams

Libretto adapted from original sources by Peter Sellars.

ACT I
Scene i
The Manhattan Project laboratory at Los Alamos, New Mexico. June 1945.

Work on the atomic bomb approaches its culminating point. Physicists, engineers, and U.S. military personnel are all laboring under intense pressure from Washington in order to have the bomb tested and ready for use within the next month. J. Robert Oppenheimer—"Oppie" to his friends—has brought the brightest minds in physics and engineering to the remote mesa in what was assumed to be a race against their German counterparts. But already Germany has surrendered, and many of the scientists are now beginning to question the necessity of the bomb's use on Japan.

General Leslie Groves, Army commander of the project, while aware of Oppenheimer's vague but troubling past involvements with the Communist Party, has up to now been able to persuade the government to look the other way because of Oppenheimer's great value to the program.

After an opening chorus describing the situation, Edward Teller approaches Oppenheimer in the lab. Teller's obsession with his dream of a thermonuclear weapon, the "Super," has caused difficulties in working with the other scientists. Teamwork is difficult for Teller, and Oppenheimer excuses him from group collaboration.

Teller shows Oppenheimer a letter he has just received from another physicist, the Hungarian Leo Szilard. Szilard is imploring all the scientists involved in atomic energy to take a moral stand on the bomb's use by signing a letter to President Truman: "We alone are in a position to declare our stand." Oppenheimer responds by admonishing Teller and all the others not to involve themselves in "political pronouncements."

Robert Wilson, an idealistic young physicist also working on the bomb, is organizing a meeting in the lab to talk about the social and moral implications of the "Gadget" (code word for the bomb). Oppenheimer, well aware of Wilson's socialist affinities, strongly objects to the idea of this meeting. "I might warn you—you could get in trouble if you had such a meeting." Wilson, too, has a petition for the President that he hopes everyone will sign: "Atomic attacks on Japan cannot be justified until we make clear the terms of peace and give them a chance to surrender."

Oppenheimer, who has just returned from Washington, describes the decision to bomb Japanese cities, including civilian targets. "We should seek to make a profound psychological impression on as many inhabitants as possible." Wilson is outraged and accuses Oppenheimer of siding with the "Establishment."

Scene ii

The Oppenheimers' house in Los Alamos.

Oppenheimer and his wife, Kitty, are alone in their house in Los Alamos. It is a warm summer night, but Oppenheimer is preoccupied with reading reports. Kitty gently chides him: "Am I in your light?" Roused, Oppenheimer responds to her by quoting a rich, atmospheric stanza by one of his favorite poets, Baudelaire. For a brief moment they are both transported into the intoxicating climate of the poem.

Kitty is seized by a vision of the struggle of war and need for love: "A world is to be fought for, sung, and built."

Scene iii

The "Trinity" Test Site at Alamogordo, New Mexico. July 15, 1945.

It is the night before the test of the first atomic bomb. Truman is already in Potsdam negotiating over the spoils of Europe with Churchill and Stalin. The pressure on Oppenheimer and General Groves to achieve a successful test is overwhelming: The Americans want to have their nuclear weapon as a trump card to play against the Russians.

The weather on the desert floor has changed abruptly. A freak summer electrical storm lashes the test site. The bomb, already partially armed for detonation and hoisted on a high tower, is in danger of being struck by lightning. Groves, beside himself with frustration and anxiety, berates the chief meteorologist, Frank Hubbard, as if the storm were Hubbard's fault. Hubbard warns the general that attempting a test in these conditions is extremely dangerous.

Captain Nolan of the Army Medical Corps impresses upon Groves the toxic and deadly properties of plutonium that are only now beginning to be understood. An accident at the test site could render hundreds of military and scientific personnel fatally ill with painful radiation poisoning. Panic is beginning to take hold, and several enlisted men have had to be removed under sedation.

Groves dismisses all staff in order to speak with Oppenheimer alone. Oppie gently humors Groves about the latter's chronic weight problems, and the general confesses many failed attempts to control his diet.

Completely alone, Oppenheimer recalls a sonnet by John Donne: "Batter my heart, three-person'd God." It is the poem that inspired him to name the test site "Trinity."

ACT II
Scene i
The Oppenheimers' house in Los Alamos.

It is the night of July 15, 1945. The scientists and Army soldiers have left Los Alamos, and are now at the Alamogordo detonation area on the desert floor, more than a hundred miles away. Women have been prohibited from the test site.

Kitty and her Tewa Indian maid, Pasqualita, are sitting in the living room, drinking. Kitty scans the dial of her radio while Pasqualita occasionally checks on the Oppenheimers' sleeping children. Kitty, in a long soliloquy, sings of the war, of death, and of the resurrection of the spirit: "Now I say that the peace the spirit needs is peace, not lack of war, but fierce continual flame."

Orchestral Interlude: Rain over the Sangre de Cristo Mountains.

Seven-month-old Katherine Oppenheimer awakens, crying. Pasqualita takes the baby and comforts her by singing a lullaby as she continues to watch the rain over the mountains.

Scene ii
The "Trinity" test site at Alamogordo, New Mexico. Midnight, July 16, 1945.

The plutonium bomb has been mounted onto the detonation tower, and all personnel have been cleared from the surrounding blast area.

Robert Wilson has to climb the tower one last time to attach a measuring instrument to the bomb. From the top of the tower he can feel the wind and rain buffet his face, and he sees flashes of lightning in the distance. Meteorologist Jack Hubbard is at the foot of the tower making wind velocity measurements ordered by Groves. Wilson confesses his extreme anxiety about being around the bomb in the middle of an electrical storm. To Hubbard a test in the middle of such weather is a "blunder of the first magnitude," and he points out that the high winds could scatter lethal radioactive debris for miles.

While Wilson and Hubbard are at the tower, Groves, Oppenheimer, and the others wait nervously at the Base Camp observation bunker for the storm to pass.

The scientists' talk returns to an unsettling concern: whether or not the detonation might trigger the destruction of the entire Earth's atmosphere. Teller muses, "Might we not be setting off a chain reaction that will encircle the globe in a sea of fire?" A rumor has it that Enrico Fermi, one of the team's most respected scientists, has been taking bets on whether such a calamity might ensue. Oppenheimer reminds them that they already have data confirming that such a result is not possible, but it hardly brightens the mood of gloom pervading the test site. With the rain still coming down, Groves disregards Hubbard's warnings about the storm and orders all to prepare for the test shot at 5:30 a.m.

Scene iii (Countdown, Part I)

The final countdown begins at 5:10 a.m.

Groves complains to his aide about the behavior of the scientists, which has caused him endless security headaches: "This program has been plagued from the start by the presence of certain scientists of doubtful discretion and uncertain loyalty."

Everyone waits, each absorbed in his own thoughts: the men in their bunkers at a distance of two miles from the explosion, Kitty and Pasqualita in the house back on the Los Alamos mesa.

Oppenheimer, whose normally thin frame has diminished even further to ninety-eight pounds, is in a state of extreme nervous exhaustion. He tries to calm himself by reading from a beaten-up book of poetry he has brought along, but he is beset by hallucinations.

Pasqualita, having drunk heavily during the night, has her own visions: "News came on the frost, 'The dead are on the march!'"

At Base Camp the men begin a betting pool. Each tries to guess the yield of the bomb. Oppenheimer surprises everyone by his pessimistic prediction of a very low yield—"a fizzle," Teller calls it. Even Groves is unable to conceal his depressed state and also guesses a low yield. Teller scoffs at their timidity and predicts a powerful explosion.

Oppenheimer is suddenly overcome by a terrifying vision of Vishnu described in the Bhagavad-Gita: "At the sight of this, your Shape stupendous, full of mouths and eyes...terrible with fangs...when I see you, Vishnu...with your mouths agape and flame-eyes staring—all my peace is gone; my heart is troubled."

Scene iv (Countdown, Part II)

Groves is concerned that Oppenheimer, "our high-strung director," is going to have a nervous breakdown.

The storm breaks, and the sky over ground zero suddenly clears. A warning rocket arches in the sky, and a siren sounds. Everyone waits in a state of uncertainty. At Zero minus two minutes another warning rocket goes off but sputters out prematurely.

At Zero minus sixty seconds a third, different rocket appears in the morning sky, signaling the final sixty-second countdown. Base Camp resembles an outpost of the dead: Scientists and Army personnel are scattered about, hunkered in their shallow bunkers. There is no movement or whisper of activity, only the rhythmic voice of the countdown announcer over the loudspeaker. At Zero minus forty-five seconds an engineer flips the switch for the automatic timer. The triggering circuits begin to fire in rapid precision.

"Zero minus one." There is an eerie silence, and then the bomb goes off.

The Complete Works of John Adams

Complete technical specifications and recommendations for synthesizer/ sampler requirements can be found under the appropriate title at http://Earbox.com/tech-guide/t-specs.htm.

STAGE WORKS

Nixon in China (1985–87)

Opera in three acts

Score: coloratura and lyric soprano, three mezzos, high tenor, lyric baritone, baritone, bass-baritone, chorus, and dancers; two flutes (both doubling piccolo), two oboes (second doubling English horn), three oboes (doubling E-flat and bass clarinets), four saxophones, three trumpets, three trombones, bass drum, pedal bass drum, woodblock, suspended cymbal, snare drum, sandpaper blocks, tambourine, hi-hat, tenor drum, sizzle cymbal, glockenspiel, slapping sound, triangle, sleigh bells, two electronic pianos, synthesizer or sampler (Kurzweil K2000), and strings.

Premiere: October 22, 1987, Houston Grand Opera. Presented by Houston Grand Opera. Alice Goodman, libretto; Peter Sellars, director; Mark Morris, choreographer; John DeMain, conductor.

Nonesuch 79177; excerpts on Nonesuch 79453 (*Earbox*)

The Death of Klinghoffer (1990–91)

Opera in two acts

Score: soprano, mezzo, countertenor, tenor, three baritones, bass, chorus, and dancers; two flutes (both doubling piccolo), two oboes (second doubling English horn), two clarinets (second doubling bass clarinet), two bassoons (second doubling contrabassoon), two horns, two trumpets, two trombones, timpani, KAT MIDI mallet controller, three keyboard samplers, and strings.

Premiere: March 19, 1991, Théâtre de la Monnaie, Brussels. Presented by Théâtre de la Monnaie. Alice Goodman, libretto; Peter Sellars, director; Mark Morris, choreographer; Kent Nagano, conductor.

Nonesuch 7928; excerpts on Nonesuch 79453 (*Earbox*); Decca 074 189-9 DH (Penny Woolcock DVD)

I Was Looking at the Ceiling and Then I Saw the Sky (1995)

Songplay in two acts

Score: three mezzos, high tenor, tenor, and two baritones; two reed players (clarinet, bass clarinet, and alto saxophone), three keyboards (piano or sampler, sampler, and synthesizer), acoustic and electric guitar, double bass (doubling electric bass), and drum kit (doubling MIDI drums).

Premiere: May 13, 1995, University of California, Berkeley. Presented by University of California, Berkeley. June Jordan, libretto; Peter Sellars, director; John Adams, conductor.

Nonesuch 79473-2; Actes Sud OMA34102; Nonesuch 79453 (*Earbox*); Naxos 8.669003

El Niño: A Nativity Oratorio (1999–2000)

Score: soprano, mezzo-soprano, and baritone soloists; a male ensemble consisting of three countertenors; mixed chorus; a children's chorus (optional); two flutes (doubling piccolo), two oboes (doubling English horn), two clarinets (first doubling bass clarinet), two bassoons (doubling contrabassoon), three horns, three trombones, glockenspiel, triangles of three sizes, gong, Alpine herd bells, guiro, maracas, high cowbell, temple block, tam-tam, chimes, claves, temple bowls, electronic sampler, two steel-string guitars, piano, celesta, harp, and strings.

Premiere: December 15, 2000, Théâtre du Châtelet, Paris. Dawn Upshaw, Lorraine Hunt-Lieberson, Willard White, soloists; Peter Sellars, director; Kent Nagano, conductor.

Nonesuch 79634-2

Doctor Atomic (2004–05)

Opera in two acts

Score: mezzo-soprano, alto, two baritones, bass baritone, bass, and chorus; three flutes (second and third doubling piccolo), three oboes (third doubling English horn), three clarinets (second doubling E-flat clarinet, third doubling bass and contrabass clarinet), three bassoons (third doubling contrabassoon), four horns, three trumpets (third doubling piccolo trumpet), three trombones, tuba, timpani, thunder sheet, glockenspiel, triangle and two high triangles, tuned gongs, crotales, suspended cymbal, medium and large tam-tam, bass drum, two roto toms, Chinese cymbals, snare drum, chimes and bass chime, celesta, harp, strings, and computer-controlled sound system.

Premiere: October 1, 2005, San Francisco Opera. Presented by San Francisco Opera. Peter Sellars, libretto and director; Lucinda Childs, choreographer; Donald Runnicles, conductor.

A Flowering Tree (2006)

Opera in one act

Score: soprano, tenor, bass, and chorus; three flutes (second and third doubling piccolo), soprano and alto recorders, two oboes (second doubling English horn), two clarinets, bass clarinet, two bassoons (second doubling contrabassoon), four horns, two trumpets, two trombones, harp, celesta, two percussionists, and strings.

Premiere: November 14, 2006, MuseumsQuartier, Vienna. Commissioned by New Crowned Hope Festival. Libretto adapted by John Adams and Peter Sellars after the ancient Indian folktale as anthologized by Attipat Krishnaswami Ramanujan. Simón Bolívar

Symphony Orchestra and Schola Cantorum of Venezuela; Peter Sellars, director; John Adams, conductor.

ORCHESTRAL WORKS

Common Tones in Simple Time (1979)
Score: three flutes (all doubling piccolo), two oboes, three clarinets, two bassoons, two horns, two trumpets, two grand pianos, two marimbas, crotales, glockenspiel, metallophones, two tuned gongs (optional), and strings.

Premiere: January 30, 1980, at Hellman Hall, San Francisco. San Francisco Conservatory of Music Orchestra, conducted by John Adams.

Nonesuch 79144-2

Harmonium for large orchestra and chorus (1980–81)
Score: Mixed chorus divisi. Four flutes (three doubling piccolo), three oboes, three clarinets (third doubling bass clarinet), three bassoons (third doubling contrabassoon), four horns, four trumpets, three trombones, tuba, glockenspiel, crotales, two marimbas, metallophone, bass drum, tubular bells, suspended cymbal, sizzle cymbal, crash cymbals, xylophone, triangle, medium and large tom-toms, anvil, cowbells, tambourine, celesta, piano (synthesizer), harp, and strings (all parts divisi).

Premiere: April 15, 1981, Davies Hall, San Francisco. San Francisco Symphony Orchestra and Chorus, conducted by Edo de Waart.

Nonesuch 79549; ECM New Series 1277; Nonesuch 79453 (*Earbox*); Telarc 80365

Shaker Loops (version for string orchestra) (1983)
The string orchestra version can be played either by a septet of soloists or by a string orchestra of any size.

Premiere: April 1983, Alice Tully Hall, New York City. American Composers Orchestra, conducted by Michael Tilson Thomas.

Nonesuch 79360; BMG/RCA 09026-68674-2; Virgin 7 91168-2; Philips 412214 2; Nonesuch 79453 (*Earbox*); Naxos 8.559031

Harmonielehre (1984–85)

Score: four flutes (three doubling piccolo), three oboes (third doubling English horn), four clarinets (two doubling bass clarinet), three bassoons and contrabassoon, four horns, four trumpets, three trombones, two tubas, timpani, two marimbas, vibraphone, xylophone, tubular bells, crotales (played both with mallets and a bow), glockenspiel, high and low suspended cymbals, sizzle cymbal, small crash cymbals, bell tree, two tam-tams, two triangles, bass drum, piano (sometimes four-hands), celesta, two harps, and strings (with violins divided into four sections, and violas and cellos each into two).

Premiere: March 21, 1985, Davies Hall, San Francisco. San Francisco Symphony, conducted by Edo de Waart.

Nonesuch 79115; EMI 55051; Nonesuch 79453 (*Earbox*)

The Chairman Dances: Foxtrot for Orchestra (1985)

Score: two flutes (both doubling piccolo), two oboes, two clarinets (second doubling bass clarinet), two bassoons, four horns, two trumpets, two trombones, bass tuba, timpani, xylophone, glockenspiel, triangle, bell tree, crotales, tambourine, snare drum, high hat cymbal, pedal bass drum, crash cymbals, medium and high woodblocks, claves, vibraphone, sandpaper blocks, castanets, piano, harp, and strings.

Premiere: January 31, 1986, Milwaukee. Milwaukee Symphony, conducted by Lukas Foss.

Nonesuch 79144-2; Argo 444 454-2; EMI 55051; Nonesuch 79453 (*Earbox*)

Tromba Lontana: Fanfare for Orchestra (1985)

Score: two flutes (both doubling piccolo), two oboes, two clarinets, four horns, two trumpets, glockenspiel, crotales, suspended cymbals, vibraphone, piano, harp, and strings.

Premiere: April 4, 1986, Jones Hall, Houston. Houston Symphony, conducted by Sergiu Commissiona.

EMI 55051; Nonesuch 79144-2

Short Ride in a Fast Machine: **Fanfare for Orchestra (1986)**

Score: two flutes (both doubling piccolo), two oboes (second doubling English horn), four clarinets, three bassoons (third doubling contrabassoon), four horns, four trumpets, three trombones, bass tuba, timpani, woodblock, triangle, xylophone, crotales, glockenspiel, suspended cymbal, sizzle cymbal, snare drum, pedal bass drum, large bass drum, large tam-tam, tambourine, two optional synthesizers (Casio 200 series or Yamaha DX series), and strings.

Premiere: June 13, 1986, Mansfield, Massachusetts. Pittsburgh Symphony Orchestra, conducted by Michael Tilson Thomas.

Nonesuch 79144-2; EMI 55051; Chandos 9363 (version for band); Naxos 8.559031

Fearful Symmetries (1988)

Score: two flutes (both doubling piccolo), two oboes (second doubling English horn), two clarinets, bass clarinet, four saxophones, bassoon, two horns, three trumpets, three trombones, timpani, synthesizer (Kurzweil K2000 or Yamaha HX-1 Electone), sampler (Kurzweil K2000), piano, and strings.

Premiere: October 29, 1988, Avery Fisher Hall, New York City. Orchestra of St Luke's, conducted by John Adams.

Nonesuch 79218; Actes Sud OMA34102; Nonesuch 79453 (*Earbox*)

Eros Piano for piano and orchestra (1989)

Score: solo piano, two flutes (both doubling piccolo), two oboes, two clarinets (second doubling bass clarinet), two bassoons, two horns, vibraphone, crotales, maracas, optional synthesizer, and strings.

Premiere: November 24, 1989, Queen Elizabeth Hall, London. Paul Crossley, piano; London Sinfonietta, conducted by John Adams.

Nonesuch 79249; Nonesuch 79453 (*Earbox*)

El Dorado (1991)

Score: three flutes (second and third doubling piccolo), two oboes, English horn, three clarinets (doubling E-flat and bass clarinet), two bassoons, contrabassoon, four horns, three trumpets (second and third doubling flugelhorn), three trombones, tuba, timpani (also plays claves and sandpaper blocks), marimba, xylophone, bowed vibraphone, claves, bowed crotales, cowbell, cabaza, snare drum, tom-toms, pedal bass drum, bongos, tenor drum, high-hat cymbal, timbales, two different lengths of metal pipe, log drum, guiro, maracas, tambourine, three temple blocks, woodblock, two keyboard samplers, harp, and strings.

Premiere: November 11, 1991, Davies Hall, San Francisco. San Francisco Symphony, conducted by John Adams.

Nonesuch 79359-2

Violin Concerto (1993)

Score: solo violin, two flutes (two doubling piccolo and alto flute), two oboes (two doubling English horn), two clarinets (two doubling bass clarinet), two bassoons, two horns, trumpet, marimba, two low tom-toms, five roto toms, tubular bells, three bongos, two congas, two bass drums, suspended cymbal, tambourine, three high timbales, guiro, bowed vibraphone, claves, high cowbell, timpani, two synthesizers (Yamaha SY99 and Kurzweil K2000), and strings.

(NB: min strength advised in 1st movement.)

Premiere: January 19, 1994, Ordway Music Theater, Saint Paul, Minnesota. Jorja Fleezanis, violin; Minnesota Orchestra, conducted by Edo de Waart.

BBC Late Junction BBCLJ30012; Telarc 80494; Nonesuch 79360; Nonesuch 79453 (*Earbox*)

Lollapalooza (1995)

Score: three flutes (second and third doubling piccolo), three oboes (third doubling English horn), two clarinets, E-flat clarinet, bass clarinet, three bassoons, contrabassoon, four horns, three trumpets, three trombones, tuba, timpani, xylophone, three large roto toms, suspended cymbal, small tam-tam, snare drum, pedal bass drum, maracas, tambourine, claves, triangle, woodblock, bongo, low floor tom-tom, piano, and strings.

Premiere: November 10, 1995, Symphony Hall, Birmingham. City of Birmingham Symphony Orchestra, conducted by Simon Rattle.

BMG/RCA 68798; Nonesuch 79453 (*Earbox*)

Slonimsky's Earbox (1996)

Score: piccolo, two flutes, two oboes, English horn, three clarinets (including E-flat clarinet), bass clarinet, three bassoons, four horns, four trumpets, three trombones, tuba, timpani, crotales, marimba, glockenspiel, xylophone, two suspended cymbals, woodblock, claves, snare drum, hi-hat, temple blocks, cast, shaker, tambourine, tam-tam, triangle, vibraphone, piano, sampler (Kurzweil K2000 or Akai; alternatively, celesta or small electronic jazz organ), harp, and strings.

Premiere: September 12, 1996, Bridgewater Hall, Manchester. Halle Orchestra, conducted by Kent Nagano.

Nonesuch 79453 (*Earbox*)

Century Rolls for piano and orchestra (1996)

Score: solo piano, piccolo, two flutes, two oboes, English horn, two clarinets, bass clarinet, two bassoons, three horns, three trumpets, two trombones, timpani, vibraphone, xylophone, woodblock, marimba, high bongos, glockenspiel, celesta, harp, and strings.

Premiere: September 25, 1997, Cleveland, Ohio. Emanuel Ax, piano; Cleveland Orchestra, conducted by Christoph von Dohnányi.

Nonesuch 79607-2

Naive and Sentimental Music (1997–98)

Score: four flutes (third and fourth doubling piccolo), three oboes (third doubling English horn), three clarinets (second doubling bass clarinet), bass clarinet, three bassoons (third doubling contrabassoon), four horns, four trumpets, three trombones, two tubas, timpani, normal and bowed vibraphone, almglocken, xylophone, marimba, triangles, three "ranch" triangles, suspended cymbals, sizzle cymbal, two small Chinese gongs, small high-pitched bells, shaker, crotales, large bass drum, chimes, high anvil, tam-tams, five Japanese temple bowls, five low gongs, large sleigh bells, piano, celesta, keyboard sampler, guitar, two harps, and strings.

Premiere: Feburary 19, 1999, Los Angeles. Los Angeles Philharmonic Orchestra, conducted by Esa-Pekka Salonen.

Nonesuch 79636-2

Guide to Strange Places (2001)

Score: two piccolos, two flutes, two oboes, English horn, two clarinets, bass clarinet, contrabass clarinet, two bassoons, contrabassoon, four horns, three trumpets, three trombones, tubas, marimba, glockenspiel, bass drum, snare drum, cowbell, chimes, claves, almglocken, woodblock, triangle, three suspended triangles, crotales, four roto toms, low roto tom, high triangle, suspended cymbal, piano, celesta, harp, and strings.

Premiere: October 6, 2001, Concertgebouw, Amsterdam. Netherlands Radio Philharmonic, conducted by John Adams.

On the Transmigration of Souls for orchestra, chorus, children's choir, and pre-recorded sound track (2002)

Score: piccolo, three flutes (third doubling piccolo), three oboes, two clarinets, bass clarinet, contrabass clarinet, two bassoons, contrabassoon, four horns, four trumpets, three trombones, two tubas, timpani, glockenspiel, crotales, high triangles, chimes, suspended cymbal, brake drums, piano, (acoustic piano tuned one-quarter tone high; a sampler may be used as an alternative), celesta, two harps, and strings, with pre-recorded tape via computer-controlled sound system.

Premiere: September 19, 2002, Avery Fisher Hall, New York City. Brooklyn Youth Chorus and New York Choral Artists, New York Philharmonic, conducted by Lorin Maazel.

Nonesuch 79816-2

My Father Knew Charles Ives (2003)

Score: three flutes (third flute doubling piccolo), two oboes and English horn, three clarinets and bass clarinet (third clarinet doubling E-flat clarinet), two bassoons and contrabassoon, four horns, four trumpets, three trombones, tuba, timpani, crotales, chimes, xylophone, glockenspiel, three triangles, small and large bass drums, snare drum, cowbell, crash cymbals, small suspended cymbals, low tom-toms, tam-tam, almglocken, marimba, high and low bowl gongs, tuned gongs, vibraphone, piano, celesta, harp, and strings.

Premiere: April 30, 2003, Davies Symphony Hall, San Francisco. San Francisco Symphony, conducted by Michael Tilson Thomas.

The Dharma at Big Sur for electric violin and orchestra (2003)

Score: solo amplified violin, two bass clarinets, four horns, three trumpets, two trombones, contrabass trombone, tuba, timpani, vibraphone, xylophone, glockenspiel, marimba, chimes, almglocken, four bowl gongs, tuned gongs, triangle, two pots, crotales, two keyboard samplers, two harps, and strings.

Premiere: October 24, 2003, Walt Disney Concert Hall, Los Angeles. Tracy Silverman, violin; Los Angeles Philharmonic, conducted by Esa-Pekka Salonen.

VOICE AND ORCHESTRA

The Nixon Tapes (1987)

Scenes from *Nixon in China* for voices and orchestra.

Score: two high baritones, lyric soprano, coloratura soprano, and bass; two flutes, two oboes, three clarinets, four saxophones, three trumpets, three trombones, two pianos, synthesizer or sampler (Kurzweil K2000), and strings.

Premiere: July 17, 1998, Aspen, Colorado. Aspen Chamber Orchestra, conducted by John Adams.

The Wound-Dresser for baritone voice and orchestra (1988)

Score: baritone, two flutes (second doubling piccolo), two oboes, clarinet, bass clarinet, two bassoons, two horns, trumpet (doubling piccolo trumpet), timpani, keyboard sampler (Kurzweil K2000), and strings.

Premiere: February 24, 1989, Saint Paul, Minnesota. Sanford

Sylvan, baritone; Saint Paul Chamber Orchestra, conducted by John Adams.

BBC Late Junction BBCLJ30012; Nonesuch 79218; Nonesuch 79453 (*Earbox*); Naxos 8.559031

CHAMBER MUSIC

Piano Quintet (1970)*
Premier: May 1970, Paine Hall (Harvard), Cambridge, Massachusetts.

Shaker Loops String Septet (1978)
Score: three violins, viola, two celli, contrabass.

Premiere: December 1978, Hellman Hall, San Francisco. New Music Ensemble of the San Francisco Conservatory, conducted by John Adams.

New Albion NA 014

Chamber Symphony (1992)
Score: flute (doubling piccolo), oboe, two clarinets (first doubling E-flat clarinet, second doubling bass clarinet), two bassoons (second doubling contrabassoon), horn, trumpet, trombone, trap set (cowbell, hi-hat cymbal, snare drum, pedal bass drum, woodblock, two bongos, three tom-toms, roto toms, tambourine, timbales, clave, conga), keyboard sampler (Yamaha SY-77/SY-99 or Kurzweil K2000/2500), and strings.

Premiere: January 17, 1993, Anton Philipszaal, The Hague. Schoenberg Ensemble, conducted by John Adams.

Nonesuch 79219-2; BMG/RCA 09026-68674-2; CCn'C 00492; Actes Sud OMA34102

John's Book of Alleged Dances (1994)
Score: string quartet and pre-recorded performance CD.

Premiere: November 19, 1994, California Center for the Arts, Escondido, California. Kronos Quartet.

Nonesuch 79465-2; Nonesuch 79453 (*Earbox*)

---

*Unpublished composition

Road Movies (1995)
Score: Violin and piano
Premiere: October 23, 1995, Kennedy Center, Washington, DC. Robin Lorentz, violin; Lorna Eder, piano.
Nonesuch 79699

Gnarly Buttons for clarinet and chamber ensemble (1996)
Score: solo clarinet, English horn, bassoon, trombone, guitar (doubling banjo/mandolin), two keyboards (including piano), and strings.
Premiere: October 19, 1996, Queen Elizabeth Hall, London. Michael Collins, clarinet; London Sinfonietta, conducted by John Adams.
Nonesuch 79465-2

OTHER ENSEMBLE WORKS

American Standard (1973)*
Premiere: March 23, 1973, San Francisco Conservatory. San Francisco Conservatory New Music Ensemble, conducted by John Adams.
Released on LP: Obscure #2 (produced by Brian Eno)

Christian Zeal & Activity (1973) (**Part II of** *American Standard*)
Score: Flute, clarinet, bassoon, pre-recorded tape (tape may also be prepared by performing organization), harp, and strings.
Premiere: March 23, 1973, San Francisco Conservatory. San Francisco Conservatory New Music Ensemble, conducted by John Adams.
Nonesuch 79144-2; Actes Sud OMA34102; Nonesuch 79453 (*Earbox*)

Grounding (1975)*
Score: six voices, three saxophones, and live electronics.
Premiere: November 1975, Hall of Flowers, Golden Gate Park, San Francisco. San Francisco Conservatory New Music Ensemble, conducted by John Adams.

Grand Pianola Music (1982)

Score: two pianos, three female voices, winds, brass, and percussion.

Premiere: February 1982, the Japan Center Theater, San Francisco. Julie Steinberg and Robin Sutherland, pianists, with the San Francisco Symphony, conducted by John Adams.

Nonesuch 79219-2; Chandos 9363; EMI CDC-7 47331 2; Nonesuch 79453 (*Earbox*)

Scratchband for amplified ensemble (1996)

Score: flute (doubling piccolo), oboe, two clarinets (second doubling bass clarinet), horn, trumpet, trombone, two samplers (first doubling piano; sampler part is Kurzweil K2000 but has also been programmed for AKAI sampler), electric guitar, bass guitar, pedal bass drum, four tom-toms, two bongos, snare drum, tambourine, hi-hat, cymbals, ride cymbal, woodblock, cowbell, three temple blocks, castanets, claves, maracas, roto tom or timpani (optional).

Premiere: April 13, 1996, Penn State University, University Park, Pennsylvania. Ensemble Modern, conducted by John Adams.

PIANO

Phrygian Gates (1977)

Solo piano.

Premiere: March 17, 1977, Hellman Hall, San Francisco. Mack McCray, pianist.

Music & Arts 604; Albany, TROY 038-2; Telarc 80513; BMG/RCA 09026-68674-2; Tall Poppies, TP 108 (Australia); Nonesuch 79699

China Gates (1977)

Solo piano.

Nonesuch 79699; Telarc 80513; Argo 436 925; Albany, TROY 038-2; BIS 1110

Hallelujah Junction (1996)
Two pianos.
Premiere: April 3, 1998, Getty Center, Los Angeles. Gloria Cheng-Cochran and Grant Gershon, piano.
Nonesuch 79699; Turtle Records TRSA0021

American Berserk (2001)
Solo piano.
Premiere: February 25, 2002, Carnegie Hall, New York City. Garrick Ohlsson, piano.
Nonesuch 79699

CHORUS

Ktaadn (1974)*
Score: mixed chorus, oscillators, and filters.

Harmonium (1980–81)
See details above.

Choruses from *The Death of Klinghoffer* (1991)
See details above.

On the Transmigration of Souls (2002)
See details above.

TAPE AND ELECTRONIC COMPOSITIONS

Heavy Metal (1970)*
Two-channel tape.

Studebaker Love Music (1976)*
Two-channel tape.

Onyx (1976)*
Four-channel tape.

Light Over Water (1983)
Two-channel tape.
New Albion 005 (LP)

Hoodoo Zephyr (1992–93)
MIDI keyboard.
Nonesuch 79311

FILM

Matter of Heart (1982)*
Music for the documentary film about C. G. Jung.

An American Tapestry (1999)
Music for the film.
Directed by Gregory Nava; produced by Barbara Martinez-Jitner;
released on the Showtime Cable Channel in November 1999.

ARRANGEMENTS AND ORCHESTRATIONS

The Black Gondola (1989)
Orchestration of *La Lugubre Gondola* by Franz Liszt.
Score: two flutes, two oboes (second doubling English horn),
two clarinets (second doubling bass clarinet), two bassoons, three
horns, timpani, harp, and strings.
Premiere: October 27, 1989, Saint Paul, Minnesota. Saint Paul
Chamber Orchestra, conducted by John Adams.
Nonesuch 79359-2; Jupiter Recordings J109

Berceuse élégiaque (1989)
Arrangement for chamber orchestra of Busoni's Berceuse No. 7
of Elegies (1907) for solo piano.
Score: two flutes, oboe, clarinet, bass clarinet, two bassoons,
two horns, timpani (doubling gong), piano (doubling celesta),
harp, and strings.
Premiere: June 8, 1989, Saint Paul, Minnesota. Saint Paul
Chamber Orchestra, conducted by John Adams.

Five Songs by Charles Ives (1989–93)
Arrangement for voice and chamber orchestra.
Originally written for a studio recording for Nonesuch, made in August 1989 with Dawn Upshaw, soprano, and the Orchestra of St. Luke's, conducted by John Adams.
Nonesuch 79249-2

Le Livre de Baudelaire (1993)
Orchestration of four songs by Claude Debussy from *Cinq poèmes de Charles Baudelaire.*
Score: three flutes (third doubling piccolo), two oboes, two clarinets, bass clarinet, two bassoons, four horns, timpani, xylophone, bell tree, low suspended cymbal, triangle, tam-tam, harp, celesta, strings, and mezzo-soprano.
Premiere: March 10, 1994, Concertgebouw, Amsterdam. Roberta Alexander, soloist; Royal Concertgebouw Orchestra, conducted by John Adams.

La Mufa (1995)
Orchestration of tango by Astor Piazzolla.
Score: two flutes, oboe, clarinet, bass clarinet, two bassoons, two horns, piano, and strings.
Premiere: January 16, 1997, Philharmonie, Cologne. Gidon Kremer, violin; Deutsche Kammerphilharmonie, Bremen.

Todo Buenos Aires (1996)
Orchestration of tango by Astor Piazzolla.
Score: flute, oboe, clarinet, bass clarinet, two bassoons, two horns, timpani, piano, and strings.
Premiere: February 19, 1997, Heidelberg. Gidon Kremer, violin; Heidelberg Philharmonic Orchestra, conducted by Thomas Kalb.

CONTRIBUTORS

EMANUEL AX is a pianist renowned for his breadth of performance interests, combining a poetic sensibility with outstanding virtuosity. He co-commissioned Adams's piano concerto *Century Rolls* and is its foremost advocate.

SARAH CAHILL is a pianist, music critic, and radio producer. She has followed John Adams's career since 1977, when he dedicated his piano piece *China Gates* to her, and has written about his music for a variety of publications.

RUPERT CHRISTIANSEN is opera critic of the *Daily Telegraph* in London and author of the *Faber Pocket Guide to Opera*.

DANIEL COLVARD is a violist and writer living in New York City. He is a graduate of Dartmouth College, where he wrote his thesis, *Three Works by John Adams*, which investigates experimentation and musical patrimony in Adams's orchestral output between 2001 and 2003.

ARTHUR C. DANTO is Johnsonian professor of philosophy at Columbia University and art critic of the *Nation*. His books include *The Transfiguration of the Commonplace*, *Nietzsche as Philosopher*, and *Narration and Knowledge*.

JUSTIN DAVIDSON won the Pulitzer Prize for criticism in 2002 and is the classical music critic for *Newsday*.

RICHARD DYER is the classical music critic for the *Boston Globe*.

BERND FEUCHTNER is editor of the German periodical *Opernwelt*.

ALICE GOODMAN is a poet and authored the librettos for *Nixon in China* and *The Death of Klinghoffer*.

JOSHUA KOSMAN is the classical music critic for the *San Francisco Chronicle*.

RENAUD MACHART is staff music critic for *Le Monde* and hosts a weekly show on France Musiques (Radio France). He is the author of the first book ever written on John Adams's music (*John Adams*, Actes Sud, 2004) and of studies and translations (George Benjamin, Francis Poulenc, Ned Rorem). His *Leonard Bernstein* is forthcoming from Actes Sud.

INGRAM MARSHALL is the composer of *Fog Tropes*, which was premiered byJohn Adams. He spent the 1970s and '80s on the West Coast, where he was a friend and colleague of Adams. He now lives in Connecticut.

THOMAS MAY is senior music editor at Amazon.com and writes regularly for San Francisco Opera. He is the author of *Decoding Wagner* (also from Amadeus Press).

TIM PAGE won the Pulitzer Prize for criticism in 1997 for his writings about music for the *Washington Post*. He is the author or editor of more than a dozen books.

ALAN RICH, music critic of *LA Weekly* since 1992, has also written for *Newsweek*, the *New York Herald-Tribune*, and the *New York Times*. His books include *Music, Mirror of the Arts, Play-by-Play* (4 volumes) and *So I've Heard*, a collection of his writings from Amadeus Press.

JOHN ROCKWELL is senior cultural correspondent of the *New York Times*. He was the founding director of the Lincoln Center Festival and is the author of *All American Music: Composition in the Late Twentieth Century* (1983), which was nominated for a National Book Critics Circle award, and *Sinatra: An American Classic* (1984).

ALEX ROSS is the music critic of the *New Yorker.* He is working on his first book, *The Rest Is Noise: Listening to the Twentieth Century,* a cultural history of music since 1900.

EDWARD ROTHSTEIN is critic at large for the *New York Times,* where he also served as chief music critic. He is the author of *Emblems of Mind: The Inner Life of Music and Mathematics* (1995, 2006) and co-author of *Visions of Utopia* (2003).

PIERRE RUHE, classical music critic of the *Atlanta Journal-Constitution* since 2000, has written for the *Washington Post* and London's *Financial Times* and served as an editor for National Public Radio's *Performance Today.* Ruhe is writing a study on the operas of Handel and Rameau (forthcoming from Amadeus Press).

DAVID SCHIFF, composer and writer, is R.P. Wollenberg professor of music at Reed College. Among his works are the opera *Gimpel the Fool,* the jazz violin concerto *4 Sisters,* and the piano trio *New York Nocturnes;* he has written books on the music of Elliott Carter and George Gershwin.

PETER SELLARS is one of the leading theater, opera, and festival directors in the world today. He is known both for his re-envisioning of classic works and as the driving force behind new works and has been a close collaborator on each of John Adams's stage works.

ROBERT SPANO is the music director of the Atlanta Symphony Orchestra and a frequent guest conductor of orchestras and opera companies around the world. He was music director of the Brooklyn Philharmonic from 1996 to 2004 and is a leading advocate of contemporary American composers.

MICHAEL STEINBERG, writer, teacher, chamber music coach, critic, and narrator, has been program annotator for the Boston Symphony, New York Philharmonic, and San Francisco Symphony. He is the author of *The Symphony: A Listener's Guide, The Concerto: A Listener's Guide,* and *Choral Masterworks: A Listener's Guide* (Oxford University Press). *For the Love of Music:*

Seductions and Discoveries, a collection of essays by Steinberg and Larry Rothe, has recently been published.

MARK SWED is the classical music critic for the *Los Angeles Times.*

RICHARD TARUSKIN is professor of musicology at the University of California, Berkeley. He is the author of *The Oxford History of Western Music* and such books as *Music in the Western World: A History in Documents* (1985), *Text & Act* (OUP, 1995), and *Stravinsky and the Russian Traditions* (1996). He is a frequent contributor to the *New York Times, New Republic,* and many other scholarly journals.

ANTHONY TOMMASINI is chief classical music critic of the *New York Times,* author of the award-winning biography *Virgil Thomson: Composer on the Aisle,* and a pianist.

KEN UENO is a composer who earned his Ph.D. from Harvard University and now teaches at the University of Massachusetts-Dartmouth, where he is assistant professor and director of the Electronic Music Studios. He is an overtone singer and laptop artist with the experimental improvisation group Onda.

DAWN UPSHAW, a three-time Grammy Award-winning soprano, was involved in the premiere performance of *El Niño* in Paris in 2000. She participated in the Nonesuch recording of the work, and has sung several subsequent performances in London, Los Angeles, New York, and San Francisco. The soprano part in *El Niño* was written specifically for Ms. Upshaw.

INDEX OF JOHN ADAMS COMPOSITIONS

Schubert, Franz, 121, 177, 368

Schumann, Robert, 12, 154, 177, 361

Scorsese, Martin, 188

Scott, Raymond, 150

Scriabin, Alexander, 166, 360

Scruggs, Jan, 369

Seeger, Pete, 4

Sellars, Peter, xvi, 15, 28, 37, 39, 43, 46–49, 56, 111, 119, 127, 129, 142, 145, 171–72, 174, 176, 185, 220–21, 238–248, 249–55 passim, 276, 278, 288–89, 291, 295, 300, 307, 313, 315, 317–18, 322, 323, 325, 335, 341–42, 345–46, 350–54, 362–64, 379, 381, 383–85

Sessions, Roger, 81

Seuss, Dr., 122

Shapiro, Harold, 8, 10

Sheng, Bright, 145

Shostakovich, Dmitri, 41, 333

Sibelius, Jean, xv, 34, 49, 55, 68, 82, 103–4, 145, 148, 152, 154, 169, 189, 192, 263

Silverman, Tracy, 65, 210, 216, 218

Sledge, Eugene, 231

Slonimsky, Nicholas, 90, 263, 390, 394–95

Sousa, John Philip, 71

Spaeth, Sigmund, 4

Spano, Robert, 55, 57, 258–263, 306, 329

Spielberg, Steven, 16, 187, 285

Springsteen, Bruce, 60

Stalin, Joseph, 230, 303, 333

Stein, Gertrude, 158

Stevens, Wallace, 37, 84

Stockhausen, Karlheinz, 8, 10, 23, 74, 92, 260

Strauss, Richard, 64

Stravinsky, Igor, xv, 7–8, 22, 82, 104, 148, 150, 152, 154, 186, 247–48, 260, 265, 266, 273, 344, 360, 395

Subramaniam, L., 157

Sylvan, Sanford, 123, 127, 226, 295, 308, 314–15, 318, 341

Takemitsu, Toru, 390

Tcherepnin, Ivan, 11, 239

Thomson, Virgil, 3, 352

Tilson Thomas, Michael, 40, 52, 60, 86, 112, 269, 358, 376

Tinguely, Jean, 122

Tippett, Michael, 130

Tolstoy, Leo, 231, 303, 333

Truman, Harry, 230, 383

Tsypin, George, 127, 129, 254, 315

Tudor, David, 69

Twain, Mark, 15, 187

Upshaw, Dawn, 43, 227, 246, 276–79, 363

Ussachevsky, Vladimir, 92

Van Gogh, Vincent, 18

Varèse, Edgar, 92, 197, 226, 274

Vaughn Williams, Ralph, 61, 198

SOURCES AND PERMISSIONS

Grateful acknowledgment is made to the following for permission to use previously published and unpublished material.

"The Harmonist" by Alex Ross. From *The New Yorker*, January 8, 2001. Reprinted by permission of the author.

"On Top, But Ever the Risk-Taker" by Mark Swed. From *Los Angeles Times*, January 28, 2001. Reprinted by permission of *Los Angeles Times*.

"Composer Captures Essence of Today" by Pierre Ruhe. From *The Atlanta Journal-Constitution*, May 23, 2003. Reprinted by permission of *The Atlanta Journal-Constitution*.

"Voice of America" by Joshua Kosman. From *San Francisco Chronicle*, May 18, 2003. Reprinted by permission of *San Francisco Chronicle*.

"Life as Music: John Adams Goes Public" by Alan Rich. From *LA Weekly*, October 3, 2003. Reprinted by permission of the author.

"*Shaker Loops*" by Ingram Marshall. Reprinted by permission of the author and the San Francisco Symphony.

"*Harmonium* for Large Orchestra and Chorus" by Michael Steinberg. Reprinted by permission of the author and the San Francisco Symphony.

"*Grand Pianola Music*" by Sarah Cahill. Reprinted by permission of the author and Lincoln Center.

"*Light over Water*: The Genesis of a Music" by Ingram Marshall. First published in Julie Lazar, ed., *Available Light* (Los Angeles: The Museum of Contemporary Art, 1983). Reprinted by permisson of the publisher and the author.

"Memory Spaces" by David Schiff. From *The Atlantic*, April 2003. Reprinted by permission of the author.

"John Adams Discusses *On the Transmigration of Souls*" by Daniel Colvard. Reprinted by permission of the author.

"*My Father Knew Charles Ives*" by Michael Steinberg. Reprinted by permission of the author and the San Francisco Symphony.

"*The Dharma at Big Sur*" by Daniel Colvard. Reprinted by permission of the author.

"Breaking Taboos" by Rupert Christiansen. From *Opera* magazine, May 2003. Reprinted by permission of the author.

"John Adams on Conducting Ives" by Ingram Marshall. Reprinted by permission of the author and the Oral History of American Music project at Yale University.

"Early Works" by Edward Rothstein. Originally titled "*Harmonielehre*," from *The New Republic*, December 2, 1985. Reprinted by permission of *The New Republic*, © 1985, The New Republic, LLC.

"Mischief" by Alan Rich. From *LA Weekly*, July 30, 2004. Reprinted by permission of the author.

"*Nixon in China*" by Edward Rothstein. From *The New Republic*, January 4, 1988. Reprinted by permission of *The New Republic*, © 1988, The New Republic, LLC.

"*Nixon in China*" by Tim Page. From *Newsday*, March 28, 1988. Reprinted by permission of *Newsday*.

"The *Klinghoffer* Debate" by Bernd Feuchtner. From *Opernwelt Jahrbuch 2004*. Reprinted by permission of the author.

"From an Episode of Terrorism, Adams's *Death of Klinghoffer*" by John Rockwell. From *The New York Times*, March 21, 1991. Reprinted by permission of *The New York Times*.

"Seeking Symmetry Between Palestinians and Jews" by Edward Rothstein. From *The New York Times*, September 7, 1991. Reprinted by permission of *The New York Times*.

"Seeking Answers in an Opera" by Mark Swed. From *Los Angeles Times*, October 7, 2001. Reprinted by permission of *Los Angeles Times*.

"Dept. of Raw Nerves: Hijack Opera Scuttled" by Alex Ross. From *The New Yorker*, November 19, 2001. Reprinted by permission of the author.

"Music's Dangers and the Case for Control" by Richard Taruskin. From *The New York Times*, December 9, 2001. Reprinted by permission of *The New York Times*.

"Born Again" by Alan Rich. From *LA Weekly*, November 10, 2003. Reprinted by permission of the author.

"Something To Say" by Alan Rich. From *LA Weekly*, November 9, 2004. Reprinted by permission of the author.

"I Was Looking at the Ceiling and Then I Saw the Sky" by Sarah Cahill. From *East Bay Express*, May 19, 1995. Reprinted by permission of the author.

"Adams, Sellars Think Smaller in New Opera" by Richard Dyer. From *The Boston Globe*, July 23, 1995. Reprinted by permission of *The Boston Globe*.

"Adams's Twentieth Century Rolls—and Rocks" by Mark Swed. From *Los Angeles Times*, February 5, 2001. Reprinted by permission of *Los Angeles Times*.

"Bigger Proves Better in Adams's Grandiose World" by Mark Swed. From *Los Angeles Times*, February 22, 1999. Reprinted by permission of *Los Angeles Times*.

"Rebirth of a Savior in *El Niño*" by Mark Swed. From *Los Angeles Times*, January 13, 2001. Reprinted by permission of *Los Angeles Times*.

"Washed in the Sound of Souls in Transit" by Anthony Tommasini. From *The New York Times*, September 21, 2002. Reprinted by permission of *The New York Times*.

"The Art of 9/11" by Arthur C. Danto. Reprinted with permission from the September 23, 2002, issue of *The Nation*. For subscription information, call 1-800-333-8536. Portions of each week's *Nation* magazine can be accessed at http://www.thenation.com.

"Symphony Premieres Adams's Splendid *Ives*" by Joshua Kosman. From *San Francisco Chronicle*, May 2, 2003. Reprinted by permission of *San Francisco Chronicle*.

"History's Unholy Trinity" by Justin Davidson. From *Newsday*, October 3, 2005. Reprinted by permission of *Newsday*.

"Learning To Love the Bomb" by Alan Rich. From *LA Weekly*, October 14, 2005. Reprinted by permission of the author.